WIND BY THE ·SEA·

Grateful acknowledgment is made to the following publishers, authors, and agents for their permission to reprint copyrighted material. Any adaptations are noted in the individual acknowledgments and are made with the full knowledge and approval of the authors or their representatives. Every effort has been made to locate all copyright proprietors; any errors or omissions in copyright notice are inadvertent and will be corrected in future printings as they are discovered.

"Ancient Mysteries" from *The Book of the Unknown* by Harold and Geraldine Woods. Copyright © 1982 by Harold and Geraldine Woods. Reprinted by permission of Random House, Inc.

"Arachne" from *The Warrior Goddess: Athena* by Doris Gates. Copyright © 1972 by Doris Gates. Reprinted by permission of Viking Penguin Inc.

"Art Must Be True" from *Maria's House* by Jean Merrill. Copyright 1974 © by Jean Merrill. Reprinted by permission of Jean Merrill.

"The Big Spring" from *Spring Comes to the Ocean* by Jean Craighead George. Copyright © 1965 by Jean Craighead George. Reprinted by permission of Harper & Row, Publishers, Inc., and of the author's agents, Curtis Brown Ltd.

Brother to the Wind by Mildred Pitts Walter, illustrated by Diane and Leo Dillon. Text copyright © 1985 by Mildred Pitts Walter. Illustrations copyright © 1985 by Diane and Leo Dillon. By permission of Lothrop, Lee & Shepard Books (A Division of William Morrow), and of the author's agents, McIntosh and Otis, Inc.

Acknowledgments continue on pages 639–640, which constitute an extension of this copyright page.

WORLD OF READING

WIND BY THE SEA

P. David Pearson   Dale D. Johnson

Theodore Clymer   Roselmina Indrisano   Richard L. Venezky

James F. Baumann   Elfrieda Hiebert   Marian Toth

Consulting Authors

Carl Grant   Jeanne Paratore

SILVER BURDETT & GINN

NEEDHAM, MA • MORRISTOWN, NJ
ATLANTA, GA • CINCINNATI, OH • DALLAS, TX
MENLO PARK, CA • DEERFIELD, IL

Everyday Heroes

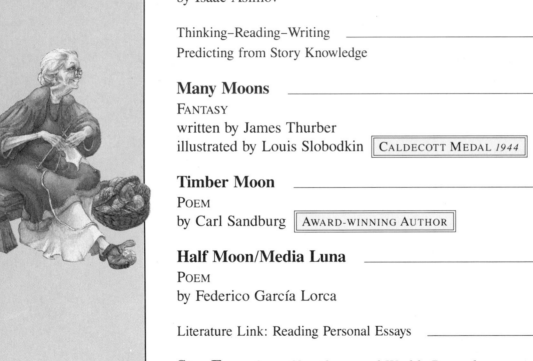

CHALLENGE OF THE SEA

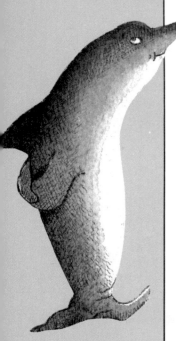

UNIT
THREE

A Way of Seeing

UNIT ONE

EVERYDAY HEROES

A hero can care for a child or save a life.

What events in everyday life bring out the heroic qualities in people?

MOTHER AND CHILD,
stone carving by Oshaweektuk-A, Eskimo Art, 1956

Dana was an ordinary girl having another average day. At least that's what she thought, until she came to the intersection of Main and North Streets.

An Unlikely
HEROINE

by Susan Beth Pfeffer

It was a pretty average day.

I got to the corner of Main and North streets, just in time to miss the traffic light. I half noticed the people who were waiting for the light with me, the way you half notice things when you really aren't thinking about anything special, just waiting to cross the street. There was a woman carrying a bag from Woolworth's, and a man in a business suit who looked a little like my father, and a mother with a half dozen packages in one hand, trying to control her little kid with the other. The kid was two or maybe three. I don't have that much experience with little kids, so it's hard for me to tell how old they are, or if they're boys or girls. This one was just a wriggling kid in overalls and a blue shirt.

But then the kid managed to wriggle away from its mother. And before she even had a chance to notice, the kid had run smack into the middle of Main and North streets, with a big blue car coming right at it.

The funny thing is I didn't even think. If I'd taken one second to think, I never would have moved. I would have stood there frozen and watched the car hit the kid. It couldn't possibly have stopped in time. I couldn't even be sure if the driver would see the kid, it was so little.

Not that any of that really registered. Instead, I ran into the street, right into the path of that big blue car, and pushed the kid out of the way. The momentum of pushing kept me going, and I stumbled along, half holding the hysterical kid and half holding my schoolbooks.

I knew the car could hit us. It was roaring at us like a blue giant. But the funny thing was I felt like a giant, too, an all-powerful one, like even if the car hit us, it wouldn't hurt us because I was made of steel, too. Like Superman. And as long as I was there, the kid was safe. I moved my giant steel legs and lifted the kid with my giant steel arms, and in what couldn't have been more than ten seconds, but felt more like ten years, I pushed both of us out of the path of the car.

By the time I'd gotten to the other side of the street with the kid, the blue car's brakes were screeching it to a halt. But over that noise, and the noise of the kid crying, I could hear its mother screaming from way across the street. It was amazing how far off she looked.

I really wanted to lean against the lamppost, but I wasn't going to let go of that kid. I'd already lost most of my books, since I wasn't about to go to the middle of the street and pick them up where I'd dropped them. So I stood there, holding on to the kid with my grip getting weaker and weaker as I started to realize just what I'd done, and just what the car could have done to the kid and me.

The man in the business suit stood in the middle of the street, holding his hand up to stop the cars, and picked up my books for me. The kid's mother, still screaming, crossed the

street, walked over to where we were, and started weeping. She was shaking pretty hard, too, but nowhere near as hard as I was. The kid ran to its mother, and the two of them hugged and sobbed. That left me free to grab onto the lamppost, which I did, with both arms.

"I couldn't see, I didn't see," the driver of the blue car cried at us. I guess she pulled her car over to the side of the street, because I watched her join us. She seemed like a nice lady, too, not the sort that drove blue giant monster cars and aimed them at kids. "I have two of my own. I never would have . . ."

"He just got away from me," the kid's mother said. "I was holding his hand, and then he just broke away from me . . ."

17

"Here are your books," the businessman said, handing them to me. That meant I had to give up the lamppost, which I did reluctantly. That car could have killed me. I risked my life for some little kid—I didn't even know if it was a boy or a girl. I could have been killed trying to save some strange kid's life.

"I have to go home now," I said, trying to sound conversational. Nobody was paying any attention to me anyway. I grabbed my books, and took about a half dozen steps away from the corner of Main and North streets before my legs gave way, and I practically sank onto the sidewalk.

"I'll drive you home," the woman with the Woolworth's bag said. "My car is right here."

I gratefully followed the woman into her car. She didn't say anything to me, except to ask where I lived. A couple of times, though, she patted me on the hand, as if to say things were going to be all right.

"Here," I said when we got to our house. What a beautiful house, too. I'd never noticed just how beautiful it was before. The grass was mowed, and there were marigolds blooming in the front garden. Marigolds. If that car had hit me, I might never have seen marigolds again.

"There's no car in the driveway," the woman said. "Are you sure your parents are home?"

"Oh, no, they aren't," I said. "They both work."

"I won't leave you here alone," she said.

"That's okay," I said. "My older sister should be in." I fumbled around, got the key from my pocket, and unlocked the front door. The woman followed me in, to make sure Jean really was there.

She was in the living room, sprawled on the sofa, watching TV and eating an apple. I wanted to hug her.

"You see?" I said instead. "She's here."

"If you want, I'll stay until your parents come," the woman said.

"No, really," I said. "I'm okay."

"Dana?" Jean asked, turning around to face us. "What's the matter? What's going on?"

"You should be very proud of your younger sister," the woman said. "She saved a little boy's life. She's quite a heroine."

And that was the first I realized that I really was one.

The next morning at the breakfast table, I was trying to finish my math homework. I hadn't felt like working the night before, and I'd had to tell the story of what happened with the kid to Jean and Mom and Dad so often that I almost believed it had happened. But I didn't think the math teacher would accept it as an excuse for my homework not being done. Jean was nibbling on her toast, and Mom was drinking her orange juice and reading the paper. Dad was upstairs shaving.

"Good grief!" Mom exclaimed, and nearly choked on her juice.

"What?" Jean asked. I didn't even look up.

"There's an article here about Dana," she said.

That was enough to arouse my attention. So I put aside the math, and got up to see what Mom was talking about.

Sure enough, the *Herald* had an article on page 28, all about what had happened. "Mystery Girl Saves Tot's Life" the headline read.

I tried skimming the article, but it wasn't easy with Mom calling to Dad to come downstairs, and Jean reading it out loud.

"Listen to this," Jean said. " 'I'd know her anywhere. She was about fourteen years old, and she was wearing a red shirt.' Fourteen."

"Do I really look fourteen?" I asked.

"No," Mom said. "The woman was in a state of shock. Bill! Come down here!"

"If Dana looks fourteen, I must look sixteen," Jean said. "That's only fair."

"I wasn't wearing a red shirt," I said. "But it's got to be me."

"Of course it's you," Mom said.

"What's all the excitement?" Dad asked. He still had lather over half his face.

"Look at this," Mom said, and she took the paper away from me before I had a chance to finish it. I didn't think that was fair, since it was about me, but Dad started reading the article before I had a chance to protest. "Would you look at that," he said. "You're famous, Dana."

"She isn't famous yet," Jean said. "Nobody knows Dana's the one who saved that kid."

"Can I tell the lady?" I asked.

"I don't see why not," Mom said. "I'm sure she wants to thank you in person."

"That's what the article says," Jean said. " 'I owe my child's life to this girl. I won't be happy until I can thank her personally.' "

"We wouldn't want her to be unhappy forever," Dad said. "I think Dana should go to the paper after school and let them know. They can contact this woman."

"Why can't I go before school?" I asked. What a great excuse not to finish my math.

"Because school is more important," Mom said. "This can wait. Now, finish your homework, and then you'd better get going."

"Do you think they'll put my picture in the paper?" I asked.

"They might," Dad said. "I guess we'd better prepare ourselves for life with a celebrity."

"All I did was . . ." I started to say. But then I realized what I did was save that kid's life. Who knows? The kid might grow up to be president. Or cure cancer. And it would all be thanks to me. I smiled.

"I think the next few days are going to be absolutely unbearable," Jean said, looking at me. "Anybody mind if I change my name?"

"No teasing," Dad said. "Face it, Jean, you're as proud of Dana as the rest of us."

"I guess," she said, and then she smiled at me. "Sure, why not? My sister, the heroine."

I have to admit I liked the sound of it.

It wasn't easy making it to lunch without telling my best friend Sharon the whole story, but every spare minute I had until then I spent on my homework. It was hard concentrating on homework when I knew I was going to go to the paper after school and become famous. The little Dutch boy with his finger in the dike probably didn't have to do his homework for a week after he'd saved Holland. But there were no such breaks for me.

"Did you see that article in the paper?" I asked Sharon as soon as we sat down with our trays.

"What article?" Sharon asked.

"This one," I said, pulling it out of my schoolbag. It hadn't been easy getting Mom and Dad to agree that I should have the one copy of it. But they decided they could buy more on their way to work, so they let me take mine to school.

Sharon skimmed the article. I practically knew it by heart. "What about it?" she asked.

"That's me," I said. "I'm the fourteen-year-old who saved that kid's life."

"What are you talking about?" she asked, and then she read the article more carefully. "You're not fourteen, Dana. And you were wearing an orange shirt yesterday, not red. How can it be you?"

"It was me," I said, grabbing the article back from her. "There are witnesses and everything."

Sharon looked at me and laughed. "You're crazy," she said.

"I am not crazy!" I cried. "That's me they're writing about. And Mom and Dad said I could go to the paper after school and let them know it was me. They might even run my picture in the paper."

"Dana, you're my best friend," Sharon said. "I've known you forever. You would never do anything that brave. I'm sorry, but you just wouldn't."

"What are you talking about?" I asked. I was too upset to start eating lunch, even though it was chili, my favorite. Instead, I fingered the article and tried not to pout.

"Dana, you're afraid of your own shadow," Sharon said. "I remember when you were afraid of a little lightning."

"I was in kindergarten then," I said. "I really did save the kid's life. I didn't think about it. I just did it. And if that kid cures cancer someday, it's going to be because of me."

"I think you've gone crazy," Sharon said, then started eating her chili. "So did you work on your book report?"

"I didn't work on anything!" I shouted. "Listen to me, Sharon. I'm the person they're looking for. I saved that kid's life. And I don't understand why you won't believe me. Have I ever lied to you before?"

"No," Sharon said. She stopped eating her chili and looked me over thoughtfully. "You're not a liar."

"Thank you," I said.

"It's just hard to believe, that's all," Sharon said, and went back to her chili.

"I'm going to the paper after school," I said. "I was going to ask you if you wanted to come with me, but since you don't believe me, I guess there isn't any point."

"You're really going?" Sharon asked.

"Of course I am," I said. "I told you my parents said I could."

"That's an awfully long walk for a practical joke," she said.

"Don't come," I said. "Don't see a mother's grateful tears."

That had been my favorite phrase in the whole article.

"If I go with you, will you really go through with it?" Sharon asked.

"If it isn't true, I'll treat you to ice cream," I said. "A sundae. Deal?"

"Deal," Sharon said.

I didn't much like the idea that Sharon believed in ice cream more than she believed in me, but I was glad to have company when I went to the paper. I could have asked Jean, but she was fourteen, and looked enough like me that I was afraid the woman might think Jean was the one who saved the kid's life. Sharon doesn't look anything like me.

School that afternoon was even harder to concentrate on than school that morning. I thought I would scream when the clock only moved one second at a time. When the final bell rang, I jumped up, grabbed my books and Sharon, and practically pushed her out of the building.

"What's the hurry?" she asked. "You'll be just as much a heroine three minutes from now."

"I want to get it over with," I said. The truth was, the longer the day had gone, the more uncertain I'd gotten. Maybe two kids' lives had been saved the day before. Maybe the lady wouldn't recognize me. The longer I waited, the more her memory would fade. I just wanted to have it done with.

So I forced Sharon to keep pace with me, and I half ran to the paper. I knew where it was, but hadn't been inside it since our class trip in second grade.

"We're going to die of heart attacks before we ever get there," Sharon said, puffing by my side. I'm in better shape than she is.

"It's only four blocks more," I said. "Come on, you can do it."

"I want to live!" she screeched at me, but I ignored her. I had my moment of destiny waiting for me four blocks away. If she couldn't make it, that was her problem.

We were both panting pretty hard by the time we got to the newspaper building. I didn't protest when Sharon raised her hand up to stop me from going in until we both caught our breath. She took out a comb and combed her hair, then offered it to me. I combed mine as well. If they were going to take a picture of me, I wanted to look neat.

"Come on," I said, and walked into the building. I straightened myself as best I could, and tried to look fourteen. But my stomach was hurting and my heart was beating and all of a sudden I started worrying that I'd dreamed the whole thing up.

"Yes?" the receptionist asked.

"I'm the person in the paper," I said. "I mean that article about the mystery girl who saved the tot's life. That's me."

"Oh," the receptionist said, raising her eyebrows. She didn't look like she believed me, and she didn't even know me.

"She really is," Sharon said. "Honest."

I turned around to face her. "Why do you believe me now?" I whispered at her.

"You're not crazy enough to do this if you didn't really do it," she whispered back.

The receptionist looked at both of us, but then she pressed a few buttons and said, "Mrs. Marsh, there's a girl here who claims she's the one who saved that child's life."

I stood there, not even breathing.

"All right," the receptionist said, and hung up. "Girls, Mrs. Marsh would like you to go to the city room and talk with her. She's waiting for you. Straight down the hallway and then it's the first left."

"Okay," I said, and Sharon and I started walking that way. Sure enough, the city room was easy enough to recognize, and Mrs. Marsh was standing there by the door. She'd written the article about me. I'd never met a reporter before, and I felt even more nervous. But Mrs. Marsh didn't look scary. Actually, she sort of looked like my mother.

"Which one of you?" she asked.

"Me," I said. "I mean I. My name is Dana Alison Parker, and I saved that kid's life."

"Come on over here," Mrs. Marsh said, leading Sharon and me to her desk. "Could you tell me a few details about what happened yesterday, Dana? Just to make sure we're talking about the same thing."

"Sure," I said, and I told her the whole story. I'd told it often enough the day before. I made sure to mention the businessman who picked up my books from the street, and the woman who'd been driving the car and had two of her own, and the woman with the Woolworth's bag who'd taken me home. "The kid was wearing overalls," I said. "And a blue shirt, but I didn't know if it was a boy or a girl. It's hard to tell sometimes."

"You certainly sound like you were there," Mrs. Marsh said. "A lot of what you told me wasn't in my article."

"Dana wouldn't lie," Sharon said. "Are you going to call the lady and let her know?"

"Yes, I think I will," Mrs. Marsh said, and sure enough, she dialed a number. Before I knew it, Mrs. Marsh was saying, "Mrs. McKay, I think we've found your heroine. Would you like to come down to the paper and meet her? Fine. We'll expect you here in ten minutes." She hung up the phone and smiled at me. "Can I get you something?" she asked us. "A soft drink, maybe?"

"No, thank you," I said, and Sharon shook her head.

"Wait here," Mrs. Marsh said. "We're going to want some photographs." She got up and went to the other end of the room.

"Do you think there'll be a reward?" Sharon asked me.

"A reward?" I asked.

"Well, you did save that kid's life," she said. "And he might cure cancer, just like you said."

"A reward," I said. What would I do with a reward? And how much might it be?

But I didn't like the way my mind was going. I didn't save that kid's life just to get some money. I didn't even do it to get my name in the paper, or to earn the respect of everybody I knew. I still wasn't sure why I did it, but it wasn't for any sort of profit.

Of course thinking about a reward made the minutes go a lot faster. Mrs. Marsh came back with a photographer, who was holding an awfully big camera with a huge flash attachment. He winked at me, but I started getting nervous again. Mrs. McKay might not recognize me. I couldn't be sure I'd recognize her, and I'd been a lot less upset than she was.

But then Mrs. Marsh started walking toward the door, and I recognized Mrs. McKay all right, and her little boy. Sharon and I both stood up, and I had this horrible thought that Mrs. McKay would walk over to Sharon and thank her by mistake.

But I didn't have to worry. With the photographer clicking and flashing away, Mrs. McKay swooped up her boy and ran to me. "It's her!" she cried as she got closer to me. "Oh, how can I ever thank you?" And soon she was hugging me and the little boy, and the photographer was going crazy, and Mrs. Marsh was taking notes, and Sharon was looking at me almost respectfully. "Oh, thank you, thank you, thank you."

And she cried grateful tears right on me.

Reader's Response

Dana realized that she enjoyed being treated like a celebrity. If you were Dana, how would you feel about all the attention you received? Describe what you might or might not like about it.

An Unlikely
HEROINE

Thinking It Over

1. Why did Dana feel that she would not have saved the child if she had stopped to think?
2. Why do you think Dana felt all-powerful as she was saving the child's life?
3. Why did Dana remark that she had never noticed how beautiful her house was before?
4. What made it so difficult for Sharon to believe that Dana was the real heroine?
5. Do you think Dana would have accepted a reward if Mrs. McKay had offered one? Explain your answer.
6. Was Sharon a good friend to Dana? Explain your answer.

Writing to Learn

THINK AND INFER How would you feel after accomplishing a brave or difficult deed? Read these quotations from the story. Copy the diagram on your paper. On the lines, supply words that describe how you think Dana felt as she spoke.

(a) "The funny thing is I didn't even think. If I had taken one second to think, I never would have moved. — *surprised* / *startled*

(b) "The truth was, the longer the day, the more uncertain I'd gotten."

WRITE Remember a time you did something that was difficult to do. Write a paragraph describing, first, *what you did*, and then, *how you felt* when you did it.

29

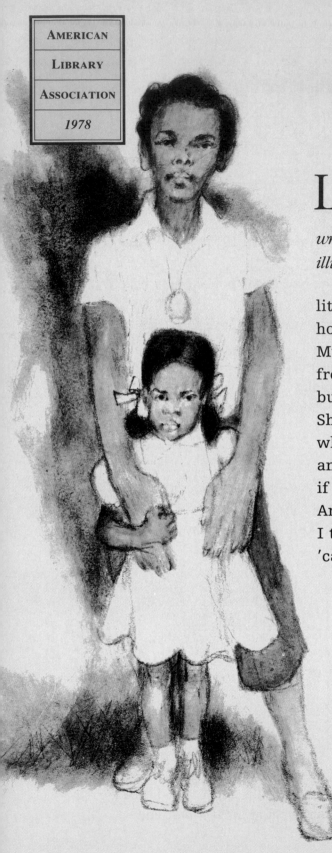

Little Sister

written by Nikki Grimes
illustrated by Tom Feelings

little sister
holds on tight.
My hands hurt
from all that squeezing,
but I don't mind.
She thinks no one will bother her
when I'm around,
and they won't
if I can help it.
And even when I can't,
I try
'cause she believes in me.

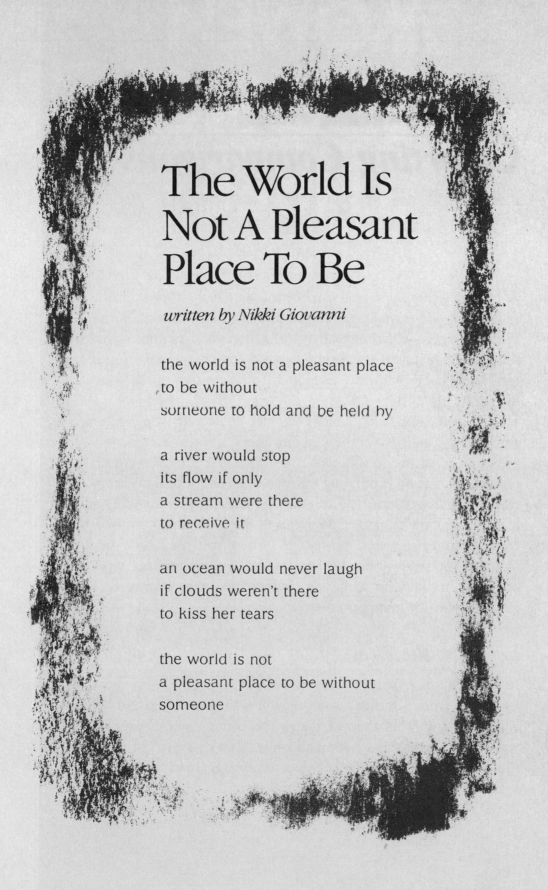

The World Is Not A Pleasant Place To Be

written by Nikki Giovanni

the world is not a pleasant place
to be without
someone to hold and be held by

a river would stop
its flow if only
a stream were there
to receive it

an ocean would never laugh
if clouds weren't there
to kiss her tears

the world is not
a pleasant place to be without
someone

Charting Comparisons

The writing you read can be as dreary as a November rain or as thrilling and stimulating as a fresh breeze on a mountain ridge. What makes good writing satisfying? Often good writing includes images that appeal to your senses; a good author can make you see, feel, hear, smell, and taste as though you were one of the characters in a story.

Read the following sentences: "He roared his reply like an angry bear" and "He shouted his reply." Both sentences say the same thing but in different ways. The first sentence creates a powerful image by comparing the man to an angry bear. When you read the first sentence, you can almost hear the roaring voice and feel the shaking ground. Comparisons like this are often used to create stronger images in writing. When you read, you might increase your enjoyment by keeping an eye out for this type of comparison, making sure you understand what it means and guessing why the author used it.

Learning the Strategy

When you come across a comparison in writing, how can you figure out what it means? Ask yourself what two things are being compared and what type of image the comparison creates. One way to help understand a comparison is to make a chart of similarities between the two things being compared. Read the following sentence from "An Unlikely Heroine."

She seemed like a nice lady, too, not the sort that drove blue giant monster cars and aimed them at kids.

What does the author use as a comparison for the blue car? Look at the chart below that shows the similarities between a car and a monster.

CAR	MONSTER
Cars are large.	Monsters are large.
Cars can be dangerous.	Monsters are dangerous.

By using a comparison, the author makes you think of a car as something large and dangerous, something monstrous! Does this comparison create a strong image for you? What other things could you compare with a car to create as strong an image?

Using the Strategy

Read the following passage from "An Unlikely Heroine." Make a chart that compares the narrator to a giant.

I knew the car could hit us. It was roaring at us like a blue giant. But the funny thing was I felt like a giant, too, an all-powerful one, like even if the car hit us, it wouldn't hurt us. . . .

Applying the Strategy to the Next Story

The next story is "Three Strong Women." As you read, you will be asked to think about how the author uses comparisons, and to make a chart for one of them.

The writing connection can be found on page 125.

Forever-Mountain, a Japanese sumo wrestler, is one of the strongest men in ancient Japan—and he knows it!

THREE STRONG WOMEN

by Claus Stamm

Long ago, in Japan, there lived a famous sumo wrestler, and he was on his way to the capital city to wrestle before the Emperor.

He strode down the road on legs thick as the trunks of small trees. He had been walking for seven hours and could, and probably would, walk for seven more without getting tired.

The time was autumn, the sky was a cold, watery blue, the air chilly. In the small bright sun, the trees along the roadside glowed red and orange.

The wrestler hummed to himself, "Zun-zun-zun," in time with the long swing of his legs. Wind blew through his thin brown robe, and he wore no sword at his side. He felt proud that he needed no sword, even in the darkest and loneliest places. The icy air on his body only reminded him that few tailors would have been able to make expensive warm clothes for a man so broad and tall. He felt much as a wrestler should—strong, healthy, and rather conceited.

◄◆►

What are the wrestler's legs compared to?

35

A soft roar of fast-moving water beyond the trees told him that he was passing above a river bank. He "zun-zunned" louder; he loved the sound of his voice and wanted it to sound clearly above the rushing water.

He thought: They call me Forever-Mountain because I am such a good strong wrestler—big, too. I'm a fine, brave man and far too modest ever to say so. . . .

Just then he saw a girl who must have come up from the river, for she steadied a bucket on her head.

Her hands on the bucket were small, and there was a dimple on each thumb, just below the knuckle. She was a round little girl with red cheeks and a nose like a friendly button. Her eyes looked as though she were thinking of ten thousand funny stories at once. She clambered up onto the road and walked ahead of the wrestler, jolly and bounceful.

"If I don't tickle that girl, I shall regret it all my life," said the wrestler under his breath. "She's sure to go 'squeak' and I shall laugh and laugh. If she drops her bucket, that will be even funnier—and I can always run and fill it again and even carry it home for her."

He tiptoed up and poked her lightly in the ribs with one huge finger.

"Kochokochokocho!" he said, a fine, ticklish sound in Japanese.

The girl gave a satisfying squeal, giggled, and brought one arm down so that the wrestler's hand was caught between it and her body.

"Ho-ho-ho! You've caught me! I can't move at all!" said the wrestler, laughing.

"I know," said the jolly girl.

He felt that it was very good-tempered of her to take a joke so well, and started to pull his hand free.

Somehow, he could not.

He tried again, using a little more strength.

"Now, now—let me go, little girl," he said. "I am a very powerful man. If I pull too hard I might hurt you."

"Pull," said the girl. "I admire powerful men."

She began to walk, and though the wrestler tugged and pulled until his feet dug great furrows in the ground, he had to follow. She couldn't have paid him less attention if he had been a puppy—a small one.

Ten minutes later, still tugging while trudging helplessly after her, he was glad that the road was lonely and no one was there to see.

"Please let me go," he pleaded. "I am the famous wrestler Forever-Mountain. I must go and show my strength before the Emperor"—he burst out weeping from shame and confusion—"and you're hurting my hand!"

The girl steadied the bucket on her head with her free hand and dimpled sympathetically over her shoulder. "You poor, sweet little Forever-Mountain," she said. "Are you tired?

Shall I carry you? I can leave the water here and come back for it later."

"I do not want you to carry me. I want you to let me go, and then I want to forget I ever saw you. What do you want with me?" moaned the pitiful wrestler.

"I only want to help you," said the girl, now pulling him steadily up and up a narrow mountain path. "Oh, I am sure you'll have no more trouble than anyone else when you come up against the other wrestlers. You'll win, or else you'll lose, and you won't be too badly hurt either way. But aren't you afraid you might meet a really *strong* man someday?"

Forever-Mountain turned white. He stumbled. He was imagining being laughed at throughout Japan as "Hardly-Ever-Mountain."

She glanced back.

"You see? Tired already," she said. "I'll walk more slowly. Why don't you come along to my mother's house and let us make a strong man of you? The wrestling in the capital isn't due to begin for three months. I know, because Grandmother thought she'd go. You'd be spending all that time in bad company and wasting what little power you have."

"All right. Three months. I'll come along," said the wrestler. He felt he had nothing more to lose. Also, he feared that the girl might become angry if he refused, and place him in the top of a tree until he changed his mind.

"Fine," she said happily. "We are almost there."

She freed his hand. It had become red and a little swollen. "But if you break your promise and run off, I shall have to chase you and carry you back."

Soon they arrived in a small valley. A simple farmhouse with a thatched roof stood in the middle.

"Grandmother is at home, but she is an old lady and she's probably sleeping." The girl shaded her eyes with one hand. "But Mother should be bringing our cow back from the field—oh, there's Mother now!"

She waved. The woman coming around the corner of the house put down the cow she was carrying and waved back.

She smiled and came across the grass, walking with a lively bounce like her daughter's. Well, maybe her bounce was a little more solid, thought the wrestler.

"Excuse me," she said, brushing some cow hair from her dress and dimpling, also like her daughter. "These mountain paths are full of stones. They hurt the cow's feet. And who is the nice young man you've brought, Maru-me?"

The girl explained. "And we have only three months!" she finished anxiously.

"Well, it's not long enough to do much, but it's not so short a time that we can't do something," said her mother, looking thoughtful. "But he does look terribly feeble. He'll need a lot of good things to eat. Maybe when he gets stronger he can help Grandmother with some of the easy work about the house."

"That will be fine!" said the girl, and she called her grandmother—loudly, for the old lady was a little deaf.

"I'm coming!" came a creaky voice from inside the house, and a little old woman leaning on a stick and looking very sleepy tottered out of the door. As she came toward them she stumbled over the roots of a great oak tree.

"Heh! My eyes aren't what they used to be. That's the fourth time this month I've stumbled over that tree," she complained and, wrapping her skinny arms about its trunk, pulled it out of the ground.

"Oh, Grandmother! You should have let me pull it up for you," said Maru-me.

"Hm, I hope I didn't hurt my poor old back," muttered the old lady. She called out, "Daughter! Throw that tree away like a good girl, so no one will fall over it. But make sure it doesn't hit anybody."

"You can help Mother with the tree," Maru-me said to Forever-Mountain. "On second thought, you'd better not help. Just watch."

Her mother went to the tree, picked it up in her two

hands and threw it—clumsily and with a little gasp. Up went the tree, sailing end over end, growing smaller and smaller as it flew. It landed with a faint crash far up the mountainside.

"Ah, how clumsy," she said. "I meant to throw it *over* the mountain. It's probably blocking the path now, and I'll have to get up early tomorrow to move it."

The wrestler was not listening. He had very quietly fainted.

"Oh! We must put him to bed," said Maru-me.

"Poor, feeble young man," said her mother.

"I hope we can do something for him. Here, let me carry him; he's light," said the grandmother. She slung him over her shoulder and carried him into the house, creaking along with her cane.

The next day they began the work of making Forever-Mountain over into what they thought a strong man should be. They gave him the simplest food to eat, and the toughest. Day by day they prepared his rice with less and less water, until no ordinary man could have chewed or digested it.

Every day he was made to do the work of five men, and every evening he wrestled with Grandmother. Maru-me and her mother agreed that Grandmother, being old and feeble, was the least likely to injure him accidentally. They hoped the exercise might be good for the old lady's rheumatism.

He grew stronger and stronger but was hardly aware of it. Grandmother could still throw him easily into the air—and catch him again—without ever changing her sweet old smile.

He quite forgot that outside this valley he was one of the greatest wrestlers in Japan and was called Forever-Mountain. His legs had been like logs; now they were like pillars. His big hands were hard as stones, and when he cracked his knuckles the sound was like trees splitting on a cold night. ◆◆

◆◆◆

What three comparisons are made here? Make a chart of the similarities between the wrestler's legs and pillars.

41

Sometimes he did an exercise that wrestlers do in Japan—raising one foot high above the ground and bringing it down with a crash. Then people in nearby villages looked up at the winter sky and told one another that it was very late in the year for thunder.

Soon he could pull up a tree as well as the grandmother. He could even throw one—but only a small distance. One evening, near the end of his third month, he wrestled with Grandmother and held her down for half a minute.

"Heh-heh!" she chortled and got up, smiling with every wrinkle. "I would never have believed it!"

Maru-me squealed with joy and threw her arms around him—gently, for she was afraid of cracking his ribs.

"Very good, very good! What a strong man," said her mother, who had just come home from the fields, carrying, as usual, the cow. She put the cow down and patted the wrestler on the back.

They agreed that he was now ready to show some *real* strength before the Emperor.

"Take the cow along with you tomorrow when you go," said the mother. "Sell her and buy yourself a belt—a silken belt. Buy the fattest and heaviest one you can find. Wear it when you appear before the Emperor, as a souvenir from us."

"I wouldn't think of taking your only cow. You've already done too much for me. And you'll need her to plow the fields, won't you?"

They burst out laughing. Maru-me squealed, her mother roared. The grandmother cackled so hard and long that she choked and had to be pounded on the back.

"Oh, dear," said the mother, still laughing. "You didn't think we used our cow for anything like *work*! Why, Grandmother here is stronger than five cows!"

"The cow is our pet," Maru-me giggled. "She has lovely brown eyes."

"But it really gets tiresome having to carry her back and forth each day so that she has enough grass to eat," said her mother.

"Then you must let me give you all the prize money that I win," said Forever-Mountain.

"Oh, no! We wouldn't think of it!" said Maru-me. "Because we all like you too much to sell you anything. And it is not proper to accept gifts of money from strangers."

"True," said Forever-Mountain. "I will now ask your mother's and grandmother's permission to marry you. I want to be one of the family."

"Oh! I'll get a wedding dress ready!" said Maru-me.

The mother and grandmother pretended to consider very seriously, but they quickly agreed.

Next morning Forever-Mountain tied his hair up in the topknot that all Japanese wrestlers wear, and got ready to leave. He thanked Maru-me and her mother and bowed very low to the grandmother, since she was the oldest and had been a fine wrestling partner.

Then he picked up the cow in his arms and trudged up the mountain. When he reached the top, he slung the cow over one shoulder and waved good-bye to Maru-me.

At the first town he came to, Forever-Mountain sold the cow. She brought a good price because she was unusually fat from never having worked in her life. With the money, he bought the heaviest silken belt he could find.

When he reached the palace grounds, many of the other wrestlers were already there, sitting about, eating enormous bowls of rice, comparing one another's weight and telling stories. They paid little attention to Forever-Mountain, except to wonder why he had arrived so late this year. Some of them noticed that he had grown very quiet and took no part at all in their boasting.

All the ladies and gentlemen of the court were waiting in a special courtyard for the wrestling to begin. They wore many robes, one on top of another, heavy with embroidery and gold cloth. The gentlemen had long swords so weighted with gold and precious stones that they could never have used them.

Behind a screen sat the Emperor—by himself, because he was too noble for ordinary people to look at. He was a lonely old man with a kind, tired face. He hoped the wrestling would end quickly so that he could go to his room and write poems.

The first two wrestlers chosen to fight were Forever-Mountain and a wrestler who was said to have the biggest stomach in the country. He and Forever-Mountain threw some salt into the ring. It was understood that this drove away evil spirits.

Then the other wrestler, moving his stomach somewhat out of the way, raised his foot and brought it down with a fearful stamp. He glared fiercely at Forever-Mountain as if to say, "Now *you* stamp, you poor frightened man!"

Forever-Mountain raised his foot. He brought it down.

There was a sound like thunder, the earth shook, and the other wrestler bounced into the air and out of the ring, as gracefully as any soap bubble.

He picked himself up and bowed to the Emperor's screen.

"The earth god is angry. Possibly there is something the matter with the salt," he said. "I do not think I shall wrestle this season." And he walked out, looking very suspiciously over one shoulder at Forever-Mountain.

Five other wrestlers then and there decided that they were not wrestling this season, either. They all looked annoyed with Forever-Mountain.

From then on, Forever-Mountain brought his foot down lightly. As each wrestler came into the ring, he picked him up very gently, carried him out, and placed him before the Emperor's screen, bowing most courteously every time.

The court ladies' eyebrows went up. The gentlemen looked disturbed and a little afraid. They loved to see fierce, strong men tugging and grunting at each other, but Forever-Mountain was a little too much for them. Only the Emperor was happy behind his screen, for now, with the wrestling over so quickly, he would have that much more time to write his poems. He ordered all the prize money handed over to Forever-Mountain.

"But," he said, "you had better not wrestle anymore." He stuck a finger through his screen and waggled it at the other wrestlers, who were sitting on the ground weeping with disappointment like great fat babies. ◆◆◆

Forever-Mountain promised not to wrestle anymore.

◆◆◆

What does the author compare the wrestlers to? Does this create a strong, vivid image for you?

Everybody looked relieved. The wrestlers sitting on the ground almost smiled.

"I think I shall become a farmer," Forever-Mountain said, and left at once to go back to Maru-me.

Maru-me was waiting for him. When she saw him coming, she ran down the mountain, picked him up, together with the heavy bags of prize money, and carried him halfway up the mountainside. Then she giggled and put him down. The rest of the way she let him carry her.

Forever-Mountain kept his promise to the Emperor and never fought in public again. His name was forgotten in the capital. But up in the mountains, sometimes, the earth shakes and rumbles, and they say that is Forever-Mountain and Maru-me's grandmother practicing wrestling in the hidden valley.

Reader's Response

What do you think was the most important thing Forever-Mountain learned from the three strong women? Explain your answer.

THREE STRONG WOMEN

Thinking It Over

1. What was Forever-Mountain's opinion of himself before he met Maru-me?
2. Why did Forever-Mountain want to forget that he had ever seen Maru-me?
3. Which do you think was the most surprising feat performed by the three women? Explain why.
4. Why did Forever-Mountain gently place the wrestlers in front of the Emperor instead of fighting them?
5. Why did the Emperor tell Forever-Mountain not to wrestle anymore?
6. If the three strong women of the title had been three strong men, how do you think the story might have been different?

Writing to Learn

THINK AND PREDICT The author of this story describes imaginative exaggerations. You, too, may exaggerate as you predict the future of Forever-Mountain and Maru-me. Read the predictions below. Then think up another adventure you might predict for Forever-Mountain and Maru-me.

Prediction 1

Maru-me and Forever-Mountain wrestle a huge sea creature.

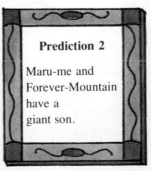

Prediction 2

Maru-me and Forever-Mountain have a giant son.

Your Prediction

WRITE In a very short story that has imaginative exaggerations, write about a future adventure for Forever-Mountain and Maru-me.

Reading Social Studies

Many facts and ideas are presented in social studies textbooks. It takes careful attention to understand and remember them. It is also important that you learn to analyze ideas and draw conclusions about the information that is presented. You must be able to form your own ideas based on your reading. You must be able to think for yourself.

Why is it important to draw your own conclusions when you read? Most important issues today have two or more sides. Two people may study the same facts about an issue but reach different conclusions. Often neither person is right or wrong, but they do have different opinions. Therefore, it is important for you to be able to study the facts and draw your own conclusions.

To draw conclusions from social studies textbooks, you should use the following steps:

- ◆ Use text clues. Read a passage and find the important ideas and facts.
- ◆ Use illustration clues. Study any pictures, diagrams, and maps, and read the captions for additional information.
- ◆ Use experience clues. Consider what you already know about the subject you are studying.
- ◆ Draw your conclusions by using clues from your textbook and clues from your own experience.
- ◆ Modify your conclusions, if necessary, based on new information gathered from further reading.

Use Text Clues

The first step in drawing conclusions is to look at the title and headings and carefully read the text. Any information or ideas that the writer states directly are called *text clues*.

Read this passage from a social studies book. As you read, look for text clues that tell you whom the passage is about.

James Watt (1736–1819)

When James Watt grew up, he became the instrument maker for the University of Glasgow. One time, he was given a model of a steam engine to repair. As Watt worked on the old model, he began to think of ways to improve it. He made a model of his own invention and it did, in fact, work much better than the old type.

Steam engines based on Watt's design were used for power in mines, factories, textile mills, and many other industries.

Watt kept working on his invention. As he explained: "It is a great thing to find out what will *not* do; it leads to finding out what *will* do."

What text clues did you find? Clues in the title and first sentence tell you the passage is about *James Watt*, who worked as an *instrument maker*. Then you learn that Watt made a model of a steam engine that was *much better than the old type*.

Use Illustration Clues

Now look at the diagram and caption that go with the passage about James Watt. What is pictured? From the caption you learn that the diagram shows a steam engine based on Watt's design. The caption also tells you that the steam engine was used in several industries.

Use Experience Clues

You have gathered clues from the text, the diagram, and the caption about James Watt and his steam engine. Now consider your experience clues. What do you know from your own experience that might help you draw conclusions about James Watt? Perhaps you once solved a tricky problem or figured out a better way to do something. Or maybe you know about other inventors, like Eli Whitney, who made life easier with their inventions. These are all clues that can help you draw a conclusion.

Draw Your Conclusions

What opinions have you reached after reading the passage, studying the picture and caption, and thinking about what you already know? You might conclude that James Watt's invention changed the world. Or you might conclude that James Watt was one of the greatest inventors of his time.

Modify Your Conclusions

As you read new information, be prepared to look for more clues. New information may support your conclusion and make it stronger or cause you to adjust your conclusion. Continue reading about James Watt.

> He continued to make improvements. . . . Watt's engines were soon being used in coal mines, flour mills, printing plants, and many other industries. The engine invented by James Watt completely changed people's lives.

Did the new information cause you to modify your conclusion, or was your conclusion reinforced by the new clues?

As You Read Read the following pages from a social studies textbook. Then answer the questions on page 55.

The Industrial Revolution

What was the Industrial Revolution?

VOCABULARY

energy
consumer goods
capital goods

capitalist
market

Another Kind of Revolution   Not all the revolutions in the eighteenth century were political revolutions, or changes in government. There were also great changes in the ways people made things. Historians have called these changes the Industrial Revolution. The Industrial Revolution began in Great Britain in the mid-1700s and gradually spread to other countries of Western Europe. In fact, by the 1890s both the United States and Germany challenged Great Britain as leading industrial nations.

The Industrial Revolution came about because of the use of new sources of **energy**. Energy is power—in this case, the power to make things work.

During the Middle Ages people worked mostly in small workshops, using simple hand tools. For the most part, the only power that was needed to work these tools was muscle power—human and animal. Even a simple machine like the spinning wheel was turned by the spinner. A weaver pushed a shuttle back and forth by hand.

People in the Middle Ages also used waterpower and wind power. They made waterwheels to harness the power of flowing water. Cloth makers used waterwheels to *full* cloth. *Fulling* is a process of beating wet cloth to thicken it. It was a backbreaking job. Waterwheels provided the power needed to move large wooden hammers up and down to pound the cloth. Windmills were also used to grind grain for flour and to work the bellows of some blacksmiths' forges.

A worker in a small workshop prepares to use a frame loom.
■ Who provided power to run this loom?

Steam Power   Waterwheels and windmills both had important drawbacks. Waterwheels could not be used everywhere. They had to be located on rapidly flowing streams or on streams that could be dammed. Windmills worked only when the wind blew. A calm day meant no power.

The idea that steam could be used as a source of power was known to the ancient Greeks. It was the British, however, who put the idea to practical use. Since the early 1700s, steam engines had been used to pump water out of British coal mines. But these steam engines did not work well.

In 1769, however, James Watt—an engineer from Scotland—developed a steam engine that was practical and effective. Watt's steam engine made it possible to have a sure source of energy wherever and whenever it was needed. Mills and factories no longer had to be located on streams nor depend on wind power. Steam engines began to provide cheap power for mines, ironworks, and factories.

Machines and Factories   James Watt's steam engine was only one of the important inventions of the time. Other clever people invented machines that could do jobs that were once done by hand. Machines were invented to spin thread, weave cloth, drill through wood or metal, and work air blowers for furnaces.

The new machines were too costly to be owned by individual workers. And they were too large to be put in small workshops. The new machines were usually set up in large buildings or factories. Large numbers of workers were brought together to operate the machines. Factories replaced many of the small shops.

These large factories amazed a visitor to Britain in the 1860s. He had come from a country where work was still done in the old-fashioned ways. The visitor wrote about the wonderful machines that he saw. On every side were "wheels, cogs, moving leather belts." Everything was "motion and action." The whole building seemed to be "toiling and turning at a fast pace."

The visitor went to a machine shop and watched an iron-cutting machine tear sheets of iron into shreds. He saw a drilling machine bore holes "through iron plates as thick as your thumb as if they were made of butter." He watched the working of a 500-pound (227 kg) steam hammer "so delicately controlled that it could crack a nut without crushing the kernel."

Machines Change the Ways People Work   The visitor thought the machines were wonderful. But he felt they made the workers seem unimportant. He wrote, "Here man is an insect and it is the army of machines which holds attention."

It was true that machines greatly affected the lives of the factory workers. Machines worked faster than humans. Machines did not get tired or have to stop and rest. The people who tended the machines could not work at their own speed; they had to keep up with the machines.

Skills that people had taken years to learn lost much of their value. Spinners and weavers in the new textile factories simply tended the machines. A child who tended several power looms could produce far more cloth in a day than a skilled adult handweaver could produce.

Before machines, people had been able to work at home or in small workshops. The steam engine made this impossible. The spinning wheel was replaced by a spinning machine. The hand loom was replaced by a power loom. These had to be connected to an engine by belts and wheels. Now, people had to work in factories.

Power looms weave cloth in this English textile factory in 1834.
☐ What kind of power ran these looms?

Machines even affected where workers lived. People had to live near the factories where they worked. So the growing use of steam brought with it the growth of factory towns and cities. Most of these towns were not attractive. The visitor who admired the wonderful machines did not admire the city near the factory. He described smoke-filled air and "endless rows of buildings along dirty, gray streets."

More Goods for More People The new factories brought problems, but they also brought benefits. Machines could produce much more than people doing the same work by hand. Goods became more plentiful. Supplies of cloth, pots, pans, and many other things increased.

As goods became more plentiful, they also became cheaper. More people could buy more goods. More goods made life more comfortable and pleasant. In fact, factory-made goods became so cheap that the British—and later other Western nations—sold their products all over the world. People everywhere could buy machine-made goods from Europe and the United States more cheaply than they could buy the handmade goods from their own countries. Among other things, Europeans produced blankets for America, ironware for Africa, and cotton cloth for Asia.

Capitalists Provide Money for the New Factories The products, or goods, produced in the new factories included all kinds of things that people make to sell. Some goods, such as food and clothing, are consumed—that is, they are used up. These are called **consumer goods**. Some goods, such as tools and machines, are used to produce other goods. These are called **capital goods**.

People who worked in their own homes or in small shops, using hand tools

Watt and Boulton made steam engines in this factory from 1775 to 1800.
■ Does this picture show capital goods?

and simple machines, needed few capital goods. The invention of machines changed that. Before a single yard of machine-made cloth could be produced for sale, someone had to provide the capital goods needed to produce it. Someone had to buy, rent, or build the factory. Someone had to pay for the power looms, the steam engines, and the other machines needed to run it.

The people who supplied the money for the capital goods are called **capitalists**. They provided the money because they hoped that the new factories would help them to make more money, or a profit.

However, the capitalists also took a risk—the chance of losing their money. Many ideas for new inventions did not work out or did not work well enough to be of use. New factories and businesses sometimes failed to make a profit. Fire sometimes destroyed other businesses. Then those who had risked their money lost it.

53

An 1876 print shows four inventions of the Industrial Revolution: the electric telegraph, the steam press, the locomotive, and the steamboat.
■ How did these inventions improve transportation and communication?

Risks were part of the new way of producing goods. This was an important difference between modern times and the Middle Ages, when guilds controlled business. Guilds had decided who could make a product, how it was to be made, and the price charged for it. The new way gave people more freedom. People were free to try new inventions and start new businesses if they wanted to and were able to take risks. Greater freedom to do business brought greater risks, but it also brought more goods and more profits.

Industry Brings Great Changes In large part, the Industrial Revolution produced the kind of world we live in today. From its beginnings in Great Britain, industrialization spread first to the countries of Western Europe and then to the United States. Today there is hardly any area of the world that has not been affected by industrialization.

In the late nineteenth century, the industrialized nations of Western Europe and the United States began to compete more and more for **markets**, or places to sell their goods, and raw materials. This led to a new kind of empire building in which European countries tried to get colonies and to control trade in all parts of the world. All this competition led to feelings of increased rivalry and nationalism in Europe. This would be one of the important causes of a war that would involve Europe and most of the countries of the world in 1914—World War I.

CHECKUP
1. What types of power did people use to make things in the Middle Ages?
2. What effect did steam power have on the way goods were produced?
3. How did factories change the ways people worked?
4. How did machines make it possible for more people to have more and cheaper goods?
5. **Thinking Critically** Why did the new factories mean greater risks as well as greater profits for capitalists?

Using What You Have Learned

1. Do written materials contain *text clues* or *experience clues?* What are experience clues?

2. Answer the question that appears in the caption of the picture on page 51. Where did you find the answer to this question?

3. Reread the first three paragraphs on page 51. What time in history does the picture on that page show? How did text clues help you in your answer?

4. Reread the section titled "Machines Change the Ways People Work." Would you conclude that the changes brought on by the Industrial Revolution made the lives of factory workers better or worse?

5. Reread the section called "More Goods for More People." How might you modify the conclusion you reached in question 4?

6. Read the first paragraph under "Machines and Factories." How did machines make producing things easier? What examples are given in the text?

7. Read the following conclusion: "The Industrial Revolution relieved workers from the tedium of making goods by hand." Do you agree with this statement? Modify the statement so it reflects your own views.

8. Imagine the day-to-day life of someone your own age who lived during the Industrial Revolution. Use text and picture clues from pages 51−54 and your own experience clues to conclude whether you would enjoy such a life. Explain your answer.

Examples and excerpts are from *The Eastern Hemisphere Yesterday and Today,* *Silver Burdett & Ginn Social Studies,* © 1988.

In this play set in ancient Sicily, a strong friendship is put to the test.

DAMON AND PYTHIAS

retold by Fan Kissen

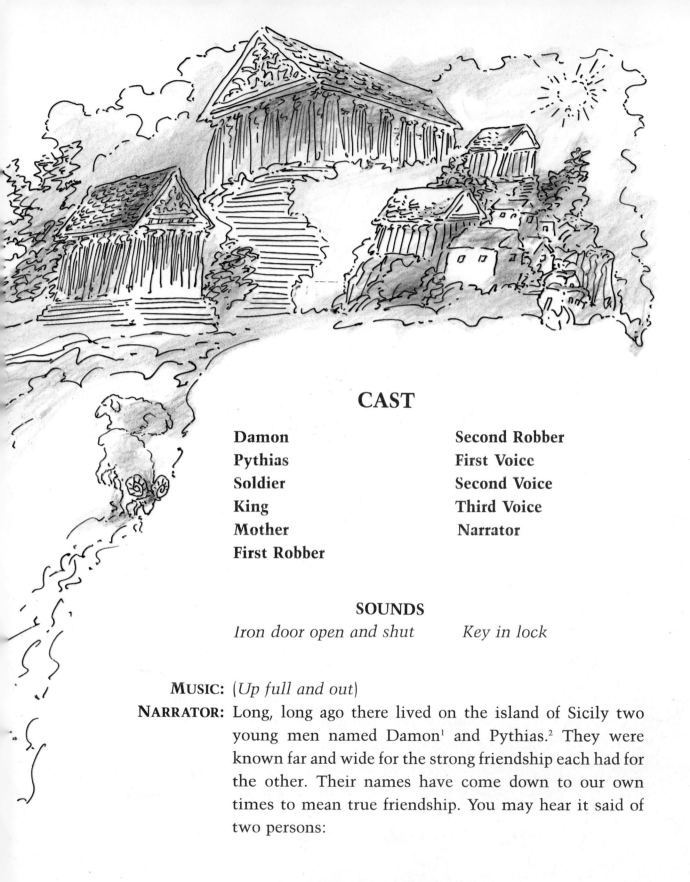

CAST

Damon	Second Robber
Pythias	First Voice
Soldier	Second Voice
King	Third Voice
Mother	Narrator
First Robber	

SOUNDS

Iron door open and shut   *Key in lock*

MUSIC: (*Up full and out*)

NARRATOR: Long, long ago there lived on the island of Sicily two young men named Damon[1] and Pythias.[2] They were known far and wide for the strong friendship each had for the other. Their names have come down to our own times to mean true friendship. You may hear it said of two persons:

---

[1]Damon (dā′ mən)   [2]Pythias (pith′ ē əs)

FIRST VOICE: Those two? Why, they're like Damon and Pythias!

NARRATOR: The King of that country was a cruel tyrant. He made cruel laws, and he showed no mercy toward anyone who broke his laws. Now, you might very well wonder:

SECOND VOICE: Why didn't the people rebel?

NARRATOR: Well, the people didn't dare rebel, because they feared the King's great and powerful army. No one dared say a word against the King or his laws—except Damon and Pythias. One day a soldier overheard Pythias speaking against a new law the King had proclaimed.

SOLDIER: Ho, there! Who are you, that dares to speak so about our King?

PYTHIAS: (*Unafraid*) I am called Pythias.

SOLDIER: Don't you know it is a crime to speak against the King or his laws? You are under arrest! Come and tell this opinion of yours to the King's face!

MUSIC: (*A few short bars in and out*)

NARRATOR: When Pythias was brought before the King, he showed no fear. He stood straight and quiet before the throne.

KING: (*Hard, cruel*) So, Pythias! They tell me you do not approve of the laws I make.

PYTHIAS: I am not alone, your Majesty, in thinking your laws are cruel. But you rule the people with such an iron hand that they dare not complain.

KING: (*Angry*) But *you* have the daring to complain *for* them! Have they appointed you their champion?

PYTHIAS: No, your Majesty. I speak for myself alone. I have no wish to make trouble for anyone. But I am not afraid to tell you that the people are suffering under your rule. They want to have a voice in making the laws for themselves. You do not allow them to speak up for themselves.

KING: In other words, you are calling me a tyrant! Well, you

58

shall learn for yourself how a tyrant treats a rebel! Soldier! Throw this man into prison!

SOLDIER: At once, your Majesty! Don't try to resist, Pythias!

PYTHIAS: I know better than to try to resist a soldier of the King! And for how long am I to remain in prison, your Majesty, merely for speaking out for the people?

KING: (*Cruel*) Not for very long, Pythias. Two weeks from today at noon, you shall be put to death in the public square, as an example to anyone else who may dare to question my laws or acts. Off to prison with him, soldier!

MUSIC: (*In briefly and out*)

NARRATOR: When Damon heard that his friend Pythias had been thrown into prison, and the severe punishment that was to follow, he was heartbroken. He rushed to the prison and persuaded the guard to let him speak to his friend.

DAMON: Oh, Pythias! How terrible to find you here! I wish I could do something to save you!

PYTHIAS: Nothing can save me, Damon, my dear friend. I am prepared to die. But there is one thought that troubles me greatly.

DAMON: What is it? I will do anything to help you.

PYTHIAS: I'm worried about what will happen to my mother and my sister when I'm gone.

DAMON: I'll take care of them, Pythias, as if they were my own mother and sister.

PYTHIAS: Thank you, Damon. I have money to leave them. But there are other things I must arrange. If only I could go to see them before I die! But they live two days' journey from here, you know.

DAMON: I'll go to the King and beg him to give you your freedom for a few days. You'll give your word to return at the end of that time. Everyone in Sicily knows you for a man who has never broken his word.

PYTHIAS: Do you believe for one moment that the King would let me leave this prison, no matter how good my word may have been all my life?

DAMON: I'll tell him that *I* shall take your place in this prison cell. I'll tell him that if you do not return by the appointed day, he may kill *me*, in your place!

PYTHIAS: No, no, Damon! You must not do such a foolish thing! I cannot—I *will* not—let you do this! Damon! Damon! Don't go! (*To himself*) Damon, my friend! You may find yourself in a cell beside me!

MUSIC: (*In briefly and out*)

DAMON: (*Begging*) Your Majesty! I beg of you! Let Pythias go home for a few days to bid farewell to his mother and sister. He gives his word that he will return at your appointed time. Everyone knows that his word can be trusted.

KING: In ordinary business affairs—perhaps. But he is now a man under sentence of death. To free him even for a few days would strain his honesty—*any* man's honesty—too far. Pythias would never return here! I consider him a traitor, but I'm certain he's no fool.

DAMON: Your Majesty! I will take his place in the prison until he comes back. If he does not return, then you may take *my* life in his place.

KING: (*Astonished*) What did you say, Damon?

DAMON: I'm so certain of Pythias that I am offering to die in his place if he fails to return on time.

KING: I can't believe you mean it!

DAMON: I do mean it, your Majesty.

KING: You make me very curious, Damon, so curious that I'm willing to put you and Pythias to the test. This exchange of prisoners will be made. But Pythias must be back two weeks from today, at noon.

DAMON: Thank you, your Majesty!

KING: The order with my official seal shall go by your own hand, Damon. But I warn you, if your friend does not return on time, you shall surely die in his place! I shall show no mercy.

MUSIC: (*In briefly and out*)

NARRATOR: Pythias did not like the King's bargain with Damon. He did not like to leave his friend in prison, with the chance that he might lose his life if something went wrong. But at last Damon persuaded him to leave, and Pythias set out for his home. More than a week went by. The day set for the death sentence drew near. Pythias did not return. Everyone in the city knew of the condition on which the King had permitted Pythias to go home. Everywhere people met, the talk was sure to turn to the two friends.

FIRST VOICE: Do you suppose Pythias will come back?

SECOND VOICE: Why should he stick his head under the King's axe, once he's escaped?

THIRD VOICE: Still, would an honorable man like Pythias let such a good friend die for him?

FIRST VOICE: There's no telling what a man will do when it's a question of his own life against another's.

SECOND VOICE: But if Pythias doesn't come back before the time is up, he will be killing his friend.

THIRD VOICE: Well, there's still a few days' time. I, for one, am certain that Pythias *will* return in time.

SECOND VOICE: And *I* am just as certain that he will *not*. Friendship is friendship, but a man's own life is something stronger, *I* say!

NARRATOR: Two days before the time was up, the King himself visited Damon in his prison cell.

SOUND: (*Iron door unlocked and opened*)

KING: (*Mocking*) You see now, Damon, that you were a fool to make this bargain. Your friend has tricked you! He will not come back here to be killed! He has deserted you.

DAMON: (*Calm and firm*) I have faith in my friend. I know he will return.

KING: (*Mocking*) We shall see!

SOUND: (*Iron door shut and locked*)

NARRATOR: Meanwhile, when Pythias reached the home of his family he arranged his business affairs so that his mother and sister would be able to live comfortably for the rest of their years. Then he said a last farewell to them before starting back to the city.

MOTHER: (*In tears*) Pythias, it will take you only two days to get back. Stay another day, I beg you!

PYTHIAS: I dare not stay longer, Mother. Remember, Damon is locked up in my prison cell while I'm gone. Please don't make it any harder for me! Farewell! Don't weep for me. My death may help to bring better days for all our people.

NARRATOR: So Pythias began his journey in plenty of time. But bad luck struck him on the very first day. At twilight, as he walked along a lonely stretch of woodland, a rough voice called:

FIRST ROBBER: Not so fast there, young man! Stop!

PYTHIAS: (*Startled*) Oh! What is it? What do you want?

SECOND ROBBER: Your money bags.

PYTHIAS: My money bags? I have only this small bag of coins. I shall need them for some favors, perhaps, before I die.

FIRST ROBBER: What do you mean, before you die? We don't mean to kill you, only take your money.

PYTHIAS: I'll give you my money, only don't delay me any longer. I am to die by the King's order three days from now. If I don't return to prison on time, my friend must die in my place.

FIRST ROBBER: A likely story! What man would be fool enough to go back to prison, ready to die.

SECOND ROBBER: And what man would be fool enough to die *for* you?

FIRST ROBBER: We'll take your money, all right. And we'll tie you up while we get away.

PYTHIAS: (*Begging*) No! No! I must get back to free my friend! (*Fade*) I must go back!

NARRATOR: But the two robbers took Pythias's money, tied him to a tree, and went off as fast as they could. Pythias struggled to free himself. He cried out for help as loud as he could, for a long time. But no one traveled through that lonesome woodland after dark. The sun had been up for many hours before he finally managed to free himself from the ropes that had tied him to the tree. He lay on the ground, hardly able to breathe.

MUSIC: (*In briefly and out*)

NARRATOR: After a while Pythias got to his feet. Weak and dizzy from hunger and thirst and his struggle to free himself, he set off again. Day and night he traveled without stopping, desperately trying to reach the city in time to save Damon's life.

MUSIC: (*Up and out*)

NARRATOR: On the last day, half an hour before noon, Damon's hands were tied behind his back and he was taken into the public square. The people muttered angrily as Damon was led in by the jailer. Then the King entered and seated himself on a high platform.

SOUND: (*Crowd voices in and hold under single voices*)

SOLDIER: (*Loud*) Long live the King!

FIRST VOICE: (*Low*) The longer he lives, the more miserable our lives will be!

KING: (*Loud, mocking*) Well, Damon, your lifetime is nearly up. Where is your good friend Pythias now?

DAMON: (*Firm*) I have faith in my friend. If he has not returned, I'm certain it is through no fault of his own.

KING: (*Mocking*) The sun is almost overhead. The shadow is almost at the noon mark. And still your friend has not returned to give you back your life!

DAMON: (*Quiet*) I am ready, and happy, to die in his place.

KING: (*Harsh*) And you shall, Damon! Jailer, lead the prisoner to the—

SOUND: (*Crowd voices up to a roar, then under*)

FIRST VOICE: (*Over noise*) Look! It's Pythias!

SECOND VOICE: (*Over noise*) Pythias has come back!

PYTHIAS: (*Breathless*) Let me through! Damon!

DAMON: Pythias!

PYTHIAS: Thank the gods I'm not too late!

DAMON: (*Quiet, sincere*) I would have died for you gladly, my friend.

CROWD VOICES: (*Loud, demanding*) Set them free! Set them both free!

KING: (*Loud*) People of the city! (*Crowd voices out*) Never in all my life have I seen such faith and friendship, such loyalty between men. There are many among you who call me harsh and cruel. But I cannot kill *any* man who proves such strong and true friendship for another. Damon and Pythias, I set you both free. (*Roar of approval from crowd*) I am King. I command a great army. I have stores of gold and precious jewels. But I would give all my money and power for one friend like Damon or Pythias.

SOUND: (*Roar of approval from crowd up briefly and out*)

MUSIC: (*Up and out*)

◆ LIBRARY LINK ◆

"Damon and Pythias" is based on an ancient Roman legend. Author Fan Kissen puts this legend, other legends, and folk tales into play form in The Bag of Fire and Other Plays.

Reader's Response

Even though the king mocked Damon's trust, Damon's faith in his friend was not shaken. What qualities exhibited in Damon and Pythias' friendship do you value?

DAMON AND PYTHIAS

 ## Thinking It Over

1. Why was Pythias imprisoned?
2. Why do you think Damon wanted to help Pythias?
3. What do you think Pythias meant when he told his mother that his death might bring better days for all their people?
4. How did Damon's and Pythias's actions change the king?
5. What do you think Pythias would have done if he had returned too late to save Damon?
6. Could there be drawbacks in having a very close friendship? Explain your answer.

 ## Writing to Learn

THINK AND EVALUATE On your paper, write the words that you think best describe Damon.

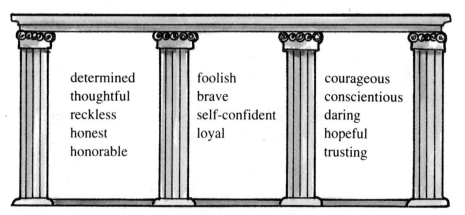

determined	foolish	courageous
thoughtful	brave	conscientious
reckless	self-confident	daring
honest	loyal	hopeful
honorable		trusting

WRITE Write a one-paragraph defense of your choice of words. Why do you think these are the best words to describe Damon?

The time is 1940, and the Germans have invaded Norway. Some Norwegians are attempting a secret mission to help their country, but there is one task no grown-up can carry out.

TREASURE
IN THE
SNOW

BY MARIE MCSWIGAN

When Germany invaded Norway during the Second World War, a group of Norwegians attempted to remove some of their country's gold to safety. This story tells how young Peter and his friends were recruited by Peter's Uncle Victor to help in the effort.

Peter was sure he had not been mistaken. But here was Thor's Rock and there was no cave anywhere that he could see.

There had been a high wall of snow in front of it, he remembered. But look as he would, all he could see were young pines.

"It was where the rock curved so you could stand in a heavy rain and not get wet. That's here," he told the others. But for all they searched they could find neither wall nor cave.

It was Lovisa who spied Per Garson's brown face framed in the branches of a young fir.

"You said you could get here without help," he teased Peter when they came close. "It's here all the time."

"There weren't any trees the other night." Peter felt ashamed. He had been so sure he knew just where to find the cave but he had to be shown after all.

"These we fixed to make it seem more real," Per Garson explained. When Peter looked again he saw that a strip of evergreens made a narrow corridor in front of the wall.

"You made it since the night I was here—since the night before last?"

"Ja."

Peter was still unbelieving. But sure enough, behind the trees was the wall of snow and back of that the cave. Per Garson led them around shrubbery to the entrance.

"Shouldn't someone stand guard over the door in case the Germans come?" Helga asked. "I'll do it."

"Is no need, I think," Per Garson answered. "Still,—is no harm to watch. Spies are everywhere."

So Helga posted herself behind the tree where Per Garson had been waiting and the others went into the cave.

There was a strange kind of white light inside. Peter thought it might be like being in one of the sepulchres of the Bible. For the strong sunlight was cut down by the wall in front of the doorway and a pearly beam fell on the sides and floor.

Per Garson went at once to the end where a stack of brown bricks rose up like a garden wall.

"Gold," Peter whispered to Michael.

"That? Gold?" Peter agreed with Michael that it was hard to believe that each of those brown bricks was money enough to buy an airplane.

Per Garson began lifting down the bricks.

He laid four of them, side by side, on Peter's sled. Then he went to the far side of the cave to a pile of rough brown sacks like potato sacks,—the bags that had covered the bricks on their journey to the cave. He carried one of these to Peter's sled. He folded it twice and laid it over the rectangle of bricks.

"Next the rope." He produced a new clothesline and with it began lashing the sack and bricks to the sled. Over and over went the rope. Then he drew out a long knife and cut the clothesline.

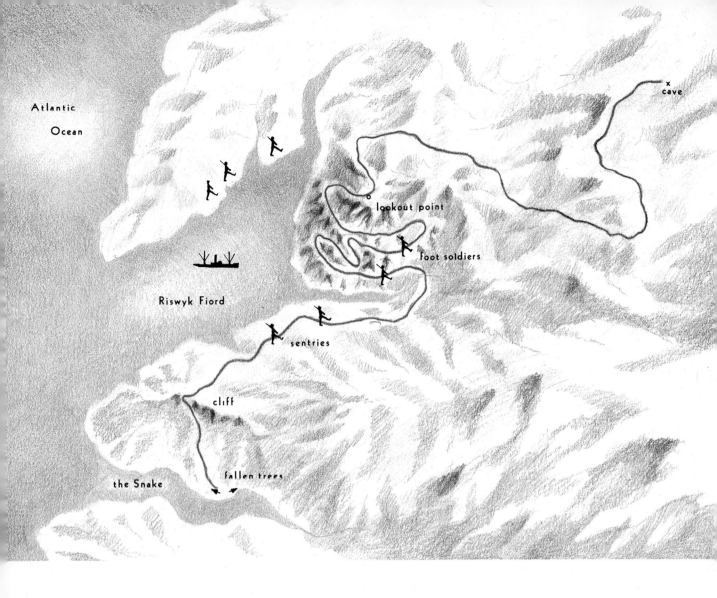

"We could help you, Per Garson," Peter suggested. "Then we could start sooner."

"Na, this must be done right."

"We could do it right."

"Na. Na. Your Uncle Victor holds me to blame if anything goes wrong. He says we can't have the rope coming loose and the bricks falling in the snow. One time for that and the Germans would have our gold."

They watched him take down more bricks for the next sled. Then more for the next and the next. For an old man he worked quickly. With each sled, the same procedure. First the bricks, then the sack folded twice, then the clothesline.

"Now you tell Helga to come here. I think we can be safe these few minutes."

Michael went to get Helga. She had seen nothing more than a few squirrels.

"Now I show you how to untie the rope," Per Garson announced. "When you get to the Snake you first look for a pair of trees that are fallen and covered with snow. They're 'bout two hundred feet apart. Be sure you find them for that's the place your uncle thinks is safest. Now you untie the knots. And so. And so!"

"Can you do it? Try." He laced the bricks onto the sled again and Peter tried to untie them. He was clumsy at first. Instead of openings he made knots. But after a time he learned how to untie the rope.

When it came Helga's turn she gave one quick pull and the rope was dangling from her hand.

"Good. You learn things fast," Per Garson praised.

Each of them had to prove she or he knew how to unload the sleds. Michael was slower than Peter to learn. He tried again and again and each time succeeded only in making the knots tighter.

"Never mind," Peter was anxious to get started. "I'll untie his for him."

"Na, he'll have to know. Next time he'll have to show his team."

The lesson went on and after a time Michael learned the trick.

"And can you show the others?"

Michael felt he could.

"All right, then. Off with you. You bring back the ropes and sacks. These we need again," Per Garson instructed. "For your pockets, here." He handed each a flat parcel. "Your lunch. For supper you go to Holms' farm where you'll get plenty good hot meal."

He led the way to the opening. "Now I think it's time you go."

Soon would come the moment the four children dreaded—
the first German sentry.

Per Garson said the Nazi[1] soldiers were on their way to the
town but the children had not seen them.

The rest of the morning had been spent pulling the heavy
sleds through the woods. They had to go almost all the way back
to the village of Riswyk before they could begin to toboggan down
the mountain.

What would happen?

What if the Nazis refused to allow them to go on?

What if, somehow, they suspected and began to search the
sled?

Peter wouldn't let himself think of what might happen. He
made up stories about the four of them. They were Vikings and
their sleds were Viking boats. They were sailing the seas. They
would go far, far away. The very nearest they would go would be
to America.

"Peter, I'm hungry. Let's eat," Michael proposed when they
were barely out of the woods. But Peter had wanted to get a
start on the long ride down the mountain. When Michael repeated
his request a little later he agreed.

It's an idea, he thought. It would postpone their first brush
with the sentinels.

"Girls, we eat," Michael yelled.

They pulled up on a bank beside the road. Their sleds in a
cluster, they sat munching the dark bread, dried fish, cheese and
cold meat.

"Come on, Michael. Race you to the lookout," Peter wiped
his mouth on the back of his mitten.

The lookout was where Peter and Michael, Helga and
Lovisa had seen Uncle Victor the day he had so strangely returned to Norway. But now, when the four companions reached
that point, it was not to be the scene of a snow battle and all the

[1]Nazi (nä´ tsē): another name for the German government of that time

fun that went with it. Instead there were solemnness and silence, and Lovisa's blue eyes were round with fright.

The lookout today revealed an entirely different sight and one to strike fear into the stoutest.

A German freighter was at anchor in the fiord. Steaming up, she might be about to sail. On the beach that lay between the Atlantic Ocean and Riswyk Fiord, there were hundreds of gray-clad soldiers and there were others on the narrow strip of land between the big fiord and the small one they called the Snake. They were unloading enormous amounts of supplies because the snow was covered with bales, boxes, crates and drums. Rifles were stacked in neat rows, and up and down the beach in front of the fishing pier, sentries were goose-stepping while their companions worked.

"Whew!" Peter drew off his cap to wipe his forehead.

And now Lovisa was not the only one to be afraid. Fear looked out of all eyes.

It was Helga who made them brave again.

"I'm not afraid of any goose-step!" She shook the curls that hung like sausages from under her hood. "What's there to be afraid of?"

"Come on, then." Peter straightened his shoulders. He drew his sled away from the others. "Let's go."

"Look!" Michael could not take his eyes off the beach. "Soldiers marching right up our sled track. How'll we get down?"

They turned back to the sight below. Michael was right. A company of men had started up the only road that led from the sea to the mountain.

"We could hide till they passed," Lovisa urged.

"Or go down over the rocks," Michael suggested.

"But what'd we do with our sleds? We couldn't take them down that way," Peter replied.

"We'll have to meet them sometime," Helga said. "It might as well be now as later."

"Right," Peter answered. "Uncle Victor said they were to see us today on our sleds. If we sail right into them they'll see us for sure. Come on. Keep to the side and try not to spill any of 'em for that'd be bad for us."

He fell face down on his sled. With a shove he began the descent to the beach.

The Germans were a long way off. The road made several turns in the miles between the lookout and the shore below and only from the lookout could any part of the road be seen. So there was no way to tell if the Germans would turn off before they met them.

"Maybe they're not coming all the way," Peter told himself. "Maybe they'll turn aside."

But when he rounded the slope's last bend he had no such hope. Directly in front was a company of gray-clad, goose-stepping soldiers. Even on the glassy surface their legs swung out straight as rods.

Peter had no way to stop himself and now he found he was headed right into the middle of them. He let out a war whoop, a warning he was coming. But the Germans were directly in his path. He didn't see how he could avoid knocking them down like ten pins.

He was going to spill them, all right, try as he might not to. It was the worst possible thing, he knew. Near at hand these grim gray marching soldiers towered like giants to the boy on his sled.

Down he flew, faster, faster.

At one hundred yards he swerved toward the bank to avoid knocking down a whole row of men.

A voice was barking a command in German and the company took three steps to the side and out of Peter's path.

His swerve drove him into the bank and stopped him as he had not dared to hope. But he had already passed the first of the troops. Only their quick side march had saved a collision.

He raised his eyes from the snow. He was looking into the smiling face of a German infantry captain.

"I turn my men aside." He spoke in Norwegian. "It is not right that we spoil your sledding. When I was a boy I liked nothing better than sledding."

The blood rushed out of Peter's head. He was certainly dizzy. He closed his eyes. When he opened them again he was looking up the slope at the heels of the last row of German goose-steppers.

Michael and the girls joined him on the bank.

"Well, what do you know about that?" Michael was open-eyed with wonder.

"He turned his whole company aside!" Lovisa found it equally hard to believe.

Peter sat up. "If he hadn't, I would have plowed right into 'em. I might have broken my sled and the bricks would have spilled, maybe."

"The least that could have happened would have been to make them angry." Helga spoke thoughtfully.

"We've been lucky, I guess," Peter admitted.

"I told you there was nothing to be afraid of." Helga shook her curls. "When they turn out for you like that they can't be so terrible. Come on. We've got to get to the Snake."

There were more German soldiers to pass before they could make the bend into the farther fiord they called the Snake. To these they would likewise have to come close.

Nearest were the sentries that patrolled between the stacked rifles and the road down from the mountains. The sleds would pass within a few feet of where they walked.

"If Uncle Victor wants them to see us today he gets what he wants," Lovisa pointed out. "They'd have to be blind to miss us."

"Uncle Victor didn't know it would be as bad as this," Peter grumbled. "He didn't say they'd be marching on the road."

"Well, we got past them, didn't we? Come on, Peter, let me go first." Helga begged. "It would look even less suspicious if a girl went first."

But Peter was head of the Defense Club and it was for him to lead them wherever they had to go. No matter what would happen, he must go first. But he was still frightened enough to want Helga to take the lead.

They got on their sleds again, with one mile to go before they would turn the bend by the cliff that hid the entrance to the Snake.

The sentries were taking their stiff-kneed walks beside the rifles. The other Germans went on with their work of unloading the supplies. Nobody so much as looked at the children on their sleds.

What if the sentries were to stop them? Peter asked himself.

What if they wouldn't let them pass?

The captain had been friendly because he himself used to like to toboggan, and anyway it was not his job to be on watch as it was these guards'.

But when he went directly in front of the first sentry, he saw only a blank face. There was not so much as a look to show if he was pleased or displeased.

Beyond the sentry Peter saw some soldiers dragging a heavy tarpaulin over the snow. One of them looked in his direction. Under the round cap and fringe of yellow hair he saw the bluest eyes he had ever seen in his life. They seemed to say that he, too, would like to be sled-riding.

Another sentry was stepping up the line over the churned snow and beyond him, another. Like the first one, they had only blank looks to give the children. None of them so much as lifted a finger to stop them.

So they were going to be allowed to go on!

Uncle Victor had been right when he said that no one would suspect boys and girls on their sleds.

Peter breathed a sigh of relief and dug his heels into the snow for a fresh start.

The cliff that hid the Snake was just ahead. Beyond it they would be safe from curious eyes. That day, anyway, would be won.

The sleds would have to be dragged the rest of the way as the ground was level. But it wasn't far to go, after the cliff was passed. There only remained to find the two fallen trees and to bury the gold and build the snowmen.

In the Snake, Peter stopped to get his breath. His sled was terribly, terribly heavy. He hadn't noticed how heavy it was when he pulled it through the woods from the cave. Now it was a fearful load.

The others were close on his heels. They, too, seemed tired. Even Helga crept along, dragging her crushing load of gold.

"But where's Uncle Victor's boat?" Peter searched both sides of the stream with his eyes. There was no boat on the black water.

"The trees!" Lovisa's eyes fell on a flat stretch that was closed in at two ends by long ridges of snow.

"Here's one of them," she poked her arm to the elbow into the crusted white. Then she ran through the deep untrodden stretch. "And here," she called, "is the other."

The four of them began burrowing in the snow. Four pits were made and into each went the brown covered bricks. Then four snowmen rose over the bricks. Each stood guard over a mound of gold worth more than eighty thousand kroner—twenty thousand dollars. So, between the trees, eighty thousand dollars in gold bullion lay buried in the snow.

"We've done it!" Peter exulted. "We passed them and they never guessed."

"Dumb stupid things," Helga's lips curled in scorn.

"We did it! We did it!" Lovisa thumped Helga on the back and then threw her arms around Peter.

And now none of them was tired. They pounded one another's backs and shoulders. They joined hands and circled around and around Peter's snowman.

"And the captain turned aside his troops because he didn't want to spoil our sled track!" Helga burst out laughing. "Oh, if he only knew!" Tears ran out of her eyes. Weak from laughter she could no longer stand and fell helplessly in the snow.

In roars the others fell down beside her.

"He said when he was a boy, there was nothing he liked better than sledding!" Peter choked with mirth. "He likes sledding and so do we."

"Oh, if he only knew!"

◆ Library Link ◆

Would you like to learn more about how Peter and his friends saved nine million dollars of their country's gold? Find out by reading Marie McSwigan's book Snow Treasure, *from which this selection was excerpted.*

Reader's Response

Which of the four children do you think was bravest? Explain your answer.

TREASURE IN THE SNOW

Thinking It Over

1. What important mission were Peter, Helga, Michael, and Lovisa asked to carry out?
2. Why were children, rather than adults, asked to carry out the mission?
3. Do you think it was wrong of Uncle Victor to risk the children's lives to get the gold out of Norway? Explain your answer.
4. If the German soldiers had not moved out of the way, what do you think might have happened to Peter?
5. What did the four children finally do with the gold bars?
6. How do you think the experience the four children went through will affect the way they behave throughout their lives?

Writing to Learn

THINK AND PLAN Read this part from "Treasure in the Snow," which has been rewritten in play form. Notice how stage directions in parentheses make the speaking parts clearer.

> Peter: (Grumbling) He didn't say they'd be marching on the road.
>
> Helga: Well, we got past them, didn't we? Come on. (Pause) Peter, let me go first.
>
> Peter: I'm to lead wherever we go. (Pause) Oh, all right. You take the lead.

WRITE Find another part from "Treasure in the Snow." Write that part in play form. Be sure there are at least three people who speak.

83

LITERATURE LINK

How can you take charge of your own reading and learning?

The story "Treasure in the Snow" is based on an event that really happened during World War II. Only the names and conversations came from the author's imagination. Did the fact that this was a true adventure make you more curious about these children? Did you wonder why the war started and how it turned out? Or did you already know something about it?

When you read about real events and people, always keep in mind what you would like to know. When you take charge of your own reading and learning, you focus on interesting things that really matter to you.

Making a K-W-L Chart

A K-W-L chart helps you focus on what you want to learn from your reading. The chart below was made by someone who was starting to read "Treasure in the Snow." You can see that the chart keeps track of three kinds of information.

K— What I already **KNOW**	W— What I **WANT** to find out	L— What I **LEARNED** from reading
World War II was fought about 50 years ago. Germany and Japan were on one side. The U.S. was on the other.	Did these Norwegian children save their country's gold? Who asked them to help?	

Here's how you can create a K-W-L chart. Look at the completed chart as you read these directions.

- Ask yourself: What do I already know about this person or event? List these facts in the **K** column.
- Ask yourself: What do I want to know? List questions in the **W** column.
- As you read, keep your questions in mind. Remember, you're in charge!
- After reading, ask yourself: Did I learn what I wanted to? List answers and any other facts that interest you in the **L** column.
- Correct any wrong information in column **K**.

Now think back to "Treasure in the Snow" and complete the sample K-W-L chart on your own piece of paper. Did you learn anything you wanted to know? What did you find out that you hadn't expected to learn?

Try making a K-W-L chart as you read "Memories of Helen Keller." Focus on gathering information and build on what you already know about this amazing woman.

Memories of
HELEN KELLER

from *The Story of My Life* by Helen Keller

Anne Sullivan came into Helen Keller's life with a gift as remarkable as life itself.

Helen Keller was born on June 27, 1880, in Tuscumbia, a little town in northern Alabama. She spent the first months of her life much like any baby. Born into a loving and caring family, she was bright and eager to learn. As early as six months she began to say a few words. One of these, which later became significant, was the word water.

Then in the winter of 1882, a mysterious illness caused her life to change forever. The morning the fever went away her family rejoiced. They did not know that she had been left both blind and deaf, never to see or hear again.

Here in her own words are Helen Keller's early memories of what it was like to be lost in her dark and silent world. But here, too, you will read about the incredible days when her teacher, Anne Sullivan, first came to her. These memories have been selected from Helen Keller's autobiography, The Story of My Life.

Memories of her early childhood home

Even in the days before my teacher came, I used to feel along the square stiff boxwood hedges, and, guided by the sense of smell, would find the first violets and lilies. There, too, after a fit of temper, I went to find comfort and to hide my hot face in the cool leaves and grass. What joy it was to lose myself in that garden of flowers, to wander happily from spot to spot, until, coming suddenly upon a beautiful vine, I recognized it by its leaves and blossoms, and knew it was the vine which covered the tumble-down summer-house at the farther end of the garden! Here, also, were trailing clematis, drooping jessamine, and some rare sweet flowers called butterfly lilies, because their fragile petals resemble butterflies' wings. But the roses—they were loveliest of all. Never have I found in the greenhouses of the North such heart-satisfying roses as the climbing roses of my southern home. They used to

"Ivy Green," The Keller Homestead

hang in long festoons from our porch, filling the whole air with their fragrance, untainted by any earthy smell.

. . . of her father

My earliest distinct recollection of my father is making my way through great drifts of newspapers to his side and finding him alone, holding a sheet of paper before his face. I was greatly puzzled to know what he was doing. I imitated this action, even wearing his spectacles, thinking they might help solve the mystery. But I did not find out the secret for several years. Then I learned what those papers were, and that my father edited one of them.

My father was most loving and indulgent, devoted to his home. . . . His special pride was the big garden where, it was said, he raised the finest watermelons and strawberries in the county; and to me he brought the first ripe grapes and the choicest berries. I remember his caressing touch as he led me from tree to tree, from vine to vine, and his eager delight in whatever pleased me.

He was a famous story-teller; after I had acquired language he used to spell clumsily into my hand his cleverest anecdotes, and nothing pleased him more than to have me repeat them at an opportune moment.

... of her early frustrations

I do not remember when I first realized that I was different from other people; but I knew it before my teacher came to me. I had noticed that my mother and my friends did not use signs as I did when they wanted anything done, but talked with their mouths. Sometimes I stood between two persons who were conversing and touched their lips. I could not understand, and was vexed. . . .

Meanwhile the desire to express myself grew. The few signs I used became less and less adequate, and my failures to make myself understood were invariably followed by outbursts of passion. I felt as if invisible hands were holding me, and I made frantic efforts to free myself. I struggled—not that struggling helped matters, but the spirit of resistance was strong within me; I generally broke down in tears and physical exhaustion. If my mother happened to be near I crept into her arms, too miserable even to remember the cause of the tempest. After awhile the need of some means of communication became so urgent that these outbursts occurred daily, sometimes hourly.

... of the day her teacher arrived

The most important day I remember in all my life is the one on which my teacher, Anne Mansfield Sullivan, came to me. I am filled with wonder when I consider the immeasurable contrasts between the two lives which it connects. It was the third of March, 1887, three months before I was seven years old.

On the afternoon of that eventful day, I stood on the porch, dumb, expectant. I guessed vaguely from my mother's signs and from the hurrying to and fro in the house that something unusual was about to happen, so I went to the door and waited on the steps. The afternoon sun penetrated the mass of honeysuckle that covered the porch, and fell on my upturned face. My fingers lingered almost unconsciously on the familiar leaves and blossoms which had just come forth to greet the sweet southern spring. I did not know what the future held of marvel or surprise for me. . . .

I felt approaching footsteps. I stretched out my hand as I supposed to my mother. Some one took it, and I was caught up and held close in the arms of her who had come to reveal all things to me, and, more than all things else, to love me.

. . . of her first lessons ———————————————————————

The morning after my teacher came she led me into her room and gave me a doll. The little blind children at the Perkins Institution[1] had sent it and Laura Bridgman[2] had dressed it; but I did not know this until afterward. When I had played with it a little while, Miss Sullivan slowly spelled into my hand the word "d-o-l-l." I was at once interested in this finger play and tried to imitate it. When I finally succeeded in making the letters correctly I was flushed with childish pleasure and pride. Running downstairs to my mother I held up my hand and made the letters for doll. I did not know that I was spelling a word or even that words existed; I was simply making my fingers go in monkey-like imitation. In the days that followed I learned to spell in this uncomprehending way a great many words, among them *pin, hat, cup* and a few verbs like *sit, stand* and *walk*. But my teacher had been with me several weeks before I understood that everything has a name.

[1] Perkins Institution: a school for the blind in Boston, Massachusetts.
[2] Laura Bridgman: a deaf and blind student, the first to be educated by Dr. Samuel Howe, a pioneer in teaching the deaf-blind.

One day, while I was playing with my new doll, Miss Sullivan put my big rag doll into my lap also, spelled "d-o-l-l" and tried to make me understand that "d-o-l-l" applied to both. Earlier in the day we had had a tussle over the words "m-u-g" and "w-a-t-e-r."

Miss Sullivan had tried to impress it upon me that "m-u-g" is *mug* and that "w-a-t-e-r" is *water,* but I persisted in confounding the two. In despair she had dropped the subject for the time, only to renew it at the first opportunity. I became impatient at her repeated attempts and, seizing the new doll, I dashed it upon the floor. I was keenly delighted when I felt the fragments of the broken doll at my feet. Neither sorrow nor regret followed my passionate outburst. I had not loved the doll. In the still, dark world in which I lived there was no strong

Part of Helen Keller's manuscript in braille code

sentiment or tenderness. I felt my teacher sweep the fragments to one side of the hearth, and I had a sense of satisfaction that the cause of my discomfort was removed. She brought me my hat, and I knew I was going out into the warm sunshine. This thought, if a wordless sensation may be called a thought, made me hop and skip with pleasure.

We walked down the path to the well-house, attracted by the fragrance of the honeysuckle with which it was covered. Some one was drawing water and my teacher placed my hand under the spout. As the cool stream gushed over one hand she spelled into the other the word *water*, first slowly, then rapidly. I stood still, my whole attention fixed upon the motions of her fingers. Suddenly I felt a misty consciousness as of something forgotten—a thrill of returning thought; and somehow the mystery of language was revealed to me. I knew then that "w-a-t-e-r" meant the wonderful cool something that was flowing over my hand. That living word awakened my soul, gave it light, hope, joy, set it free! There were barriers still, it is true, but barriers that could in time be swept away. . . .

I remember the morning that I first asked the meaning of the word "love." This was before I knew many words. I had found a few early violets in the garden and brought them to my teacher. She tried to kiss me, but at that time I did not like to have any one kiss me except my mother. Miss Sullivan put her arm gently round me and spelled into my hand, "I love Helen."

"What is love?" I asked.

She drew me closer to her and said, "It is here," pointing to my heart, whose beats I was conscious of for the first time. Her words puzzled me very much because I did not then understand anything unless I touched it.

I smelt the violets in her hand and asked, half in words, half in signs, a question which meant, "Is love the sweetness of flowers?"

"No," said my teacher.

Again I thought. The warm sun was shining on us.

"Is this not love?" I asked, pointing in the direction from which the heat came. "Is this not love?"

It seemed to me that there could be nothing more beautiful than the sun, whose warmth makes all things grow. But Miss Sullivan shook her head, and I was greatly puzzled and disappointed. I thought it strange that my teacher could not show me love.

A day or two afterward I was stringing beads of different sizes in symmetrical groups—two large beads, three small ones, and so on. I had made many mistakes, and Miss Sullivan had pointed them out again and again with gentle patience. Finally I noticed a very obvious error in the sequence and for an instant I concentrated my attention on the lesson and tried to think how I should have arranged the beads. Miss Sullivan touched my forehead and spelled, with decided emphasis, "Think."

In a flash I knew that the word was the name of the process that was going on in my head. This was my first conscious perception of an abstract idea.

For a long time I was still—I was not thinking of the beads in my lap, but trying to find a meaning for "love" in the light of this new idea. The sun had been under a cloud all day, and there had been brief showers; but suddenly the sun broke forth in all its southern splendor.

Again I asked my teacher, "Is this not love?"

"Love is something like the clouds that were in the sky before the sun came out," she replied. Then in simpler words than these; which at that time I could not have understood, she explained: "You cannot touch the clouds, you know; but you feel the rain and know how glad the flowers and the thirsty earth are to have it after a hot day. You cannot touch love either; but you feel the sweetness that it pours into everything. Without love you would not be happy or want to play."

The beautiful truth burst upon my mind—I felt that there were invisible lines stretched between my spirit and the spirits of others. . . .

The next important step in my education was learning to read.

As soon as I could spell a few words my teacher gave me slips of cardboard on which were printed words in raised letters. I quickly learned that each printed word stood for an object, an act, or a quality. I had a frame in which I could arrange the words in little sentences; but before I ever put sentences in the frame I used to make them in objects. I found the slips of paper which represented, for example, "doll," "is," "on," "bed" and placed each name on its object; then I put my doll on the bed with the words *is, on, bed* arranged beside the doll, thus making a sentence of the words, and at the same time carrying out the idea of the sentence with the things themselves.

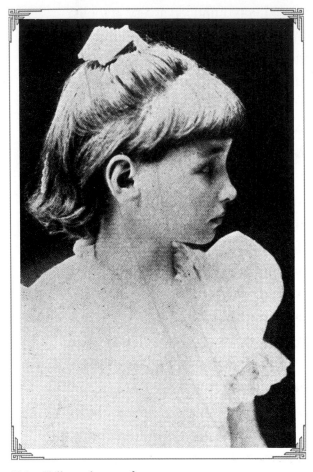

Helen Keller at the age of seven

One day, Miss Sullivan tells me, I pinned the word *girl* on my pinafore and stood in the wardrobe. On the shelf I arranged the words, *is, in, wardrobe*. Nothing delighted me so much as this game. My teacher and I played it for hours at a time. Often everything in the room was arranged in object sentences.

From the printed slip it was but a step to the printed book. I took my "Reader for Beginners" and hunted for the words I knew; when I found them my joy was like that of a game of hide-and-seek. Thus I began to read.

. . . of lessons from nature

I recall many incidents of the summer of 1887 that followed my soul's sudden awakening. I did nothing but explore with my hands and learn the name of every object that I touched; and the more I handled things and learned their names and uses, the more joyous and confident grew my sense of kinship with the rest of the world. . . .

But about this time I had an experience which taught me that nature is not always kind. One day my teacher and I were returning from a long ramble. The morning had been fine, but it was growing warm and sultry when at last we turned our faces homeward. Two or three times we stopped to rest under a tree by the wayside. Our last halt was under a wild cherry tree a short distance from the house. The shade was grateful, and the tree was so easy to climb that with my teacher's assistance I was able to scramble to a seat in the branches. It was so cool up in the tree that Miss Sullivan proposed that we have our luncheon there. I promised to keep still while she went to the house to fetch it.

Suddenly a change passed over the tree. All the sun's warmth left the air. I knew the sky was black, because all the heat, which meant light to me, had died out of the atmosphere. A strange odour came up from the earth. I knew it, it was the odour that always precedes a thunderstorm, and a nameless fear clutched at my heart. I felt absolutely alone, cut off from my friends and the firm earth. The immense, the unknown, enfolded me. I remained still and expectant; a chilling terror crept over me. I longed for my teacher's return; but above all things I wanted to get down from that tree.

There was a moment of sinister silence, then a multitudinous stirring of the leaves. A shiver ran through the tree, and the wind sent forth a blast that would have knocked me off had I not clung to the branch with might and main. The tree swayed and strained. The small twigs snapped and fell about me in showers. A wild impulse to jump seized me, but terror held me fast. I crouched down in the fork of the tree. The branches lashed about me. I felt the intermittent jarring that came now and then, as if something heavy had fallen and the shock had traveled up till it reached the limb I sat on. It worked my suspense up to the highest point, and just as I was thinking the tree and I should fall together, my teacher seized my hand and helped me down. I clung to her, trembling with joy to feel the earth under my feet once more. I had learned a new lesson—that nature "wages open war against her children, and under the softest touch hides treacherous claws." . . .

Once there were eleven tadpoles in a glass globe set in a window full of plants. I remember the eagerness with which I made discoveries about them. It was great fun to plunge my hand into the bowl and feel the tadpoles frisk about, and to let them slip and slide between my fingers. One day a more ambitious fellow leaped beyond the edge of the bowl and fell on the floor, where I found him to all appearance more dead than alive. The only sign of life was a slight wriggling of his tail. But no sooner had he returned to his element than he darted to the bottom, swimming round and round in joyous activity. He had made his leap, he had seen the great world, and was content to stay in his pretty glass house under the big fuchsia tree until he attained the dignity of froghood. Then he went to live in the leafy pool at the end of the garden, where he made the summer nights musical with his quaint love-song.

. . . of her gifted teacher, Anne Sullivan

Our favourite walk was to Keller's Landing, an old tumble-down lumber-wharf on the Tennessee River, used during the Civil War to land soldiers. There we spent many happy hours and played at learning geography. I built dams of pebbles, made islands and lakes and dug river-beds, all for fun, and never dreamed that I was learning a lesson. I listened with increasing wonder to Miss Sullivan's descriptions of the great round world with its burning mountains, buried cities, moving rivers of ice, and many other things as strange. She made raised maps in clay, so that I could feel the mountain ridges and valleys, and follow with my fingers the devious course of rivers. I liked this, too; but the division of the earth into zones and poles confused and teased my mind. The illustrative strings and the orange stick representing the poles seemed so real that even to this day the mere mention of temperate zone suggests a series of twine circles; and I believe that if any one should set about it he could convince me that white bears actually climb the North Pole. . . .

It was my teacher's genius, her quick sympathy, her loving tact which made the first years of my education so beautiful. It was because she seized the right moment to impart knowledge that made it so pleasant and acceptable to me. She realized that a child's mind is like a shallow brook which ripples and dances merrily over the stony course of its education and reflects here a flower, there a bush, yonder a fleecy cloud; and she attempted to guide my mind on its way, knowing that like a brook it should be fed by mountain streams and hidden springs, until it broadened out into a deep river, capable of reflecting in its placid surface, billowy hills, the luminous shadows of trees and the blue heavens, as well as the sweet face of a little flower. . . .

My teacher is so near to me that I scarcely think of myself apart from her. How much of my delight in all beautiful things is innate, and how much is due to her influence, I can never tell. I feel that her being is inseparable from my own, and that the footsteps of my life are in hers. All the best of me belongs to her—there is not a talent, or an aspiration or a joy in me that has not been awakened by her loving touch.

Helen Keller grew up to learn and accomplish more than anyone dreamed she ever could. This remarkable woman conquered her extreme disabilities by the power of her strong will, by her amazing intelligence, and by her endless curiosity. But the vital key that opened her world was the genius of her teacher.

Helen Keller's abilities seemed almost limitless and she came to live a life filled with many kinds of activities. Her favorite amusement was sailing, and she loved riding a bicycle! She met life with unusual joy, experiencing the world around her with senses other people are seldom aware of.

She attended Radcliffe College, graduating with honors in 1904. She traveled extensively and met and conversed with many important people of her day. She devoted her life to changing the lives of others who were deprived of sight and hearing. She did this by her lectures and writing and by her own shining example. Today her story continues to transform the way the world views the physically disabled.

◆ LIBRARY LINK ◆

You may enjoy reading more of Helen Keller's incredible experiences in her autobiography, The Story of My Life.

Reader's Response

Helen Keller tells of her most important memories and discoveries. What did you discover as a result of reading about her memories?

Memories of
HELEN KELLER

Thinking It Over

1. Since Helen Keller could neither see nor hear, how was she able to enjoy her family garden and other things in nature?
2. What was it that so troubled and upset Helen before her teacher came to live with her?
3. Why did Helen call the finger spelling she first learned finger "play"?
4. What experience gave Helen the important key to language?
5. Why was it especially hard for Helen to learn what the word *love* meant?
6. Which of Anne Sullivan's personal qualities do you think was most important in teaching Helen Keller? Explain reasons for your choice.

Writing to Learn

THINK AND ELABORATE Helen Keller does not always speak of her feelings, but we can sense them by imagining how we would feel if we were in her place. Read the passage below. On your paper, write key words that describe how the author might have felt.

> I do not remember when I first realized that I was different from other people; but I knew it before my teacher came to me. I had noticed that my mother and my friends did not use signs as I did when they wanted anything done, but talked with their mouths. Sometimes I stood between two persons who were conversing and touched their lips. I could not understand, and was vexed.

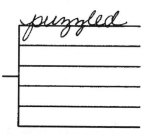

WRITE Elaborate on your discovery and compose a journal entry as Helen might have written it. Concentrate on the period in her life before she met Anne Sullivan. Let your key words suggest ideas for Helen's journal notes.

Magazine

News About Reading

Best-selling Books

The Story of My Life has been a best seller for more than eighty years.

What do Dr. Theodor Seuss Geisel and Dr. William H. Cosby have in common? Both have written best-selling books, such as *The Cat in the Hat* and *Fatherhood*. We know the authors of these best sellers better as Dr. Seuss and Bill Cosby.

A best seller has been defined as a book that sells 100,000 or more copies. Is it hard to get on a best-seller list? Figure it out for yourself: About fifty thousand books are published in the United States each year. Only about 120 reach a best-seller list. Why do some books become best sellers? One reason is that readers enjoy the book and tell their friends about it. Another reason is that people see enthusiastic reviews of the book in magazines and newspapers.

There is more than just one best-seller list. There are best-sellers for children and for adults, best-selling paperbacks,

Dr. Seuss has written many best-selling books for children.

Publishers Weekly
CHILDREN'S BESTSELLERS

BABIES & TODDLERS

MIDDLE READERS

1 **The Return of the Indian.** Lynne Reid Banks. Avon/Camelot, paper $2.95.

2 **Sarah, Plain and Tall.** Patricia MacLachlan. Harper Trophy, paper $2.50.

3 **Lincoln: A Photobiography.** Russell Freedman. Clarion, $15.95.

4 **The Whipping Boy.** Sid Fleischman, illus. by Peter Sis. Troll Associates, paper $2.95.

5 **Kristy and the Snobs (Babysitters Club #11).** Ann M. Martin. Scholastic, paper $2.75.

best-selling hardcover books, best-selling biographies, best-selling fiction, and best-selling books of information such as cookbooks and dictionaries. The best-selling book of all time, if you add together all the versions of it, is the Bible.

What are some best sellers that you might enjoy reading? *Sarah, Plain and Tall* by Patricia MacLachlan, a novel about two children and their new mother, has not only made best-seller lists but won the 1986 Newbery Award. James

Best-seller lists in *Publishers Weekly* tell which books are popular among children of different ages.

Herriot, an English veterinarian, has written several heart-warming nonfiction best sellers about animals, such as *All Creatures Great and Small.* His books were written for adults, but many children enjoy reading them, too.

Not every best seller was written recently. *The Story of My Life* by Helen Keller, parts of which you read in the last selection, was published in 1902, but people are still buying it.

Many of the very best books never reach a best-seller list, and some books on best-seller lists are fun but not noteworthy literature. So if you never read anything but best sellers, you will miss a

lot of great reading. On the other hand, there is one thing you can always count on about a best seller: It is a book that many, many people have read and enjoyed, and the chances are you will enjoy it, too.

If you were making your own best-seller list, which books would you include?

☞ **If you found this article of interest, you might enjoy reading the book reviews written by students like yourself in the magazine Stone Soup. These books may prove to be popular with other young people and turn up on a best-seller list.**

After setting records with *Fatherhood*, Bill Cosby was back "on the charts" with *Time Flies.*

Mountain climbing can be a terribly dangerous sport. If you make a wrong move, the next step could be your last. That's why teamwork is so important.

CLIMB ON!

BY ROY A. GALLANT

Have you ever thought of becoming a skilled mountain climber? Maybe you have already climbed a mountain and know the feeling of achievement it brings. Or maybe you are afraid of heights and don't much like the idea of dangling at the end of a rope halfway down a 60-foot cliff. If you are, don't worry. So is just about everyone else.

Many of the people who climb mountains do it as a challenge to themselves—to show that they are stronger than their fears. The danger and beauty of high mountains have long lured people who like adventure and who like to test their courage and skill. But there are still other reasons for climbing a mountain, which you'll find out about as you read this article,

and the story about Rudi and Teo that follows.

The first mountain I climbed was Mt. Washington, in New Hampshire, when I was 14 years old. I have climbed it several times over the years. It is not a very high mountain (6,288 feet), but sudden summer or winter storms can make it a dangerous one that has claimed lives. On April 12, 1934, the mountain was torn by the highest winds ever measured on Earth—231 miles an hour.

The climb I remember the best was up the treacherous icy slopes of Japan's famous Mt. Fuji[1] (12,388 feet high). My first view of the mountain had been from shipboard on the morning of my arrival in Japan. The grace and beauty of Fujiyama,[2] as the

[1]Fuji (fōō′ jē)

[2]Fujiyama (fōō′ je yä′ mu)

Japanese call it, are something I will never forget. I knew that one day I would climb that mountain.

Several months later four of us decided to make the climb. It was February, a time when few people would consider challenging the mountain because of the bitter cold, ice, and strong winds. At several meetings we discussed the route to the top, and the equipment and supplies we would need.

There was no shortage of danger on this climb. We set up base camp at the 5,000-foot level and spent the night in sleeping bags and small tents for shelter against the wind. The temperature dipped to -20° F that night. The plan was to continue our climb just after sunrise and to reach the top around noon. After lunch and a rest we would then make the quick descent to our base camp before dark.

As I said, that was the plan.

The climb to the top was over a seemingly endless field of soft ice blindingly bright under cloudless sky. We wore face masks, slit goggles, and down clothing. Strapped to the soles

of our bulky boots were metal frames with sharp spikes about three inches long, called crampons. These would dig into the ice and give us a firm footing as we climbed. Each of us carried an ice ax. About the height of a golf club but much stouter, it has a sharp metal point on the bottom end. At the top on one side is a curved and pointed shaft of metal about a foot long. On the other side is a shorter wide blade used to cut steps into ice or hard snow. The bottom end and curved shaft at the tip can be rammed into the ice or snow and used as an anchor.

So equipped, we made our way toward the top. We were tied to one another by rope and climbed in single file. About 25 feet of rope separated one climber from the next. For the first part of the climb we could walk as a group using our ice axes from time to time to brace ourselves against the wind.

By late morning we had reached the 11,000-foot level. Progress had been slow because of the winds, which became stronger as the day wore on. From our height the clear sky was a deep blue and the countryside stretched away far below, appearing as a toy land. The waters of Tokyo Bay glistened in the bright sunlight and the coastline snaked its way north toward Tokyo. In the lead, I signaled for a rest and with a sweep of my ice ax indicated the splendid view. Rick, the climber below me, shouted up, "So this is why we came!" I could barely hear him above the wind.

. . . I found myself suddenly signaling the others to drop to the ice and dig in with their axes to anchor themselves.

As we moved on, the wind became stronger. More and more often I found myself suddenly signaling the others to drop to the ice and dig in with their axes to anchor themselves. We would then move on until the next long gust. To keep warm we had to

keep moving. I had the grisly memory of the French climber Maurice Herzog who, in 1950, became the first to scale the famous Annapurna, 26,504 feet high. His hands and feet became so frostbitten that all of his fingers and toes had to be amputated.

By noon the top was in sight but

in my heart I knew that we would not make it, not that day. The winds were no longer gusting but howling steadily and it was almost impossible to stand. (We later learned that we had been fighting winds of 85 miles an hour.) The only way we could climb now was one at a time. The three below me would anchor, or belay, with their ice axes while I climbed until I ran out of

There are no ''loners'' in this kind of climbing.

slack rope. I would then belay and signal for the second climber to climb until he reached the end of his rope. He also would belay and signal the third climber to climb. In this way

there always were three of us belayed while one was climbing. Should a climber slip or be blown off balance, the other three could hold him until he regained his footing. Such cooperation among climbers is essential to the safety of the group. There are no ''loners'' in this kind of climbing.

As the lead climber, I was responsible for the safety of the others. I pointed to the top with my ice ax and then shook my head no. The wind was howling so much now that I was unable to hear the shouts of a climber only three feet away. I then pointed down the slope and signaled everyone to lie flat. Each of us now used the curved shaft-end of our ice ax as a brake as we let ourselves slide down over the ice. At first, we slid one at a time, one slider held by three belayers. Eventually, at lower heights the winds eased and allowed us to slide as a group, which was much faster than using our feet. At the 7,000-foot level we stopped to rest and eat lunch. The climb back down to camp was uneventful and not once, then or afterward, did one of us grumble about not reaching the top. We all had learned something from that climb—the importance of cooperation.

A week later back in Tokyo I read a story in the *Nippon Times* reporting that a group of three Japanese climbers four days earlier had attempted the climb up the same route we took. They had not used climbing rope and one of them had been blown off balance and tumbled to his death. He slid some 5,000 feet over the ice and was stripped of his clothing and equipment by the sharp points of volcanic rock sticking up out of the ice.

Although I have climbed both summer and winter, it is the summer climbing I have enjoyed most. One of the first lessons I was taught was *never* to climb alone, which brings us back to the importance of the teamwork involved in climbing, as in many other sports.

When there are only two climbers, one climbs while the other belays. The person climbing chooses a route to follow up the first pitch. You can think of the route as the "path" you are going to follow up to that next ledge where you will wait for your partner. A *pitch* is one section of a climb. The person climbing always makes sure to have three sound points of support—two footholds and one handhold, or two handholds and one foothold. As climbers make their way up a rock face they should be secure enough to lean out from the rock far enough to see their route clearly. Sometimes a climber uses a method called *jamming*. This involves jamming the toe of your boot or your fingers or hand into a vertical crack in a cliff face, and pulling yourself up bit by bit.

Mountain climbing requires good technique . . .

On reaching the first goal, that ledge, the climber changes roles and becomes the belayer or anchor. The belayer controls the rope tied to the climber below and so keeps the climber from falling if he or she slips.

the right equipment . . .

making use of crevices and projections . . .

and, on top of it all, teamwork.

One kind of belay is the *rock belay*. The belayer may hitch her or his end of the rope around a projection of rock that serves as an anchor. The belayer then keeps reeling in the rope as the climber nears. Another kind of belay is the *body belay*. When there is no handy projection of rock to tie onto, the belayer may wrap one end of the rope around the waist or up over one shoulder. As one hand pulls the rope to prevent slack, the other

Rappelling is a quick way of coming down.

hand acts as a brake by jamming the rope around the body to prevent it from slipping. In this case, the belayer must support all the weight of the climber should the climber fall. Once the climber reaches the ledge, the two change roles again and so on to the top.

A quick way of coming down off a high ledge is by *rappelling*. It looks dangerous, and may be. But it's also fun. You first make an anchor point at the top of the ledge. A chock hammered into a crevice makes a good anchor in this case. Next you thread a double thickness of your climbing rope through a ring attached to the chock and then through metal rings attached to your climbing harness. You then step off the ledge and slide down the rope, controlling your speed with your braking hand. Once down, you can look around for the next challenge and prepare to "Climb on" again.

Reader's Response

Do you agree with the author's decision to turn back during the Mount Fuji climb? Explain your answer.

CLIMB ON!

Thinking It Over

1. For what reasons do people climb mountains?
2. Why does the author feel that the first lesson of mountain climbing is never to climb alone?
3. Why do you think the author has the most vivid memories of his climb up Mt. Fuji?
4. What might have happened if the author had insisted on finishing the climb up Mt. Fuji?
5. Describe three mountain-climbing techniques.
6. Do you think the benefits of mountain climbing outweigh the risks? Explain your answer.

Writing to Learn

THINK AND UNDERSTAND Roy Gallant uses key words to make the experience of mountain climbing real. Below is an illustration of *rappelling*. Make a sketch to illustrate one of the two terms at the right.

Rappelling

jamming

rock
belaying

WRITE In your imagination, place yourself on a mountain. Write a paragraph or two about a climb in which you use the method of jamming or belaying.

*Rudi lives in Switzerland and yearns to be a mountain-climbing
guide. But a guide must be responsible for others, and on a recent
climb on Wunderhorn Rudi had risked people's lives unnecessarily.
Now he fears that he will never be given a second chance.*

MASTER AND PUPIL

by James Ramsey Ullman
from *Banner in the Sky*

It rained. For three days sun and mountains alike disappeared,
and the valley of Kurtal was wrapped in a cloak of gray mist.

On the fourth day the weather cleared. First the rain stopped.
Then the mist lifted slowly, disclosing the high world above the
valley: the meadows, the forests, the boulder-slopes, the glaciers,
and finally the great circle of the peaks. Up on the peaks, of
course, it had not been rain that had fallen, but snow, and the host
stood white and gleaming in the returning sun. High above all the
rest rose the Citadel, its summit a vast, blinding dazzle in the
cloudless sky.

Teo, the cook, stood at the open window and sniffed the air like an old bloodhound. Then he turned and looked at Rudi, who was at his usual place at the dishpan.

"Tomorrow is your day off?" he asked.

"Yes," said Rudi listlessly.

"I will make it my day off too. Gretchen can manage. Meet me at my house at eight o'clock."

The boy stared at him, uncomprehending. "Your house, sir?" he repeated.

"Yes, we will start from there."

"Start? What do you mean? Where are we going?"

"You are going to school," said Old Teo.

Leaving the town, they followed a twisting path up through the pastures. It was not the path that led toward the Citadel and Wunderhorn, but another one, on the opposite side of the valley. Old Teo went first and, in spite of his limp, kept up a strong and steady pace; and in two hours they were out of the forest and on the boulder-slope above. Directly in front of them now was a small peak known as the Felsberg. Dwarfed by the greater peaks around it, it was scarcely noticeable from the valley, and its summit was not even high enough to have caught snow in the recent storm. But, though small, it was steep and rugged, and it was often used as a "practice mountain" by guides and visiting climbers.

"Well," said Teo, peering up at its crags, "now we will see if you are a climber or a dishwasher."

Skirting the base of the Felsberg, they came to the foot of a tall cliff, and Teo sat down on a boulder. "All right," he said. "To the top and back, please. I will watch."

"Yes sir," said Rudi.

For a few minutes he studied the cliff, picking out his route. Then he started off. He did not, of course, have his fine new boots, and with smooth-soled shoes he had to be extra careful; but he concentrated closely and made good progress. He did not hug the rock, as an amateur would, but leaned well out from it, so that

114

he could see what he was doing. He tested each hand and foothold before he trusted his weight to it and made sure that, whenever possible, he had three sound points of support. After each section of the climb he paused and again studied the rocks above him, so that he would not, by haphazard climbing, get himself into some impossible position from which he could neither go on nor descend. Reaching the top of the cliff, he rested briefly. Then, with equal care and concentration, he climbed back down to where Teo was waiting.

"Was it all right?" he asked.

"Yes, of course it was all right," said the cook. "And how else should it be? On such a little thing a cow could go all right—with three legs."

They moved to another point, and he had Rudi climb again. He had him climb a cliff face, on slabs, in a steep chimney, on a knife-edged ridge. "That was a little harder," he conceded, when the boy returned to him again. "For that it would take a four-legged cow."

They circled to another side of the peak, and Teo looked up at it. "Can you do this one?" he asked.

"Yes, I think so," said Rudi.

"All right—do it with this." Unslinging his pack from his shoulders, Teo emptied out the few things that were in it and re-filled it with heavy stones.

"But—but that will throw me off balance—"

"Of course it will throw you off balance. On a real mountain, what would you rather be: a little off balance or dead from cold or starvation?"

Rudi slung on the load, and it almost buckled his knees. As he climbed, it swung maddeningly from side to side; it caught on projections and got wedged into clefts. On the steeper pitches it seemed to claw at his back like a live thing, trying to pull him loose from his delicate holds in the rock. But he made it. Up and down again. His shoulders ached, his knees shook, his body poured out sweat—but he made it.

"You want to be a guide," said Old Teo, as he rested. "A guide carries a pack. When he is a real guide he does not think of it as a load or a burden. It is as much a part of him as his rope or his boots or his clothing. It is like part of his body. Do you under-stand?"

Rudi nodded.

"All right, do it again."

Rudi did it again.

Then Teo uncoiled his rope. "Show me your knots," he said.

The boy tied and untied knots, and the old man told him what was wrong with them. He had him practice until they were right. Next they turned to belaying—the technique of holding another person on a rope. First they worked on the rock belay, in which

116

the rope is hitched around a projection in the mountain, to take the pull if a climber should fall; then on the body belay, used when there is no such projection, in which the rope is supported by the climber's own shoulders and arms. "Now let us see you rappel," said Teo when that was over. And for a half-hour, while he watched, Rudi practiced lowering himself down unclimbable cliffs by means of the doubled rope wound around his body.

By now it was past midday. Teo squinted up at the sun. "Let us eat lunch," he said. "Afterwards we will do the more important things."

Rudi had no idea what "the more important things" were, but he let it go. He would find out soon enough. Side by side, he and the old man sat on a flat rock at the foot of the Felsberg, munching their bread and sausage and looking out over the valley.

"Do you think I will ever learn, Teo?" he asked.

"Learn? To climb?" Teo rubbed a gnarled hand slowly along his jaw. "If by climbing," he said, "you mean putting one foot in front of the other and going up and down a mountain, you have learned already. Or perhaps you did not need to learn, but were born knowing." He paused, searching for the words for his thoughts. "But if you mean more than that—if you mean climbing as a guide climbs, as a true mountaineer climbs—then the answer is still to be seen."

"I want to learn, Teo. Teach me. Please teach me."

"I am not sure it is a thing that can be taught. Rather does it come with living—with growing. These climbs you have made just now: you did well on them, yes. But it is not important. It does not really matter. Do you know why it does not matter? It is because you made them alone."

Rudi started to speak, but the old man went on: "To climb alone, as one person—to find a way up steep places and not fall off: that is a part of mountaineering, of course. But only a small part. On a big mountain one does not climb alone. A guide does not climb alone. What does the word *guide* mean? It means to lead others. To help others. The other day, with that foolishness on the

Wunderhorn. How did it happen? Why did it happen? Was it not, perhaps, because you had not yet learned this? Because you were thinking, not of others, but only of yourself?''

Teo was looking at Rudi, and the old eyes were not unkindly. But the boy could not meet them.

''Yes,'' he murmured.

''And so you did a thing to be ashamed of.''

''Yes.''

They were silent awhile. The sun gleamed on the mountains. High in the sky across the valley, it struck with white fire on the crest of the Citadel, untouched and inviolate since the beginning of time.

''You did not know your father—'' said Old Teo quietly.

Rudi shook his head.

''So I will tell you something about him. Your father was the best climber there has ever been in Kurtal. He was strong. He was sure. He could go places on a mountain that other men would not even dream of. But it was not only this that made him the best. It was that—how shall I say it?—that he had a flame in him; a thing inside; not of the body but of the heart. Alone of all the guides in the valley, he believed that the Citadel could be climbed, and it was the hope of his life that he would be the one to do it.''

Teo paused and smiled a little. ''Perhaps you have heard,'' he said, ''that your father, when he climbed, always wore a red shirt?''

''Yes, I have heard,'' Rudi murmured.

''And do you know why he wore it? He wore it, he said, because he knew that someday he would stand on the summit of the Citadel. He would stand there and put a pole in the snow, and then he would take off the shirt and tie it to the pole like a flag, and the red flag in the sky would be seen from all the valleys and cities of Switzerland. When your father said this, he smiled. He pretended he was making a joke. But, inside, it was not a joke. It was what he dreamed of; what he lived for.''

Teo stared out at the great mountain. ''Then at last,'' he said, ''he had his chance. There came to Kurtal the great English climber, Sir Edward Stephenson, and he too believed the Citadel could be climbed, and wanted to do it. He and your father talked. They made their plans. They searched and explored. And then they set out. I was the only man in the valley who would go with them, and they took me along as assistant guide and porter.''

Again he paused. He looked at Rudi's face. ''Yes, you know the story. And you do not want to hear it again. But now you must hear it again, because it is the story of what I have been saying to you. It is a story that any boy who would be a guide must know and never forget as long as he lives.''

Rudi did not speak.

''We started out,'' said Old Teo. ''They had decided that the southeast ridge gave the best chance for success, so we went up the Blue Glacier and spent the night at the old hut at the top. The next morning we began climbing the ridge. It was hard, but not too hard. It went. By midday we had gained perhaps two thousand feet and an hour later were at the base of the big cliff that is called the Fortress. Here it was much harder; perhaps impossible.'' He pointed out across the blue miles of space. "Even from here you can see how the walls stand up. There was no way over them, so we looked for a way around. First we went to the right, then to the left, and on the left, far out, almost overhanging the south face, we saw what looked like an opening. We started up for it; we were nearly there. And then the accident happened. High up on the Fortress there was a great roar, and we knew that rocks were falling. We tried to run for shelter. We almost made it. But not quite. Suddenly the great rocks were crashing around us, and, though your father and I were not hit, Sir Edward was. A rock fell beside him and rolled against him, and his leg was broken.

"For an hour we stayed there. We did what we could for him, but it was not much. And of course two men alone could not get him down. Others would have to be brought up from the village, with slings and a stretcher. Your father decided that I should go down. 'And you?' I asked. 'I will stay here,' he said. It was getting late, and soon it would be dark. At the best it would be noon the next day before help could arrive. But there was nothing else to do. One of us had to stay with Sir Edward, and your father, who was chief guide, insisted that it be he. So I left them there and started down. Night came, and I lost my way. I slipped and fell.'' Teo paused and looked down at his misshapen body. "I fell, not all the way, but thirty feet, onto my left side. And since then I have been what you see now.

"But I was not dead. I was able to crawl on to the hut, and in the hut were two chamois[1] hunters, and they hurried down to Kurtal. In the morning the rescue party arrived. But meanwhile a storm had come up. For two days no one could set foot on the mountain, and on the third, when they started up, they already knew what they would find. Sir Edward and your father were in a

---

[1]chamois (sham' ē): a small goatlike mountain antelope

little cave beneath the Fortress, where I had left them. They were dead. Frozen.''

During his recital the old man had kept his eyes fixed on the mountain, but now once more he turned and looked at Rudi. ''Now do you understand,'' he said, ''why I have again made you hear this story? Your father did not die because a mountain was too steep. He did not die for conquest or for glory. Waiting there on that ridge, he himself was strong enough to go on up, or to go down. But he would not go, because he would not leave his client. He was thinking, not of himself, but of another. His red shirt—the flag that was to fly from the top of the Citadel—do you know where they found it? On Sir Edward Stephenson. While he himself was freezing to death, your father had taken it from his own back to try to keep another man warm.''

There was a long silence.

Then Teo stood up. ''Well, it is getting late,'' he said. ''And there is still one more climb to be made.''

He picked up his rope and handed one end to Rudi. Then, to the boy's astonishment he tied the other end around himself.

''You—you will climb too?'' asked Rudi.

''Yes, I will climb too.''

Rudi looked up at the sheer cliffs rising above them. Then back at Teo. He looked at the crippled leg, the hunched shoulder, the withered arm. ''But—but you cannot—'' he protested.

''I know I cannot,'' said the cook. ''Not alone, without help. . . . But I will not be alone. And you will help me.''

Rudi stared at him.

''You will be my guide,'' said Teo.

''You mean—you would trust yourself—''

''To the son of Josef Matt? Yes, of course I will trust myself.''

Seconds passed; perhaps a minute. Man and boy stood motionless, facing each other. Then they turned and walked together to the base of the cliff.

"So, up with you," said Teo.

Rudi began climbing. He climbed watchfully and carefully, while Teo payed out the rope, and presently a call from below told him that it had almost reached its full length. When he came to a good stance he turned and looked about him, and, finding a sound knob of rock, he passed the rope around it for a belay. "All right, come on!" he called. And Teo came. Rudi pulled the rope in smoothly and firmly around the rock, his body tensed for any pull or jerk. But there was none. The old man climbed slowly—very slowly—but he did not slip or stumble, and in a few minutes he was standing beside the boy on the ledge.

They went on to the next pitch. And the next. Each time Rudi went first, climbing as far as the rope would let him, and then stopped and secured it while Teo came after. Sometimes the belay was around rock, sometimes, when no rock was available, around Rudi's own body. But still Teo made no use of the support. Peering down at him from his perches, the boy marveled at how he maneuvered his crippled body on the delicate hand- and footholds: keeping his strong side always in toward the rock-face, turning his handicaps into assets, moving always at a strange lopsided angle in

order to better keep his balance. And when he came up beside
Rudi it was only to nod and say, "All right—go on."

But by now they were high on the cliff. And the going grew
harder. Rudi had to climb one stretch, first by jamming an elbow
and knee into a crevice in the rock, then by reaching up with his
free hand and pulling himself onto a ledge above. Here there was
no rock projection, and he used the body belay, bracing himself as
best he could. There will be trouble this time, he thought. And
there was. Teo got his good elbow and knee into the crevice and
somehow managed to hoist himself up, but when it came to grasp-
ing the rim of the ledge, his crippled arm could not make it. He
reached out and missed. Reached again and missed. Then his body
made a lunge. His hand touched the ledge. It clawed at it—but
could not hold it. At the same instant his voice came up to Rudi,
as quietly as if he were talking to him from the stove in the hotel
kitchen. "Steady now," he said. "Hold me."

There was a slight scratching sound: that was all. Then the
pull came. Teo's hand slipped down from the rim, his elbow and
knee lost their hold in the crevice, and he dangled free against the
mountainside. The rope bit into Rudi's body like a circular knife.
It would cut through him, he thought. But it did not cut through
him. Nor did it pull him from the ledge. Braced and straining, he

123

held fast. Then he pulled. He pulled in a foot of rope and hitched it around him; pulled again, hitched again; and again. He could hear Teo's feet scraping for support on the wall below. His hand reappeared on the rim, and then his other hand: the good hand. Rudi pulled and hitched, pulled and hitched. And then suddenly it was over; the strain and bite and tearing pressure were gone, and Teo crawled up onto the ledge beside him.

"That was not bad, boy," the old man said to him, "for a young *Lausbube,*[2] not bad at all."

Twice more he slipped before they reached the top of the Felsberg. And three times on the way down. But each time Rudi held him; and each time, though he sweated and strained, the shock and the fear were less. Where did *he* come off to be afraid, he thought grimly, when Old Teo, struggling and dangling below, was trusting his life to him without a murmur?

At the bottom, they untied themselves from the rope. Teo coiled it carefully and stowed it in his pack.

"Not bad," he said again.

And that was all he said.

[2]Lausbube (lous′ bo͞o bə): rascal

◆ LIBRARY LINK ◆

Did Rudi manage to conquer the Citadel, the mountain that his father dreamed of climbing? To find out, read Banner in the Sky *by James Ullman, from which this selection is excerpted.*

Reader's Response

What do you think was the most valuable lesson that Rudi learned from Teo?

MASTER AND PUPIL

Thinking It Over

1. Why did Teo have Rudi climb small peaks again and again?
2. What had Rudi done to feel ashamed of?
3. Why was the story Teo told about Rudi's father important to Rudi?
4. Why was Teo willing to trust Rudi on their climb together?
5. Do you think Rudi would have learned Teo's lesson if Teo had not entrusted his life to him? Explain your answer.
6. Do you think Rudi will become a mountain-climbing guide? Explain your answer.

Writing to Learn

THINK AND COMPARE In "Master and Pupil," James Ramsey Ullman wrote that when Rudi wore the backpack filled with stones, it felt "like a live thing, trying to pull him loose from his delicate holds in the rock." Make a chart like the one below that compares the backpack to a live thing.

Backpack	Live Thing

WRITE In a paragraph explain why the backpack felt like a live thing to Rudi.

125

LITERATURE LINK

How do authors express personal attitudes and feelings in stories?

What do you see in each illustration? A man and a mountain? Look again. One shows a comical character, full of pride. What does the other show? Can you feel the tension and drama of a treacherous mountain climb?

An Author's Tone

Artists convey their feelings about a subject partly by using sharp or fuzzy lines and different kinds of paint. Authors also convey their feelings about characters and events in their stories by choosing words that add a certain tone to a description. The tone may reflect a feeling such as anger, excitement, or admiration.

An author chooses words carefully to describe things vividly and also to reveal tone. For example, *monstrous* describes something large and also expresses horror. On the other hand, *colossal* also describes something large but expresses admiration. Here are ways you can detect the author's tone:

- Notice the words that are used to describe characters and events. Are they positive or negative?
- Be aware of the way the writer "talks" to you. Is it friendly, serious, foreboding, proud?
- Ask yourself: How does the writer feel about this?

The writer's tone can be a guide to the story. A disapproving tone can be a hint of future trouble. A friendly, warm tone can tip you off that things will all work out for the best. How would you describe the tone in this scene from "An Unlikely Heroine"?

> I knew the car could hit us. It was roaring at us like a blue giant. But the funny thing was I felt like a giant, too, an all-powerful one, like even if the car hit us, it wouldn't hurt us because I was made of steel, too. Like Superman. And as long as I was there, the kid was safe. I moved my giant steel legs and lifted the kid with my giant steel arms, and in what couldn't have been more than ten seconds, but felt more like ten years, I pushed us both out of the path of the car.

The writer describes a brave and likable character. Look again at her choice of words: *all-powerful, like Superman, giant.* Do you agree that the writer is expressing admiration?

Look for details the writer uses to set the tone in "To the Blue Beaches." What are the writer's attitudes toward the characters? Does the tone change as the story unfolds?

Money is made in many different ways. Carlota and
her father are particularly resourceful in finding a way to
get the money they need.

To the
BLUE BEACHES

by Scott O'Dell
from *Carlota*

*Carlota's sister was getting married, but money was
scarce on the California ranch in the 1840s. Carlota and
her father had a secret supply of gold coins in the waters
off the Blue Beach—but getting to the coins was risky.*

My father wore the heaviest of his leather breeches,
his thickest jacket, and a pair of high horsehide boots. It
was gear for the wild country that lay between the Ranch
of the Two Brothers and Blue Beach. He carried his best
musket, his tinderbox, and his powder horn. I dressed
accordingly, but carried no weapon except a knife.

There were four horses saddled and waiting for us. I
rode my stallion, Tiburón, and I rode astride.

The river would still be running a torrent. It was much
easier to cross close to the ranch and go down the south
bank, but we had no desire to get soaked so early on the
journey.

Accordingly, we chose the north bank and followed it through heavy chaparral and patches of cactus until we had ridden for two hours.

Where the river widened and ran knee-deep, we crossed to the south bank. It was still a good hour's ride from the Blue Beach. But it was here that we took the first precaution.

My father and I had been coming to Blue Beach for two years. On the three journeys we had made, we had always been followed. Sometimes by one or two Indians, sometimes by more. But to this day, no one had followed us farther than this west crossing. Here we had managed to elude them.

One thing that helped was that we never told anyone our secret—the story of the Blue Beach.

We told none of the *vaqueros*[1] or the *mayordomo*.[2] Nor Rosario, though Rosario could be trusted. Nor my sister, who could not be. Nor even Doña Dolores, whom we could trust most of all. Dolores you could hang by her thumbs and still not hear one word that she did not wish to speak.

There was no way to find the Blue Beach except by following the river, either down from the mountains or up from the sea. From the sea no one would ever find it because of a series of lagoons. From the direction of the mountains you would need to be very lucky, as lucky as we had been in the beginning.

The river at this point, where it fanned out into the deep lagoons, ran narrow, between two sheer walls of granite, where even a mountain goat would be lost. At the bottom of these cliffs were two beaches, one facing the other across a distance of a hundred steps.

The beaches were strips of fine sand, finer than the sand you find on the sea beach itself. Both had a bluish

[1]vaqueros (vä kä' rōs): cowboys   [2]mayordomo (mī yər dō' mō): foreman

130

cast, like pebbles you see through clear-running water. But they also had another color, a lighter blue that had a look of metal, as if there were copper deposits in the cliffs that had been washed down by the river and the rain and had mixed with the lighter color.

Someone might call the beaches green or the color of turquoise, but to us they were blue and this is what we called them—the Blue Beaches, more often, the Blue Beach.

On this day, as on the three other journeys we had made to the Blue Beach, we tied our horses and climbed up from the stream to a towering rock. This was where we took our second precaution, for from this high place we could survey the trails, one coming along the river, and one from the sea.

"What do you see?" my father said. He liked to test my eyesight. "Are we followed?"

"I see nothing on the trail," I said, "either from the river or from the sea."

"What is the brown spot among the oaks?"

"Where?"

"Up the river about a hundred *varas*."[3]

"I see nothing."

"Look once more."

"Does it move?"

"Judge for yourself. But first you need to find it."

I looked hard and at last made out the brown spot among the oaks. "It is a cow grazing," I said.

"There are two, and one is not a cow but a yearling fawn. What do you hear?"

"The stream."

"What else?"

"A crow somewhere."

"Is that all?"

"Yes."

"Listen."

"A woodpecker behind us."

"Yes. And what else do you hear?"

"Nothing."

"Besides the stream and the surf at the mouth of the river and gulls fishing?"

"You have good ears."

"And you will have them someday."

[3]varas (vä' rus): a unit of measurement equal to about 33 inches

"Never so good as yours."

"Better. *Mucho màs.*"[4]

Don Saturnino was silent for a while. Then he said, "Tomorrow is Carlos's birthday. He would have been eighteen had he lived."

"He would have liked these journeys," I answered.

"Perhaps. Perhaps not. Who knows? It is sufficient that you like them. You do like them, Carlota?"

"Everything, Father," I said. "Everything."

Here we sat for an hour, to make sure that we had not been followed.

When the sun was overhead, we crawled down from the pinnacle. We reached the Blue Beach and took off our boots and stepped out into the middle of the stream. We made our way for a distance of some fifty paces, leaving no tracks behind us. A clump of willows grew amidst a pile of driftwood and boulders at this place. Here the river divided and ran in two smaller streams on both sides of the willows.

The boulders could not be seen at high tide. But the tide was low now and they stuck up in two crescents, facing each other and leaving a clear space between them. The water was cold, both the sea water that met the river at this point and likewise the river water itself.

Stripped to my singlet, I splashed water on my legs, on my arms and chest. I had found that the best way to approach cold water was by small shivers, suffered one at a time.

Throwing out my arms, I took in a great gulp of air, held it for a minute, counting each second. Then I let out all the air in a quick whoosh. Then I raised my arms again and took in a greater gulp.

This air I held for two minutes, still counting the seconds in my mind—one second, two seconds, and so forth. I

[4]mucho màs (mōō′ chō mäs′): much better

133

repeated this three times. The third time I counted up to four minutes.

It had taken me two years to build up to where I could hold my breath for this length of time. My father had heard of pearl divers in La Paz who could hold their breath for five minutes and even longer. I had tried this but had fainted.

Carefully we stepped into the wide pool between the two crescents of stone, beneath the canopy of willows. We inched our way to the center of the pool, cautious not to rile the sand.

As my foot touched a smooth slab of stone, I stooped down, lifted it with much care, and set it to one side. Beneath it was a rock-lined hole filled with water, the size of my body and twice its height.

At the bottom of this hole was something that, when we first saw it, seemed to be the trunk of a tree—a tree washed down from the mountains. Undoubtedly, it once had risen above the water, but over the years floods had worn it away to a worm-eaten stump.

It had been the mainmast of a ship, which my father said was some seventy feet in length. It had the wide beam, the high stern, of the galleons that two centuries before had sailed the seas between China and the coast of California and Mexico.

These ships, my father said, came on favorable winds and currents to northern California, then along the coast south to the ports of San Blas and Acapulco. They carried great treasures from the Indies, these galleons, so great that they became the prey of American and English pirates.

Some of these treasure ships had been captured. On some, their crews had died of scurvy. Others had run aground through careless navigation. Others were driven ashore by storms. Still others had sought refuge from their pursuers by hiding in lagoons such as the one at Blue Beach.

"This must have been a large lagoon at one time," my father said when we first discovered the galleon. "A good place to hide a ship. But when it was once inside, something happened to the ship and it never returned to the sea."

Hidden in the galleon's hold, near the stump of the mainmast, were two chests filled with coins. The coins were of pure gold. They showed three castles and the two flying doves that meant they had been struck in the mint at Lima, Peru. The date marked upon each coin that we carried away on the trips we had made was the year of Our Lord 1612.

The two chests—each made of hard wood banded with iron straps and sealed with a hasp that had rusted and fallen off—were well beneath the surface of the water, whether at low tide or in the summer, when the stream ran low. This was fortunate, for had the chests been exposed, some passing Indian or *vaquero* would have discovered them.

There were many things to do before the chests could be reached. Usually it took me half a day to bring up a pouch of coins from the sunken ship.

The place where I dove, which was surrounded by the jagged rocks and driftwood, was too narrow for my father. He had tried to squeeze through when we first discovered the galleon, but partway down he got stuck and I had to pull him back. It was my task, therefore, to go into the cavelike hole. My father stood beside it and helped me to go down and to come up.

I buckled a strong belt around my waist and to it tied a *riata*[5] that was ten *varas* long and stout enough to hold a stallion. I fastened my knife to my wrist—a two-edged blade made especially for me by our blacksmith—to protect myself against spiny rays and the big eels that could sting you to death. In the many dives I had made, I never had seen a shark.

[5]riata (rē ä' tä): a leather or rawhide rope

136

Taking three deep breaths, I prepared to let myself down into the hole. In one hand I held a sink-stone, heavy enough to weigh me down. I let out all the air in my chest, took a deep breath, and held it. Then I began the descent.

The sink-stone would have taken me down fast, but the edges of the rocky hole were sharp. I let myself down carefully, one handhold at a time. It took me about a minute to reach the rotted deck where the chests lay. I now had two minutes to pry the coins loose and carry them to the surface. We had tried putting the coins in a leather sack and hoisting them to the surface. But we had trouble with this because of the currents that swept around the wreck.

The coins lay in a mass, stuck together, lapping over each other and solid as rock. They looked, when I first saw them, like something left on the stove too long. I always expected to find them gone, but now as I walked toward the chests, with the stone holding me down, I saw that they were still there. No one had come upon them during the seven months since our last visit.

The first time I had dived and brought up a handful of coins, I said to my father that we should empty both the chests and take the coins home.

"Then everyone would talk," Don Saturnino said. "As soon as they saw the gold coins the news would spread the length of California."

"We don't need to tell anyone. I can hide them in my chest at home."

"The news would fly out before the sun set. At the ranch there are many eyes."

I still thought it was a better idea to empty the chests before someone else did, but I could see that my father enjoyed these days, when the two of us went to the Blue Beach, so I said no more.

The sun was overhead and its rays slanted down through the narrow crevice. There were many pieces of debris on the deck and I had to step carefully. With my knife I pried loose a handful of coins. They were a dark green color and speckled here and there with small barnacles. I set the coins aside.

My lungs were beginning to hurt, but I had not felt the tug of the *riata* yet, the signal from my father that I had been down three minutes. I pried loose a second handful and put my knife away. Before the tug came I dropped my sink-stone and took up the coins. Gold is very heavy, much heavier than stones of the same size.

Fish were swimming around me as I went up through the hole of rocks and tree trunks, but I saw no sting rays or eels. I did see a shark lying back on a ledge, but he was small and gray, a sandshark, which is not dangerous.

On my third trip down, I hauled up about the same number of coins as the other times. The pouch we had brought was now full. I asked my father if we had enough.

"Are you tired?" he said.

"Yes, a little."

"Can you go down again?"

"Yes."

"Then go."

I dived twice more. It was on the last dive that I had the trouble. The tug on the *riata* had not come, but I was tired, so I started away from the chest with one handful of coins. Close to the chests, between them and the hole, I had noticed what seemed to be two pieces of timber covered with barnacles. They looked as if they might be part of a third and larger chest.

I still held my knife and I thrust it at a place where the two gray timbers seemed to join. It was possible that I had found another chest filled with coins.

As the knife touched them, the two timbers moved a little. Instantly, I felt pressure upon my wrist. I drew back the hand that held the knife. Rather, I tried to draw it back, but it would not move. The tide had shifted the timbers somehow and I was caught. So I thought.

I felt a tug upon the *riata* fastened to my waist. It was the signal from my father to come to the surface. I answered him with two quick tugs of the leather rope.

Now I felt a hot pain run up my arm. I tried to open my fingers, to drop the knife, but my hand was numb. Then as I stared down into the murky water I saw a slight movement where my hand was caught. At the same moment I saw a flash of pink, a long fleshy tongue sliding along my wrist.

I had never seen a burro clam, but I had heard the tales about them, for there were many on our coast. Attached to rocks or timbers, they grew to half the height of a man, these gray, silent monsters. Many unwary fishermen had lost their lives in the burros' jaws.

The pain in my arm was not so great now as the hot pains in my chest. I gave a long, hard tug on the *riata* to let my father know that I was in trouble. Again I saw a flash of pink as the burro opened its lips a little, and the fat tongue slid back and forth.

I dropped the coins I held in my other hand. The burro had closed once more on my wrist. But shortly it began to open again, and I felt a sucking pressure, as if the jaws were trying to draw me inside the giant maw.

Putting my knees against the rough bulge of the shell, as the jaws opened and then began to close, I jerked with all my strength. I fell slowly backward upon the ship's deck. My hand was free. With what breath I had I moved toward the hole. I saw the sun shining above and climbed toward it. The next thing I saw was my father's face and I was lying on the river's sandy bank. He took my knife in his hand.

After I told him what had happened, my father said, "The knife saved your life. The burro clamped down upon it. See the mark here. The steel blade kept its jaws open. Enough to let you wrench yourself free."

He pulled me to my feet and I put on my leather pants and coat.

"Here," he said, passing the reins of his bay gelding to me, "ride Santana. He goes gentler than Tiburón."

"I'll ride my own horse," I said.

"Good, if you wish it."

"I wish it," I said, knowing that he didn't want me to say that my hand was numb.

"Does the hand hurt?"

"No."

"Some?"

"No."

"You were very brave," he said.

My father wanted me to be braver than I was. I wanted to say that I was scared, both when the burro had hold of me and now, at this moment, but I didn't.

"It was good fortune," I said.

"Fortune and bravery often go together," Don Saturnino said. "If you do not hurt, let us go."

I got on the stallion and settled myself in the saddle. "Yes, let us go," I said, though I could not grip the reins well with but one hand.

◆ LIBRARY LINK ◆

If you want to find out more about how Carlota and her family lived, read Carlota *by Scott O'Dell, from which this selection is excerpted.*

Reader's Response

Do you think Carlota's risk was worth the money she found?

To the
BLUE BEACHES

Thinking It Over

1. How did Carlota and her father find the Blue Beaches?
2. Why was their discovery important to them?
3. Why did Carlota's father question her closely about the sights and sounds of their trip to the Blue Beaches?
4. Summarize the events of Carlota's last dive.
5. If Carlota had admitted her fear to her father, how do you think he would have reacted? Why do you think so?
6. What do you think Carlota's father meant when he said, "Fortune and bravery often go together"?

Writing to Learn

THINK AND VISUALIZE   If you were going to produce "To the Blue Beaches" as a movie, what scene would be the most exciting? Close your eyes and visualize it. Copy the chart shown below onto your paper, and fill in the information for the scene you chose.

	Action	Character	Place	Time	Lighting
Scene:					

WRITE   Look at the information you wrote in the chart. Then write a paragraph that communicates the feelings of the characters in the scene you, the producer, have selected to film.

BETSY BYARS

A NEWBERY AWARD BOOK

THE SUMMER OF THE SWANS

*S*he felt she would like to stand
there pointing out the swans to
Charlie for the rest of the summer.

from *The Summer of the Swans* by Betsy Byars

Sara's fourteenth summer is turning out to be the worst she can remember. Her love-hate relationship with her orange sneakers symbolizes her mood: One minute she is happy, the next she is miserable. But mostly, she is confused and discontented. If only she could fly away and escape, like the swans that have suddenly appeared on a nearby lake—and will just as suddenly go away.

Sara, the mixed-up heroine of *The Summer of the Swans,* is so caught up in her own life that she hardly has time for Charlie, her mentally retarded brother. Though Sara loves Charlie, lately she thinks he is more a bother than a brother, especially the day she takes Charlie to see the swans on the lake. But Sara quickly forgets about herself when Charlie goes looking for the swans and disappears. What seems like an endless day is really the start of a new self-confidence for Sara.

Betsy Byars's idea for *The Summer of the Swans* came from a newspaper article about an elderly man who was lost in the mountains. But the author developed the character of Charlie partly from research and partly from her experiences tutoring two children with learning difficulties. Her careful eye and subtle humor make characters like Sara and Charlie as believable and memorable as your best friends.

Times are hard in the United States during the 1930s. Meg's family can barely make a living on their Arkansas farm. Even so, Meg is determined to help her parents celebrate their anniversary in a special way.

It's the Loving That Counts

by Emily Crofford

Mother opened the steamer trunk and took out her old dresses. They were wrinkled and smelled like mothballs. Daddy's suit had mothballs in the pockets.

Sighing, Mother said, "Men's clothes don't change that much, but my dresses are just not in style."

The dresses did look different from the ones the teachers wore, but I didn't want Mother to give up the anniversary celebration. Daddy would be disappointed. Also, I knew now what I

146

was going to do for them and they would have to be away for me to do it.

"I like old-fashioned dresses," I told her.

She studied a dark blue dress, laying it out on the bed.

"I like this one better," I said holding up a black dress with a fringe on the bottom.

Mother laughed. "My Charleston dress," she said. "I can't imagine why I keep it."

I didn't want to give Daddy's and my secret away, but I had begun to worry about something. I ambled over to the dresser and took the glass stopper out of the empty perfume bottle. The stopper still smelled like rose petals. Nonchalantly, as if it were not an important question, I asked, "Did you ever go to dances in the afternoon in the old days?"

Mother, studying the blue dress, nodded absently. "Tea dances. I loved them. You know, if I made some tucks in the waist and let out the hem. . . . Run get me the catalog please, Meg."

A tea dance, a tea dance, my mind sang as I danced into the front room for the catalog.

Mother opened the catalog to Ladies Dresses.

I didn't particularly like the dresses—they were neither long nor short—but the ladies had an attitude about them that made it clear that their clothes were stylish.

Mother, glancing up from the catalog, seemed surprised that I was still there. I generally spent as little time inside as possible. I liked to play outside, and I liked outside work. Except for cooking. I liked to cook, especially baking. That was why I had decided to make Mother and Daddy a cake for their anniversary.

"Do you want to help?" Mother asked.

I nodded, and she gave me a pleased smile. "You can take the mothballs out of Daddy's suit pockets," she said. "Turn the pockets inside out, and put the coat on one hanger and the pants on another and hang them out to air."

I wasn't too crazy about the job. I could understand why the moths didn't bother to get into the steamer trunk. The mothballs made my nose smart.

Mother went into the front room, sat down at her sewing machine, and started ripping out a seam.

As soon as I had hung the suit on the clothesline, I went back in. Mother had opened the sewing machine. I stood at one end of

it, watching her work the treadle with her foot while she operated the balance wheel with her right hand and somehow managed to guide the material beneath the needle at the same time. I had never paid any attention before, but now that I had, it looked challenging. Maybe, I thought, I could help remake the dress.

Mother came to a stopping point and gave me another smile. "I'm glad to see you taking an interest in sewing."

I smiled back at her.

"You're not tall enough yet," Mother said. "You could run the needle through your finger. But the next time I have to fill a bobbin, you can do it."

I glanced at the machine needle and she said, "The needle doesn't operate when you're filling the bobbin. In the meantime, how about sweeping the house." She sighed and began to sew again. "Not that it does any good."

By Friday night Mother had finished the dress and aired and pressed it and Daddy's suit. I had helped quite a bit. I had washed dishes without grumbling. I had even sung while I did them. Mother said it was the sweetest sound she'd ever heard. And I'd taken Correy for a long walk to keep him out of Mother's hair.

On Saturday, after Daddy had left for the store to get Mr. Weatherby's pickup truck, Mother went into the bedroom to get dressed. By that time I was in a tizzy. I could hardly wait for them to leave so I could start making the cake. Keeping my plan secret had been hard, but I'd decided not to tell Bill until Mother and Daddy were gone. I was afraid he would get excited and let it slip out.

Mother's cheeks were flushed and her eyes were sparkling when she came out of her room. I told her she looked prettier than the ladies in the catalog.

When Daddy returned with the truck, he told her she was more beautiful than ever.

Already wearing the suit pants and a white shirt, it only took him a few minutes to comb his hair again and put on a necktie and the suitcoat.

Bill and Correy and I went out to the footbridge and waved good-bye until the truck was far down the road. Bill and I started back to the house, but Correy stayed at the end of the footbridge, looking down the road as if he expected the truck to turn around and come back.

"I have a wonderful surprise," I told Bill. "While Mother and Daddy are out dancing,"—I did a little jig—"we are going to make a cake for them. An anniversary cake."

Bill looked at me skeptically.

"A fancy three-layer cake. We're going to decorate it and everything."

"We've never made a cake before," Bill said. "We're probably going to make a mess and Mother will be upset."

Bill had absolutely no imagination, I thought, but I didn't say it aloud. The last time I'd told Bill he had no imagination, he'd put a grass snake in my bed to prove that he did.

Correy had finally given up on the truck coming back, and with his head down and his hands shoved in his pockets he walked glumly across the yard.

"It's time for your nap, Correy," I said. I didn't want to put up with Correy while we were making the cake. He was too little to help and would just get in the way.

"I don't wanta take a nap."

"I'm taking Mother's place while she's gone," I said. "You have to mind me. Come on in and go to bed. Right now!"

Correy's chin trembled. "I'm not sleepy right now. I don't wanta take a nap."

I grabbed his arm and he began crying and screeching, "No, no, no! I don't wanta take a nap."

If the sound carried to Aunt Louise's house, she would think I was torturing Correy. I let go of his arm and yelled, "Stop! You hear me. Stop!"

Bill rolled his eyes. "Taking Mother's place, huh?"

He was right. Mother never yelled. Of course, Correy didn't screech at her either.

I took a deep breath. "You may wait awhile for your nap," I said calmly and patiently. "Bill and I are going to make a cake for Mother and Daddy. You can watch if you'll be nice."

In the kitchen I put on one of Mother's bib aprons.

"Put in enough stovewood to get the oven good and hot," I directed Bill while I started setting out the mixing bowl and a sifting bowl and measuring cups and spoons. Mother didn't cook with recipes, but I had often helped her make cakes. I knew exactly what to do.

Bill frowned, but he picked up an armload of wood from behind the stove, brought it around to the front, and began laying sticks on the bedded coals.

When he had put in several sticks, I said, "That's enough. Now grease and flour the cake pans."

Bill dumped the remaining wood back behind the stove, crossed his arms over his chest, drew his eyebrows down, and glowered at me. "I don't have to mind you," he said.

"Yes, you do. I'm the oldest. I'm in charge."

"Come on, Correy," Bill said. "Let's go outside."

I did some quick thinking. Bill wasn't being fair, but I couldn't make him do anything. It would be miserable to have to do everything by myself.

The screen slammed behind Bill and Correy.

Quickly, I went to the door and said meekly, "I'm sorry. I guess I was being a little bit bossy."

Bill and Correy came back in and let some flies in with them. I didn't yell at them. I calmly opened the door and shooed the flies back out.

Bill threw me a mean look for good measure and got down the lard can. I got the milk and four eggs and the sugar. The hardest part would be breaking the eggs on the edge of the bowl and getting them inside instead of outside, but I didn't have to worry about that yet. Mother always sifted the flour and baking powder together first. And salt. A pinch of salt. I particularly remembered that because it seemed strange to put salt in a cake.

Bill leaned his elbows on the table to watch. Correy was kneeling in a chair. I had just gotten the dry ingredients measured into the sifter when Correy closed his hand around the handle.

"Give me the sifter, please, Correy," I said.

"I wanta sift."

"You're too little to sift," I said and tried to pry his fingers loose.

"I wanta sift, I wanta sift," Correy screeched and yanked the sifter hard. Some of the flour sifted out on the table. I closed my eyes and sighed. Sifting was what I had wanted to do most. But if I tried to take the sifter away from Correy, all the flour would get spilled.

Correy concentrated so hard on sifting that beads of perspiration popped out on his forehead, but he just couldn't do it. Instead of turning the handle smoothly, he jerked it and some of the flour spilled on the table and some spilled on the floor. Besides, at the rate he was going it would be tomorrow before we finished the cake.

"You can lick the spoon and the bowl all by yourself if you'll let me sift," I told him.

"All right," Correy said, and climbed down from the chair.

I congratulated myself just before he turned the chair over. "Uh-oh," he said, and looked up at me innocently.

I didn't say a word. I didn't give him a mean look. I just picked up the chair.

After I had sifted the flour, I thought a prayer that I could break the eggs in the bowl. The prayer worked except for one egg. The one that missed plopped on the table and the yellow broke and mixed with the white.

"I'll wipe it up," Bill said.

He tried, then I tried. We had to keep rinsing the dishcloth and wiping, and each time the egg oozed through the dishcloth and felt slimy. My hands still smelled eggy after I washed them. "Three eggs are almost as good as four," I said.

Bill and I chased the pieces of shell that were in the bowl until we finally caught them. I brushed my sweat-damp hair out of my face with the back of my hand and beat the eggs with a spoon, then let Bill put in the milk and sugar. Bill stirred while I dumped in the flour.

Correy climbed back up in the chair. "I wanta stir," he said.

I mopped my face with the apron. Between the oven and the sun beating on the back of the house, it had become terribly hot. I didn't know how Mother could stand working in the kitchen so much.

"I wanta stir," Correy said again.

"We're all through," I told him. But I had a feeling I was forgetting something. The vanilla! I had almost forgotten the vanilla. After I stirred in a capful of vanilla, I opened the oven door a crack and held my hand above it to check the temperature the way Mother did. Waves of heat flowed around my fingers, but since I had never checked the oven temperature before I didn't know whether it was right or not. "What do you think?" I asked Bill.

Bill held his hand above the door. "I don't know," he said. "Maybe I'd better put in some more stovewood."

"Okay. Three more pieces."

The cake mixture looked creamy and delicious when I poured it into the baking pans and slid them into the oven. I gave the bowl to Correy and he sat down on the floor. When he couldn't get any more of the batter with the spoon, he ran his finger around the sides and the bottom of the bowl. He didn't leave a smidgen for Bill and me. Then he went to sleep—just stretched out in the middle of the floor and went sound asleep.

I swept up the floor the best I could with him lying there. I was not about to try to put him in bed and chance awakening him. Bill put the bowls and the cup and the spoons in cold water to soak. He didn't mention putting Correy in bed either.

"And now," I said, taking off my apron, "comes the best part. The bride and bridegroom."

"Aren't you going to make an icing?"

I shook my head. "I've changed my mind. I think they'll like the cake better without icing."

Bill's eyes crinkled at the corners like Daddy's did when something tickled him. "Besides, you'd have to crack some more eggs."

"Okay, smarty pants," I said. I'd not only have to break the eggs, I'd have to separate the whites from the yellows. When Mother did it, it looked easy, but after making the cake I knew it would be impossible for me.

We couldn't find a bride and a bridegroom in the mail order catalog, but we found a lady who looked something like Mother and a man that reminded us of Daddy. We cut them out, glued them to the pasteboard back of one of Bill's old tablets, and cut around them again. By then, we figured the cake would be done. I opened the oven door and peeked. The cake had risen and turned tan.

"It smells good," Bill said.

With hot pads I carefully took out the three pans and set them on the side of the stove to cool.

A puzzled line appeared on Bill's forehead. "The cake looks kind of funny," he said.

"It may *look* a little funny," I said, "but it's going to taste delicious."

To myself I admitted that there was something wrong with the cake. All three layers had the right color except for being pale, and they didn't sink in the middle, but they looked leathery. I didn't see how missing just one egg could have caused that. Probably, I decided, the oven hadn't been hot enough.

Turning the cake out on a plate would be the trickiest part, I told Bill. I worked a spatula around the inside of the first pan, flipped it over quickly, and tapped the bottom with the spatula handle.

Bill, from eye-level with the plate, said, "You did it, Meg. It's out."

I lifted the pan and sure enough, the cake had not broken in a single place.

"It looks better upside down," Bill said.

The other two layers came out just as smoothly. We stacked them neatly. When the lady and the man wobbled after Bill stuck their feet in the cake, he propped them up with kitchen matches.

I stood back from the cake, on the side without the matches, and squinted. It was not exactly what I had envisioned, but it wasn't too bad. Actually, I decided when I squinted a little more, it was a very pretty cake.

Correy woke up, rubbed his eyes, and said, "I don't wanta take a nap."

"Come look at the cake, Correy," I said.

"I don't wanta look at the cake." He stood up and put his arms on the wall and leaned his head on them. "And I don't wanta take a nap. I told you—I don't wanta take a nap." He kicked the wall, then sat down and squalled because he had hurt his bare toes. In his whole life, Correy had never behaved as badly as he had today.

"Come on, Correy," Bill said. "We're going outside."

I didn't know whether Bill was mad at me or not, and I didn't care.

By that time it was 3:45, and I expected Mother and Daddy to drive up any minute. I tried to read my *Black Beauty* book, but my mind kept straying. The day hadn't gone the way I'd planned it. Bill hadn't let me be in charge. Making the cake had been hot, hard work. Correy had been impossible. But Mother and Daddy were having fun. They had to be to stay away so long. I imagined them whirling around the dance floor, Mother laughing, Daddy smiling tenderly down at her.

And there was still the cake. The grand finale to their anniversary celebration. Every time I went to check the clock, I stopped to admire the cake.

The minutes crawled by with all the speed of a lazy inchworm. I was beginning to worry that Mother and Daddy had had a wreck when Bill came running inside to tell me they were coming. It was 4:32.

The three of us and our dog, Brownie, waited by the footbridge while Daddy pulled the pickup to the side of the road. Before Mother reached the footbridge, Correy, with his arms outstretched, ran to her. She cuddled and kissed him.

"Could you still dance good?" I asked as we started across the yard.

Mother looked blank.

Daddy started to laugh, but he evidently saw the expression on my face because he suddenly stopped. "I'm sorry, honey," he said. "I didn't realize that you actually thought we were going dancing."

"But, oh," Mother sighed, "we had a wonderful time. We went to department stores, we had a soda at the drugstore—and we watched the people."

They had watched people?! What kind of celebration was that? All afternoon I had been picturing them dancing, and they had just been watching people. It was like expecting a peppermint stick and getting a biscuit instead. It was worse. It was like thinking there was a beautiful horse in your yard and it turned out to be a homely mule. I was so let down I could have bawled. Now there was only the cake to make this anniversary special.

As we stepped inside, Correy said, "We have a s'prise."

He had been awful and now he was happy and about to ruin everything anyway.

Correy looked at me and put his hand over his mouth. I could tell that he was sorry he had almost given away the surprise. It was hard to believe that only a little while ago he had been making ugly faces at me.

"Close your eyes," I told Mother and Daddy.

Bill and I took their hands and led them to the kitchen.

"You can open them," I said, and Bill and I did a leap and presented the cake with a sweep of our hands. "Ta-da."

"Oh, Harth," Mother said softly, "look what our children did for us."

She brought in saucers, and a knife to cut the cake with. Daddy poured glasses of milk. When we were ready, Mother removed the lady and man cutouts. "I want to keep them," she said.

Slowly, as if she were sawing through wood, Mother cut the cake. She kept smiling. One by one she put wedges of cake on the saucers and each one made a thump.

Before I took the first bite I knew the cake was a disaster. I chewed and chewed and chewed. I swallowed. Even Brownie would scorn this cake—and Brownie loved cake.

161

Numbly, I stared down at my saucer. From start to finish, my plans for Mother and Daddy's anniversary had been a failure.

"How much butter did you put in, Meg?" Mother asked. "I think that's the only thing wrong—that you didn't put in quite enough butter."

I dropped my face into my hands so they wouldn't see the dumb tears. I hadn't put in any butter. I had gotten the flour and baking powder and milk and eggs and sugar right. I had even remembered the salt and vanilla. But I had forgotten all about butter.

"Meg, darling, it doesn't matter," Mother said in such a warm positive voice that I stopped crying and lifted my head. "It's the loving that counts." As I looked at them, I realized that Mother and Daddy were glowing—they looked as happy as they had in the old photographs.

"It's not so bad if you crumble it up in your milk," Bill said.

"I don't see anything wrong with it," Correy said.

"It's a fine cake," Daddy said. "Just the kind we need. People's teeth don't get enough exercise nowadays."

The windows were wide open. The sounds of June—birds singing, chickens clucking, Dolly's new calf bleating—floated in with the breeze and mingled with our laughter.

◆ LIBRARY LINK ◆

If you liked this story by Emily Crofford, you may enjoy reading her book Stories from the Blue Road, *where this story first appeared.*

Reader's Response

What do you think was the best part of Meg's surprise for her parents?

WRITING ABOUT READING

Writing a Character Sketch

The stories in this unit introduced you to people who helped others in some way. Any of these characters could have been the subject for a character sketch. A character sketch describes what makes a particular person unique. It creates a strong impression of the person in the reader's mind by using carefully chosen details that emphasize personality traits. For example, you could write a character sketch about any one of the four young people in "Treasure in the Snow." To write the character sketch, you would use information from the story.

In addition to being about characters in stories, character sketches can be about real people. You may have read such sketches in newspapers and magazines. Now you will have the opportunity to write a character sketch about someone you know.

Prewriting

Think of someone you know who fits the characteristics of an everyday hero. It might be someone who is especially helpful to others or who has done something brave. It could be a friend, a relative, a neighbor, or a member of your community.

Make a word cluster like the one on the next page for the person you have chosen to write about. Begin by writing the person's name in the center of your page. Write down the words that come to mind when you think about that person. Let each word suggest another word. Carry the cluster as far as you can.

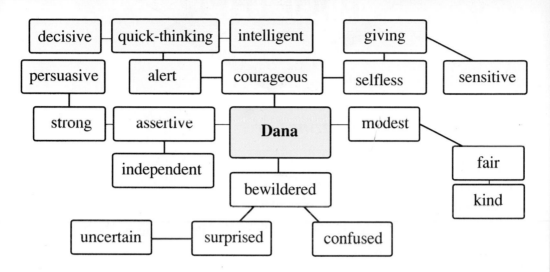

Writing

Use your word cluster to write a three-paragraph character sketch. Explain why you think your character is an everyday hero. Describe ways the person is unique. As you write, try to refer to specific things your character did or said. Using examples will help readers get to know and understand the everyday hero you have chosen.

Revising

Read your character sketch to a partner. Do the details you have included in the sketch help explain why you admire the person? What specific examples might you add to make your sketch more interesting? As you revise, use a variety of sentence types, and vary the lengths of your sentences. Add a title that sums up your character sketch.

Proofreading

Check for spelling, grammar, and punctuation errors. Make a clean, neat final copy.

Publishing

Put together a class booklet that contains many character sketches. Add pictures of the people, and entitle it *Everyday Heroes*.

Designing a News Magazine Cover

The story characters in this unit reached out to others. In the process they became "everyday heroes." News magazines often honor people by naming them "Men or Women of the Year." Do you remember Dana Parker from the story "An Unlikely Heroine"? Imagine her picture on the cover of a national news magazine.

Your group will now design a news magazine cover for one of the people in this unit. As you work, take responsibility for one or more of these tasks:

♦ Encouraging others in the group to participate

♦ Building on other people's ideas

♦ Responding to other people's suggestions

♦ Staying on the job

Before beginning, have one person from your group collect the materials you will need for the project.

Discuss the people you read about in this unit. Which one would you most want to honor on the cover of a news magazine? As a group, decide on one person. Then discuss that person's most important achievement. Was he or she very brave, unselfish, or generous?

Together, decide what your magazine cover will look like. Choose a name for the magazine and a caption that explains why the person is being honored. Each person can then be responsible for drawing or writing the different parts of the cover, such as the person's picture, the caption, the name of the magazine, and the border of the cover. Then, paste each part on a sheet of paper the size of a news magazine. Display your finished cover.

The Whipping Boy by Sid Fleischman *(Greenwillow, 1986)* A prince and a peasant boy have little reason to be friends—until adventures throw them together. The boys learn to see each other in a new light.

Over Sea, Under Stone by Susan Cooper *(Harcourt Brace Jovanovich, 1966)* On a holiday in Cornwall, the three Drew children find an ancient map. But they are not the only ones searching for the treasure. The race is on, and more than the thrill of the hunt is at stake.

The Sign of the Beaver by Elizabeth G. Speare *(Houghton Mifflin, 1983)* It is the 1700s, and Matt is alone in the Maine wilderness, with little means of finding food. Attean teaches him the Beaver clan's ways of surviving in the forest.

Trapped by Roderic Jeffries *(Harper, 1972)* Two teenage boys are lost on the mud flats of a river in England during a blizzard. Their fate lies in the decision of a commander of a police river patrol boat.

Bridge to Terabithia by Katherine Paterson *(Avon, 1979)* Leslie the newcomer isn't like the other kids. Still, Jess has never met anyone with such imagination. Together they create a make-believe kingdom in the woods, where Jess learns to conquer real-life fears.

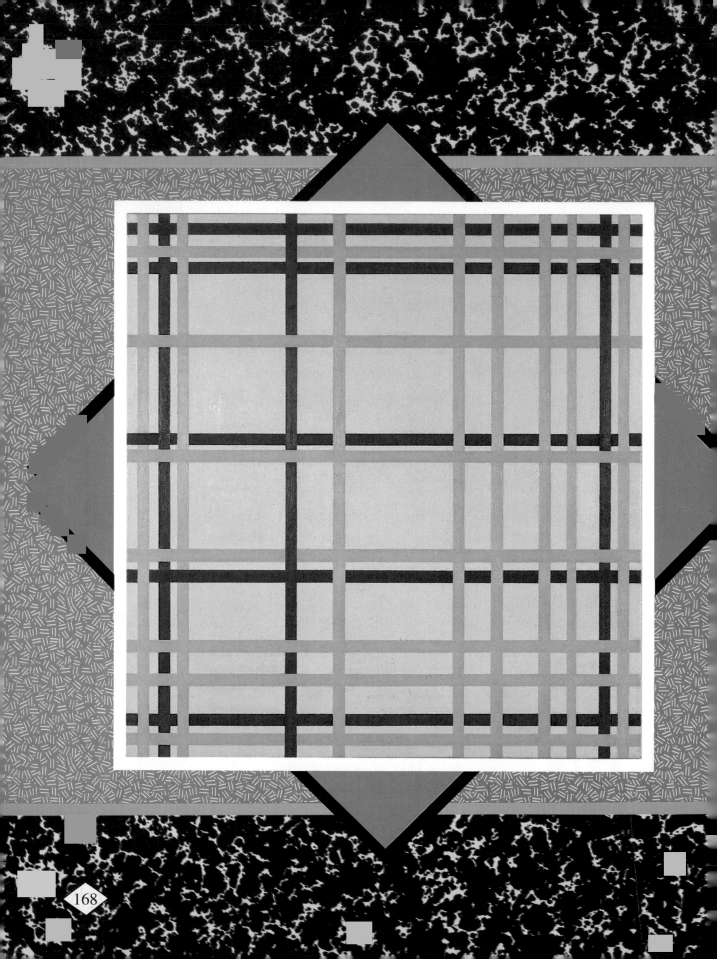

UNIT TWO

PROBLEMS AND PUZZLES

Detectives, scientists, and dreamers all look for clues.

Why do we enjoy reading about how they solve tough problems?

NEW YORK CITY I,
oil on canvas by Piet Mondrian, Dutch, 1942

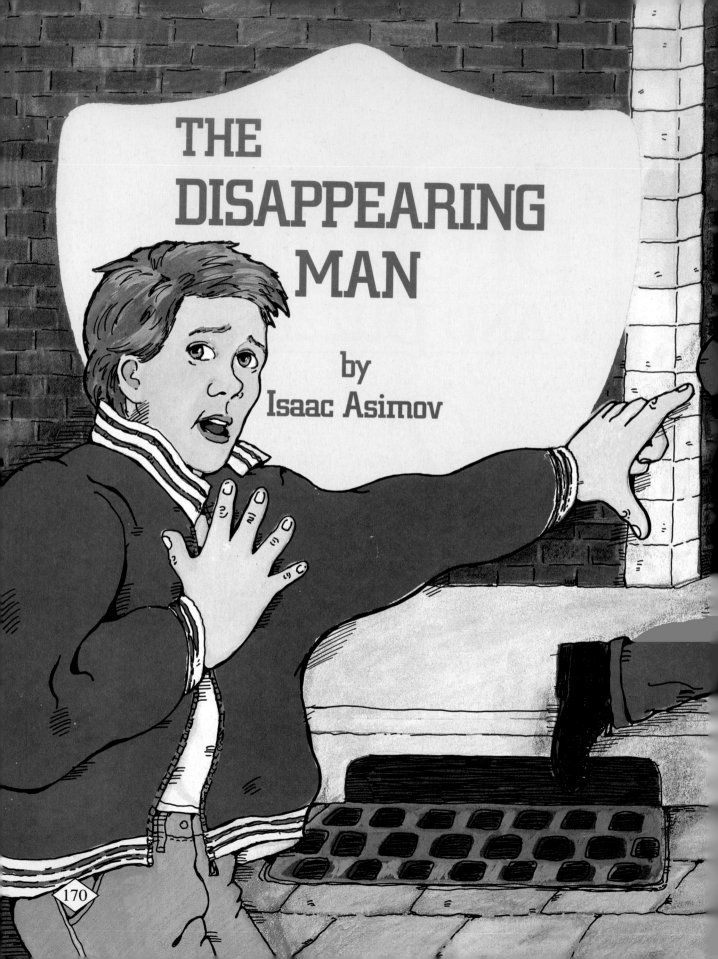

THE DISAPPEARING MAN

by
Isaac Asimov

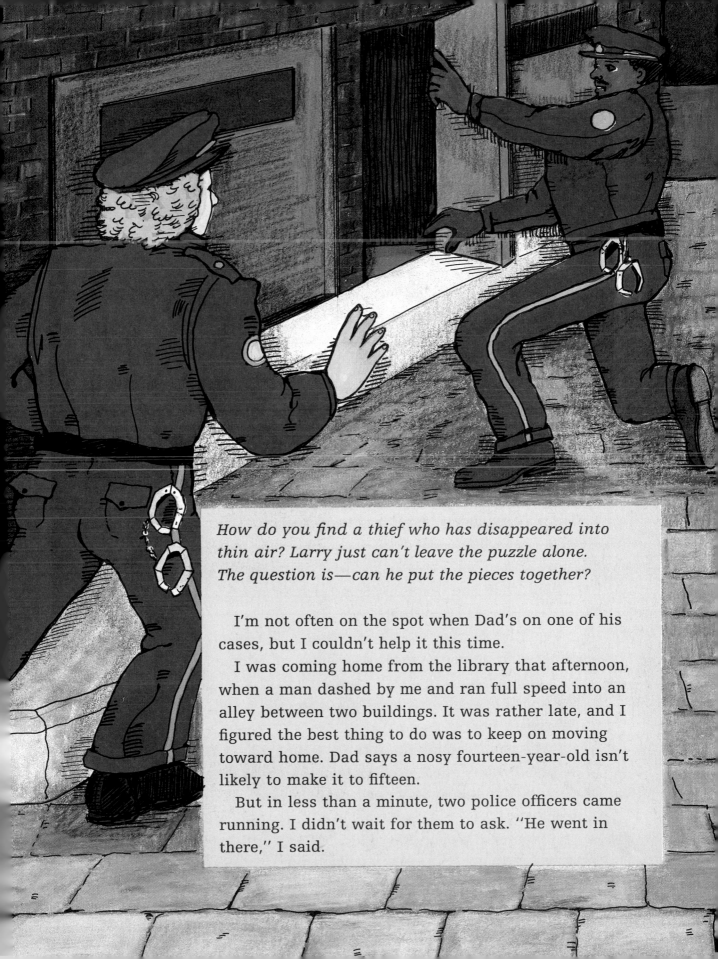

How do you find a thief who has disappeared into thin air? Larry just can't leave the puzzle alone. The question is—can he put the pieces together?

I'm not often on the spot when Dad's on one of his cases, but I couldn't help it this time.

I was coming home from the library that afternoon, when a man dashed by me and ran full speed into an alley between two buildings. It was rather late, and I figured the best thing to do was to keep on moving toward home. Dad says a nosy fourteen-year-old isn't likely to make it to fifteen.

But in less than a minute, two police officers came running. I didn't wait for them to ask. "He went in there," I said.

One of them rushed in, came out, and shouted, "There's a door open. He went inside. Go 'round to the front."

They must have given the alarm, because in a few minutes, three police cars drove up, there were plainclothes officers on the scene, and the building was surrounded.

I knew I shouldn't be hanging around. Innocent bystanders get in the way of the police. Just the same, I was there when it started and, from what I heard the police saying, I knew they were after this man, Stockton. He was a loner who'd pulled off some pretty spectacular jewel robberies over the last few months. I knew about it because Dad is a detective on the force, and he was on the case.

"Slippery fellow," he said, "but when you work alone, there's no one to double-cross you."

I said, "Doesn't he have to work with someone, Dad? He's got to have a fence—someone to peddle the jewels."

"If he has," said Dad, "we haven't located him. And why don't you get on with your homework?" (He always says that when he thinks I'm getting too interested in his cases.)

Well, they had him now. Some jeweler must have pushed the alarm button.

The alley he ran into was closed on all sides but the street, and he hadn't come out. There was the door there that was open, so he must have gone in. The police had the possible exits guarded. They even had a couple of police officers on the roof.

I was just beginning to wonder if Dad would be involved, when another car came up, and he got out. First thing he saw me and stopped dead. "Larry! What are you doing here?"

"I was on the spot, Dad. Stockton ran past me into the alley."

"Well, get out of here. There's liable to be shooting."

I backed away, but I didn't back off all the way. Once my father went into the building, I got into his car. The driver knew me, and he said, "You better go home, Larry. I'm going to have to help with the search, so I can't stay here to keep an eye on you."

"Sure, you go on," I said. "I'll be leaving in a minute." But I didn't. I wanted to do some thinking first.

Nobody leaves doors open in New York City. If that door into the alley was open, Stockton must have opened it. That meant he had to have a key; there wasn't time to pick the lock. That must mean he worked out of that building.

I looked at the building. It was an old one, four stories high. It had small businesses in it, and you could still see the painted signs in the windows in the fading light.

On the second-floor window, it said, "Klein and Levy, Tailors." Above that was a theatrical costumer, and on the top floor was a jeweler's. That jeweler's made sense out of it.

If Stockton had a key to the building, he probably worked with that jeweler. Dad would figure all that out.

I waited for the sound of shots, pretty scared Dad might get hurt. But nothing happened. Maybe Stockton would see he was cornered and just give in. I hoped so. At least they didn't have to evacuate the building. Late on Saturday, I supposed it would be deserted.

After a while, I got tired of waiting. I chose a moment when no police officers were looking and moved quickly to the building entrance. Dad would be hopping mad when he saw me, but I was curious. I figured they had Stockton, and I wanted to see him.

They didn't have him.

There was a fat man in a vest in the lobby. He looked scared, and I guess he was the security guard. He kept saying, "I didn't see *any*body."

Police officers were coming down the stairs and out of the old elevator, all shaking their heads.

My father was pretty angry. He said. "No one has anything?"

A police sergeant said, "Donovan said no one got out on the roof. All the doors and windows are covered."

"If he didn't get out," said my father, in a low voice that carried, "then he's in the building."

"We can't find him," said the sergeant. "He's nowhere inside."

My father said, "It isn't a big building—"

"We had the security guard's keys. We've looked everywhere."

"Then how do we know he went into the building in the first place? Who saw him go in?"

There was a silence. A lot of police officers were milling about the lobby now, but no one said anything. So I spoke up. "I did, Dad."

Dad whirled and looked at me and made a funny sound in the back of his throat that meant I was in for it for still being there. "You said you saw him run into the alley," he said. "That's not the same thing."

"He didn't come out, Dad. There was no place else for him to go."

"But you didn't actually see him go in, did you?"

"He couldn't go up the side of the buildings. There wouldn't have been time for him to reach the roof before the police—"

But Dad wasn't listening. "Did *anyone* actually see him go in?"

Of course no one said anything, and I could see my father was going to call the whole thing off, and then when he got me home I was going to get the talking-to of my life.

The thought of that talking-to must have stimulated my brain, I guess. I looked about the lobby desperately, and said, "But, Dad, he *did* go into the building, and he didn't disappear. There he is right now. That man there." I pointed, and then I dropped down and rolled out of the way.

There wasn't any shooting. The man I pointed to was close to the door—he must have been edging toward it—and now he made a dash for it. He almost made it, but a police officer who had been knocked down grabbed his leg and then everyone piled on him. Later they had the jeweler, too.

I went home after Stockton was caught, and when my father got home much later, he did have some things to say about my risking my life. But he also said, "You got onto that theatrical costume bit very nicely, Larry."

I said, "Well, I was sure he went into the building and was familiar with it. He could get into the costumer's if he had to, and they would be bound to have police uniforms. I figured if he could dump his jacket and pants and get into a police uniform quickly, he could just walk out of the building."

Dad said, "You're right. Even after he got outside, he could pretend he was dealing with the crowd and then just walk away."

Mom said, "But how did you know which police officer

it was, Larry? Don't tell me you know every police officer by sight."

"I didn't have to, Mom," I said. "I figured if he got a police uniform at the costumer's, he had to work fast and grab any one he saw. And they wouldn't have much of an assortment of sizes anyway. So I just looked around for a police officer whose uniform didn't fit, and when I saw one with trouser legs stopping above his ankles, I knew he was Stockton."

Reader's Response

What kind of work do you think Larry will be doing ten years after this story ends? What makes you think so?

THE DISAPPEARING MAN

Thinking It Over

1. When Larry saw a man dash into the alley, what did he first decide to do? Why?
2. What character traits and talents did Larry show in the story?
3. What made Larry sure that Stockton had a key to the building?
4. What part did the jeweler play in the robber's work? How do you know?
5. Why was Larry so sure that the robber was inside the building?
6. Why was Larry able to figure out the solution to the mystery while his father and the police were unable to?

Writing to Learn

THINK AND SUMMARIZE How did Larry solve the mystery? Gather all the facts about Stockton's actions that Larry knew or figured out from what he observed. On your paper, write short answers to complete the fact report.

Fact Report	
who?	_____
what?	_____
where?	_____
when?	_____
how?	_____
why?	_____

WRITE Use your fact report to write a headline and the lead paragraph of a news article about "The Disappearing Man."

Predicting from Story Knowledge

"**O**nce upon a time . . . and they all lived happily ever after." How many times have you read a tale that began and ended with those words? As a reader, you have come to expect certain things in this kind of tale. Although the details within one tale are different from the details within another tale, they often have very similar elements. Think how many tales you have read that have a handsome prince, or a cruel king, or an evil magician. In all likelihood, the next tale you read will also have one or more of these elements.

Your predictions about a story are often based on the stories you have read in the past. By recognizing that fables, myths, and fairy tales often have elements that are repeated from one story to another, you can start to look for particular events to occur. When you do this, you are using what you already know to make predictions about the plot. Often, when you predict something will happen, it is easier to understand when it does happen. This may make the whole story easier to understand.

Learning the Strategy

Think back to the play based on the legend "Damon and Pythias." Do you remember what happened in the play? Let's look at some of the elements and events of this legend.

ELEMENT	EVENT IN "DAMON AND PYTHIAS"
A powerful monarch	The king is cruel to Damon and Pythias.
Conflict	Pythias challenges the king's power by speaking out against an unfair law.
Generous gesture	Damon offers to take Pythias's place in jail so Pythias can visit his mother and sister one last time.
Complication	Pythias is attacked by thieves and tied to a tree.
Happy resolution	The king is so impressed by the strength of their friendship that he frees both Damon and Pythias.

Using the Strategy

Make a chart of the elements and events in "Three Strong Women." List the same elements found in the chart above. Then describe an event from "Three Strong Women" that corresponds to each element.

Applying the Strategy to the Next Story

When you read the next selection, a fairy tale called "Many Moons," look for the elements this story has in common with "Damon and Pythias." At several points in the story, you will be asked to identify specific story events and then to make a chart to compare them with elements in "Damon and Pythias."

◆◆◆ The writing connection can be found on page 275.

When a king tells his daughter he will get her anything she desires, he should be able to keep his promise . . . unless she asks the impossible!

MANY MOONS

written by James Thurber
illustrated by Louis Slobodkin

Once upon a time, in a kingdom by the sea, there lived a little Princess named Lenore. She was ten years old, going on eleven. One day Lenore fell ill of a surfeit of raspberry tarts and took to her bed.

The Royal Physician came to see her and took her temperature and felt her pulse and made her stick out her tongue. The Royal Physician was worried. He sent for the King, Lenore's father, and the King came to see her.

"I will get you anything your heart desires," the King said. "Is there anything your heart desires?"

"Yes," said the Princess. "I want the moon. If I can have the moon, I will be well again."

Now the King had a great many wise men who always got for him anything he wanted, so he told his daughter that she could have the moon. Then he went to the throne room and pulled a bell cord, three long pulls and a short pull, and presently the Lord High Chamberlain came into the room.

The Lord High Chamberlain was a large, fat man who wore thick glasses which made his eyes seem twice as big as they really were. This made the Lord High Chamberlain seem twice as wise as he really was.

"I want you to get the moon," said the King. "The

Princess Lenore wants the moon. If she can have the moon, she will get well again."

"The moon?" exclaimed the Lord High Chamberlain, his eyes widening. This made him look four times as wise as he really was.

"Yes, the moon," said the King. "M-o-o-n, moon. Get it tonight, tomorrow at the latest." ◄◆►

The Lord High Chamberlain wiped his forehead with a handkerchief and then blew his nose loudly. "I have got a great many things for you in my time, Your Majesty," he said. "It just happens that I have with me a list of things I have got for you in my time." He pulled a long scroll of parchment out of his pocket. "Let me see, now." He glanced at the list, frowning. "I have got ivory, apes, and peacocks, rubies, opals, and emeralds, black orchids, pink elephants, and blue poodles, gold bugs, scarabs, and flies in amber, hummingbirds' tongues, angels' feathers, and unicorns' horns, giants, midgets, and mermaids, frankincense, ambergris, and myrrh, troubadours, minstrels, and dancing women, a pound of butter, two dozen eggs, and a sack of sugar—sorry, my wife wrote that in there."

"I don't remember any blue poodles," said the King.

"It says blue poodles right here on the list, and they are checked off with a little check mark," said the Lord High Chamberlain. "So there must have been blue poodles. You just forget."

"Never mind the blue poodles," said the King. "What I want now is the moon."

"I have sent as far as Samarkand and Araby and Zanzibar to get things for you, Your Majesty," said the Lord High Chamberlain. "But the moon is out of the question. It is 35,000 miles away and it is bigger than the room the Princess lies in. Furthermore, it is made of molten copper. I cannot get the moon for you. Blue poodles, yes; the moon, no."

◄◆►

How is this king similar to or different from the king in "Damon and Pythias?"

The King flew into a rage and told the Lord High Chamberlain to leave the room and to send the Royal Wizard to the throne room.

The Royal Wizard was a little, thin man with a long face. He wore a high red peaked hat covered with silver stars, and a long blue robe covered with golden owls. His face grew very pale when the King told him that he wanted the moon for his little daughter, and that he expected the Royal Wizard to get it.

"I have worked a great deal of magic for you in my time, Your Majesty," said the Royal Wizard. "As a matter of fact, I just happen to have in my pocket a list of the wizardries I have performed for you." He drew a paper from a deep pocket of his robe. "It begins: 'Dear Royal Wizard: I am returning herewith the so-called philosopher's stone which you claimed—' no, that isn't it." The Royal Wizard brought a long scroll of parchment from another pocket of his robe. "Here it is," he said. "Now, let's see. I have squeezed blood out of turnips for you, and turnips out of blood. I have produced rabbits out of silk hats, and silk hats out of rabbits. I have conjured up flowers, tambourines, and doves out of nowhere, and nowhere out of flowers, tambourines and doves. I have brought you divining rods, magic wands, and crystal spheres in which to behold the future. I have compounded philters, unguents, and potions, to cure heartbreak, surfeit, and ringing in the ears. I have made you my own special mixture of wolfbane, nightshade, and eagles' tears, to ward off witches, demons, and things that go bump in the night. I have given you seven-league boots, the golden touch, and a cloak of invisibility—"

"It didn't work," said the King. "The cloak of invisibility didn't work."

"Yes, it did," said the Royal Wizard.

"No, it didn't," said the King. "I kept bumping into things, the same as ever."

"The cloak is supposed to make you invisible," said the Royal Wizard. "It is not supposed to keep you from bumping into things."

"All I know is, I kept bumping into things," said the King.

The Royal Wizard looked at his list again. "I got you," he said, "horns from Elfland, sand from the Sandman, and gold from the rainbow. Also a spool of thread, a paper of needles, and a lump of beeswax—sorry, those are things my wife wrote down for me to get her."

"What I want you to do now," said the King, "is to get me the moon. The Princess Lenore wants the moon, and when she gets it, she will be well again."

"Nobody can get the moon," said the Royal Wizard. "It is 150,000 miles away, and it is made of green cheese, and it is twice as big as this palace."

The King flew into another rage and sent the Royal Wizard back to his cave. Then he rang a gong and summoned the Royal Mathematician.

The Royal Mathematician was a baldheaded, nearsighted man, with a skullcap on his head and a pencil behind each ear. He wore a black suit with white numbers on it.

"I don't want to hear a long list of all the things you have figured out for me since 1907," the King said to him. "I want you to figure out right now how to get the moon for the Princess Lenore. When she gets the moon, she will be well again."

"I am glad you mentioned all the things I have figured out for you since 1907," said the Royal Mathematician. "It so happens that I have a list of them with me."

He pulled a long scroll of parchment out of a pocket and looked at it. "Now let me see. I have figured out for you the distance between the horns of a dilemma, night and day, and A and Z. I have computed how far is Up, how long it takes to get to Away, and what becomes of Gone. I have discovered the length of the sea serpent, the price of the priceless, and the square of the hippopotamus. I know where you are when you are at Sixes and Sevens, how much Is you have to have to make an Are, and how many birds you can catch with the salt in the ocean—187,796,132, if it would interest you to know."

"There aren't that many birds," said the King.

"I didn't say there were," said the Royal Mathematician. "I said if there were."

"I don't want to hear about seven hundred million imaginary birds," said the King. "I want you to get the moon for the Princess Lenore."

"The moon is 300,000 miles away," said the Royal Mathematician. "It is round and flat like a coin, only it is made of asbestos, and it is half the size of this kingdom. Furthermore, it is pasted on the sky. Nobody can get the moon."

The King flew into still another rage and sent the Royal Mathematician away. Then he rang for the Court Jester. The Jester came bounding into the throne room in his motley and his cap and bells, and sat at the foot of the throne.

"What can I do for you, Your Majesty?" asked the Court Jester.

"Nobody can do anything for me," said the King mournfully. "The Princess Lenore wants the moon, and she cannot be well till she gets it, but nobody can get it for her. Every time I ask anybody for the moon, it gets larger and farther away. There is nothing you can do for me except play on your lute. Something sad." ◆◇◆

"How big do they say the moon is," asked the Court Jester, "and how far away?"

"The Lord High Chamberlain says it is 35,000 miles away, and bigger than the Princess Lenore's room," said the King. "The Royal Wizard says it is 150,000 miles away, and

◆◇◆
**What conflict or
problem does the
king face?**

189

twice as big as this palace. The Royal Mathematician says it is 300,000 miles away, and half the size of this kingdom."

The Court Jester strummed on his lute for a little while. "They are all wise men," he said, "and so they must all be right. If they are all right, then the moon must be just as large and as far away as each person thinks it is. The thing to do is find out how big the Princess Lenore thinks it is, and how far away."

"I never thought of that," said the King.

"I will go and ask her, Your Majesty," said the Court Jester. And he crept softly into the little girl's room.

The Princess Lenore was awake, and she was glad to see the Court Jester, but her face was very pale and her voice very weak.

"Have you brought the moon to me?" she asked.

"Not yet," said the Court Jester, "but I will get it for you right away. How big do you think it is?"

"It is just a little smaller than my thumbnail," she said, "for when I hold my thumbnail up at the moon, it just covers it."

"And how far away is it?" asked the Court Jester.

"It is not as high as the big tree outside my window," said the Princess, "for sometimes it gets caught in the top branches."

"It will be very easy to get the moon for you," said the Court Jester. "I will climb the tree tonight when it gets caught in the top branches and bring it to you."

Then he thought of something else. "What is the moon made of, Princess?" he asked.

"Oh," she said, "it's made of gold, of course, silly."

The Court Jester left the Princess Lenore's room and went to see the Royal Goldsmith. He had the Royal Goldsmith make a tiny round golden moon just a little smaller than the thumbnail of the Princess Lenore. Then he had him string it on a golden chain so the Princess could wear it around her neck.

"What is this thing I have made?" asked the Royal Goldsmith when he had finished it.

"You have made the moon," said the Court Jester. "That is the moon."

"But the moon," said the Royal Goldsmith, "is 500,000 miles away and is made of bronze and is round like a marble."

"That's what you think," said the Court Jester as he went away with the moon.

The Court Jester took the moon to the Princess Lenore, and she was overjoyed. The next day she was well again and could get up and go out in the gardens to play.

But the King's worries were not yet over. He knew that the moon would shine in the sky again that night, and he did not want the Princess Lenore to see it. If she did, she would know that the moon she wore on a chain around her neck was not the real moon. ◆◆

◆◆

There is a complication to the king's plan. What is it?

So the King sent for the Lord High Chamberlain and said: "We must keep the Princess Lenore from seeing the moon when it shines in the sky tonight. Think of something."

The Lord High Chamberlain tapped his forehead with his fingers thoughtfully and said: "I know just the thing. We can make some dark glasses for the Princess Lenore. We can make them so dark that she will not be able to see anything at all through them. Then she will not be able to see the moon when it shines in the sky."

This made the King very angry, and he shook his head from side to side. "If she wore dark glasses, she would bump into things," he said, "and then she would be ill again." So he

192

sent the Lord High Chamberlain away and called the Royal Wizard.

"We must hide the moon," said the King, "so that the Princess Lenore will not see it when it shines in the sky tonight. How are we going to do that?"

The Royal Wizard stood on his hands and then he stood on his head and then he stood on his feet again. "I know what we can do," he said. "We can stretch some black velvet curtains on poles. The curtains will cover all the palace gardens like a circus tent, and the Princess Lenore will not be able to see through them, so she will not see the moon in the sky."

The King was so angry at this that he waved his arms around. "Black velvet curtains would keep out the air," he said. "The Princess Lenore would not be able to breathe, and she would be ill again." So he sent the Royal Wizard away and summoned the Royal Mathematician.

"We must do something," said the King, "so that the Princess Lenore will not see the moon when it shines in the sky tonight. If you know so much, figure out a way to do that."

The Royal Mathematician walked around in a circle, and then he walked around in a square, and then he stood still. "I have it!" he said. "We can set off fireworks in the garden every night. We will make a lot of silver fountains and golden cascades, and when they go off, they will fill the sky with so many sparks that it will be as light as day and the Princess Lenore will not be able to see the moon."

The King flew into such a rage that he began jumping up and down. "Fireworks would keep the Princess Lenore awake," he said. "She would not get any sleep at all and she would be ill again." So the King sent the Royal Mathematician away.

When he looked up again, it was dark outside and he saw the bright rim of the moon just peeping over the horizon.

He jumped up in a great fright and rang for the Court Jester. The Court Jester came bounding into the room and sat down at the foot of the throne.

"What can I do for you, Your Majesty?" he asked.

"Nobody can do anything for me," said the King, mournfully. "The moon is coming up again. It will shine into the Princess Lenore's bedroom, and she will know it is still in the sky and that she does not wear it on a golden chain around her neck. Play me something on your lute, something very sad, for when the princess sees the moon, she will be ill again."

The Court Jester strummed on his lute. "What do your wise men say?" he asked.

"They can think of no way to hide the moon that will not make the Princess Lenore ill," said the King.

The Court Jester played another song, very softly. "Your wise men know everything," he said, "and if they cannot hide the moon, then it cannot be hidden."

The King put his head in his hands again and sighed. Suddenly he jumped up from his throne and pointed to the windows. "Look!" he cried. "The moon is already shining into the Princess Lenore's bedroom. Who can explain how the moon can be shining in the sky when it is hanging on a golden chain around her neck?"

The Court Jester stopped playing his lute. "Who could explain how to get the moon when your wise men said it was too large and too far away? It was the Princess Lenore. Therefore, the Princess Lenore is wiser than your wise men and knows more about the moon than they do. So I will ask *her*." And before the King could stop him, the Court Jester slipped quietly out of the throne room and up the wide marble staircase to the Princess Lenore's bedroom.

The Princess was lying in bed but she was wide awake and she was looking out the window at the moon shining in the sky. Shining in her hand was the moon the Court Jester had got for her. He looked very sad, and there seemed to be tears in his eyes.

"Tell me, Princess Lenore," he said mournfully, "how can the moon be shining in the sky when it is hanging on a golden chain around your neck?"

The Princess looked at him and laughed. "That is easy, silly," she said. "When I lose a tooth, a new one grows in its place, doesn't it?"

"Of course," said the Court Jester. "And when the unicorn loses his horn in the forest, a new one grows in the middle of his forehead."

"That is right," said the Princess. "And when the Royal Gardener cuts the flowers in the garden, other flowers come to take their place."

"I should have thought of that," said the Court Jester, "for it is the same way with the daylight."

"And it is the same way with the moon," said the Princess Lenore. "I guess it is the same way with everything." Her voice became very low and faded away, and the Court Jester saw that she was asleep. Gently he tucked the covers in around the sleeping Princess.

But before he left the room, he went over to the window and winked at the moon, for it seemed to the Court Jester that the moon had winked at him.

How does this story reach a happy resolution? Make a chart of story elements to compare "Many Moons" with "Damon and Pythias." What do the two stories have in common?

Reader's Response

How do you feel about Lenore?

MANY MOONS

Thinking It Over

1. What was the demand Lenore made of her father?
2. What kind of man was the King? What makes you think so?
3. Why did the King turn to the Jester?
4. What was the solution that helped Lenore recover? Who thought of the solution?
5. At the end of the story, why do you think the Jester winked at the moon?
6. Do you think the King should have tried to fulfill Lenore's wish? Explain your answer.

Writing to Learn

THINK AND EVALUATE What message is the author of "Many Moons" sending to his readers? Copy the statements below and use this rating scale to evaluate your agreement or disagreement:

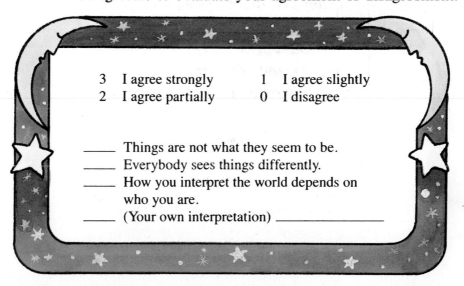

3 I agree strongly	1 I agree slightly
2 I agree partially	0 I disagree

_____ Things are not what they seem to be.
_____ Everybody sees things differently.
_____ How you interpret the world depends on who you are.
_____ (Your own interpretation) _____

WRITE Choose one of the statements above or the one you wrote. In one paragraph, write why you think it is the message of "Many Moons."

Timber Moon

There is a way the moon looks into the timber at night
And tells the walnut trees secrets of silver sand—
There is a way the moon makes a lattice work
Under the leaves of the hazel bushes—
There is a way the moon understands the hoot owl
Sitting on an arm of a sugar maple throwing its
One long lonesome cry up the ladders of the moon—
There is a way the moon finds company early in the fall time.

Carl Sandburg

Half Moon

The moon goes over the water.
How tranquil the sky is!
She goes scything slowly
the old shimmer from the river;
meanwhile a young frog
takes her for a little mirror.

Federico García Lorca
Translated by W.S. Merwin

Media Luna

La luna va por el agua.
¡Cómo está el cielo tranquilo!
Va segando lentamente
el temblor viejo del río
mientras que una rana joven
la toma por espejito.

Federico García Lorca

LITERATURE LINK

What do authors write about in personal essays?

You're a writer. Your challenge is to write something that makes your readers think and entertains them at the same time. What do you write? You might write a mystery like "The Disappearing Man" or a fantasy with a message like "Many Moons." What would you write to share your feelings or tell what happened to you? Some writers, like Helen Keller, choose the autobiography. Others choose the personal essay.

Characteristics of Personal Essays

Personal essays are nonfiction, but unlike informational articles they include the writer's feelings, opinions, and ideas.

Here are some other features you may find in a personal essay.

- Confined to one topic, combining facts and author's opinions
- Brief with a casual, conversational style
- Based on an author's experiences, often humorous

Here is part of a personal essay by Natalie Babbitt. In this essay, Ms. Babbitt writes about her early, perplexing experiences with the alphabet.

I can remember my feelings of amazement and power when I began to recognize words in the magazines my mother and father had around the house. I had always liked looking at the pictures in those magazines, but the print had never been anything but a dense jumble of letters. And then one day I found that some of that jumble was beginning to form itself into words that I knew, words I'd learned in school. It was a little like bringing a blurry television into focus—suddenly things made sense. And I was hooked.

The alphabet is still a miracle to me—how those twenty-six funny shapes can group themselves in endlessly different ways to make words with endlessly different meanings. I still play alphabet games with myself, games like trying to think of five words that are

exactly the same except for the vowels, like *bAg, bEg, bIg, bOg* and *bUg*. Just by changing the vowels, you can utterly change the meaning. And another game I like is trying to find words that contain letters in alphabetical order. For instance, *ABsConD* and *DEFoG*, and my favorite, *HIJacK*.

My mother and I used to play a game called Anagrams where you made words out of letters printed on small, tidy squares of thick cardboard. Every once in a while, one would drop on the floor, and Dingo, our dog, would chew it. We didn't mind so much if it was a *J* or a *Q* because those were hard letters to use, but it was bad if an *E* or an *S* got chewed. Still, we just let them dry out and used them anyway, rumpled though they were with tooth marks.

Ms. Babbitt's essay describes some of the difficulties of learning to read. Yet, it also contains some of Ms. Babbitt's personal thoughts. How has Ms. Babbitt blended these two aspects of the topic together? Do you get a strong sense about Ms. Babbitt's feelings about reading? How do you think Ms. Babbitt feels about reading?

The next selection is a personal essay entitled "Star Fever." The author gives you an opportunity to see stars as she sees them. How do you think she feels about her subject?

STAR

FEVER

by Judith Herbst

"Silver galaxies swirling far . . . blazing stars born from interstellar dust . . . comets and meteors and a milky way path. . . ." These are some of the exciting things that give the author of this selection "star fever."

Stargazing and Star Fever

I LOVE THE STARS. Sometimes I lie awake at night and think about them. I imagine that they all have planets with strange forms of life. I see red, rugged landscapes bathed in the glare of two suns, one swollen and scarlet, the other a cold steel blue. I see steamy tropical planets covered with silver vines that snake in and out of silver trees. I see planets with methane oceans and iron mountains. It's not so crazy. They could be out there, you know.

Of course I don't spend every night dreaming star dreams. All summer long I haunt the campgrounds of New England disguised as the midnight phantom. I wait until the other campers have turned down their lanterns and gone to sleep. Then, ever so quietly, I sneak out of my tent. In the sweet, clean air of a pine forest the stars are gold glitter. The campgrounds are still and silent except for the rustle of a raccoon in the leaves. It's a very special time.

In a while my eyes grow used to the darkness, and those faraway suns begin to show their colors. Many people are surprised to learn that stars come in colors. They think that all stars are yellow like our sun, but stars burn their material at different temperatures. The very hottest stars glow bluish-purple with temperatures as high as 90,000° Fahrenheit. Cooler stars burn blue, green, white, yellow, orange, and finally red when their temperature is only 6,300° Fahrenheit.

If you didn't know that stars come in colors then you've never really looked at them. All you need is a little patience and a very dark sky and, before long, you'll begin to pick out the delicate shades of rose, turquoise, emerald green, and lavender.

Sirius, in the Big Dog constellation, is the brightest star in the sky.

Many of the stars have names—first names, I mean—and I think that's a very good idea. I always like to know whom I'm talking to.

"Hi, Vega," I whisper. "My, my Sirius, you're looking well tonight. Keep the home fires burning, Alcor!"

Sometimes the other campers hear my conversations and I get a little embarrassed. If only they could understand that I'm not responsible for my actions. Years ago I developed a severe case of star fever, and when an attack comes on I'm simply not myself. Maybe you think I'm making this up about star fever, but human beings have had it for thousands of years.

Even the earliest cave dwellers took note of the moon and stars.

Star Fever's Beginnings

It began with the earliest cave people. We know they were looking at the stars because scientists have found some interesting paintings on the walls of many ancient caves. Next to the woolly mammoths and wild bison are pictures of the moon in its different phases. There are also five-pointed objects that look like crude drawings of stars. Some of the stars are larger than others. This suggests that the cave dwellers knew the stars differed in brightness.

It's a pretty safe bet that very early on some of the cave people got curious about all those stars. Sure, the stars were beautiful, but they were also a little annoying. They kept showing up night after clear night. What were they, anyway? The cave people, of course, had no way to answer this tremendous question, so they had to be content with just watching. But watching is a very important part of astronomy. Galileo,[1] the inventor of the telescope, spent hours doing nothing but watching.

[1]Galileo (gal′ ə lē′ ō)

It's likely that after a while some of the more creative cave people began to imagine that the stars formed pictures. They weren't very obvious pictures. You had to "connect the dots" before you saw anything, but with a little imagination you could see lions, and birds, and lizards, and even people. These star pictures came to be known as *constellations*. Constellation means "with stars." Today there is a grand total of eighty-eight constellations, ranging from my favorite, Orion,[2] the great hunter of Greek mythology, to an air pump (of all things!) named Antlia.[3]

It was a small jump from seeing pictures in the sky to telling stories about the pictures. We don't know any of the tales the cave dwellers made up, but they probably had to do with hunting, the chief occupation of the times. A good storyteller could have kept the people coming back every evening to hear more, but the star author had a little problem. Just when he or she got a ripping good yarn going, Zam! The main character started to slip into the western horizon.

This is because the earth turns on its axis like a spinning basketball. So the sky we see changes over the course of a night. All the constellations "march" from east to west. You can prove this to yourself by going out after the sun has set and finding a constellation like Ursa Major.[4] Take a close look at where Ursa Major is in the sky at sundown. Is it near the horizon? Is it high overhead? Try to be as accurate as you can. Then pop outside a couple of hours later, say ten o'clock. Now where's Ursa Major? You'll see that it has moved and moved quite a bit.

Although the cave people probably didn't understand the rotation of the earth, they had certainly discovered it.

[2]Orion (ō rī′ ən)   [3]Antlia (ant′ lē ə)
[4]Ursa Major (ər′ sə mā′ jər): Latin for "Great Bear"

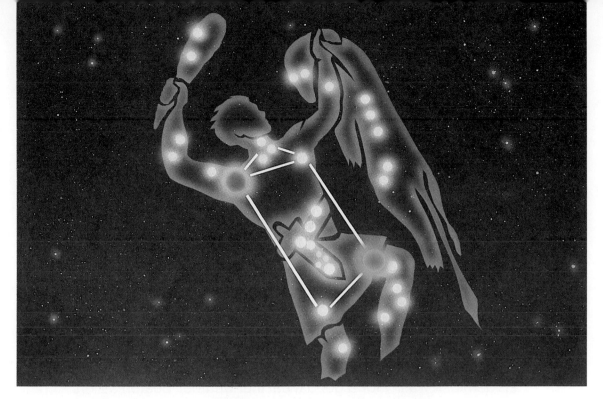

The stars Betelgeuse and Rigel help make Orion easy to identify.

Star Fever Continues!

Let's jump ahead of the cave people. The Age of Farming has begun. People are no longer wandering from place to place chasing wild herds for food. They've settled down and are learning how to plant some of the food they need.

Enter Orion. Orion signals the start of the cold months. It pops up over the eastern horizon in late November and hangs on throughout December, January, February, and part of March. Orion contains two stars that are gloriously bright. One, named Betelgeuse,[5] is in Orion's shoulder. Betelgeuse is a brilliant red and you don't even need a telescope or binoculars to see the color. This star is so big that, if it took the place of our sun, all the planets out to Jupiter would be swallowed up.

At Orion's knee lies Rigel,[6] a blue hot sparkler. With Betelgeuse and Rigel, plus Orion's distinctive shape, this constellation is one of the easiest to identify. So Orion could very neatly

[5]Betelgeuse (bēt′ əl jōōz)   [6]Rigel (rī jəl)

have been used as a kind of calendar. Its rising marked the start of cold weather. To a farmer this is important information. Many other constellations might have served the same purpose. Constellations that rise at night in the spring, like Corvus, the crow, would have been the signal to begin planting. A fall constellation—the great square of Pegasus, the flying horse—told the farmer to gather in the crops.

Those early farmers had star fever, all right, and who could blame them? Being able to "read" the stars meant food on the table.

Understanding the Stars

When people took to the sea, star fever became an epidemic. It wasn't for a good meal that weather-beaten sailors kept track of the sky. It was for saving their lives. If they lost their way in the middle of the ocean, they could easily die of starvation, exposure, thirst, or disease.

The stars not only mark the seasons, they also tell you where north, south, east, and west are. Stars "rise" in the east and "set" in the west, so all you have to do is look for the appearance of a new constellation. If you see one that wasn't there an hour before, you're facing east. Once you know east it's a snap to find the other three directions. Just look behind you for west, to the right side for south, and to the left for north.

As you can imagine, without the compass the early sailors absolutely relied on the stars to find their way around. There are no landmarks on the high seas.

You may be thinking that the sailors had big trouble during the day without the stars, but that wasn't the case. The sun was out and the sun, like the stars, rises in the east and sets in the west. So it was clear sailing day or night. Clear sailing, that is, as long as there was clear sailing. Fog, rain, and cloudy skies were the only drawbacks of navigating by the stars. Well, nothing is perfect.

It stands to reason that with all this sky-watching, people would start to wonder what stars were. One guess was as good as another, since nobody had the equipment to do an in-depth study, but it was perfectly obvious that the stars were far away indeed. Surely they must have been created by some remarkable being who had access to the entire sky.

Without true science to explain natural events such as rain, snowstorms, wind, and lightning, the early people developed a whole community of gods and goddesses, each of whom was responsible for one or more aspects of nature. It rained because there was a rain god. The sun moved across the sky because it was being pushed by none other than the sun god. It was a very tidy system—if not very scientific.

Before long, various bright stars and planets came to be associated with certain gods. The Mayans were very keen on Venus because they thought the planet actually was Kulkulcan, their chief god. They soon became quite good at charting Venus's movements. The Mayans knew the rising and setting times to the exact second. That was pretty fancy footwork for people who had no notion at all of what a telescope was.

The Mayans could study Venus from El Caracol, this observatory in Mexico.

Stars and People

Somewhere along the line an interesting idea took root. It was so interesting, in fact, the idea still persists today. People started thinking that the stars themselves directly affected people's lives. It was the position of the stars that indicated the game plan, so you had to know what was where in order to interpret the message.

Kings and other government officials were most anxious to learn what the stars had in store for them. They were in positions of power and wealth and they wanted to stay there. At the same time, politics didn't leave them much of an opportunity to watch the sky, so they had to hire experts to do it for them. Astronomy became a paying job and a rather cushy one at that. More often than not, the royal astronomer lived in the palace because the king wouldn't make a move without him. While the rest of the population froze and starved, the astronomer wore glittering robes and dined on roast chicken. However, being a professional astronomer wasn't all glamour. Goof-ups were not allowed, as two Chinese astronomers painfully discovered when they failed to predict a solar eclipse (and lost their heads).

The ancient people never accepted the fact that the stars couldn't be used to predict the future. They continued to search the sky for comets, which were supposed to foretell great events. (They don't.) They persisted in charting the paths of planets as they moved through the constellations. They monitored Mars and studied Saturn. And, for all the wrong reasons, the ancients developed an excellent knowledge of the heavens.

Star Fever and Science

Fortunately for science, there were a few nonbelievers in the bunch. Fellows like Philolaeus,[7] Heraclides,[8] and Aristarchus[9] didn't swallow that stuff about the stars having magical properties. Instead, these Greeks wanted to know what the stars were made of, how far away they were, and what kept them from falling out of the sky.

Philolaeus was the first to suggest that the stars were globes. By saying this he was actually recognizing the blackness overhead as three-dimensional space, and space that was very large indeed. Heraclides discovered the rotation of the earth. This must certainly rank in the Top Ten of Great Astronomical Brain Storms. Here's why:

If you watch the sky for any length of time you will see that the sun, moon, planets, and stars are moving from east to west above you. If you could somehow speed up the action, the sky would look like a big rotating dome. You, meanwhile, would think you are standing still. This is just an illusion, however, but an illusion we can't escape from unless we launch ourselves into space for an outside look. So how did Heraclides figure out the illusion? No doubt it was a brainstorm, a stroke of genius. He looked at the big picture and said, "Hey, wait a minute! There's another way the sky could be made to seem like it was rotating. What if . . ." Heraclides hit the nail on the head with his original thinking.

Aristarchus, who was born three years after Heraclides died (312 B.C.), put the sun in the center of the solar system and then tried to measure the distance to it. He was off by quite

---

[7]Philolaeus (fi lō lā′ əs)   [8]Heraclides (her′ ə klī dēz)   [9]Aristarchus (er əs tär′ kəs)

a bit, but the method he used was correct—a new-fangled math the Greeks had just invented called geometry.

There were a lot of other star fever victims in Greece at that time, and they seem to have been suffering from a new strain of the disease. It wasn't enough just to watch the stars anymore. People needed to know what exactly it was they were watching.

At last the astronomer had become a scientist.

The rest, as they say, is history. Today we know some extraordinary things about the universe in which we live. We have built telescopes the likes of which Galileo never dreamed of. We have stood on an alien world and have sent starships to other planets. The early scientists who first guessed the nature of stars would faint if they could hear our description of a black hole.

Star fever has taken us right into the unknown, and it's a very exciting place to be.

Silver galaxies swirling far . . . blazing stars born from interstellar dust . . . comets and meteors and a milky way path . . .

It's madness! It's star fever madness!

And I love every minute of it.

◆ LIBRARY LINK ◆

If you've caught "star fever," you'll enjoy Sky Above, World Beyond, *from which this selection is excerpted.*

Reader's Response

What feelings about the stars do you share with the author?

STAR FEVER

Thinking It Over

1. What does the author mean by the term "star fever"?
2. The cave people tried to explain the stars in creative ways. What were these ways?
3. Why has the observation of stars, from early times through today, been important to people?
4. If no one had discovered that the earth rotates, what might be different today?
5. What is the author's point of view about the stars? How do you know?

Writing to Learn

THINK AND IMAGINE   Many scientists study the stars. What five questions about the stars would you like to investigate? Draw a star on your paper. Write a question next to each point of the star.

WRITE   Write a paragraph telling why you think the stars have inspired so many poets and artists through the years.

The man with red hair brings Sherlock Holmes one of the most unique and perplexing cases of his career.

THE RED-HEADED LEAGUE

by Sir Arthur Conan Doyle
adapted by Catherine Edwards Sadler
from *The Adventures of Sherlock Holmes*

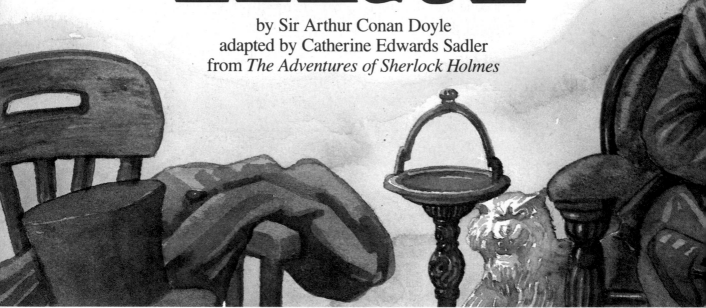

Last autumn I visited my friend, Mr. Sherlock Holmes, in the rooms we used to share at 221B Baker Street, London. I found him deep in conversation with a very stout, ruddy-faced gentleman with fiery red hair. I was about to leave when Holmes pulled me into the sitting room and closed the door behind me.

"You could not possibly have come at a better time, my dear Watson," he said cordially. "Mr. Jabez Wilson here has been telling me a most interesting story. Perhaps, Mr. Wilson, you would repeat your tale, so that Dr. Watson can hear it from the beginning and I can acquaint myself with every detail of the case. As a

rule, after I've heard the basic facts, I can guide myself by the thousands of other similar cases set in my memory. But I must admit, your tale is unique.''

The red-headed client puffed out his chest in pride and pulled a dirty and wrinkled newspaper from the inside pocket of his coat.

As he scanned the advertisement column, I took a good look at him and tried to learn something from his dress and manner . . . as my friend Sherlock was so skilled at doing. However, I did not learn much. He looked like a typical English tradesman. He wore rather baggy check trousers and a not-too-clean black coat which was unbuttoned in the front. Beneath was a drab waistcoat from which a heavy brass watch chain and a square bit of metal dangled. A frayed top hat and faded brown overcoat with a wrinkled velvet collar lay on a chair beside him. Altogether, there was nothing very remarkable about the man except his blazing red head!

Sherlock Holmes' quick eye soon took in my occupation. Answering my thoughts, he said, "Beyond the obvious—that he has done manual labor at some time, that he has been in China, and that he has done a considerable amount of writing lately—I can deduce nothing at all."

With that, Mr. Jabez Wilson started up in his chair. His forefinger was still on the newspaper column, but his eyes were set on my companion.

"How did you know all that, Mr. Holmes?" he asked. "How did you know, for example, that I did manual labor? It's true as Gospel, for I began as a ship's carpenter!"

"Your hands, my dear sir. Your right hand is a size larger than your left. You have worked hard with it and so the muscles are more developed."

"Well, the writing then?"

"What else can be indicated by your right coat-cuff being so very shiny and your left coat-elbow so very smooth, where you must rest it on the desk."

"And China?"

"The fish you have tattooed above your right wrist could only have been done in China. I have made a small study of tattoo marks and have even contributed to literature on the subject. That trick of staining the fish scales a delicate pink is quite peculiar to China. When in addition I see a Chinese coin hanging from your watch chain, the matter becomes even more simple."

Mr. Jabez Wilson laughed heartily. "Well, I never!" he said. "I thought at first that you were very clever, but now I see there was nothing to your deductions after all!"

Holmes turned toward me. "I begin to think, Watson, that I make a mistake explaining my reasoning. I must protect my reputation!" Then turning back to his client he said, "Can you find the advertisement?"

"Yes, I have it now," Wilson answered, his thick red finger planted halfway down the column. "Here it is. This is what began it all. You can read it for yourselves."

I took the paper from him and read the following words:

TO THE RED-HEADED LEAGUE.

THERE IS NOW ANOTHER VACANCY OPEN WHICH ENTITLES A MEMBER OF THE LEAGUE TO A SALARY OF FOUR POUNDS A WEEK FOR LIGHT SERVICES. ALL RED-HEADED MEN WHO ARE SOUND IN BODY AND MIND AND ABOVE THE AGE OF TWENTY-ONE ARE ELIGIBLE.

APPLY IN PERSON ON MONDAY AT ELEVEN O'CLOCK TO DUNCAN ROSS AT THE OFFICES OF THE LEAGUE, ROOM NUMBER FOUR, 17 POPES COURT, FLEET STREET, LONDON.

"What on earth does it mean?" I exclaimed in amazement.

Holmes chuckled and wriggled in his chair, as was his habit in high spirits. "It is a little off the beaten track, isn't it?" he said. "And now, Mr. Wilson, tell us about yourself, your household, and the effect this advertisement had upon your fortunes."

"I have a small pawnbroker's business at Saxe-Coburg Square near the business district," Mr. Jabez Wilson began. "It's not a very large enterprise. Lately it's barely provided me with a living. I used to keep two assistants, but now I keep only one and I'd be hard put to pay him his full wages. Luckily, he is willing to work for half-pay so as to learn the business."

"What is the name of this obliging youth?" asked Holmes.

"His name is Vincent Spaulding and he's not such a youth. I could not wish for a smarter assistant. He could earn twice what I pay him elsewhere. But if he is satisfied, why should I put ideas in his head?"

"Why, indeed?" asked Holmes. "You seem most fortunate in having an employee who comes under the market price. It is not common experience among employees these days. I don't know that your assistant isn't as remarkable as your advertisement."

"Oh, he has his faults," said Mr. Wilson. "He loves photography. He's always snapping away with his camera and diving down into the cellar, like a rabbit into a hole, to develop his pictures. That's his main fault. But he's a good worker."

"He is still with you, I presume?"

"Yes, sir. He and a girl of fourteen who does a bit of simple cooking and keeps the place clean. That's all I have in the house. I am a widower and never had any family. The three of us live quietly. We keep a roof over our heads and pay our debts, if nothing more.

"Then eight weeks ago Spaulding came down into the office with this very paper in hand, saying: 'I wish,

Mr. Wilson, that I was a red-headed man. Here's another vacancy on the League of Red-headed Men. I understand there are more vacancies than there are men to fill them. The trustees are at their wits' end what to do with all the money!'

"'What's this?' I asked him.

"'Why, have you never heard of the League of Red-headed Men?'

"'Never!'

"'Why, I wonder at that, for you are eligible yourself. They pay a couple of hundred pounds a year, the work is slight and need not interfere with one's usual business.'

"'Well, that made my ears prick up. As I said, business has not been good and the extra money would be helpful. So I asked him to tell me about it.

"'Well,' he replied, showing me the advertisement,'you can see for yourself. The League has a vacancy and there is the address where you should apply. As far as I can make out, the League was founded by an American millionaire named Ezekiah

Hopkins. He was red-headed and had a great sympathy for all red-headed men. When he died, he left an enormous fortune in the hands of trustees. They were instructed to help out needy men with the same hair color as was his.'

"'But there are millions of red-headed men who could apply,' I interrupted.

"'Not as many as you might think,' he answered. 'I have heard that it is no use applying if you have light or dark red hair. Or any other color but bright, blazing, fiery red.'

"Now," continued Mr. Wilson, "my hair is a very full and rich tint as you can see. It seemed to me that I stood as good a chance as any in such a competition. So since it was Monday—the day for applying—Vincent and I quickly shut up shop and started off for the address in the advertisement.

"Well, you've never seen so many red-headed men. The area was packed with red-headed folk. Every shade of color was there: straw, lemon, orange, brick, Irish setter, liver, clay. But not many had truly vivid red hair like mine. Somehow Vincent pushed and pulled and butted through the crowd right up to the office steps. We soon found ourselves inside.

"There was nothing in the office

but a couple of wooden chairs and a card table. Behind the table sat a small man with a head even redder than mine. There were other candidates in the room but he managed to find fault with each. However, when my turn came he exclaimed, 'I cannot recall when I have seen anything so fine!' He took a step backward, cocked his head to one side, and stared at my head. Then he plunged suddenly forward, shook my hand and congratulated me on my success. Then he stopped, added, 'One last precaution!' and seized my hair in both his hands and tugged till I yelled in pain. 'There is water in your eyes,' he said happily as he released me. 'I see all is as it should be!' He stepped over to the window and shouted that the position had been filled. The crowd gave a groan of disappointment and trooped away until there was not a red head to be seen except that of the manager and my own.

''The job involved remaining in the office from ten to two o'clock each morning. I was to copy the Encyclopaedia Britannica. Now, a pawnbroker's business is mostly in the evenings so it suited me well to earn a little extra in the morning. Besides, I knew my assistant could handle any problems that came up in the shop. I had to supply the ink, pens, and blotting paper, while Mr. Ross provided the table and chair.

'''Could you be ready to start tomorrow?' the manager asked.

'''Certainly,' I answered, and went home very pleased at my good fortune. But later that night I began to worry about the entire affair. I felt sure it was some kind of strange hoax. Still, in the morning I decided to go and see for myself. I bought a penny bottle of ink, a quill pen, and seven sheets of paper and went to the office of the Red-headed League.

''Sure enough, there was Mr. Ross! He soon started me off with the letter A. From time to time he dropped in to see how I was getting on. This went on day after day. I never dared leave the office for fear he might drop in at any moment. On Saturday he came in and plunked down four golden coins in payment for my week's work. It was the same the next week and the week after. Eight weeks passed like this and I wrote about Abbotts and Archery and Armor and Architecture and hoped to be onto the Bs before too long. I had filled a shelf with my writings when suddenly the whole business came to an end.''

"Came to an end?" questioned Sherlock.

"Yes, sir. This very morning. I went to work as usual to find the door shut and locked. A little square of cardboard was hammered onto it. You can read it yourself."

He held it up to us to read. It said:

THE RED-HEADED LEAGUE IS DISSOLVED OCT. 9, 1890

Sherlock Holmes and I looked at the brief announcement and the disappointed face behind it. Suddenly the whole matter seemed so funny that we burst out laughing.

"I cannot see that there is anything very funny about it!" cried our client, rising from his chair. "If you can do nothing better than laugh at me, I can go elsewhere!"

"No, no!" assured Sherlock, shoving the man back into his chair. "I really wouldn't miss this case for the world. It is most refreshingly unusual. But there really is something comical about it. Now, what did you do upon finding this note?"

"I was staggered, sir. I did not know what to do. I inquired about it at the offices on the floor but they knew nothing. So I went to the landlord on the ground floor and asked him what had become of the Red-headed League. He said he had never heard of such an organization. Nor had he heard of the manager, Mr. Duncan Ross.

"'Well,' said I, 'what about the gentleman in room number four?'

"'The red-headed man? His name was William Morris,' he replied. 'He was a lawyer and was using number four as a temporary office until his new one was ready. He moved out yesterday. I believe his new address is 17 King Edward Street.'

"So I went to that address. It was a company that manufactured artificial kneecaps. No one worked there named Morris or Ross."

"And what did you do next?" asked Holmes.

"I went home and asked the opinion of my assistant. He thought I would probably hear by post. But that was not good enough, Mr. Holmes. I did not wish to lose such a good-paying job without a struggle. I had heard that you gave advice to poor folk in need of it. So I came to you."

"And you did very wisely," said Holmes. "From what you have told me I think graver issues are involved in this case than one would suspect!"

"Grave enough!" said Mr. Jabez Wilson. "Why, I have lost four pounds a week!"

"As far as you are personally concerned," remarked Holmes, "you should have no grievance with this extraordinary league. On the contrary, you are some thirty pounds richer because of it. To say nothing of the minute knowledge you have gained on every subject starting with the letter A. You have lost nothing!"

"No, sir. But I want to find out more about it. Who are they and what was their object in playing a prank on me, if it was a prank. . . ."

"We shall endeavor to clear up these points for you. But first a few questions. How long had your assistant worked for you at the time of the advertisement?"

"About a month."

"And how did he come to you?"

"He came in answer to an advertisement I placed in the newspaper."

"Was he the only applicant?"

"No, I had a dozen."

"Why did you pick him?"

"Because he was handy and would come cheap."

"At half-wages, in fact?"

"Yes."

"What is he like, this Vincent Spaulding?"

"Small, stout, but very quick in his ways," replied Wilson. "He has no hair on his face but must be close to thirty. He has a mark on his forehead from a splash of acid."

Holmes suddenly sat up in his chair in considerable excitement.

"I thought as much! Is one of his ears pierced?"

"Yes! He told me that a gypsy pierced it for him when he was a lad."

"Hum!" exclaimed Holmes. "Is he still with you?"

"Oh yes, sir! I have only just left him."

"And has your business been attended to properly in your absence?"

"Nothing to complain of, sir. There's never much to do in the mornings."

"I shall be happy to give you an opinion on the subject in a day or two," Holmes said. "Today is Saturday. I hope to have solved the mystery by Monday."

"Well, Watson, what do you make of it all?" Sherlock asked me after his client had left.

"I make nothing of it," I answered frankly. "What are you going to do?"

"I beg you not to speak to me for fifty minutes." He then curled himself up in his armchair with his knees drawn up to his hawklike nose. There he sat contemplating the matter. Just as I was nodding off and thought he was as well, he suddenly sprang up from his chair.

"There is a good concert at the auditorium in the Strand this afternoon. We can go through the business district on our way!" In moments he had gathered up our coats and was pushing me out the door.

It was not long before we arrived at Saxe-Coburg Square where Mr. Wilson lived and worked. It was a shabby street with rows of two-story brick houses looking out on an enclosed park where a lawn of weedy grass and a few clumps of faded bushes struggled for survival. Above a corner house hung a board on which was lettered in white the name JABEZ WILSON. Sherlock Holmes looked it all over, walked across the street and

then back to the corner, always keeping an eye on the pawnbroker's shop. Then he walked right up to it and pounded the pavement with his stick. Finally he went up to the door and knocked. It was instantly opened by a bright-looking, clean-shaven young man who invited him in.

"Thank you," said Holmes. "I only wish to ask you the way from here to the Strand."

"Third right, fourth left," said the assistant and closed the door.

"Smart fellow, that," observed Holmes as we walked away. "He is, in my judgment, the fourth smartest man in London and for daring he might be the third. I have known something of him before."

"It seems so," I replied. "Mr. Wilson's assistant obviously plays a key role in the League. You asked directions then, to observe him."

"Not him. The knees of his trousers."

"And what did you see?"

"What I expected to see."

"Why did you beat the pavement?"

"My dear Watson, this is a time for observation, not talk. We are spies in enemy country! Now that we know

something of Saxe-Coburg Square, let us explore the area behind it."

The road behind Saxe-Coburg was much its opposite. It was a main thoroughfare with heavy traffic and swarms of pedestrians walking past the fine shops and business offices.

"Let me see," said Holmes, standing at the corner. "I should like to remember the exact order of the houses here. It's a hobby of mine to have an exact knowledge of London. There is the little newspaper shop, the Coburg branch of the City and Suburban Bank, the Vegetarian restaurant,

and McFarlan's Carriage-building Depot. And now, Doctor, since our business is done, let us go.''

After the concert Holmes said, ''You want to go home, no doubt, Watson. I have some business to attend to which will take some hours. This business at Saxe-Coburg Square is serious.''

''Why serious?''

''A considerable crime is in contemplation. I have every reason to believe we shall be in time to stop it. But today is Saturday, which complicates matters. I shall want your help tonight. Ten o'clock should be early enough.''

''Then I shall be at Baker Street at ten,'' I replied.

That night I found two hansom cabs waiting outside Holmes' house. Within I discovered Holmes deep in conversation with two men.

''Ha, our party is complete!'' exclaimed Holmes on seeing me. He buttoned his pea jacket and took up his riding crop. ''Watson, I think you know Mr. Jones of Scotland Yard? Let me introduce you to Mr. Merryweather, who is to be our companion on tonight's adventure.

''I think you will find, Mr. Merryweather, the stake tonight will be some 30,000 pounds. And for you, Mr. Jones, it will be the man you wish to lay your hands on. . . .''

"John Clay, the murderer, thief, and forger,'' said Jones of Scotland Yard. "He's young but at the head of his profession. I would rather have my handcuffs on him than any other criminal in London. I've been on his track for years and have never set eyes on him!''

"I hope I may have the pleasure of introducing you tonight,'' remarked Holmes. "It is past ten and time we started. If you two will take the first cab, Watson and I will follow in the second.''

Holmes did not speak until we were close to our destination. Finally he said, "This fellow Merryweather is a bank director and personally interested in this matter. I thought it as well to have Jones with us also. He's not a bad fellow, brave as a bulldog, and once he has his claws on someone he holds on tight. Here we are and they are waiting for us.''

We had arrived at the same busy thoroughfare we had visited earlier that day. After we dismissed the cabs, Mr. Merryweather led us down a narrow passage, through a side door, and into a small corridor. At its end was a massive iron gate. Beyond was a flight of

winding stone steps and at their base yet another gate. Mr. Merryweather then stopped to light a lantern before leading us down a dark, earth-smelling passage to a huge vault or cellar. Crates and massive boxes were piled high.

"You are not very vulnerable from above," Holmes said, looking up.

"Nor from below," said Mr. Merryweather. And he struck his stick on the flagstone floor. "Why, dear me, it sounds quite hollow!" he exclaimed in surprise.

"I must ask you to be a little more quiet," said Holmes severely.

"You have already endangered the success of our expedition. Please sit down on one of these boxes and do not interfere."

The solemn Mr. Merryweather perched himself on a crate with a very injured expression on his face. Meanwhile, Sherlock Holmes got down on his knees and pulled a large magnifying glass from his pocket. He then examined the cracks between the floorstones. After a few seconds he got back on his feet and put the magnifying glass away.

"We have at least an hour to wait," he remarked. "They can hardly act until the good pawnbroker is safely in bed. Then they will move quickly. The sooner they do their work, the more time they will have for their escape! As you may have figured out, Watson, we are at present in the cellar of the Coburg branch of one of the principal London banks. Mr. Merryweather is the chairman of the bank directors. He will explain to you why some of the most daring criminals in London should be interested in this particular cellar."

"It is our French gold," whispered the director. "We have had several warnings that an attempt might be made upon it."

"Your French gold?" I asked.

"Yes. We recently had an opportunity to strengthen our resources and so borrowed 30,000 gold napoleons from the Bank of France. Unfortunately, it has become known that the money has never been unpacked and that it is still lying here in our cellar. The crate I am sitting on right now contains 2000 napoleons packed between layers of lead foil. Our reserve of bullion is much larger at present than is usually kept in a single branch office. The directors have had considerable misgivings about it."

"Which were very well justified," observed Holmes. "And now it is time to arrange our plans. We must put the screen down over the lantern."

"And sit in the dark?" Merryweather asked.

"I am afraid so. We cannot risk the presence of light. We must choose our positions. These are daring men. Even though we take them by surprise, they could still do us harm. I shall stand behind this crate. You conceal yourselves behind those. When I flash the light on them, close in swiftly."

Holmes closed the screen on the lantern. We were in pitch darkness. The smell of hot metal remained. It reminded us that the light was still there, ready to flash out at a moment's notice.

"They have but one retreat," whispered Holmes. "Back through the house into Saxe-Coburg Square. I hope you have done what I asked, Jones?"

"I have an inspector and two officers waiting at the front door."

"Then we have stopped the holes. Now we must be silent and wait."

What a time it seemed! It was actually only an hour and a quarter but it seemed like the entire night had passed. My limbs were weary and stiff, but I dared not shift position. My nerves were on end. My hearing was so acute that I could distinguish between the deeper, heavier breath of the bulky Jones and the thin sighing breath of the bank director. Then suddenly the wait was over and my eyes caught sight of a glint of light.

At first it was just a spark in the cracks of the floorstones. Then it lengthened out and became a yellow light. Then without warning, a gash seemed to open and a white, almost womanly hand appeared. Suddenly a rending, tearing sound could be heard. One of the broad white stones turned over on its side. It left a square, gaping hole. Light shone through. Over the edge peered a clean-cut, boyish

face. He looked about and then drew himself up and into the cellar. In another instant he was hauling his companion up as well. The companion was small and pale as well with a shock of very red hair.

"It's all clear," the first rogue whispered. "Have you the chisel and the bag? Great Scott! Jump, Archie, jump!"

Sherlock Holmes had opened the light, sprung out and seized the first intruder by the collar. The other dived down the hole. I heard the sound of ripping cloth as Jones clutched at his coattails.

"It's no use, John Clay!" said Holmes. "You have no chance at all!"

"So I see," the other answered with the utmost coolness. "I guess my friend at least got away . . . though I see you have his coattails."

"There are three men waiting for him at the pawnbroker's front door," said Holmes blandly.

"Indeed! You seem to have done the thing very completely. I must compliment you."

"And I you," Holmes answered. "Your red-headed idea was very new and effective."

Jones placed his handcuffs on John Clay and marched him upstairs.

A cab was waiting to take him and his red-headed accomplice to the police station.

"Really, Mr. Holmes," said Mr. Merryweather. "I do not know how the bank can thank you or repay you. There is no doubt you have detected and defeated one of the most determined attempts at bank robbery ever!"

"I have had one or two little scores of my own to settle with

Mr. John Clay," said Sherlock Holmes. "The matter cost me a small amount which I shall expect the bank to refund. But beyond that, I am amply repaid by having had a unique experience and for hearing the very remarkable tale of the Red-headed League."

"You see, Watson," Holmes explained back at Baker Street, "it was perfectly obvious to me that the purpose of the Red-headed League was to get the pawnbroker out of the way a number of hours each day. It was a curious way of managing it, but really it would be difficult to suggest one better. The method was no doubt suggested to Clay's ingenious mind by the color of both his accomplice's and his employer's hair. The four pounds a week was a lure to draw the pawnbroker out of his shop. What was four pounds a week when they were after thousands? They first placed the advertisement in the newspaper. Then Ross-Morris rented a temporary office while Clay persuaded his boss to apply for the position. Together they managed to get the pawnbroker out of his shop each morning. From the moment I heard that the assistant worked for half-pay, I knew he had some strong motive for wanting the job."

"But how could you guess what that motive was?"

"The man's business was a small one, and there was nothing in his house of great value to steal. What did these two rogues want then? It must be something outside the house. I thought of the assistant's fondness for photography and his habit of vanishing into the cellar. The cellar! There was the clue! I made inquiries into this mysterious assistant and recognized his description. I was dealing with one of the coolest and most daring criminals in London! He was doing something in the cellar. . . . Something which took many hours each day for weeks on end. What could it be? The only thing I could think of was that he was running a tunnel to some other building.

"That is as far as I got when we visited Saxe-Coburg Square. I surprised you by beating on the pavement with my stick. I was trying to find out whether the cellar stretched in front or behind the building. It was not in front. I then rang the bell. As I hoped, the assistant answered it. We have had some near encounters, but we have never set eyes on each other before. I hardly looked into his face. His knees were what I wished to see. You must yourself have noticed how worn, wrinkled, and stained they were. They spoke of those long hours of digging. But what were they digging for? I walked around the corner. The City and Suburban Bank abutted the pawnbroker's shop. I felt sure I had solved the case. When you drove home after the concert, I called on Scotland Yard and the chairman of the bank directors. You witnessed the result.''

"And how could you tell they would make their attempt tonight?'' I asked.

"Well, they closed their League offices. That was a sign that they no longer needed Mr. Wilson out of the house. In other words, they had completed their tunnel. But they had to use it as quickly as possible—before it was discovered or the bullion was removed. Saturday was the best choice of days as the bank was closed and they would have the weekend to make their escape. For all these reasons I expected them to come tonight.''

"You reasoned it out beautifully!'' I exclaimed in admiration. "It is so long a chain and yet every link rings true.''

"Elementary, my dear Watson,'' replied Mr. Sherlock Holmes.

Reader's Response

What do you think it is about Sherlock Holmes that has made him so popular with readers?

THE RED-HEADED LEAGUE

Thinking It Over

1. Why did Mr. Wilson seek out Sherlock Holmes? Give a summary of the events that led up to that meeting.
2. What were Watson's and Holmes' impressions of Mr. Wilson? How did their impressions differ?
3. Which part of Mr. Wilson's story first made Holmes suspicious? What led you to that conclusion?
4. How would you describe Clay's and Holmes' attitudes toward each other?
5. Do you think Clay's scheme would have succeeded if he had paid Mr. Wilson for one more week of work in the Red-headed League?
6. If Mr. Wilson's hair had not been red, what do you think Clay might have done to get Mr. Wilson out of the shop?

Writing to Learn

THINK AND CONNECT   Sherlock Holmes was a master at making connections. You can do it, too. Copy and supply the missing information in the "thought links" below.

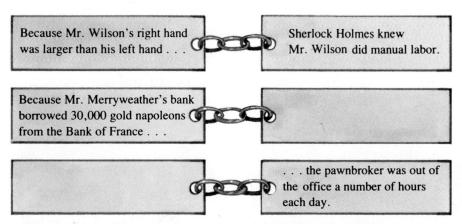

WRITE   Find two connected ideas in this story. Write them in the form of a "thought link" like the ones shown above.

Tales and Puzzles

by George Shannon

When is a folktale not a folktale? When it's a puzzle! Each of these folktales has a puzzle to solve. And if you use your imagination and try to visualize the story's events, maybe you can figure out the answer to the puzzle.

A DRINK FOR CROW

Once there was a crow who had grown so thirsty he could barely caw. He flew down to a big pitcher where he had gotten a drink of water the day before, but there was only a little bit of water remaining at the bottom. He tried and tried to reach it with his beak, but the pitcher was too deep and his beak was too short. But just as he was about to give up, he knew what to do. He flew back and forth from the garden to the pitcher until he was able to drink easily from the pitcher while sitting on its edge.

From Aesop's Fables

What did the crow do?

THE CLEVEREST SON

Once there lived a man who had three sons. When he grew old and ill and knew that he soon would die, he called all three sons into his room.

"There is no way I can divide the house and farm to support all three of you. The one who proves himself the cleverest will inherit the house and farm. There is a coin on the table for each of you. The one who can buy something that will fill this room will inherit all I own."

The eldest son took his coin, went straight to the marketplace, and filled his wagon full of straw. The second son thought a bit longer, then also went to the marketplace, where he bought sacks and sacks of feathers. The youngest son thought and then quietly went to a little shop. He bought two small things and tucked them into his pocket.

That night the father called them in to show what they had bought. The eldest son spread his straw about the floor, but it filled only one part of the room. The second son dumped out his sacks of feathers, but they filled only two corners of the room. Then the youngest son smiled, pulled the two small things out of his pocket, and soon filled the room.

"Yes," said the father, "you are indeed the cleverest and have filled the room when the others could not. You shall inherit my house and farm."

An Ethiopian Tale

What had the youngest son bought and with what did he fill the room?

WHICH FLOWER?

Once long ago there lived two rulers of different lands famed for their wisdom as well as their beauty, the Queen of Sheba and King Solomon. Upon his visit to her land, the queen decided to test King Solomon's wisdom by a series of tests and riddles. He passed each one with ease until she led him to a room filled with flowers of every shape and color. The queen had had the finest craftsmen and magicians in her land construct the flowers so that they looked exactly like the real flowers from her garden.

"The test," she told King Solomon, "is to find the ONE real flower amongst all the artificial ones."

King Solomon carefully looked from flower to flower and back again, searching for even the smallest of differences. He looked for any sign of wilted leaves or petals, but found lifelike leaves and petals in all conditions on every flower. And fragrance was of no help, for the room was filled with fragrances.

"Please," said King Solomon. "This room is so warm. Could we open the curtains and let in the breeze? The fresh air will clear my head for thinking."

The Queen of Sheba kindly agreed, and within minutes after the curtains had been opened King Solomon knew which of the many was the one real flower.

A King Solomon Tale

How did he suddenly know?

DIVIDING THE HORSES

Once there lived a farmer, his wife, and their three sons. When the farmer died, his will said that the eldest son was to receive one-half of what he owned, the middle son was to receive one-third, and the youngest son was to receive one-ninth. All the farmer owned, however, was seventeen horses. And try as they might, the three sons could not figure out any way to divide the seventeen horses by their father's wishes.

"Don't worry," their mother told them. "We can solve this with a little help."

She went to the neighboring farm and borrowed a horse. Then with a total of eighteen horses, she gave the eldest son one-half, or nine horses. She gave the middle son one-third, or six of the horses. And she gave the youngest son one-ninth, or two of the horses.

"There," she said. "Nine plus six plus two makes the seventeen horses your father left you." And she returned the eighteenth horse to the neighbor.

A Eurasian Tale

How did she do it?

FISHING

One fine summer day two fathers and two sons went fishing at their favorite lake. They fished and talked all morning and by noon everyone had caught one fish. As the two fathers and two sons walked back home, everyone was happy because each had a fish, even though only three fish were caught.

Two fathers and two sons. Only three fish and no fish were lost.

A United States Folk Tale

How can this have happened?

CROSSING THE RIVER

Once there was a man who had to take a wolf, a goat, and a cabbage across a river. But his boat was so small it could hold only himself and one other thing. The man didn't know what to do. How could he take the wolf, the goat, and the cabbage over one at a time, so that the wolf wouldn't eat the goat and the goat wouldn't eat the cabbage?

A Worldwide Tale

How did the man solve his problem?

HOW IT WAS DONE

A Drink for Crow

The crow gathered pebbles, one by one, and dropped them into the pitcher until the water rose to the top.

The Cleverest Son

The youngest son bought a match and a candle, and he filled the room with light.

Which Flower?

A bee flew in the window and immediately went to the real flower.

Dividing the Horses

1/2 plus 1/3 plus 1/9 does not equal one or all of anything.

The mother used their common denominator, which was eighteen, and changed the fractions to 9/18 plus 6/18 plus 2/18 which equaled 17/18.

So by borrowing the eighteenth horse she was creating a situation that matched the fractions.

Fishing

Only three people went fishing: a boy, his father, and his grandfather. This made two sons and two fathers.

Crossing the River

Solution 1. He could: (1) take the goat over and go back alone, (2) take the wolf over and bring the goat back, then (3) take the cabbage over and leave the goat behind, and finally (4) make one last trip and take the goat over to join the wolf and the cabbage.

Solution 2. He could: (1) take the goat over and go back alone, (2) take the cabbage over and bring the goat back, then (3) take the wolf over and leave the goat behind, and finally (4) go back and get the goat on the last trip.

◆ LIBRARY LINK ◆

Test your puzzle-solving skills by reading Stories to Solve: Folktales from Around the World, *from which these tales are excerpted.*

Reader's Response

Which folktale-puzzle did you enjoy most? What intrigued you about it?

Tales and Puzzles

Thinking It Over

1. How did the crow manage to drink water from the pitcher?
2. What else might the sons have bought to fill their father's room? How did you think of your answer?
3. Do you think the father's test of his sons was fair? Explain your answer.
4. What knowledge of King Solomon's enabled him to solve the Queen of Sheba's puzzle?
5. Why couldn't the man leave the goat, the wolf, and the cabbage alone together?
6. Briefly describe the settings of two of the stories.

Writing to Learn

THINK AND INVENT   Read the riddle below, and then choose an object about which you could write a riddle of your own. It should be an object you can see. Plan your riddle by making notes about how the object looks.

A Riddle

It looks like a tiny bolt of lightning.
It's found in even the strongest wall.
It can be short or long.
What is it?

crack in the wall

WRITE   Compose a riddle about the object you chose. Describe, but do not name the object.

Magazine

News About Reading

Movable Type — It Changed the World

Johann Gutenberg

What one single invention changed the world more than any other? The automobile? The electric light bulb? Television? It is true that those inventions have all greatly affected our lives. However, the one invention that caused greater change than any of them was the invention of movable type. That's right. In approximately the year 1450, Johann Gutenberg forever changed the way books were printed, and at the same time, he changed the whole world.

Before then, books had to be copied by hand, word for word. Copying a single book took months or years. As a result, books were very rare, and so were people who could read them. That time in history was called the Dark Ages because people lived largely in ignorance.

What Gutenberg did was invent a way to make individual letters on little blocks of metal. He could arrange those blocks, called *type*, into words and lines, cover them with ink, and print a page. After he printed many copies of the page, he could take the type apart, clean it, and make new words and lines for

This is one example of metal movable type.

A museum in Mainz, Germany, shows a re-creation of Gutenberg's workshop.

other pages. Gutenberg's first printed book was the Bible. Copies of this beautiful book still exist in rare book collections.

Johann Gutenberg gave us the world of reading.

Gutenberg's invention had an immediate effect upon the world. Other people soon began printing books, and many more people learned to read. As soon as new ideas about science, geography, government, and history were discovered, people everywhere could read about them. People could read about explorations in the New World, for example, and use that knowledge to plan their own voyages. The world began to change and grow—and it has never stopped.

Since Gutenberg's time, even the process of printing has changed. First, huge metal printing presses driven by steam took the place of his small hand press. Today, computers are used to set type that was once set by hand. Hundreds of thousands of copies of a newspaper can be printed in only a few hours.

What if movable type had never been invented? Not only would we have to live without books, newspapers, and magazines, we would have no light bulbs, automobiles, or television. For without print as a way to get and share information, modern technology could not have been developed. With movable type, Johann Gutenberg gave us the world of reading, which in turn has given us the modern world we live in.

Today, a person working with a computer can design a page of pictures and words faster than ever—without using paste or paper! This electronic method is called desktop publishing.

☛ **If you enjoyed reading about the history of Gutenberg's invention, you might enjoy the articles in the magazine Cobblestone, which is a history magazine for young people. You may also find articles about new technologies in a magazine such as 3-2-1 Contact.**

Ancient Mysteries

by Harold and Geraldine Woods

An artist's conception of how Stonehenge looked when it was originally built.

In this article, three mysteries are presented. But don't look for the answers! They are buried somewhere in the past, in another time and another culture. Perhaps some day the answers will come to light. In the meantime, it is fun to guess what they might be.

The first mystery concerns Stonehenge, an ancient stone monument on Salisbury Plain in Wiltshire, England. Archeologists believe that Stonehenge was built about 2000 B.C., but for hundreds of years they have puzzled over why, and even how, it was built.

Ancient Mystery One: Stonehenge

Take fifty or sixty blocks from a toy chest. Carry them one at a time to your local park. Arrange them into two circles and two horseshoes. Now imagine doing the same thing with stones that weigh as much as 80,000 pounds (36,287 kilograms) each. That should give you some idea of the effort that went into building Stonehenge.

The ancient rocks of Stonehenge are in southern England. They were originally arranged on a flat piece of land. See the illustration on page 250.

Many of the stones have fallen or cracked by now. Even so, they are an amazing sight. Visitors from all over the world come to see Stonehenge. They wonder, as people have wondered through the ages, how Stonehenge was built.

This is not an easy question to answer, since work on Stonehenge began over four thousand years ago. The people who lived in Britain at that time kept no written records. They didn't have metal tools or machines or horses or carts. They didn't even have wheels! Yet somehow they managed to change tens of thousands of pounds of rock into Stonehenge.

Only the outline of the giant stone circle can be seen in the ruins of Stonehenge today.

It must have been an incredibly difficult job. Scientists think that as many as forty generations of people worked for a thousand years before Stonehenge was finished. The huge stone blocks had to be made with stone tools. Then they had to be moved to the place where they now stand. Some of the stones, called Sarcens, come from an area about 24 miles (39 kilometers) from Stonehenge. Others, called bluestones, were cut 250 miles (402 kilometers) away! That's quite a distance to move tons of rock. After they were moved, the stones had to be raised to a standing position. Then the blocks that formed the top of the circle had to be set in place.

No one will ever know for sure, but scientists have figured out how this work might have been done. First of all, the cutting of the blocks may have been made easier with the use of fire. The workers may have laid burning branches on the rock along the line they wanted to cut. When the stone was red hot, the workers may have poured cold water over it. The quick change from hot to cold would have strained the rock, making it easier for a stone tool to crack it. The workers may then have rubbed the block with small stones for endless hours until it was the proper shape.

As for moving the blocks, the bluestones might have been floated on rafts. There is a river that flows quite near Stonehenge. The overland travel was probably done with wooden sleds. The sleds might have been placed on top of dozens of logs to help them slide more smoothly. Even so, each block would have had to be pulled by hundreds of people.

Why Was Stonehenge Built?

The greatest mystery of Stonehenge is not really how but *why* it was built. Why should all those people put so much work into such a project? Why carry stones for 250 miles? Why use stones at all, when lightweight wood was all around? And finally, what was the giant stone circle used for?

People have been puzzling over these questions for hundreds of years. They've come up with some pretty wild answers. At various times Stonehenge has been described as a cattle pen, a palace, and an altar. One person even said the huge stones were foundations for the tents of Julius Caesar!

Today we're quite certain that none of these theories is right. The most popular explanations for Stonehenge are rooted in science and math. A man named Alexander Thom spent many years measuring Stonehenge and other ancient stone circles. He thinks Stonehenge may have been a sort of solid math problem. The ancient people, he says, may have used it to figure out the measurements of triangles and other shapes. Professor Thom also suggests that Stonehenge was an early laboratory for the study of the sun and the stars. He bases this theory on the fact that the sun rises directly above one of the stones on the longest day of the year. Among many early peoples, that day was considered important.

Scientist Gerald Hawkins also thinks that Stonehenge was used to study the sky. He fed the measurements of Stonehenge into a computer. The computer said that Stonehenge could have been used to predict eclipses of the sun and the moon.

Many people also think that Stonehenge was part of an early religion. The gigantic stones may have been an offering to a god. Or the circle itself may have been a temple for some ancient celebrations.

None of these theories, however, can be proved. So Stonehenge remains a puzzle—a great, silent mystery of stone!

Ancient Mystery Two: Atlantis

Suppose someone told you that the Atlantic Ocean once had a huge island in it instead of being open water.

Would you believe it? If so, you probably believe in the lost kingdom of Atlantis.

The first person to write about Atlantis was a Greek philosopher named Plato. Over two thousand years ago he described a fabulous island-empire where the palaces were covered with silver and gold. According to Plato, Atlantis was located "beyond the Pillars of Hercules." The Pillars of Hercules is the name the Greeks gave to the Strait of Gibraltar. That would place Atlantis in the Atlantic Ocean, right between America and Europe.

Of course, there's no island in the Atlantic today like the one Plato described. That also fits the Atlantis story, because Atlantis was supposed to have been destroyed about

Plato's description would have put Atlantis in the middle of the Atlantic Ocean.

twelve thousand years ago. According to Plato, the Atlanteans were very rich and happy for a number of years. But after a while they became greedy. They began to war against other countries, in search of power and wealth. As a punishment the gods sent disaster to Atlantis. First terrible heat, then tidal waves and earthquakes rocked the island. After only twenty-four terrible hours, Plato wrote, Atlantis sank to the bottom of the sea. This all happened, he said, about nine thousand years before his time.

The Evidence of Thera

Ever since Plato wrote about the island-empire, people have been searching for Atlantis. After all, who wouldn't want to find a sunken island filled with treasure? And the searchers *did* find Atlantis—over and over again. They found it in the Bahamas, in the North Sea, around the Azores islands, and in many other parts of the globe. After their search was over, most of the Atlantis hunters wrote

Thera is much smaller than Atlantis was believed to be, and is also not located "beyond the Pillars of Hercules."

books proving that their place was the *real* lost empire. Most of them also tried to prove that everyone else who had found Atlantis was completely wrong.

But historians expect to see some coins, pottery, or perhaps a few ruins at the location of an ancient empire. Yet none of the searchers has ever produced an object that was definitely Atlantean. Scientists who study the rocky crust of Earth have never found a trace of the large sunken island Plato described. For these reasons most historians think that Atlantis is just a legend.

However, there is one interesting possibility. An island called Thera was once part of a rich, ancient empire. A little over three thousand years ago (about nine hundred years before Plato), a volcano erupted there with tremendous force. The explosion caused much of Thera's land to sink beneath the sea. Scientists think that Thera's disaster took place in a single day and night. That's exactly what Plato said about Atlantis.

Could Thera be the lost kingdom of Atlantis? A few historians think so. But there are problems with this theory. Thera is not located "beyond the Pillars of Hercules," as Plato reported. It is in the Mediterranean Sea. And the island, even before the eruption, was much smaller than Atlantis was supposed to be. It was also destroyed much too recently.

One scholar claims that the difference in size and dates might have been caused by a confusion of numbers. The Theran symbols for ten and one hundred are almost the same. If all the numbers in Plato's story are changed from hundreds to tens, Thera fits the description of Atlantis almost exactly.

The sunken areas of Thera have not been completely explored yet. So evidence may turn up someday to prove that it really was Atlantis. Even if that doesn't happen, the legend of Atlantis will live on. People will continue to hunt for the lost empire. Perhaps someday you will join the search.

Ancient Mystery Three: Linear A

 日 ΥΥ↲ㅋ Don't feel badly if you don't understand this writing — no one else does either! It may be the name of a goddess, though no one is really sure. It is written in "Linear A," a type of writing used on the island of Crete more than three thousand years ago. Linear A has about seventy-five signs and a few picture symbols, and most of them are a puzzle to historians.

If you are good at codes and have a few years to spare, you might try cracking the secret of ancient Cretan writing. That's what Michael Ventris did, although he worked on Linear B, a form the Cretans used a little later than Linear A.

Michael had heard about the mysterious symbols when

he was still a schoolboy. He decided that working on Cretan writing would be a fine hobby, and for the next seventeen years he spent all his spare time on the project. And his work paid off. In 1953 Michael Ventris was able to announce that the mystery of Cretan Linear B was finally solved!

Unfortunately Michael Ventris died before he was able to decode Linear A, as well as an even earlier form of Cretan writing. They remain a puzzle. So do several other types of writing.

The language of the ancient Mayan Indians of Central America, for example, has never been completely understood. Researchers have decoded some of the Mayan calendar system, but much of the writing is still a mystery. So are the words carved on some statues made by the Olmecs, who lived in Mexico around three thousand years ago. Nor can anyone read Etruscan, the language of the people who lived in Italy before the ancient Romans. This is particularly annoying, since an attempt was made to avoid the problem nineteen hundred years ago! Claudius, the Roman emperor at that time, had an Etruscan wife. Claudius was afraid that the Etruscan language was dying out, so he wrote an Etruscan/Latin dictionary. Unfortunately the book was lost.

So if you are good at languages and like mysteries, there's plenty of work for you. Good luck!

 Reader's Response

Which one of these mysteries was most interesting to you? Give reasons for your choice.

Ancient Mysteries

Thinking It Over

1. How many years ago do scientists think the construction of Stonehenge was begun?
2. What makes Stonehenge such an amazing structure?
3. Do you believe Atlantis actually existed, or do you believe it was a legend? Why?
4. If historians do find traces of Atlantis, where do you think they will find them? (Use details to support your opinion.)
5. Do you think specialists will ever crack the code of Linear A? What leads you to believe they will or won't?
6. Why does the author feel it is particularly annoying that no one can read Etruscan?

Writing to Learn

THINK AND QUESTION   Suppose that you have been asked to lead a discussion of one of the ancient mysteries. Choose one of the mysteries. Create three original questions about it. Include a "how," a "why," and an "opinion" question.

Questions for Discussion
How: How was Michael able to solve the mystery of Cretan Linear B?
Why: Tell one reason why Stonehenge may have been built.
Opinion: In your opinion, did Atlantis exist?

WRITE   Copy your favorite question and write your answer to it.

LITERATURE LINK

How can you figure out unfamiliar words and phrases?

Stonehenge—why was it built? What messages do these weatherbeaten rocks have for us? Although for years scientists, historians, and puzzle lovers have pondered these questions, none has unlocked the mystery.

Sometimes your reading can seem as mysterious as the boulders of Stonehenge, particularly when you face one word after another that you don't understand. Sometimes it's not just words but whole phrases or sentences that don't seem to make sense. Unlike Stonehenge mystery solvers, though, readers have strategies to use when the going gets rough.

Look for Structural Clues

If a particular word is giving you trouble, one strategy is to look at the structure of the word itself. Does it have a base word that you know? Do any word-parts or spelling patterns give you a hint? As an example, the word *Cretan* looks very much like *Crete*, the name of an island in Europe. The capital letter tells that it's a proper name. When you look for word-parts, you'll see that *Cretan* is made from the base word *Crete* and the suffix *-an*, meaning "one who lives."

Context Clues Might Help

Another strategy for figuring out words — or even phrases — that don't make sense is to use context clues. For unfamiliar words, reread the sentence or paragraph and look for synonyms or even definitions the author might have included. Sometimes authors describe how something looks or works; you can use this description to guess at word meaning. Whatever the word, take a minute and think about it. Most of the time you'll be able to figure out a meaning that makes sense.

Using context clues to figure out the meaning of a whole phrase is trickier, because there usually aren't as many clues. Often the phrase is a figurative expression, and you have to think about the meaning the author intended. Take this example from "The Red-headed League":

> "What on earth does it mean?" I exclaimed in amazement.
>
> Holmes chuckled and wriggled in his chair, as was his habit in high spirits. "It is a little off the beaten track, isn't it?" he said.

Clearly Holmes doesn't mean that the advertisement has wandered off the path and into the woods. The context shows that Watson is puzzled and Holmes is in agreement. *Off the beaten track* must mean "unusual" or "out of the ordinary."

Ask for Help

A third strategy for understanding unfamiliar words or phrases is to ask someone — or something — for help. Check with a friend or your teacher. A dictionary is also a gold mine of word information, and many also give meanings of common idioms — phrases whose meanings are very different from what you'd expect from the individual words. To find the meaning of an idiom, look up what seems to be the most important word. Idioms are usually explained near the end of the entry for that key word.

For example, when you say you are going to "turn over a new leaf," no one expects you to pick up a leaf and turn it over. This phrase is an idiom, and the key word seems to be *leaf*. Check *leaf* in the dictionary: What does the idiom mean? It means that you are going to make a new start or begin to change your habits.

Sounds easy, and it is! Once you discover the meaning of a new word or expression, chances are that you'll be able to remember it if it pops up again. Not only that, but you'll be able to use it in your own writing.

Here's part of "The Night the Bed Fell," a humorous story by James Thurber. It has some words and phrases that may be unfamiliar to you.

I suppose the high-water mark of my youth in Columbus, Ohio, was the night the bed fell on my father. It makes a better recitation (unless, as some friends of mine have said, one has heard it five or six times) than it does a piece of writing, for it is almost necessary to throw pieces of furniture around, shake doors, and bark like a dog to lend the proper atmosphere and verisimilitude to what is admittedly a somewhat incredible tale. Still, it did take place.

It happened, then, that my father had decided to sleep in the attic one night, to be where he could think. My mother

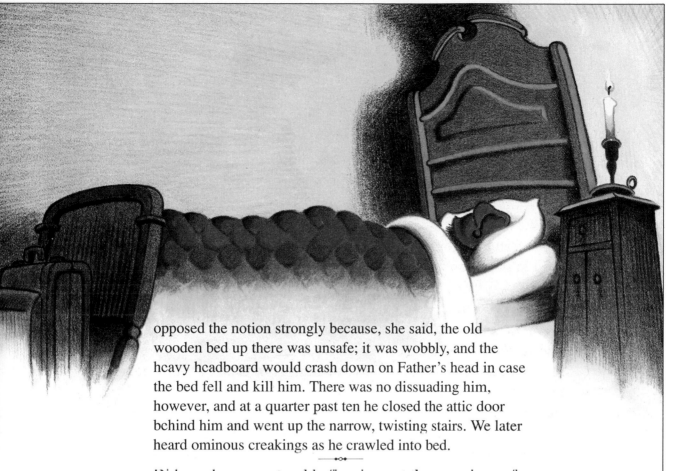

opposed the notion strongly because, she said, the old
wooden bed up there was unsafe; it was wobbly, and the
heavy headboard would crash down on Father's head in case
the bed fell and kill him. There was no dissuading him,
however, and at a quarter past ten he closed the attic door
behind him and went up the narrow, twisting stairs. We later
heard ominous creakings as he crawled into bed.

———◦◇◦———

Did you have any trouble figuring out the meanings of any
words or phrases? How about *recitation?* You could use structural
clues to figure out this word. You know the base word *recite.* A
recitation must be something that's repeated aloud and possibly
from memory.

Verisimilitude is a word you can guess at from context.
Thurber admits that the tale is incredible and suggests that acting
out the story with all the motions makes it seem more real.
Verisimilitude must mean something like "truth" or "reality."

What about *high-water mark?* It seems to indicate an
important event. Since this is an idiom, it's the kind of expression
a dictionary can help you with. Try finding it under *high.*

There are many interesting words and expressions in "The
Cat and the Golden Egg." Some may be unfamiliar to you. If you
need help with any new words, try using the strategies suggested
in this lesson.

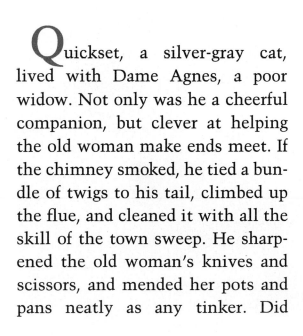

Dame Agnes lives only with her cat, Quickset. Now it looks as if neither of them will see another meal.

The Cat and the Golden Egg

by Lloyd Alexander

Quickset, a silver-gray cat, lived with Dame Agnes, a poor widow. Not only was he a cheerful companion, but clever at helping the old woman make ends meet. If the chimney smoked, he tied a bundle of twigs to his tail, climbed up the flue, and cleaned it with all the skill of the town sweep. He sharpened the old woman's knives and scissors, and mended her pots and pans neatly as any tinker. Did

Dame Agnes knit, he held the skein of yarn; did she spin, he turned the spinning wheel.

Now, one morning Dame Agnes woke up with a bone-cracking rheumatism. Her joints creaked, her back ached, and her knees were so stiff she could no way get out of bed. "My poor Quickset," she moaned, "today you and I must both go hungry."

At first, Quickset thought

Dame Agnes meant it was the rheumatism that kept her from cooking breakfast, so he answered:

"Go hungry? No, indeed. You stay comfortable; I'll make us a little broiled sausage and soft boiled egg, and brew a pot of tea for you. Then I'll sit on your lap to warm you, and soon you'll be good as new."

Before Dame Agnes could say another word, he hurried to the pantry. But, opening the cupboard, he saw only bare shelves: not so much as a crust of bread or crumb of cheese; not even a dry bone or bacon rind.

"Mice!" he cried. "Eaten every scrap! They're out of hand, I've been too easy on them. I'll settle accounts with those fellows later. But now, mistress, I had best go to Master Grubble's market and buy what we need."

Dame Agnes thereupon burst into tears. "Oh, Quickset, it isn't mice, it's money. I have no more. Not a penny left for food or fuel."

"Why, mistress, you should have said something about that before now," replied Quickset. "I never would have let you come to such a state. No matter, I'll think of a way to fill your purse again.

Meantime, I'll have Master Grubble give us our groceries on credit."

"Grubble? Give credit?" Dame Agnes exclaimed. "You know the only thing he gives is short weight at high prices. Alas for the days when the town had a dozen tradesmen and more: a baker, a butcher, a greengrocer, and all the others. But they're gone, thanks to Master Grubble. One by one, he's gobbled them up. Schemed and swindled them out of their businesses! And now he's got the whole town under his thumb, for it's deal with Grubble or deal with no one."

"In that case," replied Quickset, "deal with him I will. Or, to put it better, he'll deal with me."

The old woman shook her head. "You'll still need money. And you shall have it, though I must do something I hoped I'd never have to do."

"Go to the linen chest," Dame Agnes went on. "At the bottom, under the good pillowslips, there's an old wool stocking. Fetch it out and bring it to me."

Puzzled, Quickset did as she asked. He found the stocking with a piece of string tied around the toe and carried it to Dame Agnes, who undid the knot, reached in and drew out one small gold coin.

"Mistress, that's more than enough," said Quickset. "Why did you fret so? With this, we can buy all we want."

Instead of being cheered by the gold piece in her hand, Dame Agnes only sighed:

"This is the last of the small savings my dear husband left to me. I've kept it all these years, and promised myself never to spend it."

"Be glad you did keep it," said Quickset, "for now's the time you need it most."

"I didn't put this by for myself," Dame Agnes replied. "It was for you. I meant to leave it to you in my will. It was to be your legacy, a little something until you found another home. But I see I shall have to spend it. Once gone, it's gone, and that's the end of everything."

At this, Dame Agnes began sobbing again. But Quickset reassured her:

"No need for tears. I'll see to this matter. Only let me have that

gold piece a little while. I'll strike such a bargain with Master Grubble that we'll fill our pantry with meat and drink a-plenty. Indeed, he'll beg me to keep the money and won't ask a penny, that I promise."

"Master Grubble, I fear, will be more than a match even for you," Dame Agnes replied. Nevertheless, she did as Quickset urged, put the coin in a leather purse, and hung it around his neck.

Quickset hurried through town to the market, where he found Master Grubble sitting on a high stool behind the counter. For all that his shelves were loaded with victuals of every kind, with meats, and vegetables, and fruits, Grubble looked as though he had never sampled his own wares. There was more fat on his bacon than on himself. He was lean-shanked and sharp-eyed, his nose narrow as a knife blade. His mouth was pursed and puckered as if he had been sipping vinegar, and his cheeks as mottled as moldy cheese. At sight of Quickset, the storekeeper never so much as climbed down from his stool to wait on his customer, but

only made a sour face; and, in a voice equally sour, demanded:

"And what do you want? Half a pound of mouse tails? A sack of catnip? Out! No loitering! I don't cater to the cat trade."

Despite this curdled welcome, Quickset bowed and politely explained that Dame Agnes was ailing and he had come shopping in her stead.

"Sick she must be," snorted Master Grubble, "to send a cat marketing, without even a shopping basket. How do you mean to carry off what you buy? Push it along the street with your nose?"

"Why, sir," Quickset answered, "I thought you might send your shop boy around with the parcels. I'm sure you'll do it gladly when you see the handsome order to be filled. Dame Agnes needs a joint of beef, a shoulder of mutton, five pounds of your best sausage, a dozen of the largest eggs—"

"Not so fast," broke in the storekeeper. "Joints and shoulders, is it? Sausage and eggs? Is that what you want? Then I'll tell you what I want: cash on the counter, paid in full. Or you, my fine cat, won't have so much as a wart from one of my pickles.''

"You'll be paid," Quickset replied, "and very well paid. But now I see your prices, I'm not sure I brought enough money with me."

"So that's your game!" cried Grubble. "Well, go and get enough. I'll do business with you then, and not before."

"It's a weary walk home and back again," said Quickset. "Allow me a minute or two and I'll have money to spare. And, Master Grubble, if you'd be so kind as to lend me an egg."

"Egg?" retorted Grubble. "What's that to do with paying my bill?"

"You'll see," Quickset answered. "I guarantee you'll get all that's owing to you."

Grubble at first refused and again ordered Quickset from the shop. Only when the cat promised to pay double the price of the groceries, as well as an extra fee for the use of the egg, did the storekeeper grudgingly agree.

Taking the egg from Master Grubble, Quickset placed it on the floor, then carefully settled himself on top of it. "Fool!" cried Grubble.

"What are you doing? Get off my egg! This cat's gone mad, and thinks he's a chicken!"

Quickset said nothing, but laid back his ears and waved his tail, warning Grubble to keep silent. After another moment, Quickset got up and brought the egg to the counter:

"There, Master Grubble, that should be enough."

"What?" shouted the storekeeper. "Idiot cat! You mean to pay me with my own egg?"

"With better than that, as you'll see," answered Quickset. While Grubble fumed, Quickset neatly cracked the shell and poured the contents into a bowl. At this, Grubble ranted all the more:

"Alley rabbit! Smash my egg, will you? I'll rub your nose in it!"

Suddenly Master Grubble's voice choked in his gullet. His eyes popped as he stared into the bowl. There, with the broken egg, lay a gold piece.

Instantly, he snatched it out. "What's this?"

"What does it look like?" returned Quickset.

Grubble squinted at the coin, flung it onto the counter and listened to it ring. He bit it, peered closer, turned it round and round in his fingers, and finally blurted:

"Gold!"

Grubble, in his fit of temper, had never seen Quickset slip the coin from the purse and deftly drop it into the bowl. Awestruck, he gaped at the cat, then lowered his voice to a whisper:

"How did you do that?"

Quickset merely shook his head and shrugged his tail. At last, as the excited storekeeper pressed him for an answer, he winked one eye and calmly replied:

"Now, now, Master Grubble, a cat has trade secrets just as a storekeeper. I don't ask yours, you don't ask mine. If I told you how simple it is, you'd know as much as I do. And if others found out—"

"Tell me!" cried Grubble. "I won't breathe a word to a living soul. My dear cat, listen to me," he hurried on. "You'll have all the victuals you want. For a month! A year! Forever! Here, this very moment, I'll have my boy take a cartload to your mistress. Only teach me to sit on eggs as you did."

"Easily done," said Quickset. "But what about that gold piece?"

"Take it!" cried Grubble, handing the coin to Quickset. "Take it, by all means."

Quickset pretended to think over the bargain, then answered:

"Agreed. But you must do exactly as I tell you."

Grubble nodded and his eyes glittered. "One gold piece from one egg. But what if I used two eggs? Or three, or four, or five?"

"As many as you like," said Quickset. "A basketful, if it suits you."

Without another moment's delay, Grubble called his boy from the storeroom and told him to deliver all that Quickset had ordered to the house of Dame Agnes. Then, whimpering with pleasure, he filled his biggest basket with every egg in the store. His nose twitched, his hands trembled, and his usually sallow face turned an eager pink.

"Now," said Quickset, "so you won't be disturbed, take your basket to the top shelf and sit on it there. One thing more, the most important. Until those eggs hatch don't say a single word. If you have anything to tell me, whatever the reason, you must only cluck like a chicken. Nothing else, mind you. Cackle all you like; speak but once, and the spell is broken."

"What about my customers? Who's to wait on them?" asked Grubble, unwilling to lose business even in exchange for a fortune.

"Never fear," said Quickset. "I'll mind the store."

"What a fine cat you are," purred Grubble. "Noble animal. Intelligent creature."

With that, gleefully chuckling and licking his lips, he clambered to the top shelf, hauling his heavy burden along with him. There he squatted gingerly over the basket, so cramped that he was obliged to draw his knees under his chin and fold his arms as tightly as he could; until indeed he looked much like a skinny, long-beaked chicken hunched on a nest.

Below, Quickset no sooner had taken his place on the stool than Mistress Libbet, the carpenter's wife, stepped through the door.

"Why, Quickset, what are you doing here?" said she. "Have you gone into trade? And can that be Master Grubble on the shelf? I swear he looks as if he's sitting on a basket of eggs."

"Pay him no mind," whispered Quickset. "He fancies himself a hen. An odd notion, but harmless. However, since Master Grubble is busy nesting, I'm tending shop for him. So, Mistress Libbet, how may I serve you?"

"There's so much our little ones need." Mistress Libbet sighed unhappily. "And nothing we can afford to feed them. I was hoping Master Grubble had some scraps or trimmings."

"He has much better," said Quickset, pulling down one of the juiciest hams and slicing away at it with Grubble's carving knife. "Here's a fine bargain today: only a penny a pound."

Hearing this, Master Grubble was about to protest, but caught himself in the nick of time. Instead, he began furiously clucking and squawking:

"Cut-cut-cut! Aw-cut!"

"What's that you say?" Quickset glanced up at the agitated store-keeper and cupped an ear with his paw. "Cut more? Yes, yes, I understand. The price is still too high? Very well, if you insist: two pounds for a penny."

Too grateful to question such generosity on the part of Grubble, Mistress Libbet flung a penny onto the counter and seized her ham without waiting for Quickset to wrap it. As she hurried from the store, the tailor's wife and the stonecutter's daughter came in; and, a moment later, Dame Gerton, the laundrywoman.

"Welcome, ladies," called Quickset. "Welcome, one and all. Here's fine prime meats, fine fresh vegetables on sale today. At these prices, they won't last long. So, hurry! Step up!"

As the delighted customers pressed eagerly toward the counter, Master Grubble's face changed from sallow to crimson, from crimson to purple. Cackling frantically, he waggled his head and flapped his elbows against his ribs.

"Cut-aw-cut!" he bawled. "Cut-cut-aw! Cuck-cuck! Cock-a-doodle-do!"

Once more, Quickset made a great show of listening carefully:

"Did I hear you a-right, Master

Grubble? Give all? Free? What a generous soul you are!"

With that, Quickset began hurling meats, cheese, vegetables, and loaves of sugar into the customers' baskets. Grubble's face now turned from purple to bilious green. He crowed, clucked, brayed, and bleated until he sounded like a barnyard gone mad.

"Give more?" cried Quickset. "I'm doing my best!"

"Cut-aw!" shouted Grubble and away went a chain of sausages. "Ak-ak-cut-aak!" And away went another joint of beef. At last, he could stand no more:

"Stop! Stop!" he roared. "Wretched cat! You'll drive me out of business!"

Beside himself with fury, Master Grubble forgot his cramped quarters and sprang to his feet. His head struck the ceiling and he tumbled back into the basket of eggs. As he struggled to free himself from the flood of shattered yolks, the shelf cracked beneath him and he went plummeting headlong into a barrel of flour.

"Robber!" stormed Grubble, crawling out and shaking a fist at Quickset. "Swindler! You promised I'd hatch gold from eggs!"

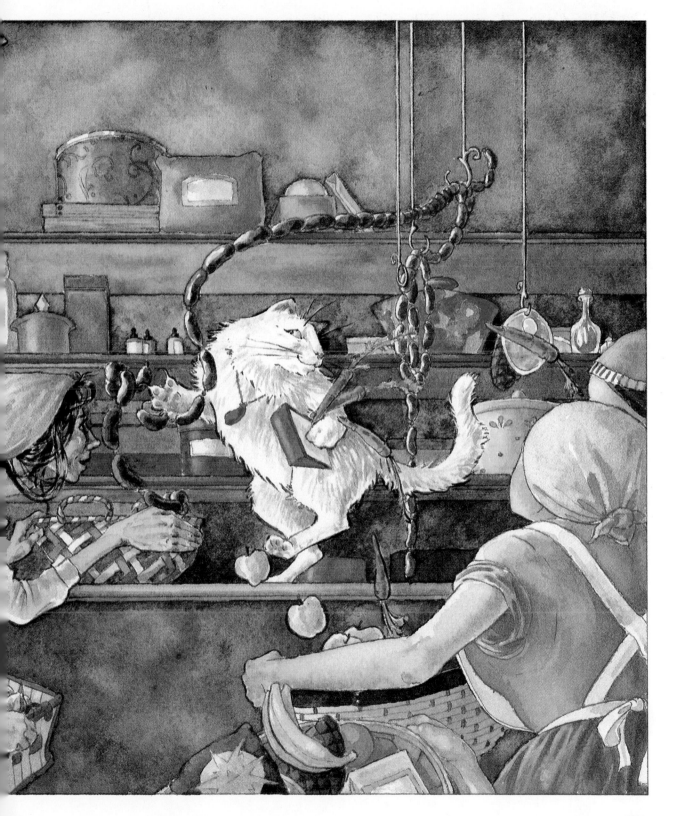

"What's that?" put in the tailor's wife. "Gold from eggs? Master Grubble, you're as foolish as you're greedy."

"But a fine cackler," added the laundrywoman, flapping her arms. "Let's hear it again, your cut-cut-awk!"

"I warned you not to speak a word," Quickset told the storekeeper, who was egg-soaked at one end and floured at the other. "But you did. And so you broke the spell. Why, look at you, Master Grubble. You nearly turned yourself into a dipped pork chop. Have a care. Someone might fry you."

With that, Quickset went home for breakfast.

As for Master Grubble, when word spread that he had been so roundly tricked, and so easily, he became such a laughingstock that he left town and was never seen again. At the urging of the towns-folk, Dame Agnes and Quickset took charge of the market, and ran it well and fairly. All agreed that Quickset was the cleverest cat in the world. And, since Quickset had the same opinion, it was surely true.

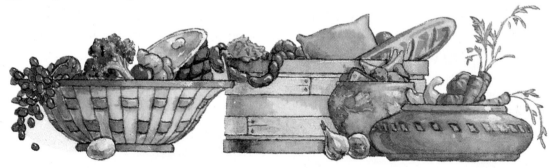

◆ LIBRARY LINK ◆

You don't have to be a cat fancier to enjoy reading more tales of shrewd cats who manage to outsmart humans in The Town Cats and Other Tales, *where this story first appeared.*

Reader's Response

What is your opinion of the trick Quickset played on Master Grubble?

The Cat and the Golden Egg

Thinking It Over

1. Why was Dame Agnes so unhappy?
2. Why did Master Grubble agree to sit on the eggs and cackle like a chicken?
3. Why did Quickset offer to tend store for Master Grubble?
4. If Quickset had been unable to trick Grubble, how might Quickset have assisted Dame Agnes?
5. How would you describe Quickset?
6. Did you feel sorry for Master Grubble? What made you feel the way you did?

Writing to Learn

THINK AND DESCRIBE   Does "The Cat and the Golden Egg" have any similarities to other fairy tales or fables you have read? Copy the chart onto your paper and describe the parts of "The Cat and the Golden Egg" that go with each story element.

Element	Episode in "The Cat and the Golden Egg"
Conflict	
Generous gesture	
Complication	
Happy resolution	

WRITE   Write a paragraph that describes how the story follows and includes each of the story elements.

Michael Built a Bicycle

by Jack Prelutsky

Michael built a bicycle
unsuitable for speed,
it's crammed with more accessories
than anyone could need,
there's an AM-FM radio,
a deck to play cassettes,
a refrigerator-freezer,
and a pair of TV sets.

There are shelves for shirts and sweaters,
there are hangers for his jeans,
a drawer for socks and underwear,
a rack for magazines,
there's a fishtank and a birdcage
perched upon the handlebars,
a bookcase, and a telescope
to watch the moon and stars.

There's a telephone, a blender,
and a stove to cook his meals,
there's a sink to do the dishes
somehow fastened to the wheels,
there's a portable piano,
and a set of model trains,
an automatic bumbershoot
that opens when it rains.

There's a desk for typing letters
on his fabulous machine,
a stall for taking showers,
and a broom to keep things clean,
but you'll never see him ride it,
for it isn't quite complete,
Michael left no room for pedals,
and there isn't any seat.

LITERATURE LINK

How can you discover and explore the moral of a story?

Remember how Quickset the cat outsmarted Master Grubble in "The Cat and the Golden Egg"? The grouchy grocer learned that greedy people finally get punished. That could be the lesson, or moral, of the story.

Many stories, particularly folk tales and fables, contain strong lessons that are intended to be applied to life. You may not agree with the lesson of a story, but it is always interesting to explore and discuss it.

Lesson About Life

Sometimes the moral of a story is quite obvious. At other times, you need to explore the story events. Let's consider this Aesop's fable, "The Fox and the Stork."

One day the mischievous fox invited the stork to dinner. When the hungry stork arrived and sat down to eat, he found before him some soup in a flat dish. The stork dipped his long bill into the shallow dish, but came away with little more than a taste of the soup. Meanwhile, the fox lapped up his soup and even had a second helping.

A week later, the stork invited the fox to dinner. The fox, still laughing about the joke, accepted. When the fox arrived, the stork served him a delicious-smelling stew in a long-necked glass, which was so narrow that the fox was unable to get at the food. But the stork just dipped his long bill into the glass and gobbled up the stew. The fox made no complaint, but he was no longer laughing.

This chart shows one way to discover the moral of the fable you just read.

Events	Character Reaction
Fox invites stork to dinner and serves a meal in a shallow dish. Stork cannot eat with his long bill.	Fox laughs because the stork goes hungry.
Stork invites fox to dinner and serves a meal in a tall, narrow glass. Fox cannot eat.	Fox leaves hungry. He does not laugh this time.

The stork, of course, found a solution to the fox's practical joke. The fox did not think it was so funny when the joke was on him. What lesson do you think he learned about playing practical jokes? Is this a lesson that could apply to people in real life?

When you want to discover and explore the moral of a story, try making a chart like the one above. Follow these steps:

- List the story's main events.
- Next to each event, note how characters reacted to it.
- Find the event that is the solution to a problem.
- Notice how a story character reacted to this event.
- Ask yourself: What lesson might the character learn? Do you think this lesson can apply to real life?

Next you will read the folk tale "Brother to the Wind." Try making a chart to explore the story events. What is the moral of this tale? How does this message apply to real life?

Discovering the Moral of a Story 279

Have you ever dreamed of floating through the air, gliding with the wind? Emeke, a shepherd boy from a small village in Africa, has such a dream.

BROTHER
TO
THE
WIND

written by Mildred Pitts Walter
illustrated by Diane and Leo Dillon

"Good Snake can make any wish come true," Emeke's[1] grandmother often said. And every day in the village of Eronni,[2] Emeke herded his family's goats and dreamed of finding Good Snake. He wanted to make a wish to fly.

Emeke rose early to herd the goats high up on the mountain. Dark clouds clung to the earth. Morning was almost like night. The rains would soon come.

"Say, Emeke," Ndumu[3] shouted in the dim light, "still want to fly like a bird?" Other boys on the road laughed.

¹Emeke (ē me′ kē)
²Eronni (er on′ ē)
³Ndumu (dōō′ mōō)

"Our friend thinks he can move like the wind," Mongo[4] said.

"No, he really thinks he will find Good Snake and that Good Snake will help him fly." Nizam's[5] words brought great bursts of laughter.

High up on the mountain, alone with his goats, Emeke looked out at the farms and his village below. Fires blazed and sent up smoke as the men cleared thick brush for new farmland. They worked hard to beat the rains. Their clothes, the colors of the rainbow, flowed with the wind.

Finally Emeke sat watching his goats eat greedily. Then, with his knees drawn to his chest and chin, he closed his eyes. He tried to imagine now what he had often felt in dreams. He wanted to feel the wind, to soar up, up, up, then wheel off like a bird. But his mind filled only with the laughter of his friends.

Then he remembered his grandmother's words: "If you find Good Snake, he will help you fly."

If only I could leave my goats for one day, he thought. I would go searching deep in the bush for Good Snake. But Father would never let me do that.

Maybe he should go into the bush at night when the village was asleep. No boy would go there after dark. Secrets of the bush unfold, and the silence of ghosts grows loud in the dark. No. No boy would do that. "But no boy in my village can fly," Emeke said aloud.

He would find Good Snake and make his wish.

Suddenly he heard a low rumbling noise. What could it be? Not thunder. Thunder came only with the rains. Emeke put his ear closer to the ground and heard the sound of many feet.

Then Emeke saw the strangest thing. A swarm of fireflies moved in a circle in the distance. In their light Emeke saw

[4]Mongo (mon′ gō)
[5]Nizam (nē′ zäm)

animals moving toward a tree, not too far from where his goats were feeding.

Emeke jumped up. He saw Elephant, Rhinoceros, Giraffe, and Zebra. He moved closer and saw smaller animals: Turtle, Hyena, Wild Dog, and Hare. There were many birds too. How peacefully and quietly they all moved together. Emeke's goats were calm, still eating the short grass. They will be safe for a little while, Emeke thought.

Curious, he hurried.

Cautiously he fell in line with the animals.

When they reached the tree he saw an unusual thing. A huge snake was wrapped around the biggest branch. His tail was hidden in the leaves, but his head hung down toward the ground. Emeke's heart beat wildly, his skin went hot, then cold, and his scalp tingled. This is Good Snake, he thought. Emeke wanted to run away, but his feet felt rooted to the spot.

Hyena, Elephant, Rhinoceros, and all the animals, one by one, made wishes. But Turtle stood off to the side, laughing. He did not believe in Good Snake.

As Emeke watched Turtle laughing, he thought of Ndumu, Nizam, and Mongo. Would he dare ask to fly like a bird?

Finally Good Snake nodded at him. Emeke knew it was now his turn. "Oh, Good Snake, I would like to fly."

Good Snake uncurled his tail and brought forth a rock. "Are you sure you want to fly?"

"Oh, yes, Good Snake," Emeke whispered, hardly able to speak.

Good Snake held out the rock. "This is what you must do: Before the rains come, find the bark of a baobab[6] tree and three large bamboo poles. Then make a kite exactly like the one on the back of this rock."

[6]baobab (bā′ ə bab)

Emeke took the rock and placed it in his pouch. But what did a rock and kite have to do with flying, Emeke wondered. He wanted to say, Why make a kite? All I want to do is fly like a bird. Instead he listened as Good Snake went on: "Before the feast of the harvest, you must find the right wind for the kite."

"Good Snake, how will I know the right wind?" Emeke asked.

Good Snake curled up his tail again and looked at Emeke. "The right wind will whisper words that will let you know for sure. Then, on the day of the feast, meet me high on the mountaintop. If you have done all the things that I have asked, then on that day you will fly. One other thing: Keep that rock with you always. It will help you."

Emeke was so happy and excited he almost forgot to thank Good Snake as he hurried back to his goats.

Good Snake called after him. "Be sure you find the bark and bamboo before the rains come."

Turtle laughed. "He, he, he. Beware! Things without wings don't fly."

The dark heavy clouds threatened to overflow. Emeke hurried toward his goats, wondering how he would find bark and bamboo before it rained. He touched the rock and remembered: *The rock will help you.*

When he reached the place where his goats were feeding, he saw Hyena lurking nearby. Emeke hurriedly gathered his goats together to protect them. His goats did not seem at all alarmed. They kept right on eating greedily.

Hyena moved closer.

Emeke became more frightened, and touched the rock.

"Do not be scared," Hyena shouted. "I have come to herd your goats."

"*You?* Herd my goats?" Emeke asked in disbelief.

"Yes. I wished to have more patience and less greed. Be off to the bush to find your bamboo and bark. I'll care for your goats until you return."

Emeke did not trust Hyena.

He was still afraid.

Hyena sensed Emeke's fear and said, "Do you believe Good Snake can help you fly?"

Emeke realized he did not know whether he could trust

Good Snake. But his grandmother believed in Good Snake. "Yes," he said. "I believe Good Snake can help me fly."

"Then believe that he can make me a goat herder."

Every few feet Emeke turned to look back, thinking his goats would be eaten. But Hyena was moving among the goats as a caring herder should. I must trust Hyena, he thought, and hurried on toward the bush.

The clouds made the bush almost as dark as night. Emeke stumbled along in the unfriendly quiet.

He must find the bark and bamboo before the rains came.

Suddenly he walked into something that felt like a wall. It moved. Emeke's heart beat wildly. Then he knew. It was not a wall at all. It was Elephant. Emeke was frightened; he squeezed the rock for comfort.

"I am here to help you find the baobab tree," Elephant said.

"How do you know I need bark from the baobab tree?"

"I made a wish too. I wished to be kind and helpful. My wish can come true, if I can help you." Elephant led the way into the bush.

Soon Emeke had enough bark for his kite. Emeke thanked Elephant. Now he must hurry to find the bamboo. His father would be furious if he found the goats left in Hyena's care.

At last Emeke found the watering hole where bamboo grew. To his surprise, Rhinoceros was waiting for him with three neatly cut poles.

"I knew you would come," Rhinoceros said. "I made a wish to be gentle and of service. My wish has come true."

It was night when Emeke returned to the pasture. His goats were gone! Emeke's heart skipped beats. He felt weak and his head seemed to swell. He ran here and there, every-where, looking. Then, around a curve, he saw his goats. Hyena had gathered them all together.

The goats pushed and shoved around Emeke. Hyena was glad to see Emeke too. Emeke thanked Hyena and hurried down the mountain.

He had not gone far when he saw his father with men from the village. Emeke's friends were with them.

"Where were you?" his father demanded.

"On the mountain."

"No, you were not!" Ndumu shouted.

"We looked all over for you," Nizam said.

"And what is this burden you are carrying?" His father pointed to the bark and bamboo.

"I want to fly, Father, so—"

An explosion of laughter interrupted Emeke. Emeke looked at his father and knew his father was humiliated. The men laughed because they thought Emeke was a lazy, careless boy who did not take his duties seriously.

"Why do you say foolish things, Emeke?" his father demanded. "Did you ever see humans fly?"

Emeke felt his father was more hurt than angry. He wanted to move closer to his father, but it was as though the laughter had turned him to stone.

Finally, with tears in his voice and with great respect, Emeke tried to explain again.

"Father, I did not leave the goats alone. Hyena cared for them. . . ."

There was another explosion of laughter. Over the laughter Emeke's father shouted, "Let me hear no more of this foolishness. Now, I want you to promise that you will never leave the goats unattended again."

Emeke remembered that he still had to find the right wind. He did not want to promise.

"Emeke," his father said, "if you leave the goats again, I will have to punish you. I want your word that you will not."

"I promise," Emeke said sadly.

Later that night, thunder rumbled and lightning lit up the village. Emeke heard the sound of drops like small pebbles pelting the roof. The rains had come. He had found the bark and bamboo just in time.

Rain fell in gray sheets, soaking the earth, filling the streams. Emeke could not herd his goats. While other children sat around the fire roasting maize and groundnuts, Emeke sat alone working on his kite.

With the rock close by, he worked every day. Soon word spread about the huge kite. Emeke's friends called him bird boy, wing-flapper. People in the village said Emeke was a foolish boy. His family was ashamed of him. Only his grandmother believed he might fly one day.

"Why such a heavy kite?" his mother asked.

"You will never fly that one on a string," his father said.

"It will fly me. I will soar in the wind, dive and wheel like a bird without falling," Emeke said proudly.

His grandmother beamed, but his father said, "Put the kite away. Forget this flying foolishness."

Finally the rain fell in drops as thin as needles against the sunlight. White clouds raced away, leaving the sky clean and blue. The sun shone bright and the wind blew cold. Emeke herded his goats at the foot of the mountain and wondered where he would ever find the right wind.

Days grew warmer. After many days and nights, the growing season ended and it was time for the harvest to begin.

The night before the harvest festival, the moon rose like a giant orange ball. The night slowly turned almost as bright as day.

Emeke lay listening to the wind. "Come out, come out, you don't have to break your promise," the wind sighed.

Emeke rushed outside. He hurried to the edge of his

village. The grass grew tall, and the wind sang like the sound of the sea. The grass bowed left and right, moving like women's skirts in the dance. Emeke stood still, listening.

Then softly as the flutter of a bird's wing came a whisper: "My brother." Emeke trembled with the excitement that comes with dancing. Be still and listen, he told himself. Again the whisper: "My brother." That is the right wind! He felt light with happiness.

The rest of the night, Emeke slept without dreaming.

The morning of the festival came with the sound of many drums. The air was heavy with excitement. Today I will fly, Emeke thought when he awoke.

Emeke walked with his family to the center of the village. His friends gathered around him, excited about the games and races to be held at the festival.

"I will fly today," Emeke said matter-of-factly. "Look up and you will see me."

"Then look down," Ndumu said. "Oooh, no more Emeke! He is splattered like a bird's egg." Ndumu fell to the ground, arms and legs spread. All the boys bent with laughter.

"I will fly. You will see," Emeke said.

When the center of the village was overrun with people, Emeke slipped away with his kite and rock. He hurried up the mountain to meet Good Snake.

As he came near the top of the mountain, he heard a plodding sound. He looked around and saw Turtle struggling to join him.

"Hey," Turtle shouted. "Beware! Boys were not made to fly."

"With the help of Good Snake, I can, and I will."

"What if you drift to the end of the earth or land on your feet in the mouth of Crocodile, or in Lion's lair?"

Emeke became frightened. He had thought only of flying. Then suddenly he heard the wind sighing softly. Emeke's confidence returned. "I am not afraid, Turtle." He hurried to find Good Snake.

High up on the mountain Good Snake was waiting.

"I made the kite and found the wind," Emeke said to Good Snake.

Good Snake turned the kite this way and that to make

sure it was made well, safe for flying. Then he led Emeke to the edge of the mountain. "You will fly from here down into your village."

Emeke heard the drums from the distance. He looked down and saw the cloud of dust from dancing feet. He thought of Ndumu's words and of his friends' laughter. Turtle's words echoed: "Boys are not made to fly." Emeke hurriedly backed away from the edge. He looked at Good Snake and said, "I cannot fly."

"But everything is ready."

"With all those people in the center of the village, where will I land safely?" Emeke cried.

"You must think of nothing but flying. Trust me with the rest. Give me the rock. I leave you with the wind."

Emeke pointed the nose of his kite up slightly. Should he trust Good Snake? Would he really fly? He waited. He listened.

"My brother," the wind sighed.

Emeke felt the easy, steady wind. He forgot his fear. He balanced his kite and started running toward the edge of the mountain.

He kept his mind on running and keeping his kite's nose up.

Suddenly he was in the air. He flowed up, then floated down, gliding with the wind. His body seemed to disappear. There was only wind, sky, and the earth far below. He was flying! Soaring, turning, streaming down, then lightly, easily floating. "I am brother to the wind," he shouted.

He floated to his feet as lightly as a feather. His grandmother was the first to reach him. She hugged him, beaming with love. His mother and father smiled with pride. All of his friends rushed to examine the kite. "He did fly like a bird," Nizam said.

Drummers beat their drums, sending up sounds as great as all the thunder in the world. Dancing feet sent up clouds of dust. Emeke danced to the rhythms with his grandmother.

 ### Reader's Response

Do you think Emeke was brave or foolish when he ignored the warnings of Turtle and the teasing of friends?

BROTHER ᴛᴏ ᴛʜᴇ WIND

Thinking It Over

1. How was Emeke different from the other village boys?
2. What led Emeke to Good Snake?
3. If Hyena had betrayed Emeke and eaten his flock, what would have happened to Emeke's dream?
4. Why was Emeke upset after he explained his wish to his father?
5. How do you think Emeke felt after his flight?
6. What obstacles did Emeke have to overcome to achieve his dream? How did you arrive at your answer?

Writing to Learn

THINK AND CREATE   The author of "Brother to the Wind" created word pictures by using exact color and shape details. Read the word picture from the story in the first frame. Then find a second word picture in the story and copy it on your paper.

Finally the rain fell in drops as thin as needles.

WRITE   Look out the window or think of a scene from nature you remember. Write a word picture of a flower, a bird, a branch, or any natural object you choose. Use color and shape details in your word picture.

A PUFFIN BOOK

Charlie Pippin

Candy Dawson Boyd

NO NUKES

Charlie knows
that dreams
can die...
but she won't
give up hers
without a fight

*W*hat did Mama mean about the Vietnam War changing Daddy's dreams?

from *Charlie Pippin* by Candy Dawson Boyd

In Candy Dawson Boyd's dramatic novel *Charlie Pippin*, a new school year is beginning in Berkeley, California. It will turn out to be an important year for Chartreuse "Charlie" Pippin, a smart and determined sixth grader with many things on her mind. To begin with, Charlie has a secret school business to run, selling pencils and paper animals intricately folded in the Japanese way called origami. Then the bright businesswoman must deal with the troublesome consequences when the principal and her furious father find out. In fact, her father presents the biggest puzzle: Why is he often so rigid and angry? Charlie's mother tells her that he wasn't always that way, that fighting in the Vietnam War changed him. But what happened in the war and why it changed Charlie's father are subjects no one in the family will discuss.

In her struggle to understand her father, Charlie decides to study the Vietnam War. Despite her father's objections, she volunteers for the war and peace committee that is one of the sixth grade social studies projects. Charlie learns all about the war, but it is a mysterious 15-year-old newspaper clipping and a surprise trip that lead her to the real answers about her father.

Nicodemus and his friends are trapped in a laboratory
where they are being used for experiments. The doors of their
cages are bolted, and there's no way out!

THE
RATS
OF
NIMH

by Robert O'Brien
from *Mrs. Frisby and the
Rats of NIMH*

The one important phase of training began one day after
weeks of really hard work at the "shape recognition" that I mentioned before. But this was different. For the first time they used
sounds along with the shapes, and pictures, real pictures we
could recognize. For example, one of the first and simplest of
these exercises was a picture, a clear photograph, of a rat. I suppose they felt sure we would know what that was. This picture
was shown on a screen, with a light behind it. Then, after I had
looked at the picture and recognized it, a shape flashed on the
screen under it—a sort of half circle and two straight lines, not
like anything I had seen before. Then the voice began:

"Are."

"Are."

"Are."

It was Julie's voice, speaking very clearly, but it had a tinny sound—it was a record. After repeating "are" a dozen times or so, that particular shape disappeared and another one came on the screen, still under the picture of the rat. It was a triangle, with legs on it. And Julie's voice began again:

"Aiee."

"Aiee."

"Aiee."

When that shape disappeared a third one came on the screen. This one was a cross. Julie's voice said:

"Tea."

"Tea."

"Tea."

Then all three shapes appeared at once, and the record said:

"Are."

"Aiee."

"Tea."

"Rat."

You will already have recognized what was going on: they were teaching us to read. The symbols under the picture were the letters R-A-T. But the idea did not become clear to me, nor to any of us, for quite a long time. Because, of course, we didn't know what reading *was*.

Oh, we learned to recognize the shapes easily enough, and when I saw the rat picture I knew straight away what symbols would appear beneath it. In the same way, when the picture showed a cat, I knew the same shapes would appear, except the first one would be a half-circle, and Julie's voice would repeat "See—see—see." I even learned that when the photograph showed not one but several rats, a fourth shape would appear under it—a snaky line—and the sound with that one was "ess—ess—ess." But as to what all this was for, none of us had any inkling.

It was Jenner who finally figured it out. By this time we had developed a sort of system of communication, a simple enough thing, just passing spoken messages from one cage to the next, like passing notes in school. Justin, who was still next to me, called to me one day:

"Message for Nicodemus from Jenner. He says it is important."

"All right," I said, "what's the message?"

"Look at the shapes on the wall next to the door. He says to look carefully."

My cage, like Jenner's and those of the rest of A group, was close enough to the door so I could see what he meant: Near the doorway there was a large, square piece of white cardboard fastened to the wall—a sign. It was covered with an assortment of black markings to which I had never paid any attention (though they had been there ever since we arrived).

Now, for the first time, I looked at them carefully, and I grasped what Jenner had discovered.

The top line of black marks on the wall were instantly familiar: R-A-T-S; as soon as I saw them I thought of the picture that went with them; and as soon as I did that I was, for the first time, reading. Because, of course, that's what reading is: using symbols to suggest a picture or an idea. From that time on it gradually became clear to me what all these lessons were for, and once I understood the idea, I was eager to learn more. I could scarcely wait for the next lesson, and the next. The whole concept of reading was, to me at least, fascinating. I remember how proud I was when, months later, I was able to read and understand that whole sign. I read it hundreds of times, and I'll never forget it:

RATS MAY NOT BE REMOVED FROM THE LABORATORY WITHOUT WRITTEN PERMISSION. And at the bottom, in smaller letters, the word NIMH.

RATS MAY NOT BE REMOVED FROM THE LABORATORY WITHOUT WRITTEN PERMISSION.

NIMH

But then a puzzling thing came up, a thing we're still not sure about even now. Apparently Dr. Schultz, who was running the lessons, did not realize how well they were succeeding. He continued the training, with new words and new pictures every day; but the fact is, once we had grasped the idea and learned the different sounds each letter stood for, we leaped way ahead of him. I remember well, during one of the lessons, looking at a picture of a tree. Under it the letters flashed on: T-R-E-E. But in the photograph, though the tree was in the foreground, there was a building in the background, and a sign near it. I scarcely glanced at T-R-E-E, but concentrated instead on reading the sign. It said:

NIMH. PRIVATE PARKING BY PERMIT ONLY. RESERVED FOR DOCTORS AND STAFF. NO VISITORS PARKING. The building behind it, tall and white, looked very much like the building we were in.

I'm sure Dr. Schultz had plans for testing our reading ability. I could even guess, from the words he was teaching us, what the tests were going to be like. For example, he taught us "left," "right," "door," "food," "open," and so on. It was not hard to imagine the test: I would be placed in one chamber, my food in another. There would be two doors, and a sign saying: "For food, open door at right." Or something like that. Then if I—if all of us—moved unerringly toward the proper door, he would know we understood the sign.

As I said, I'm sure he planned to do this, but apparently he did not think we were ready for it yet. I think maybe he was even a little afraid to try it; because if he did it too soon, or if for any other reason it did not work, his experiment would be a failure. He wanted to be sure, and his caution was his undoing.

Justin announced one evening around the partition: "I'm going to get out of my cage tonight and wander around a bit."

"How can you? It's locked."

"Yes. But did you notice, along the bottom edge there's a printed strip?"

I had not noticed it. I should perhaps explain that when Dr. Schultz and the others opened our cages we could never quite see how they did it; they manipulated something under the plastic floor, something we couldn't see.

"What does it say?"

"I've been trying to read it the last three times they brought me back from training. It's very small print. But I think I've finally made it out. It says: To release door, pull knob forward and slide right."

"Knob?"

"Under the floor, about an inch back, there's a metal thing just in front of the shelf. I think that's the knob, and I think I can reach it through the wire. Anyway, I'm going to try."

"Now?"

"Not until they close up."

"Closing up" was a ritual Dr. Schultz, George, and Julie went through each night. For about an hour they sat at their desks, wrote notes in books, filed papers in cabinets, and finally locked the cabinets. Then they checked all the cages, dimmed the lights, locked the doors, and went home, leaving us alone in the still laboratory.

About half an hour after they left that night, Justin said: "I'm going to try now." I heard a scuffling noise, a click and scrape of metal, and in a matter of seconds I saw his door swing open. It was as simple as that—when you could read.

"Wait," I said.

"What's the matter?"

"If you jump down, you won't be able to get back in. Then they'll know."

"I thought of that. I'm not going to jump down. I'm going to climb up the outside of the cage. It's easy. I've climbed up the inside a thousand times. Above these cages there's another shelf, and it's empty. I'm going to walk along there and see what I can see. I think there's a way to climb to the floor and up again."

"Why don't I go with you?" My door would open the same way as his.

"Better not this time, don't you think? If something goes wrong and I can't get back, they'll say: It's just A-9 again. But if two of us are found outside, they'll take it seriously. They might put new locks on the cages."

He was right, and you can see that already we both had the same idea in mind: that this might be the first step toward escape for all of us.

And so it was.

By teaching us how to read, they had taught us how to get away.

Justin climbed easily up the open door of his cage and vanished over the top with a flick of his tail. He came back an hour later, greatly excited and full of information. Yet it was typical of Justin that even excited as he was, he stayed calm, he thought clearly. He climbed down the front of my cage rather than his own, and spoke softly; we both assumed that by now the other rats were asleep.

"Nicodemus? Come on out. I'll show you how." He directed me as I reached through the wire bars of the door and felt beneath it. I found the small metal knob, slid it forward and sideward, and felt the door swing loose against my shoulder. I followed him up the side of the cage to the shelf above. There we stopped. It was the first time I had met Justin face to face.

He said: "It's better talking here than around that partition."

"Yes. Did you get down?"

"Yes."

"How did you get back up?"

"At the end of this shelf there's a big cabinet—they keep the mouse cages in it. It has wire mesh doors. You can climb up and down them like a ladder."

"Of course," I said. "I remember now." I had seen that cabinet many times when my cage was carried past it. For some reason—perhaps because they were smaller—mice were kept in cages-within-a-cage.

Justin said: "Nicodemus, I think I've found the way to get out."

"You have! How?"

"At each end of the room there's an opening in the baseboard at the bottom of the wall. Air blows in through one of them and out the other. Each one has a metal grid covering it, and on the grid there's a sign that says: Lift to adjust air flow. I lifted one of them; it hangs on hinges, like a trapdoor. Behind it there is a thing like a metal window—when you slide it wide open, more air blows in.

"But the main thing is, it's easily big enough to walk through and get out."

"But what's on the other side? Where does it lead?"

"On the other side there's a duct, a thing like a square metal pipe built right into the wall. I walked along it, not very far, but

I can figure out where it must go. There's bound to be a duct like it leading to every room in the building, and they must all branch off one main central pipe—and that one has to lead, somewhere, to the outside. Because that's where our air comes from. That's why they never open the windows. I don't think those windows *can* open."

He was right, of course. The building had central air conditioning; what we had to do was find the main air shaft and explore it. There would have to be an intake at one end and an outlet at the other. But that was easier said than done, and before it was done there were questions to be answered. What about the rest of the rats? There were twenty of us in the laboratory, and we had to let the others know.

So, one by one, we woke them and showed them how to open their cages. It was an odd assembly that gathered that night, under the dimmed lights in the echoing laboratory, on the shelf where Justin and I had talked. We all knew each other in a way, from the passing of messages over the preceding months; yet except for Jenner and me, none of us had ever really met. We were strangers—though, as you can imagine, it did not take long for us to develop a feeling of comradeship, for we twenty were alone in a strange world. Just how alone and how strange none of us really understood at first; yet in a way we sensed it from the beginning. The group looked to me as leader, probably because it was Justin and I who first set them free, and because Justin was obviously younger than I.

We did not attempt to leave that night, but went together and looked at the metal grid Justin had discovered, and made plans for exploring the air ducts. Jenner was astute at that sort of thing; he could foresee problems.

"With a vent like this leading to every room," he said, "it will be easy to get lost. When we explore, we're going to need some way of finding our way back here."

"Why should we come back?" someone asked.

"Because it may take more than one night to find the way out. If it does, whoever is doing the exploring must be back in his cage by morning. Otherwise Dr. Schultz will find out."

Jenner was right. It took us about a week. What we did, after some more discussion, was to find some equipment: first, a large spool of thread in one of the cabinets where some of us had seen Julie place it one day. Second, a screwdriver that was kept on a shelf near the electric equipment—because, as Jenner pointed out, there would probably be a screen over the end of the air-shaft to keep out debris, and we might have to pry it loose. What we really needed was a light, for the ducts, at night, were completely dark. But there was none to be had, not even a box of matches. The thread and the screwdriver we hid in the duct, a few feet from the entrance. We could only hope they would not be missed, or that if they were, we wouldn't be suspected.

Justin and two others were chosen as the exploration party. They had a terrible time at first: Here was a maze to end all mazes; and in the dark they quickly lost their sense of direction. Still they kept at it, night after night, exploring the network of shafts that laced like a cubical spiderweb through the walls and ceilings of the building. They would tie the end of their thread to the grid in our laboratory and unroll it from the spool as they went. Time and time again they reached the end of the thread and had to come back.

"It just isn't long enough," Justin would complain. "Every

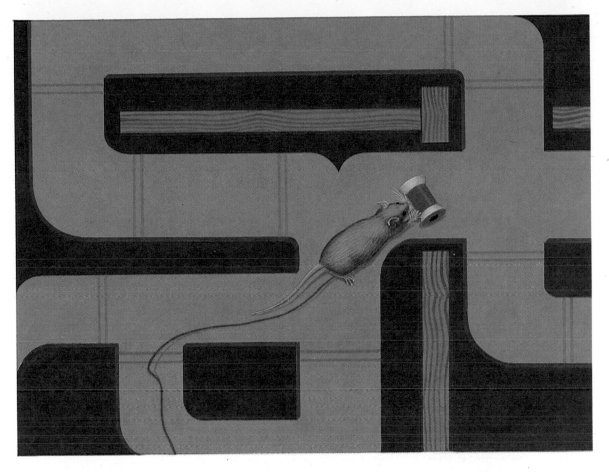

time I come to the end, I think: if I could just go ten feet farther. . . ."

And finally, that's what he did. On the seventh night, just as the thread ran out, he and the other two reached a shaft that was wider than any they had found before, and it seemed, as they walked along it, to be slanting gently upward. But the spool was empty.

"You wait here," Justin said to the others. "I'm going just a little way farther. Hang on to the spool, and if I call, call back." (They had tied the end of the thread around the spool so they would not lose it in the dark.)

Justin had a hunch. The air coming through the shaft had a fresher smell where they were, and seemed to be blowing harder

than in the other shafts. Up ahead he thought he could hear the whir of a machine running quietly, and there was a faint vibration in the metal under his feet. He went on. The shaft turned upward at a sharp angle—and then, straight ahead, he saw it: a patch of lighter-colored darkness than the pitch black around him, and in the middle of it, three stars twinkling. It was the open sky. Across the opening there was, as Jenner had predicted, a coarse screen of heavy wire.

He ran toward it for a few seconds longer, and then stopped. The sound of the machine had grown suddenly louder, changing from a whir to a roar. It had, obviously, shifted speed; an automatic switch somewhere in the building had turned it from low to high, and the air blowing past Justin came on so hard it made him gasp. He braced his feet against the metal and held on. In a minute, as suddenly as it had roared, the machine returned to a whisper. He looked around and realized he was lucky to have stopped; by the dim light from the sky he could see that he had reached a point where perhaps two dozen air shafts came together like branches into the trunk of a tree. If he had gone a few steps farther he would never have been able to distinguish which shaft was his. He turned in his tracks, and in a few minutes he rejoined his friends.

We had a meeting that night, and Justin told all of us what he had found. He had left the thread, anchored by the screwdriver, to guide us out. Some were for leaving immediately, but it was late, and Jenner and I argued against it. We did not know how long it would take us to break through the screen at the end. If it should take more than an hour or two, daylight would be upon us. We would then be unable to risk returning to the laboratory, and would have to spend the day in the shaft—or try to get away by broad daylight. Dr. Schultz might even figure out how we had gone and trap us in the air shaft.

Finally, reluctantly, everyone agreed to spend one more day in the laboratory and leave early the next night. But it was a hard decision, with freedom so near and everyone thinking as I did: "Suppose. . . ." Suppose Dr. Schultz grew suspicious and put locks on our cages? Suppose someone found our thread and pulled it out? (This was unlikely—the near end, tied to the spool, was six feet up the shaft, well hidden.) Just the same, we were uneasy.

Then, just as we were ending our meeting, a new complication arose. We had been standing in a rough circle on the floor of the laboratory, just outside the two screen doors that enclosed the mice cages. Now, from inside the cabinet, came a voice:

"Nicodemus." It was a clear but plaintive call, the voice of a mouse. We had almost forgotten the mice were there, and I was startled to hear that one of them knew my name. We all grew quiet.

"Who's calling me?" I asked.

"My name is Jonathan," said the voice. "We have been listening to your talk about going out. We would like to go, too, but we cannot open our cages."

As you can imagine, this caused a certain consternation, coming at the last minute. None of us knew much about the mice, except what we had heard Dr. Schultz dictate into his tape recorder. From that, we had learned only that they had been getting the same injections we were getting, and that the treatment had worked about as well on them as on us. They were a sort of side experiment, without a control group.

Justin was studying the cabinet.

"Why not?" he said. "If we can get the doors open."

Someone muttered: "They'll slow us down."

"No," said the mouse Jonathan. "We will not. Only open our cages when you go, and we will make our own way. We won't even stay with you if you prefer."

"How many are you?" I asked.

"Only eight. And the cabinet doors are easy to open. There's just a simple hook, halfway up."

But Justin and Arthur had already figured that out. They climbed up the screen, unhooked the hook, and the doors swung open.

"The cages open the same way as yours," said another mouse, "but we can't reach far enough to unlatch them."

"All right," I said. "Tomorrow night, as soon as Dr. Schultz and the others leave, we'll open your cages, and you can follow the thread with us to get out. After that you're on your own."

"Agreed," said Jonathan, "and thank you."

"And now," I said, "we should all get back to the cages. Justin, please hook the doors again."

The next day was terrible. I kept expecting to hear Dr. Schultz say: "Who took my screwdriver?" And then to hear Julie add: "My thread is missing, too." That could have happened and set them to thinking—but it didn't, and that night, an hour after Julie, George, and Dr. Schultz left the laboratory, we were out of our cages and gathered, the whole group of us, before the mouse cabinet. Justin opened its doors, unlatched their cages, and the mice came out. They looked very small and frightened, but one strode bravely forward.

"You are Nicodemus?" he said to me. "I'm Jonathan. Thank you for taking us out with you."

"We're not out yet," I said, "but you're welcome."

We had no time for chatting. The light coming in the windows was turning gray; in less than an hour it would be dark, and we would need light to figure out how to open the screen at the end of the shaft.

We went to the opening in the baseboard.

"Justin," I said, "take the lead. Roll up the thread as you go. I'll bring up the rear. No noise. There's sure to be somebody awake somewhere in the building. We don't want them to hear us." I did not want to leave the thread where it might be found: the more I thought about it, the more I felt sure Dr. Schultz would try to track us down, for quite a few reasons.

Justin lifted the grid, pushed open the sliding panel, and one by one we went through. As I watched the others go ahead of me, I noticed for the first time that one of the mice was white. Then I went in myself, closing the grid behind me and pushing the panel half shut again, its normal position.

With Justin leading the way, we moved through the dark passage quickly and easily. In only fifteen or twenty minutes we had reached the end of the thread; then, as Justin had told us it would, the shaft widened; we could hear the whir of the machine ahead, and almost immediately we saw a square of gray daylight. We had reached the end of the shaft, and there a terrible thing happened.

Justin—you will recall—had told us that the machine, the pump that pulled air through the shaft, had switched from low speed to high when he had first explored through there. So we were forewarned. The trouble was, the forewarning was no use at all, not so far as the mice were concerned.

We were approaching the lighted square of the opening when the roar began. The blast of air came like a sudden whistling gale; it took my breath and flattened my ears against my head, and I closed my eyes instinctively. I was still in the rear, and when I opened my eyes again I saw one of the mice sliding past me, clawing uselessly with his small nails at the smooth metal beneath him. Another followed him, and still another, as one by one they were blown backward into the dark maze of tunnels we had just left. I braced myself in the corner of the shaft and grabbed at one as he slid by. It was the white mouse. I caught him by one leg, pulled him around behind me and held on. Another blew face-on into the rat ahead of me and stopped there—it was Jonathan, who had been near the lead. But the rest were lost, six in all. They were simply too light; they blew away like dead leaves, and we never saw them again.

In another minute the roar stopped, the rush of air slowed from a gale to a breeze, and we were able to go forward again.

I said to the white mouse: "You'd better hold on to me. That might happen again."

He looked at me in dismay. "But what about the others? Six are lost! I've got to go back and look for them."

Jonathan quickly joined him: "I'll go with you."

"No," I said. "That would be useless and foolish. You have
no idea which shaft they were blown into, nor even if they all went
the same way. And if you should find them—how would you find
your way out again? And suppose the wind comes again? Then
there would be eight lost instead of six."

The wind did come again, half a dozen times more, while we
worked with the screwdriver to pry open the screen. Each time
we had to stop work and hang on. The two mice clung to the
screen itself; some of us braced ourselves behind them, in case
they should slip. And Justin, taking the thread with him as a
guide-line, went back to search for the other six. He explored
shaft after shaft to the end of the spool, calling softly as he went—
but it was futile. To this day we don't know what became of those

six mice. They may have found their way out eventually, or they may have died in there. We left an opening in the screen for them, just in case.

The screen. It was heavy wire, with holes about the size of an acorn, and it was set in a steel frame. We pried and hammered at it with the screwdriver, but we could not move it. It was fastened on the outside—we couldn't see how. Finally the white mouse had an idea.

"Push the screwdriver through the wire near the bottom," he said, "and pry up." We did, and the wire bent a fraction of an inch. We did it again, prying down, then left, then right. The hole in the wire grew slowly bigger, until the white mouse said: "I think that's enough." He climbed to the small opening and by squirming and twisting, he got through. Jonathan followed him; they both fell out of sight, but in a minute Jonathan's head came back in view on the outside.

"It's a sliding bolt," he said. "We're working on it."

Inside we could hear the faint rasping as the two mice tugged on the bolt handle, working it back. Then the crack at the base of the screen widened; we pushed it open, and we were standing on the roof of NIMH, free.

◆ LIBRARY LINK ◆

You can find out what happens to Nicodemus and his friends by reading the book Mrs. Frisby and the Rats of NIMH *by Robert O'Brien.*

Reader's Response

Would you recommend this story to a friend? Why or why not?

Writing a Research Proposal

In this unit you met characters who were capable of solving problems. Larry found the jewel thief who had disappeared. Sherlock Holmes solved the mystery of the Red-headed League, and Emeke learned how to fly. Now you will explore ways to solve a problem by writing a research proposal.

A research proposal is a written request to a company or agency, asking them to investigate a new idea. The proposal first identifies and describes the problem that the idea is supposed to solve. It then explains the idea in detail and tells how it will solve the problem. Next it suggests what kind of research will be needed to prove the idea works. For example, if the idea is a new product, models of the product will have to be made out of various materials and then tested. Special personnel, such as chemists, may be required. Finally, the proposal states how much time and money should be allotted.

Prewriting

Emeke wanted to fly; his problem was that he didn't know how. The solution to the problem was the invention of the hang glider that Emeke used to float down the mountain.

Often solving a problem means creating something new. For example, people frequently lock their keys in their cars. An invention that would solve this problem is a car door lock that opens only at the owner's touch.

Think of a problem that is interesting to you. Then think of an invention that would solve the problem. Plan how you would describe the invention. The diagram on the next page may help you plan.

Problem	Invention
People lock their keys in their cars.	A car door lock that doesn't require a key.
How It Will Work It will be a sensory device that reacts only to the owner's finger-print.	**Appearance** It will be a disk slightly larger than a quarter with a thin band of silver around the edge and plastic sensory material in the middle.

Writing

Write a three-paragraph research proposal to a manufacturing firm, asking them to consider your invention. First, explain the problem. Second, describe your invention and tell how it could solve the problem. Be sure to explain how the invention would work. Finally, describe the research that will be needed, and ask the company to conduct it.

Revising

Examine your proposal for details. Did you describe the problem you are trying to solve as clearly as possible? Add descriptive words to give a precise picture of your invention.

Proofreading

Look carefully at any technical words to make sure they are spelled correctly.

Publishing

Make a class catalogue entitled *Problems and Puzzles: Solutions*. Add sketches, measurements, and prices of your inventions.

Making a Jigsaw Puzzle

You met many different kinds of characters in this unit. A character is a little bit like a jigsaw puzzle; he or she has different personality traits that fit together to make a whole person. Which unit character is described by the puzzle parts shown below? If you guessed Sherlock Holmes, you are right!

Your group will now make a jigsaw puzzle in which the different pieces

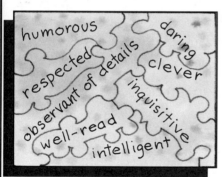

describe different parts of a story character's personality. As you work, take responsibility for one or more of these tasks:

♦ Contributing ideas

♦ Recording the group's ideas

♦ Encouraging others' ideas

♦ Helping others follow directions

Begin by collecting the materials you will need for this project. As a group, decide on one character in this unit you think is particularly interesting. Suggest words that describe the character, and together choose eight words for your puzzle.

Before you make your puzzle, write the character's name in big letters on the back of a stiff piece of paper. Turn the paper over and draw the outline of an eight-piece puzzle. Take turns cutting out the puzzle pieces. Then divide the pieces among your group. Each of you should write one of the eight descriptive words on your puzzle piece.

When everyone has finished, take turns fitting your pieces back together to make your jigsaw puzzle. Flip the puzzle over. If you put the puzzle back together correctly, you will see the character's name.

Dragonsong by Anne McCaffrey *(Macmillan, 1976)* Menolly has a talent for music, but her family won't allow her to study. Then one day she finds some strange and beautiful creatures that change her life forever.

The Treasure of Alpheus Winterborn by John Bellairs *(Bantam, 1985)* Is there really a treasure hidden in the Hoosac Public Library? Anthony is intent on finding out, even when the clues lead to eerie experiences.

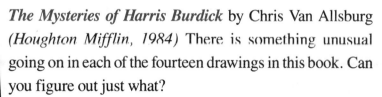

The Mysteries of Harris Burdick by Chris Van Allsburg *(Houghton Mifflin, 1984)* There is something unusual going on in each of the fourteen drawings in this book. Can you figure out just what?

Philip Hall Likes Me. I Reckon Maybe. by Bette Greene *(Dial Press, 1974)* A year in the life of Beth Lambert carries plenty of excitement and triumph. Her only problems come from liking that Philip Hall....

My Side of the Mountain by Jean C. George *(Dutton, 1967)* Sam Gribley's diary records the story of the year he spent in the Catskill Mountains. Sam learns to find not only food and shelter, but companionship as well.

CHALLENGE OF THE SEA

For centuries people have told stories of the sea.

What is the special power of the sea that draws us to these tales?

STARTING OUT AFTER RAIL,
oil on canvas by Thomas Eakins, American, 1874

When Mafatu, a Polynesian boy, is stranded on an island, his life depends upon his ability to conquer what he fears most—the sea.

MAFATU
AND THE MA'O

by Armstrong Sperry
from *Call It Courage*

Mafatu, son of the great Polynesian chief of Hikueru, was scorned by his people because of his fear of the sea. To earn his proper place among them, he set out in his canoe, alone except for his dog, Uri, and his pet albatross—determined to conquer his fear or to be conquered. When a storm wrecked his canoe and tossed him onto a deserted island, Mafatu first had to find food and shelter. Then he had to build a canoe to take him home.

Mafatu[1] set about building his canoe. He had banked his fire the night before in the natural shelter of a cave and he resolved never to let the sparks die out. For it was altogether too difficult to make fire with the firestick, and it required too much time. In Hikueru,[2] for that reason, the fires were always kept burning, and it was the special charge of the younger members of a family to see that fuel was ever at hand. Woe unto the small boy who let the family fires go out!

While his breakfast roasted in the coals, the boy cleared the brush away from the base of the great tamanu. There was no wood better for canoe building than this. It was tough, durable, yet buoyant in the water. Mafatu could fell his tree by fire, and burn it out, too. Later he would grind an adze out of basalt for the finished work. The adze would take a long time, but he had made them often in Hikueru and he knew just how to go about it. The boy was beginning to realize that the hours he had spent fashioning utensils were to stand him now in good stead. Nets and knives and sharkline, implements and shell fishhooks—he knew how to make them all. How he had hated those tasks in

[1]Mafatu (mä fä′ tōō)   [2]Hikueru (hē kwer′ ōō)

Hikueru! He was quick and clever with his hands, and now he was grateful for the skill which was his.

The fire crackled and snapped about the base of the tamanu tree. When at length it had eaten well into the trunk, Mafatu climbed aloft and crept cautiously out upon a large branch that overhung the beach. Then taking firm hold of the branches above his head, he began to jump up and down. As the fire ate deeper into the trunk, the tree began to lean under the boy's weight. With a snap and a crash it fell across the sand. As it fell, Mafatu leaped free of the branches, as nimbly as a cat.

"That's enough for today, Uri," he decided. "Tomorrow we'll build our fires down the trunk and start burning it out."

In the meantime there were many other things to do: a fish trap of bamboo, a net of sennit,[3] a fishhook, too, if only he could find some bone. And while the canoe was building, how could Mafatu get out to the distant reef to set his trap, unless first he made a raft of bamboo?

The boy decided that the raft was of first importance. He chose a score or more of fine bamboos as large around as his arm, felling them by fire; then he lashed them together with strips of *purau*[4] bark, making a sturdy raft of two thicknesses. It would serve him well until his canoe should be finished.

As he worked, his mind returned again and again to the wild pig he was determined to kill. How could he go back to Hikueru without a boar's-tooth necklace? Why, that necklace was almost as important as a canoe! For by that token men would know his strength and courage. When the day came that he should leave this high island, he would sail to the north and east. Somewhere in that quarter lay the Cloud of Islands; the great Tuamotu[5] Archipelago which extends across a thousand

[3]sennit (sen' it): a plant fiber
[4]purau (po͞o' rä o͞o): a tropical tree
[5]Tuamotu (to͞o u mō' to͞o): a group of islands in Polynesia

324

miles of ocean and ten degrees of latitude. Within those reef-spiked channels floated Hikueru, his homeland. . . . There was no doubt in his mind that he would find it; for Maui,[6] who had led him safe to this shore, would someday guide him home again. But first, Mafatu knew, he must prove himself worthy. Men should never again call him Mafatu, the Boy Who Was Afraid. And Tavana Nui[7] should say with pride: "Here is my son, come home from the sea."

Kivi, the albatross, came and went on his mysterious errands, emerging out of blue space, vanishing into it again. At sundown, regularly, the white bird came wheeling and circling, to alight clumsily on the beach almost at Mafatu's side, while Uri pranced about and greeted his friend after his own fashion. As for Uri, he was having the time of his life; for there were countless sea birds nesting along the shore to be chased and put to rout; and wild goats and pigs in the mountains to make life exciting enough for any dog.

Mafatu had discovered a mulberry tree. He stripped off the bark and removed the inner white lining. Then he wet the fiber and laid it upon a flat stone and set about beating it with a stick of wood. The fiber spread and grew thinner under the per-

[6]Maui (mä' $\overline{oo}$ ē)   [7]Tavana Nui (tu vä' nu n$\overline{oo}$' ē)

sistent beating. The boy added another strip, wet it, and beat it into the first one; then another and another. Soon he had a yard of "cloth" to serve as a *pareu*.[8] It was soft and white, and now at last he was clothed.

"Before I go home I will make a dye of *ava*[9] and paint a fine design on my *pareu*," the boy promised himself. "I must not go back ill-clothed and empty-handed. Men must know that I have conquered the sea, and made the land serve me as well."

The days passed in a multitude of tasks that kept Mafatu busy from dawn till dark. His lean-to grew into a three-sided house with bamboo walls and a thatch of palm leaves. The fourth wall was open to the breezes of the lagoon. It was a trim little house and he was proud of it. A roll of woven mats lay on the floor; there was a shelf in the wall with three bowls cut from coconut shells; bone fishhooks dangled from a peg; there was a coil of tough sennit, many feet long; an extra *pareu* of tapa waterproofed with gum of the *artu*[10] tree, for wet weather. All day long the wind played through the openings in the bamboo walls and at night lizards scurried through the thatch with soft rustlings.

[8]pareu (pa' ra $\overline{oo}$): loin cloth   [9]ava (ä' vä)   [10]artu (är' t$\overline{oo}$)

One morning, wandering far down the beach, Mafatu came upon a sheltered cove. His heart gave a leap of joy; for there, white-gleaming in the sun, was all that remained of the skeleton of a whale. It might not have meant very much to you or to me; but to Mafatu it meant knives and fishhooks galore, splintered bone for darts and spears, a shoulder blade for an ax. It was a veritable treasure trove. The boy leaped up and down in his excitement. "Uri!" he shouted. "We're rich! Come—help me drag these bones home!"

His hands seemed all thumbs in his eagerness; he tied as many bones as he could manage into two bundles. One bundle he shouldered himself. The other Uri dragged behind him. And thus they returned to the camp site, weary, but filled with elation. Even the dog seemed to have some understanding of what this discovery meant; or if not, he was at least infected with his master's high spirits. He leaped about like a sportive puppy, yapping until he was hoarse.

Now began the long process of grinding the knife and the ax. Hour after long hour, squatting before a slab of basalt, Mafatu worked and worked, until his hands were raw and blistered and the sweat ran down into his eyes. The knife emerged first, since that was the most imperative. Its blade was ten inches long, its handle a knob of joint. It was sharp enough to cut the fronds of coconut trees, to slice off the end of a green nut. *Ai*,[11] but it was a splendid knife! All Mafatu's skill went into it. It would be a fine weapon as well, the boy thought grimly, as he ground it down to a sharp point. Some sea robber had been breaking into his bamboo trap and he was going to find out who the culprit was! Probably that old hammerhead shark who was always cruising around. . . . Just as if he owned the lagoon!

Fishing with a line took too long when you were working against time. Mafatu could not afford to have his trap robbed.

[11]ai (ä′ ē)

Twice it had been broken into, the stout bamboos crushed and the contents eaten. It was the work either of a shark or of an octopus. That was certain. No other fish was strong enough to snap the tough bamboo.

Mafatu's mouth was set in a grim line as he worked away on his knife. That old hammerhead—undoubtedly *he* was the thief! Mafatu had come to recognize him; for every day when the boy went out with his trap, that shark, larger than all the others, was circling around, wary and watchful. The other sharks seemed to treat the hammerhead with deference.

Hunger alone drove Mafatu out to the reef to set his trap. He knew that if he was to maintain strength to accomplish all that lay ahead he must have fish to add to his diet of fruit. But

often as he set his trap far out by the barrier-reef, the hammer-head would approach, roll over slightly in passing, and the cold gleam of its eye filled Mafatu with dread and anger.

"Wait, you!" the boy threatened darkly, shaking his fist at the *ma'o*.[12] "Wait until I have my knife! You will not be so brave then, Ma'o. You will run away when you see it flash."

But the morning that the knife was finished, Mafatu did not feel so brave as he would have liked. He hoped he would never see the hammerhead again. Paddling out to the distant reef, he glanced down from time to time at the long-bladed knife where it hung about his neck by a cord of sennit. It wasn't, after all, such a formidable weapon. It was only a knife made by a boy from a whale's rib.

Uri sat on the edge of the raft, sniffing at the wind. Mafatu always took his dog along, for Uri howled unmercifully if he were left behind. And Mafatu had come to rely upon the companionship of the little yellow dog. The boy talked with the animal as if he were another person, consulting with him, arguing, playing when there was time for play. They were very close, these two.

This morning as they approached the spot where the fish trap was anchored, Mafatu saw the polished dorsal of the hated hammerhead circling slowly in the water. It was like a triangle of black basalt, making a little furrow in the water as it passed.

"*Aiá*, Ma'o!" the boy shouted roughly, trying to bolster up his courage. "I have my knife today, see! Coward who robs traps—catch your own fish!"

The hammerhead approached the raft in leisurely fashion; it rolled over slightly, and its gaping jaws seemed to curve in a yawning grin. Uri ran to the edge of the raft, barking furiously; the hair on the dog's neck stood up in a bristling ridge. The shark, unconcerned, moved away. Then with a whip of its powerful tail it rushed at the bamboo fish trap and seized it in its

---

[12]ma'o (mä' ō)

jaws. Mafatu was struck dumb. The hammerhead shook the trap as a terrier might shake a rat. The boy watched, fascinated, unable to make a move. He saw the muscles work in the fish's neck as the great tail thrashed the water to fury. The trap splintered into bits, while the fish within escaped only to vanish into the shark's mouth. Mafatu was filled with impotent rage. The hours he had spent making that trap—But all he could do was shout threats at his enemy.

Uri was running from one side of the raft to the other, furious with excitement. A large wave sheeted across the reef. At that second the dog's shift in weight tipped the raft at a perilous angle. With a helpless yelp, Uri slid off into the water. Mafatu sprang to catch him but he was too late.

Instantly the hammerhead whipped about. The wave slewed the raft away. Uri, swimming frantically, tried to regain it. There was desperation in the brown eyes—the puzzled eyes so faithful and true. Mafatu strained forward. His dog. His companion. . . . The hammerhead was moving in slowly. A mighty rage stormed through the boy. He gripped his knife. Then he was over the side in a clean-curving dive.

Mafatu came up under his enemy. The shark spun about. Its rough hide scraped the flesh from the boy's shoulder. In that instant Mafatu stabbed. Deep, deep into the white belly. There was a terrific impact. Water lashed to foam. Stunned, gasping, the boy fought for life and air.

It seemed that he would never reach the surface. *Aué,*[13] his lungs would burst! . . . At last his head broke water. Putting his face to the surface, he saw the great shark turn over, fathoms deep. Blood flowed from the wound in its belly. Instantly gray shapes rushed in—other sharks, tearing the wounded hammerhead to pieces.

[13] aué (ä o͞o wā′)

331

Uri—where was he? Mafatu saw his dog then. Uri was trying to pull himself up on the raft. Mafatu seized him by the scruff and dragged him up to safety. Then he caught his dog to him and hugged him close, talking to him foolishly. Uri yelped for joy and licked his master's cheek.

It wasn't until Mafatu reached shore that he realized what he had done. He had killed the *ma'o* with his own hand, with naught but a bone knife. He could never have done it for himself. Fear would have robbed his arm of all strength. He had done it for Uri, his dog. And he felt suddenly humble, with gratitude.

◆ LIBRARY LINK ◆

Would you like to know if Mafatu and Uri reach home safely? You can find out by reading Armstrong Sperry's book Call It Courage. *The book is a Newbery Award winner.*

Reader's Response

Of all the things Mafatu did, which do you think took the most courage?

332

MAFATU
AND THE MA'O

Thinking It Over

1. What things did Mafatu have to do to survive on the island? How would you decide which was most important?
2. What did Mafatu hope to prove by his actions on the island?
3. Why was Mafatu so excited when he found the skeleton of a whale on the beach?
4. What finally gave Mafatu the courage to attack the shark?
5. Do you think Mafatu will be able to make it home? What about his character tells you this?
6. If Mafatu returns home to his people, do you think he will still be called the Boy Who Was Afraid? Explain your answer.

Writing to Learn

THINK AND EVALUATE What was most important to Mafatu's success? Select three items from the list below.

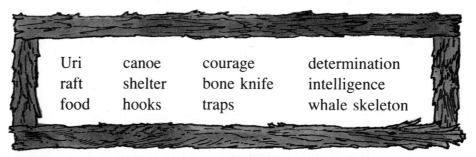

Uri	canoe	courage	determination
raft	shelter	bone knife	intelligence
food	hooks	traps	whale skeleton

WRITE In a brief composition, explain why you chose these three items as Mafatu's most important assets.

Writing Essay Questions

Have you ever had a time when people were talking to you and their words went "in one ear and out the other"? You heard the words but they didn't make sense to you. Sometimes this happens when you read, as well.

One way to understand and remember what you read is to put the ideas in each paragraph into your own words. A fun way to do this is to make up questions based on your reading and then try to answer your own questions. When you do this, you will change the words around and put them together in a way that makes the most sense for you.

The best kind of question to help you learn is an essay question. An essay is longer than just a word or a sentence. An essay question is one that requires at least a one-paragraph answer.

Learning the Strategy

Read the following paragraph about toads and frogs. Then look at the essay question and answer that follow. In real life, of course, most essay questions and answers that you write will be based on much longer selections.

Both toads and frogs begin life in water. Once they are grown, however, toads live on land, while frogs usually stay around water. Most frogs are thinner than toads and have a smoother skin. Toads and frogs both move very fast, but frogs can jump longer distances because they have longer hind legs. Of course, neither frogs nor toads give warts!

Question: How are toads and frogs different?

Answer: Frogs and toads live in different environments: frogs live near water, but toads live on land. Frogs are thinner and smoother than toads. Frogs can also jump farther because their hind legs are longer than the hind legs of toads.

Using the Strategy

Practice making sense of information you read by writing an essay question. On a separate sheet of paper, write an essay question about "Mafatu and the Ma'o" and answer it in a short paragraph. As you write your question and answer, keep in mind that this strategy can work just as well with fiction as it does with nonfiction.

Question:

Answer:

Applying the Strategy to the Next Selection

As you read the next article, "How a Shark Finds Its Food," you will be asked at several key points to think of an essay question that would cover the material you have just read. Then you will answer one of your own questions.

The writing connection can be found on page 421.

The shark has been called "a very efficient eating machine." When you read this article, you will learn why.

HOW A SHARK FINDS ITS FOOD

by Wyatt Blassingame

Hunting its food in the vast open sea, the shark has three senses on which it chiefly relies. These are smell, sight, and the vibration of the water—the shark's "hearing." Of these, the sense of smell is usually thought to be the most important. Although the shark's brain is small for the size of its body—some persons believe the shark's brain does not even record the sense of pain—a very large part of that brain is given to the sense of smell. Some scientists refer to the shark as a "swimming nose."

337

The shark's nostrils are on the underside of its snout, just ahead of the mouth. But they have no connection with the mouth. In fact, they have nothing to do with breathing. They are for smelling only, and they do an excellent job. Each nostril is a kind of cup filled with olfactory cells, the cells that sense odors. As the shark moves, or even when it lies still, water constantly flows in and out of each nostril, constantly bathing the olfactory cells.

Dr. Perry Gilbert has studied sharks for over thirty years. In one experiment he learned that where a strong sea current is flowing, sharks could detect the odor of blood more than a quarter of a mile away. Also a very small bit of tuna—one of the shark's favorite foods—was smelled by sharks seventy-five feet away. At that distance there was about one part of tuna juice to every 1.5 million parts of water! ◆◆◆

◆◆◆
What essay question could you ask to cover the material in this section? How would you answer that question?

"Hearing"

The hunting shark has another sense to rely on that is almost as keen as its sense of smell. This is called the lateralis system. It consists of very fine canals, just beneath the skin, that run along each side of the shark from tail to head, and across the head. These canals are filled with a watery fluid. Scattered along the canals are small pores that open to the surface.

Any noise or motion in water causes a vibration. When that vibration strikes the open pores of the lateralis system, a message is sent to the shark's brain just as if the shark had been touched by some solid object. This helps the shark find its prey at night or in murky water where it cannot see.

Moreover, the shark can tell the vibrations made by a healthy fish that would be hard to capture from those of an injured one. William Beebe, the famous naturalist, proved

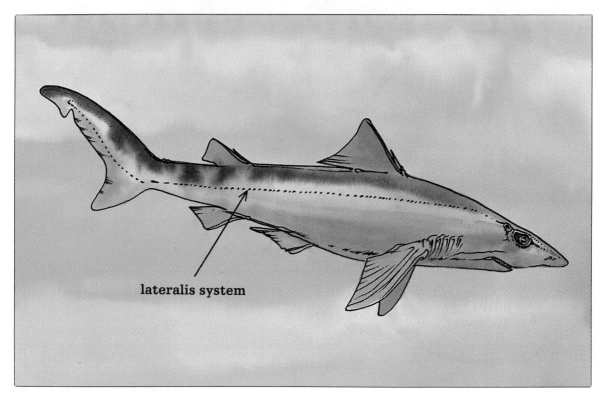

The shark "hears" when its lateralis system detects vibrations in the water.

this in the Galápagos Islands. Looking down through clear water he saw a number of sharks. Small fish swam all around them, unnoticed. Beebe let down a hook and caught one of the small fish. It began to struggle—and instantly the sharks whirled toward it, whether or not they had been looking in that direction. He repeated the experiment over and over, always with the same result.

During World War II, it was learned that whenever a ship was sunk by torpedoes, sharks came from long distances to investigate. But exactly how sensitive the lateralis system is, no one yet knows. This will require some imaginative research by future scientists.

Other fish also have similar systems, but because the shark sometimes attacks human beings, more research has been done on it than on other species. ◄◆►

◄◆►

What essay question could you ask to cover the material in this section? How would you answer that question?

339

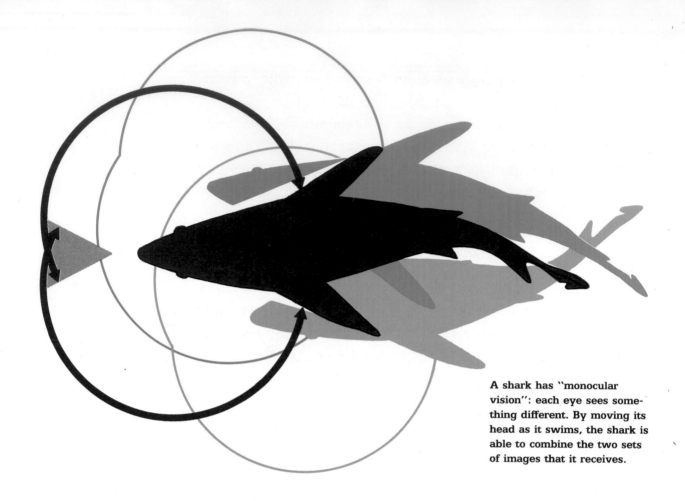

A shark has "monocular vision": each eye sees something different. By moving its head as it swims, the shark is able to combine the two sets of images that it receives.

The Eyes

The shark has another aid in finding its prey—its eyes. For a long while it was believed that the shark's eyesight was very poor. But actually the shark sees better than most people had believed. In fact, it is unusually sensitive to light. Hunting at night or in the depths of the ocean it needs to be. And its eyes have a special aid, one it shares with cats and some other night-prowling animals. This is something called the *tapetum lucidum*. It is a mirrorlike layer in the back of the eye: Light comes through the eye and is reflected back again. In this way the part of the eye sensitive to light is stimulated twice.

Usually, then, the hungry shark will first locate its prey by either smell or by vibrations in the water. As it draws closer, the shark swings its head from side to side, picking up the smell first in one nostril, then the other.

As it draws still closer, its eyes take over. The exact distance is largely determined by the amount of light and the clarity of the water. But certainly sharks use their eyes in the final moments of attack. ◄◆►

◄◆►
What essay question could you ask to cover the material in this section? How would you answer that question?

The Ampullae of Lorenzini

Human beings may use sight and smell, and even vibrations of the air, in hunting. But the sharks have one sense that is foreign to the human body—at least in the everyday meaning. Every living animal gives off a small field of electricity. Dr. Eugenie Clark has found that the shark is more sensitive to this electrical field than any animal yet studied. Many sharks like to feed on their relatives, the stingrays. And stingrays often lie buried in the sand, invisible, motionless. But the cruising shark can sense the electric field of the stingray, nose it out of the sand, and eat it.

The shark does this by means of something called the ampullae of Lorenzini. The ampullae are the swollen parts

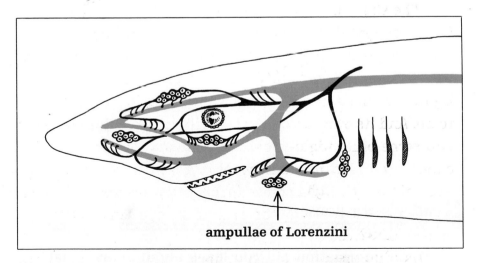

ampullae of Lorenzini

The ampullae of Lorenzini helps the shark find food, serves as a built-in compass, and may even help it determine whether an object is edible.

of canals that lie just under the skin of the shark's head and open to the surface. Lorenzini is the scientist who discovered them. The ampullae of Lorenzini is something very much like the shark's lateralis system, but it is confined to the shark's head. It not only helps the shark find food, but it acts as a kind of built-in compass. With it some species navigate the trackless wastes of the ocean, knowing exactly where they are at all times.

This ampullae of Lorenzini may still have another use. Sharks often rub their heads against objects before biting them, or before turning away without biting. Some naturalists believe that with this bumping the shark uses the ampullae of Lorenzini to taste, or in some other way determine whether or not the object is edible. ◆◆◆

Write one of the essay questions you thought of while reading this article. Then write your answer to that question.

In what other subjects in school would this strategy of writing and answering essay questions be helpful? Why?

◆ LIBRARY LINK ◆

To learn more about sharks, read the rest of Wonders of Sharks *by Wyatt Blassingame.*

Reader's Response

What information did you learn about sharks that surprised you?

HOW A SHARK FINDS ITS FOOD

Thinking It Over

1. Some scientists refer to the shark as a "swimming nose." How do you know what they mean by this?
2. When scientists say a shark "hears," what do they really mean?
3. Why might a shark go after a bleeding fish a quarter of a mile away instead of a healthy fish one foot away?
4. How are a shark's eyes like a cat's eyes?
5. Do you think scientists should continue to study sharks? State your reasons.
6. What good advice could you give ocean swimmers based on what you have learned about sharks?

Writing to Learn

THINK AND ANALYZE How does a shark find food? Copy this picture of a shark. Label the parts of its body that help it to smell, see, and sense the movement of its prey.

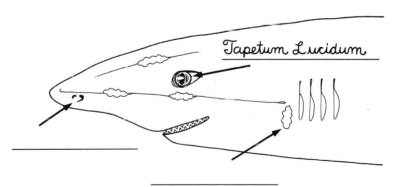

Tapetum Lucidum

WRITE Beneath your drawing, write a paragraph telling why you think people are so fascinated by sharks.

A boat is often all that separates us from the dangers of the sea. When Paloma's boat is damaged, she knows that she will be tested to the fullest.

PALOMA

by Peter Benchley
from *The Girl of the Sea of Cortez*

Paloma had learned a special understanding of the sea and its challenges from Jobim, her father. She was at home in its waters, and spent hours in her boat. But when her brother Jo, jealous of her closeness to the sea and to their father, jabbed a hole in her anchored boat and left her stranded alone, she knew that getting back to shore would require every bit of skill and understanding that she possessed.

Paloma was alone on the sea.

She pulled herself up onto the overturned bottom of the pirogue[1] and examined the hole Jo had dug with his harpoon. It was about the size of her fist, easy enough to patch with wood once ashore, but big enough to keep her from getting to shore.

She tried to think through her choices. She could stay with the overturned boat until she drifted onto land—tonight or tomorrow or the next day, or. . . . It might be many days, and she might succumb to thirst or exposure. And suppose the weather went bad. To try to ride out a *chubasco*[2] by straddling a hollow log was suicidal.

She could abandon the boat and swim for home. Absolutely, positively not. Not worth considering.

Or, she could try to patch the pirogue here and now.

With what? She had no wood, no canvas, no leather, no nails or tacks, no hammer. She could plug the hole with herself: She could sit on it. But then she couldn't paddle, because every time she moved the hole would open and water would rush in. She pictured everything she had brought with

[1]pirogue (pǝ rōg′): a hollowed-out log canoe
[2]chubasco (choo bäs′ kō): a sudden violent windstorm

345

her, analyzing its potential to be shaped into a plug. Her hat? No, the straw fibers were too loosely woven; water would pour through them. Her flippers? She could cut one up and fit the piece of rubber into the hole. But the rubber wouldn't stay; it would float free. The glass faceplate of her mask? She had no way of securing it to the wood.

Her mind evaluated every item and discarded it. And then, as she looked at the wood fibers, she saw beside them other fibers, closely woven though not as thick as the wood, and she had the answer: her dress. She could stuff her dress into the hole, and it would keep the water out. The fabric was already saturated with salt water, so no more could penetrate it. And packed tightly in a ball, the cloth fibers would bind and become nearly waterproof.

She peeled the sodden shift up over her head, then ducked under the pirogue and, from the inside, packed the cloth into the hole. It made a tight plug—nothing that could survive a pounding in a heavy sea, but secure enough for an easy paddle on calm water.

She ducked out again, hauled herself up onto the bottom, and reached over and grabbed the far edge. Bracing herself on one knee, she pulled, and there was a liquid sucking sound and a pop as the suction broke and the pirogue jumped free of the water and righted itself. It was still full of water, though; only an inch of freeboard stuck above the surface. Since the boat was a hollow log, it would not sink, but if Paloma were to climb aboard, her weight would drive the pirogue's sides down flush with the surface. Every minuscule movement she made would tip the boat and allow more water to slosh aboard. She could not bail it out from inside.

So she clung to one side with one arm, and with the other hand began methodically to splash water overboard. She forced herself not to be impatient, for she knew that this was what she was going to be doing for the next several

hours, probably well into the night. And she did not hurry, for she didn't want to tire herself and risk a cramp in an arm or leg. She could stop a cramp, but a muscle that had once gone into spasm was sure to cramp again unless it was rested for hours. Each succeeding cramp would be harder to relieve than the one before, and she did not want to be forced too early to use extreme remedies. It was said that the only way to relieve a terrible cramp was to cause worse pain elsewhere in your body, the theory being that the mind can only focus on one pain center at a time and it will concentrate on the most severe, and will thus stop sending cramp signals to the afflicted muscle.

Everyone, Paloma included, agreed that cramps could be affected dramatically by the mind. No matter what caused the cramp initially, you made it worse if you panicked, and you relieved it, to a greater or lesser degree, by detaching yourself from it and regarding it rationally as a muscle that has contracted and must be commanded to relax. Icy calm, of course, was a prescription more easily issued than filled, especially if you were swimming and the cramp knotted you up into a ball that reduced your buoyancy to a point where you could barely stay afloat, or if you were running, being chased by somebody or something, and a cramp knocked you to the ground.

As she continued to bail, the muscles in her upper arm began to stiffen and ache. To be free to massage that arm with her other hand, she had to release her grip on the boat. Immediately the tide caught her and dragged her away from the pirogue, but she was confident of her strength as a swimmer and was not worried.

She was more than fifty yards away from the pirogue when she finally felt the fibers in her arm muscles relax and soften, and she stopped massaging the tissue. Unhurriedly, she began to breaststroke against the tide.

To anything observing her from below, she appeared to be a sizable, healthy animal going about its business, emitting no signs of vulnerability, no signals of prey. After ten or fifteen minutes, it had seemed she was not moving at all; she seemed no closer to her boat than when she had started.

But she had marked her beginning against a set of peculiarly shaped rocks on the bottom, and she knew she was making progress—very slowly, probably no more than a couple of feet with each stroke, and half of that she was losing before she could take her next stroke; but she was gaining ground. She was not tiring; she could swim like this indefinitely, and eventually—it might be a couple of hours from now—the tide would ease and she would gain a little more with each stroke. Then it would go slack, and she would gain still more. Finally it would turn, and she would make it to her boat in a few strokes.

Her left leg went first. She had a split second warning, and then she felt her toes begin to roll over one another and snarl. She reached down with her hand and tried to squeeze the lower calf muscle, but it was too late. The muscle fibers had already balled into a knot the size of an orange. She rolled onto her back and used both hands to squeeze her leg. Kneading with her fingertips, she softened the knot and felt it begin to relax. Suddenly the knot dissolved and she thought the cramp was finished and she straightened out her leg and then, before she knew what was happening, with a violent, almost audible spasm an even bigger knot lashed itself into the back of her thigh. Her heel snapped back, like the blade of a jackknife closing.

She was drifting fast, was already much farther away from her boat. She told herself not to think about it, but to make an effort not to think about it was to think about it even harder.

She tried to use her hands to straighten out her leg, but her arms weren't long enough to give her adequate leverage. So she brought up her other foot and forced the toes between heel and buttock and pushed down.

Then the other leg went, a perfect mimic of the first one. She had no balance, she was top-heavy, and she rolled in the water like a trussed hog.

At first she thought she would faint from the pain. She *hoped* she would faint, for she was one of those people who tend to float on their backs, and as soon as she lost consciousness the cramps would disappear and she would roll onto her back with her head out of water.

When she didn't faint, she tried to swim toward her boat, using only her arms, but that was hopeless; she lost ground and grew quickly tired. She knew she had to attack the cramps with her mind.

So she stopped swimming and said to herself: You're drifting away. What is the worst thing that can happen? You'll drift so far that you can't get back to your boat on this tide.

349

You won't drown because you know how to float forever (unless a *chubasco* comes along, and there's no use worrying about that now). So you'll drift and drift, and sometime the tide will turn and take you back toward your boat. Even if you drift wide of your boat, all that will happen is that you'll travel until either you strike land or someone picks you up. So, really, you have nothing to worry about. (Somewhere, in the far recesses of her mind, she knew she could not float forever, or even for more than a few days. She would fall victim to thirst or hunger or the sun. But her mind did not let that knowledge intrude.)

Then she looked down through the water and saw that there was one "worst thing" she had neglected. She had drifted far off the seamount by now, and way down, in the blue shadows just before darkness, were two sharks, circling slowly. They were not the familiar hammerheads. Even from this distance she could discern the bullet shapes and the pointed snouts, and she knew they were a kind of bull shark—quick, bold, aggressive, ill-tempered, and completely unpredictable.

Each circle brought the sharks a bit closer to the surface; each circle was a bit quicker than the one before. And Paloma knew immediately what was happening: She was

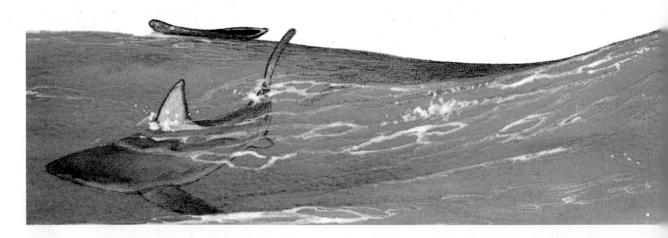

sending new signals, signals that said she was no longer a sizable, healthy animal going about its business—now she was a wounded, panicked animal that could not defend itself and might make easy prey.

All right, she told herself: I've got to stop behaving like this or they'll home in on me and tear me to pieces. As she heard the words in her brain, she felt a rush of panic, and so she tried even harder to straighten out her legs; and the harder she tried the tighter they knotted.

What would it be like to be attacked by a big fish? Would it hurt, or would it be so quick it wouldn't hurt so much at all? No, it would probably hurt. What kind of pain would it be? What's the worst pain you can imagine?

She bit her tongue. How that hurt! She bit harder. Nothing could hurt worse than this. She bit still harder, and now she tasted blood in her mouth and saw little puffs of red seep from between her lips into the water. The blood might draw the sharks closer.

But all she could focus on was the pain in her tongue. It was a blade, a flame, a needle.

The cramps collapsed.

She didn't know it until she stopped biting her tongue. As when you ease off of the throttle of an outboard motor, she expected the pain in her mouth to fade to a background, idle-speed sensation, and the pain in her legs to accelerate and take over. The pain in her mouth did fade, but nothing replaced it. She looked down and saw that her legs had unlocked themselves and the muscles in her calves were no longer twitching.

Very tentatively, she began to swim, aiming vaguely in the direction of her boat but more to test her muscles than to accomplish much. She used her arms and shoulders and let her legs follow along in a weak scissor-kick.

There was no pain, but there was no progress either. Her arms alone were not enough to move her body against the tide. Still, she kept swimming, to exercise the muscles and restore circulation to the tissue. She maintained a smooth and easy stroke, conveying calm and control.

After a few minutes, she looked down again, and she searched the edge of the gloom for the circling sharks. She saw only one and only part of that one, a flicker of gray shadow, heading away. She was a healthy animal once more, and to the sharks' perceptions a formidable foe instead of vulnerable prey.

She swam on for more than one hour, watching her boat grow smaller and smaller against the sea. Once in a while, a small muscle would give a warning twinge, a threat of spasm, and she would stop and massage the muscle and shake it. She did not want to stop for long, though, for continual exercise kept her warm, and warmth encouraged her blood to circulate. If she allowed herself to grow cold, her circulation would drop, her muscles would be starved for oxygen and they would cramp.

She swam without thinking, focusing on each stroke as an act of its own, independent of every other stroke and of all other acts, to be begun and completed with mechanical perfection toward an overall end that did not exist. She forced all other thoughts from her mind, for they could generate emotions that could alter her body chemistry and cause trouble— a cramp, a stitch in her side, a knot of gas in her stomach, or superhyperventilation, which could make her faint.

The first sign she had that the tide was changing was a feeling of warm, still water on her skin. She had swum into a mid-sea current that slackened with the tide and was lying on the surface like curdled milk on a cup of coffee. She stopped swimming and looked around. The sea, which had been merely calm, was now flat and slick. Such swells as there were were so slow and lazy that she could not perceive them.

She saw a piece of floating weed and swam to it and threw it as hard as she could toward her faraway boat. It landed ten feet away and lay still. It didn't move to her, away from her, or off to one side. The tide was dead slack. Now if she swam she could not lose, she could only gain, and soon the new tide would begin and would push her along. Her pirogue was anchored, so it would not move.

With every stroke she took she imagined the boat growing infinitesimally larger. She traveled about a mile in the first hour, swimming on the slack tide. The second mile took her twenty minutes, for the tide had turned and begun to run. In another fifteen minutes she was sitting in her pirogue, working her fingertips into the soft tissue of her thighs.

She had been frightened, but now she felt proud, too, for she had survived on her own. Every decision had been hers alone to make, and every decision had been correct. True, Jobim had taught her the skills and given her the knowledge that helped her survive, but putting it all into practice, actually *doing* it, felt wonderful.

She shivered. The sun had dropped so far that the pirogue cast a sharp shadow on the sea. During the hours
around midday, the sun had added heat to the water, and in
a few hours more water would retain that heat. But then the
cooling air would leech the heat from the water. Paloma
guessed that the temperature of the water had fallen five degrees or more since her boat had capsized.

Kneeling in the bottom of the boat, she scooped with her
hands and splashed with her paddle, and scooped some
more and splashed some more. She saw the sun slide to the
horizon, then seem to hesitate, then plunge beneath it, leaving a sky of richer blue dotted in the east by faint stars. She
saw a light or a campfire wink on a distant island. Nearby,

somewhere behind her in the twilight, a small ray jumped into the air and slapped back down with a stinging splash, and Paloma started at the knowledge that out here she was never alone, day or night.

The boat was dry now, as dry as it would be until the sun could get at it tomorrow and evaporate the water from the wood. She had not been on the sea at night for a long time, so she double-checked the landmarks she could still see and stood up in the pirogue to search for the first lights of Santa Maria. Then she started to paddle.

A three-quarter moon had risen in the black sky, and it cast a path of gold before the pirogue, a path that led Paloma home.

Reader's Response

Which part of the story surprised you or startled you most? Explain why.

PALOMA

Thinking It Over

1. How did Paloma plan to get back to shore?
2. What three problems did Paloma face after she had patched her boat?
3. When Paloma bit her tongue, she described the pain as "a blade, a flame, a needle." Explain how these words helped you understand what she was feeling.
4. What do you think was the source of Paloma's courage to keep on?
5. If Paloma had tired while swimming back to her boat, what could she have done to rest? How did you think of your answer?
6. To survive, Paloma used her special skills and knowledge of the sea. What do you think helped her the most?

Writing to Learn

THINK AND ANALYZE   Paloma survived because she remained calm and tried to reason. Copy the diagram below and think about the steps Paloma took to resolve her problem.

> Resolution: *Paloma is able to paddle to shore.*
>
> Third Step:
> Reason:
>
> Second Step:
> Reason:
>
> First Step: *Pulls self up on pirogue*
> Reason: *To examine hole*
>
> Problem: *Paloma is all alone in the sea with a damaged pirogue.*

WRITE   Complete the diagram. Use at least three or as many steps as you wish. At each step write what Paloma did and the reason for her action.

ONE GREAT THING

written by
Kitlinguharmiut Eskimos,
illustrated and
adapted by Aline Amon

I think over again
my small adventures,
when I drifted out with a shore wind
in my kayak
and thought I was in danger.
My fears,
those small ones,
that I thought so big,
were for all the vital things
I had to get and to reach.

And yet, there is only
one great thing—
to live to see, at home or on journeys,
the great day that dawns,
and the light that fills the world.

Magazine

News About Reading

Journals of the Sea

Everyone knows that Christopher Columbus discovered the New World in 1492. What many people don't know is that Columbus was also a writer. He kept a daily written record of his journey, called a *logbook* or *log*. His purpose was to document where he had been and what he had discovered. Today we can read his log as a fascinating account of a dangerous and exciting adventure, one of the world's most famous journals of the sea.

Columbus's logbook for October 12, 1492, describes his first landing in the New World. "I went ashore in the armed boat and took the royal standard. And we saw the trees very green, and much water and fruits of diverse kinds. Presently many of the inhabitants

Christopher Columbus kept two logbooks. A secret one recorded the true distance. The one shown to the crew made the distance seem shorter so the men would not grow fearful.

assembled. I gave to some red caps and glass beads to put round their necks, and many other things of little value. They came to the ships' boats afterward, where we were, swimming and

One of Columbus's ships has been reconstructed.

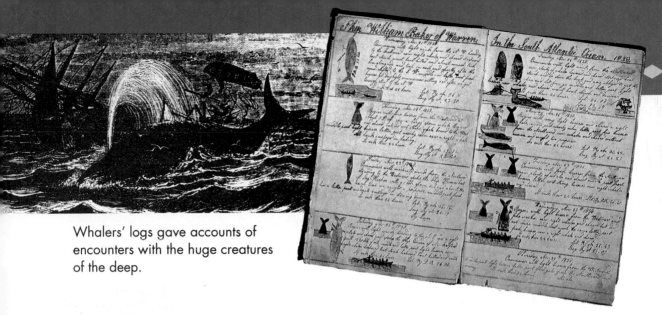

Whalers' logs gave accounts of encounters with the huge creatures of the deep.

Sea journals are some of the most thrilling stories ever told.

bringing us parrots, cotton threads in skeins, darts—what they had with good will."

Ships' captains and sailors have kept records of their sea voyages for centuries. Some, like Columbus, wrote them to document their explorations. Captains of whaling vessels used their logs to record their successes and failures in capturing whales. Sailors recorded the terrible hardships and cruel treatment they experienced at the hands of their captains.

Thor Heyerdahl is a modern sailor who made a long voyage to prove a theory. He thought that Native South Americans had sailed on balsawood rafts 1,500 years ago to settle islands in the middle of the Pacific Ocean. To prove that such a journey was possible, Heyerdahl built a balsa-wood raft and sailed the same route from South America with five companions and a parrot. His book, *Kon-Tiki*, written in 1950, was named after the raft. It became a best seller all over the world, and it is still popular reading for people who love sea stories.

Clare Francis, an English woman, was one of four women who competed in the 1976

Singlehanded Transatlantic Race. Her book, *Woman Alone*, tells of her epic voyage from Plymouth, England, to Newport, Rhode Island, in twenty-nine days.

Over the centuries sailors have kept logs and journals of their voyages. Only a small number of them were ever published. They are, however, some of the most thrilling stories ever told.

☛ **Many people love exploring the sea. Look into the Cousteau Society magazines Dolphin Log and Calypso Log, which are filled with fascinating, up-to-date articles about the sea.**

TIDES at the

If you've been to the seashore, you've watched the tides roll in and out. Now discover the secret of the sea's restlessness.

Along the edges of the ocean, water crashes toward shore! If you live near the sea, you know that the water sometimes comes high up on the shore. At other times the ocean is quite far out on the beach. These daily forward and backward motions of the sea are the high tides and the low tides.

Day after day, year after year, tides come in and go out, constantly following the same pattern over and over. Windstorms make the seas temporarily rise higher on beaches and against cliffs. However, the constant rise and fall of the tides follows a steady routine. The daily rise and fall of the sea surface is a continuing and never-ending process.

SEASHORE

by Elizabeth Clemons

High and Low Tides

In most places, for approximately six continuous hours of any given day, the water of the sea moves in toward land. As it comes in closer to shore, the water rises higher and higher on the beach. This incoming water is called the *flood tide*. When the water stops rising, it is *high tide*.

Then the water moves away from shore. It "turns," or starts to go out. This is called the *ebb tide*. At the end

of the next six hours, the water stops going out. Once the water reaches its lowest point, it is *low tide*.

As soon as low tide is reached, the water starts to move toward shore again. The change from low tide to high tide is not sudden. It is steady and constant. The same vertical rise and fall and the horizontal flow-and-ebb pattern of the moving sea water is repeated during the next twelve hours and twenty-five minutes of the day or night.

Range and Times of Tides

There are two high tides and two low tides each twenty-four hours in most places along the ocean. In some places the difference between high tide and low tide is less than one foot. In other places it may be as great as fifty feet. The difference between the water levels at high tide and low tide is called the *range* of the tides.

In some places the difference between high tide and low tide is less than one foot. In other places it may be as great as fifty feet.

The time between the two high tides is about twelve hours and twenty-five minutes. If we have high tide at 7 a.m. on Monday morning, the next high tide will be that night at 7:25 p.m. Then the next high tide will be

Tuesday morning at 7:50 a.m. Every twenty-four hours the tide is about fifty minutes later. Many people think of it as about an hour later each day.

Tides Along Flat Shores

Tides are very noticeable in an area of shallow water. At low tide you may see just a wide strip of mud flats. When the tide comes in, the entire mud flat will no longer be land but will actually be covered with water. This often happens where there is low land or a flat area near the sea. The range of the tide in shallow water spreads out over a wide flat area.

You can see the mark of the highest part of the water on the damp sand.

If there is a sloping beach along the shore, the water runs up on the beach. It comes in higher and higher and then recedes, or goes back toward the sea. You can see the mark of the highest part of the water on the damp sand. Broken shells, seaweeds, and small pieces of driftwood mark the place of the high tide.

Where the bits of material are left by the outgoing tide, you will be able to see that the water has run up higher on some places on the beach. This is because the water had more force or energy when it came in at that particular place.

Notice these various places as you go along the beach and try to figure out why the range of the tide is not in a straight line on the beach where you are walking.

Tides Along Steep Shores

Where the coastal area is steep, with cliffs near the beach, the range of tide is seen to be quite different. The tides along these areas make a definite water line on the straight sides of the cliffs. These marks show the actual rise in tide-water. The sea comes up on the cliff, covering the rocks along the shore. The sea rises in height against the cliff. It is not spread out horizontally over land or mud flats. It does not run up on a sloping beach. The range of a tide against a cliff is almost the same as mercury rising in a thermometer. You can see the height of the tidewater on the cliff or on steep rocky shores, just as you can see the line rising with warmer temperatures on a thermometer.

Where the shore is rocky and extends into the sea, the tide comes in and fills small tide pools and covers rocky boulders.

Tidal Pools

When the tide goes out, the tide pools, rocks, and masses of seaweed that lie between the rocks along the shore are uncovered. The range of the tide can often be judged by how much of the rock is covered, or how completely the tide pools are filled at high tide.

Even if the rocky shore does not extend into the sea, waves with wind behind them are strong enough to crash over high rocky areas. Use caution when walking near the edges of such rocky places. Waves come in with great force.

What Causes the Tides?

Gravitational attraction causes tides. Because water, which covers about three fourths of the earth's surface, is a liquid and free to move around, it shows the effect of the moon's gravitational pull upon the earth.

The moon's gravitational pull lifts the sea like a wave. Actually, that is what a tide really is. The rise of the water is slow because it is a very long moving wave. The wave's motion reaches to the bottom of the sea.

The moon pulls hardest on the part of the earth nearest it. The pull lifts the water on that part of the earth. The water bulges out toward the moon. Where the bulge is greatest, it is known as high tide. When the moon is on the horizon, and the bulge is the lowest, it is low or ebb tide.

At the same time that the moon lifts the water up on the part of the earth nearest it, the moon pulls *least* on the opposite side of the earth. The water on the opposite part of the earth bulges *away* from the moon, because of the lessening of the pull.

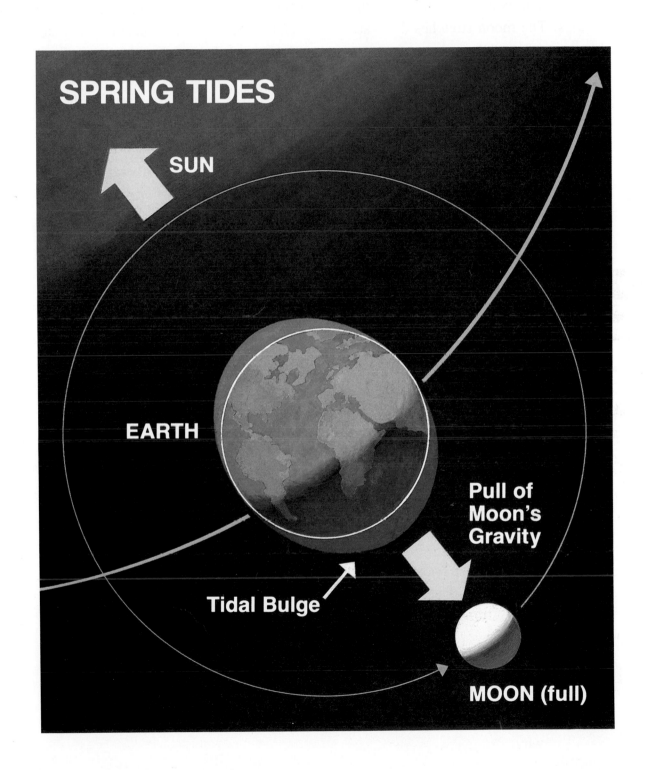

SPRING TIDES

SUN

EARTH

Pull of Moon's Gravity

Tidal Bulge

MOON (full)

367

Sometimes this is explained by thinking of it as a "stretching" along the axis. The moon stretches the water along one part of the axis, and the sun stretches it along the other part.

As the moon circles the earth, it pulls the waters on different parts of the earth into high tides. These high tides, as you know, occur fifty minutes later each day. This takes place because the moon rises fifty minutes later each night. The moon rotates about the earth in approximately twenty-nine days and so is about fifty minutes later each day in reaching the same position.

The earth constantly spins around, bringing another part of the globe beneath the moon. Each part of the water of the earth is pulled toward the moon. This bulge toward the moon, or high tide, moves around the earth as the earth continues turning.

There are times when the sun and the moon both pull in a straight line, and then the tides are *very* high. People who study the tides know that the highest ones of the month occur when the moon is full and again two weeks later at the new moon. At these times, the sun and the moon are in a straight line with the earth.

◆ LIBRARY LINK ◆

This selection is from the nonfiction book Waves, Tides, and Currents *by Elizabeth Clemons. In it, you'll find many other fascinating facts about the sea.*

Reader's Response

What did you find most interesting about the tides? Explain why.

TIDES at the SEASHORE

Thinking It Over

1. In your own words, define each of these terms: *flood tide*, *high tide*, *ebb tide*, and *low tide*.
2. If high tide occurred at 6 A.M. on Wednesday morning, when would the next high tide occur? How do you know?
3. Describe the way the tide rises in each of these areas: a mud flat, a sloping beach, and a steep cliff.
4. What would a full moon in the night sky tell you about the tides?
5. Do you feel that the pictures and headings added to your understanding of this selection? Give reasons for your answer.

Writing to Learn

THINK AND CONTRAST   How is the low tide different from the high tide? Copy the contrast chart below and fill it in to show the differences between the tides.

Coastal Area	High Tide	Low Tide
flat coast		water reaches lowest point
steep cliff	water rises against cliff	
rocky shore		

WRITE   Imagine that you took a walk along the beach at low tide today. Write an entry for your diary telling what you observed that led you to believe it was low tide.

Tides

The tide is high! The tide is high!
The shiny waves go marching by
Past ledge and shallow and weedy reach
Up the long gray lengths of shingle beach;
Like an army storming height on height
With green-blue armor and banners white
On, on they charge to the farthest line
Of scattered seaweed brown and fine—
So far, then, grumbling, back creep they,
And the tide has turned for another day.

The tide is low! The tide is low!
Weed-decked and gaunt the ledges show
With mussel shells in blues and blacks
And barnacles along their backs.
Now kelp shines like mahogany
And every rock pool brims with sea
To make a little looking glass
For sky and clouds and birds that pass.

Rachel Field

The Tide Rises, the Tide Falls

The tide rises, the tide falls,
The twilight darkens, the curlew calls;
Along the sea-sands damp and brown
The traveller hastens toward the town,
    And the tide rises, the tide falls.

Darkness settles on roofs and walls,
But the sea, the sea in the darkness calls;
The little waves, with their soft, white hands,
Efface the footprints in the sands,
    And the tide rises, the tide falls.

The morning breaks; the steeds in their stalls
Stamp and neigh, as the hostler calls;
The day returns, but nevermore
Returns the traveller to the shore,
    And the tide rises, the tide falls.

Henry Wadsworth Longfellow

Reading Mathematics

When you read problems in mathematics textbooks, you must read carefully to understand the problem. Making a drawing can help you understand the problem and help point the way to a solution.

Before you start to solve the problem, you need to make sure you understand all the information given. Asking yourself the following questions will help you understand the problem completely.

1. What question does the problem ask?
2. What facts are provided that are important in answering the question?
3. How can you put these facts into a drawing?
4. How does the drawing help you find the answer?

Using a Drawing

Making a drawing can help you understand and solve the problem below. Read the problem carefully.

Two boats leave a river dock and travel in opposite directions. Boat A travels 6 km east, where its passengers disembark. Boat B travels 5 km west, where its cargo is unloaded. By noon, Boat A has traveled 2 km west to its next stopping place, and Boat B has traveled 3 km west of its first stop. How far apart are the boats at noon?

What question does the problem ask? The final sentence of the word problem states the question. You have to find out how far apart the boats are at noon.

What facts are provided? When you read a mathematics problem, decide what facts are necessary to solve the problem and what facts are unnecessary. Here are the important facts: The boats leave from the same place. Boat A goes 6 km east, then 2 km west. Boat B goes 5 km west, then an additional 3 km west.

Now put these facts into a drawing. Draw a river on your paper that runs east-west. In the middle, put a dock. Then, show where Boat A traveled. Use arrows to help you keep track of the direction of travel. Boat A went 6 km east, then turned around and went 2 km west. Now draw the course Boat B followed. Boat B went 5 km west, then continued another 3 km west. Your drawing should look similar to the drawing below.

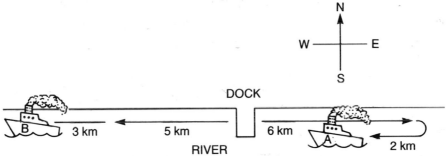

Now you can compute the answer from your drawing. Add the distances the boats went away from each other. Then subtract the distance that Boat A traveled back toward Boat B.

$$3 + 5 + 6 - 2 = 12 \text{ km}$$

The boats are 12 km apart at noon. Did the drawing help you figure out the solution?

As You Read   The following page is from a mathematics textbook. Read problems 1–8. Then answer the questions on page 375.

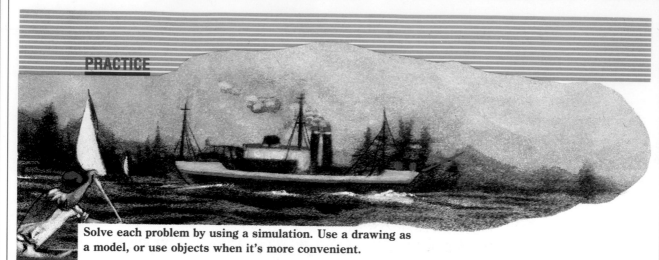

Solve each problem by using a simulation. Use a drawing as a model, or use objects when it's more convenient.

1. Randi paddles her canoe 3 km east, then 2 km north. After that she paddles 6 km west, then 2 km south. How far is she from her starting point?

2. Mario paddles his canoe 2 km east, then 5 km west. He then paddles 4 km east. How far is Mario from his original starting point?

3. A section of the river is roped off because of dangerous rocks. The section is a square, 32 meters on each side. Marker buoys are placed every 4 meters. How many buoys are there?

4. There are 4 boats on the river. The yellow boat is in front of the red boat. The blue boat is behind the green boat. The yellow boat is behind the blue boat. What is the order of the boats?

5. Boat X and Boat Y leave a dock and travel in opposite directions. Boat X travels 6 km east to drop off its passengers. Boat Y travels 8 km west, where its passengers disembark. Then Boat X travels 3 km east, and Boat Y travels 8 km east. How far apart are the boats?

6. Dennis has 4 uncles who have offices on different floors in the Harbor Office Building. One day, Dennis visits his uncles. First, he goes up to the 12th floor, then down 5 floors. Later, he goes up 3 floors and down 7 floors. What floor is he on when he visits the last uncle?

★7. A rubber ball is dropped from a height of 12 meters. It bounces up 9 meters on the first bounce. It bounces back up 5 meters on the second bounce. What is the total distance the ball has traveled when it hits the ground the third time?

★8. Inez places 20 pennies in a row on her desk. She replaces every third coin with a nickel. Next, she replaces every fourth coin with a dime. Finally, she replaces every fifth coin with a quarter. What is the value of the 20 coins now in a row?

CREATE YOUR OWN PROBLEM

This table gives the distances that Pierre sails his boat on Monday through Friday. Assume that the pattern continues for the next two days. Create two problems using his sailing data from Monday through Sunday. Solve each problem.

Day	Distance in km
Monday	7
Tuesday	5
Wednesday	8
Thursday	6
Friday	9

Using What You Have Learned

1. Read problem 1 on the previous page.
   a. What question does the problem ask?
   b. Make a drawing to help you understand the problem.

2. Read problem 3 on the previous page.
   a. What question does the problem ask?
   b. What facts are important to solve the problem?
   c. Make a drawing to help you solve the problem.
   d. How does making the drawing help you solve the problem?
   e. How many buoys are there?

3. Make a drawing to help you solve problem 4 on the previous page.

4. Read problem 6 on the previous page.
   a. What questions does the problem ask?
   b. What information is necessary to solve the problem?
   c. Make a drawing to help you find the solution.
   d. What is the solution to the problem?

5. Write a word problem of your own that can be solved using a drawing. Exchange papers with a friend and solve each other's problems.

Enemy ships are about to challenge the Tiny Kingdom, a poor peace-loving country that has neither weapons nor warships.

The
Princess
and·the
Admiral

written by Charlotte Pomerantz
illustrated by Tony Chen

A very long time ago, there was a small patch of dry land called the Tiny Kingdom. Most of its people were poor farmers or fisherfolk. Their bodies were lean and brown and strong from working long hours in the sun. They built the thatched mud huts in which they lived. They wove the simple earth-colored clothing they wore. And everyone, even the children, helped to plow the fields, harvest the rice, and catch the fish that they ate.

The land of the Tiny Kingdom was as poor as its people. The soil had neither gold nor silver, which was why no country, in the memory of the oldest man or woman, had ever made war against them. The people were good-humored about the poverty of the land. It had given them a hundred years of peace.

The ruler of the Tiny Kingdom was Mat Mat, a dark-eyed young princess, as lean and brown as her people. One night, almost a thousand years ago, the Princess looked out the window of her

377

royal bedchamber at the fishing boats in the harbor below, then up at the pale sliver of a moon. Sometimes when the Princess was wakeful, she would follow the moon's slow silent journey upwards across the sky into morning.

Tonight the young Princess was too excited to sleep. For this month marked the anniversary of One Hundred Years of Peace in the Tiny Kingdom. It would be celebrated, as were all great events, with a Carnival and Fireworks Display. Tomorrow morning, at the Council of Three Advisers, the Princess would choose the date.

There would be all kinds of firecrackers—flares, petards, and pinwheels that burst into flowers and waterfalls and fishes. Birds and butterflies would flit among trees of green fire. Then, at midnight, one—no, three—fantastic red dragons would slither and writhe across the night sky.

"Beautiful!" murmured the Princess, her dark eyes shining.

The next morning, the Princess was the first to arrive at the Council Chamber. The three advisers followed. First, the Elder, a man of ninety years. Then, the Younger, a man of eighty years. And finally, In-Between, who was exactly eighty-five.

The Princess greeted them. "Joyful tidings, my dear advisers. This month marks the anniversary of One Hundred Years of Peace in the Tiny Kingdom. I think you will agree that this calls for a very special Carnival and Fireworks display."

The three advisers were strangely silent and stone-faced.

The Elder broke the silence. "Excuse me, Your Highness, but there can be no celebration."

"Why not?" demanded the Princess.

"There are rumors of invasion," said the Younger.

"It looks like war," said In-Between.

The Princess stared at them, unbelieving. "But we have no enemies."

"I fear we do," said the Elder. "We have just had a report from our fishing boats that a large fleet of warships is at this very moment sailing toward our kingdom."

"How terrible!" said the Princess. "How many ships are coming?"

"Our fishing boats report twenty ships of war," said In-Between, "including the flagship of the Admiral."

"How large are the ships?"

"I would judge each to be about five times the size of the Royal Swanboat," said the Elder.

"More like four times the size of the largest fishing boat," said the Younger.

"Mmmm," said In-Between. "I'd say the truth lies somewhere in the middle."

"Never mind," said the Princess impatiently. "How long will it be before the enemy reaches the harbor of the Tiny Kingdom?"

"Two days, more or less," the advisers replied in chorus.

The Princess settled herself on her throne. "Let us review our capabilities," she said, "and make some contingency plans."

The Elder spoke first. "We have no ships of war."

"We have no men or women under arms," said the Younger.

"We do have an inexhaustible supply of firecrackers," said In-Between. "Totally useless in the present emergency."

The Princess stepped down from her throne, walked to the window, and looked at the harbor below. "No forts, no soldiers, no weapons, no sinews of war," she mused. "Clearly, we shall have to rely on . . . other things." She walked briskly back to the throne. "Call in the Court Astrologer," she said.

The three advisers shrugged. "With all due respect," said the Younger, "astrology is no substitute for weapons."

"We shall see," said the Princess.

An ancient and withered old woman tottered into the Council Chamber.

"Your Highness wants me?" she asked. "I haven't been consulted since your great-grandmother swallowed a chicken neck."

"I seek information about the position of the sun and the moon," said the Princess.

"With pleasure," said the old woman. "When the moon is in her first or third quarter, it's as if she were a stranger to the sun. But when it is a new moon or a full moon, there is a special, rather remarkable attraction. We feel it on earth, in plants and oceans. I often feel it in my bones."

"And what of the moon tonight?"

"Tonight it is a new moon which hangs its fragile lantern over your Tiny Kingdom."

"Interesting," said the Princess. "You may return to your tower."

The Princess beckoned her three advisers to come close. "Our course is clear," she said. "As clear as the lantern moon." The four of them huddled together while the Princess whispered her plan.

"And so," she concluded, "the first order of business is to send out a dozen of our fishing boats to tease the enemy. Their ships are bound to chase ours, and if everything goes well, the enemy ships should get here at the right time."

The next day, upon orders of Princess Mat Mat, hundreds of farmers, fisherfolk, and children gathered in a nearby forest to cut down the tallest trees. The strongest men and women sawed through the trunks. The less strong sharpened both ends of the fallen trees, and the children stripped off the branches.

Then everyone helped to haul the tree poles to the riverbed. When the tide had gone down enough for them to drag the poles into the water, they hammered them—dozens and dozens of them—into the muddy bottom of the riverbed.

The Princess watched from the window of her royal bedchamber. When she had counted 253 poles jutting out of the water like a crazy, staggered picket fence, she gave orders for the people to return to their huts.

The next morning, when the Princess and her advisers stood on the Royal Balcony, not a single pole was visible.

"I thought the tide would be higher," said the Elder.

"I thought it would be lower," said the Younger.

"Your Highness," said In-Between, "I think you guessed just right."

"It was no guess," said the Princess. "Not after I talked to the Court Astrologer. We know the tides are caused by the attraction of the sun and the moon. Therefore, when I learned that these two celestial bodies are especially close at this time, I knew that the tides would be exceptionally high. High enough to cover the tree poles." She smiled. "The moon is a faithful ally."

Just then, the first ships of the enemy fleet were sighted approaching the mouth of the riverbed. They were in full chase of the twelve fishing boats that had been sent out to tease them.

The enemy fleet sailed up the middle of the river. As they faced the village, fifty more fishing boats appeared from all directions and surrounded them.

Aboard the flagship of the enemy fleet, the Admiral gave the command: *"Furl sails and drop anchor! Get ready to fight!"*

From the Royal Balcony the Princess looked down at the enemy ships and clapped her hands.

"He did it! The Admiral did just what I hoped he would do!" she exclaimed, trying hard not to jump up and down.

Even the Elder adviser could not hold back a smile. "Your plan is working perfectly," he said.

On the river, the Admiral peered uneasily at all the fishing boats. "It looks as if they are going to climb aboard."

As he spoke, the fisherfolk began to hurl cooking pots, soup ladles, coconuts, mangoes, melons, chickens—whatever they had been able to lay hold of—at the enemy fleet. One tall fisherman, in his enthusiasm, took a whole pail of eels and threw it aboard the Admiral's flagship. Then the little fishing boats turned around and quickly sailed past the harbor, leaving the Admiral and his warships in full command of the river.

The Admiral chortled. "Did they really think they could conquer our mighty armada with coconuts and cooking pots?"

"It would seem they are a rather primitive people, sir," said the Helmsman.

The Admiral surveyed the village and the castle. "No trouble here," he said smugly. "The fishing boats have disappeared behind a bend in the river. Not a living soul on the streets, except for a few scrawny chickens and goats. It's clear the natives are terrified." He looked down at the water. "The tide is going out, but there's still plenty of depth here in the middle of the river. We'll wait for low tide to make sure we can dock."

Settling comfortably into his deck chair, he said, "Tomorrow, first thing, we'll surround the palace, search and destroy the arsenal, seize the crown jewels, and behead the Princess."

"Princess?" said the Helmsman. "What makes you think it's a Princess?"

The Admiral snickered. "Only a girl would be silly enough to fight a great naval battle with fruits and vegetables." He spotted an eel at his feet and kicked it scornfully. "Even fish! Ridiculous."

An hour later, a tremendous shout came from below deck. *"Shipping water!"*

"What's that supposed to mean?" barked the Admiral.

"It means there's a leak," said the Helmsman.

From all over the fleet came the cry, *"Shipping water! We're shipping water!"*

The Admiral dashed down to the hold. There, an extraordinary sight greeted his eyes: What appeared to be the trunk of a tree was poking through the bottom of the ship! Even as the Admiral watched, the tree top was slowly coming upward. Then another tree . . . and another . . . and another. By Neptune, more than a dozen were coming through the bottom! And where the wood had splintered around the tree trunks, the water was seeping in, slowly but steadily.

"Start bailing and saw off those trees," bawled the Admiral.

"Beg pardon, sir," said the Helmsman, "but if you get rid of the trees, the water will rush through. The trees are like corks. Take away the corks, and we'll all drown in the onrushing waters."

"Never mind," said the Admiral testily. "Send a message to the fleet. *'All ships continue bailing. All ships' captains to report to my cabin for a Council of War.'*"

Some two hours later, when the captains were all assembled aboard the Admiral's flagship, the Helmsman stuck his head in the cabin door. "Sorry to interrupt, sir, but the water is draining out of the ships."

"Naturally, you blockhead," said the Admiral. "The men are bailing."

"No, no," said the Helmsman. "It's happening all by itself."

"Ye gods and little fishes!" gasped the Admiral. "I'd better have a look."

He strode out on the deck, stumbled on a coconut, then stopped and stared goggle-eyed at the astounding spectacle. All around, his whole fleet was stuck up on tree poles! The air resounded with loud crackings and bangings coming from the bottoms of all the ships as they settled firmly onto the tree trunks. And, of

course, the seawater was drip-dripping out of all the elevated ships' bottoms.

Suddenly everything became clear to the Admiral. He had been trapped. These devilish fisherfolk had used the tide against him. They had put in poles at low tide. He had come in with his ships at high tide. Then, when the tide went out, he was left stuck up on the poles.

Now he could hear a muted roar of laughter from the farmers, fisherfolk, and children who crowded the riverbank and docks.

From around the bend, the little fishing boats reappeared and surrounded the fleet. At their head was a golden swanboat, flying a flag of truce under the royal standard. It sailed up alongside the Admiral's flagship.

"Ahoy, mate," said a fisherman. "Ready to surrender?"

The Admiral looked down and shook his fist. "Never! You just wait till we come ashore."

The tall fisherman grinned. "If you're thinking of sending your men swimming or wading to shore, think again. Because any man found in the water will be whacked on the head with an oar."

"Who the devil are you?" thundered the Admiral.

"I'm a fisherman. In fact, I'm the best fisherman around. Because I sacrificed a whole pail of eels for the glory of the Tiny Kingdom, the Princess has bestowed on me the honor of taking you to shore to negotiate the terms of peace."

"Never!" said the Admiral. "I will go down with my ship."

"Your ship isn't going to go down," said the fisherman. "It will stay stuck up there on the tree poles until the ebb and flow of the tide breaks the fleet to smithereens."

The Admiral sighed, climbed down, and settled gloomily into the stern of the Royal Swanboat. The tall fisherman rowed him to shore.

After the Admiral had changed into dry socks, he was summoned to the Council Chamber to face Princess Mat Mat and her three advisers.

The Princess led the Admiral to the window overlooking the harbor.

"It's a quaint sight, isn't it?" she said.

The Admiral turned red. "Quaint!" he groaned. "It's a nightmare."

"Try and get hold of yourself," said the Princess.

"What humiliation!" cried the Admiral. "To be defeated by a woman!" He glanced at the young princess. "Not even a woman. A slip of a girl." He drooped miserably. "What's the difference. I shall be beheaded at dawn."

"Certainly we will behead you," said the Elder.

"I would cut off his feet," said the Younger.

"In my opinion," said In-Between, "justice lies somewhere in the middle."

The Princess clucked her tongue in disapproval. "Are you such old men that you have forgotten the story of the widow and her chickens?"

"Your highness," said the Elder, "every child in this kingdom knows it by heart."

"Perhaps it is time to tell it again," said the Princess. She faced them all and commenced her tale.

"Once upon a time, there was a poor old widow who saw a young man sneak into her yard and steal two chickens. She knew very well who the young man was, but she did not report him to the authorities. Instead, that evening, when everyone, including the young man, had gathered in the village square to watch a carnival and fireworks display, the widow called out: 'What kind of person steals two chickens from a poor old woman? I'll tell you—a no-good thief with a heart of stone. Shame on this person. Shame! Shame!'

"The young man listened and was indeed ashamed. That very night, he sneaked into the widow's yard and returned one of the chickens. (He had, alas, cooked and eaten the other one.) The widow saw him and hid. 'It is good,' she said. 'I got back one of my chickens, and the young man did not lose face in the village.' "

When the Princess had finished her tale, she turned to the Admiral and said, "So you see, sir, revenge is not our way. We do not believe that those who have wronged us should be punished or humiliated beyond what is necessary."

"You are not going to behead me?" said the Admiral.

"Ugh," said the Princess. "How distasteful."

The Admiral was completely fogbound. "Your Highness, what are you going to do?"

"Simple," said the Princess. "I shall supply you with two guides to take you and your men through the harsh mountainous terrain that leads back to your country and your Emperor. I shall also provide you with a two-week supply of food and water, as well as five water buffaloes to help carry your provisions." The Princess was thoughtful. "Of course, we would appreciate your returning the water buffalo."

The Admiral knelt down before the Princess and kissed her hand. "Be assured, your animals shall be returned." His voice trembled with gratitude and relief. "Your Highness, I shall never forget you, nor the kind and gentle ways of your kingdom." Tears filled his eyes, rolled down his cheeks and onto his medals. "If there is anything I can ever do for you . . ."

"As a matter of fact, there is," said the Princess.

"Anything," repeated the Admiral.

The Princess eyed him coolly and said, "I would ask you not to make unkind remarks about women and girls—especially princesses."

That evening, from the Royal Balcony, Princess Mat Mat and her three advisers watched the long winding caravan of enemy soldiers and sailors. The water buffaloes pulled carts

heavy-laden with food and water. At the front, leading his men, the Admiral, bedecked with medals and sniffling from a head cold, sat astride the fattest water buffalo. All along the winding road into the mountains, the farmers, fisherfolk, and children waved them goodbye.

"It is good," said the Princess to her advisers. "We won the battle, and since the Admiral is returning home with his men, he will not lose too much face with his Emperor." She sighed wistfully. "How close we came to celebrating One Hundred Years of Peace."

"Dear Princess," said the Elder, "what happened this morning could hardly be called a battle. The only casualty was a sailor who got bonged on the head with a mango."

"It was more like a skirmish," said the Younger. "But I thought the sailor got bonged on the toe."

"That's odd," said In-Between. "I was quite sure it was a coconut."

"My dear advisers," said the Princess, "do I understand you to mean that we can go ahead with the celebration?"

The Elder shrugged. "If the poor widow could forget about one of her chickens, surely we can forget one small incident in a hundred years of peace."

"For the first time," said the Younger, "the three of us are in agreement about the number of firecrackers, flares, torches, Bengal lights, petards, Roman candles and pinwheels for the celebration. One thousand."

The Princess was jubilant. "Why that's more than I ever dreamed of! . . . And will there be three dragons?"

"Concerning dragons," said the Elder, "we don't think three is the right number."

"Alas," said the Princess. "How many, then?"

"We shall see," said In-Between.

Thus it came to pass that within the week the Tiny Kingdom celebrated One Hundred Years of Peace—well, almost—with the biggest Carnival and Fireworks Display in its history. Not one, not three, but twelve fantastic red dragons slithered and writhed across the night sky.

And of all the happy farmers, fisherfolk, and children in the Tiny Kingdom, not one was happier than Princess Mat Mat.

Reader's Response

How would you have treated the Admiral if you had been Princess Mat Mat?

The Princess and the Admiral

Thinking It Over

1. Why was the Tiny Kingdom planning a celebration?
2. Why was the celebration postponed?
3. How did Princess Mat Mat save her kingdom?
4. Suppose Princess Mat Mat had not forgiven the Admiral. How might that have changed her country's future?
5. If the Elder, the Younger, and In-Between each gave you a description, which would you expect to be most accurate? How do you know?
6. Do you think that the Tiny Kingdom should have had its celebration at the end of the story? Explain your answer.

Writing to Learn

THINK AND INFER   What made the Princess such a capable leader? Copy each action the Princess took, listed below. On the lines, write what each action suggests about the Princess.

The Princess listens to her advisers.

considerate
thoughtful
respectful

The Princess decides to aid instead of punish the invaders.

The Princess's plans include farmers, fisherfolk, and children.

WRITE   Write a paragraph telling why the Princess was a good leader. Use your list of actions and characteristics to give you ideas.

Literature Link

How can you make a plan to guide your reading?

Do you remember your first day in your present school? Perhaps you got lost trying to find the gym or the cafeteria. But after a few weeks, with the help of a map or a friend, the layout became clear and you were getting around with no trouble.

Like a school, a nonfiction article has its own special layout, or structure. The author planned it that way, based on the kind of information to be presented. There's no need for you to get lost in an article just because it's new to you. You can figure out the structure before you begin reading. Then you can make a reading plan to guide you on your way.

Look at the Structure

Let's look at the structure of "Ancient Mysteries," an article from Unit 2, and make a plan for reading it as if you were reading it for the first time. First read the introduction for some clues.

In this article, three mysteries are presented. But don't look for the answers! They are buried somewhere in the past, in another time and another culture. Perhaps some day the answers will come to light. In the meantime, it is fun to guess what they might be.

The big clue to structure is the fact that there are three mysteries. The article will probably be divided into three parts. If you turned the pages, you'd find that there are indeed three sections, one about each mystery: Stonehenge, Atlantis, and Linear A.

Using the introduction and the layout of the article, you might make a plan like this for reading "Ancient Mysteries."

1. Divide reading into 3 blocks.
2. Don't expect answers to the mysteries.
3. Guide questions for each mystery:
   What is this mystery about?
   Who has tried to solve it? How?
   What might happen in the future?

Here's how to make a reading plan for any nonfiction article:

- Preview the article. Read any introduction and look through the article for other clues to its structure.
- Notice the layout. Look for headings, numbers, or other ways the information is divided up.
- Plan how you will read each section. Compose questions.

Before reading "The Monterey Bay Aquarium," preview the pages to figure out the structure of the article. Then make a reading plan, using the steps you learned in this lesson.

Visitors admire the world's only indoor kelp forest.

Sharks and killer whales may challenge the imagination, but they aren't the only fish in the sea . . . or at the Monterey Bay Aquarium.

THE MONTEREY BAY AQUARIUM

by Paul Fleischman

You walk through the door—and immediately freeze. Overhead, to your left, a thresher shark whips its tail. To your right are three huge killer whales. Have you wandered into a nightmare? Hardly. You've just entered the Monterey Bay Aquarium.

The shark and whales, lifesize and hanging from the ceiling, are fiberglass. The other 6,000 creatures you'll meet are not. On a visit to the aquarium, on the shores of California's Monterey Bay, you'll have a chance not only to see them swim, scurry, hunt, and court, but to pick up and handle a few as well.

One of the aquarium's most spectacular exhibits is the three-story-high kelp forest—the world's only kelp forest growing indoors. Clinging to the bottom with a rootlike "holdfast," the yellow-brown kelp reaches up through 28 feet of water, spreading out on the tank's sunlit surface. With "stipes" instead of trunks, and "blades" in place of leaves, the kelp forest resembles an underwater redwood grove. Sunbeams slant down from above, while the kelp sways gently

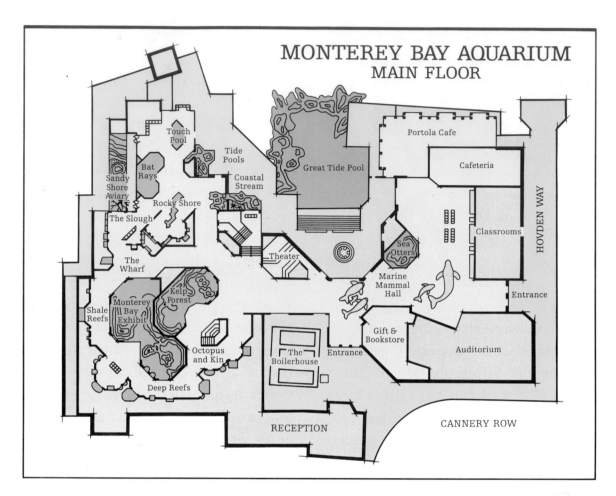

back and forth. With a patient eye, you will begin to spot some of the many creatures that call the kelp forest home.

Long-legged brittle stars and crabs can be seen within the tangled holdfast. Watch for turban snails higher up. The fish of the kelp forest aren't as fast as those of the open ocean, but they're better at playing hide-and-seek. Special air sacs allow some of them to hover in hiding within the maze of blades. Many are completely camouflaged. Golden señoritas[1] match the color of the kelp. Spiny rockfishes blend in with the rocks on the bottom. Most of the kelp fishes have mouths made for nibbling the many tiny creatures that feed upon the kelp.

On the forest's floor, look for fallen kelp fronds being eaten by prickly sea urchins and abalone.[2] These in turn are preyed on by starfish, the champion arm-wrestlers of the deep, who spend hours prying

[1]señoritas (se nyō rē' täs)
[2]abalone (a bu lō' nē): a large shellfish

396

open a shell. Sea cucumbers, looking like giant orange worms, dine on the crumbs resulting from all these meals.

Like a forest on land, the kelp forest changes with the seasons. In summer, the kelp grows up to ten inches a day in the wild. In winter, it may be damaged or ripped out entirely by storms. In spring, new fronds grow, filling in the forest's gaps. All year around, the kelp offers food, housing, and shelter from the waves to a vast array of inhabitants.

Among the animals who depend on the kelp are the aquarium's most playful residents, the sea otters. Floating on their backs, doing somersaults in the water, taking part in high-speed games of tag, these smallest of the marine mammals charm every audience.

Their two-story tank lets you view them from above as well as from below the water's surface. In the wild, though, their home is the kelp beds. They live on creatures who live on the kelp. They depend on it for shelter during storms. Before sleeping, they wrap themselves in it to keep from drifting out to sea.

Why are otters so playful? No one knows, though part of the answer might lie in the fact that their constant motion helps to keep them warm. Unlike the whales and other marine mammals, otters have no layer of blubber between their warm-blooded insides and the cold water outside. So they move around a lot, which requires a lot of energy, which in turn requires a lot of eating. Could you eat 25 hamburgers a day? That's the equivalent of what an otter swallows, eating up to one-quarter of its body weight daily. If you're present at feeding time, you'll be amazed at how much fish, squid, and abalone an otter can eat. Wild otters eat so many purple sea urchins that their bones eventually turn purplish as well.

Otters have another defense against the cold—their coats. When you touch the soft sample of fur on the wall by their tank, you'll understand why they were hunted until they were nearly extinct. Fifty years ago, there were fewer than 100 sea otters left. They are now protected and have increased in number to around 1,500. Watch and you'll see them carefully groom the coats that were so highly prized. By cleaning its coat and blowing air into the spaces between the hairs, the otter keeps the cold water away from its skin.

Sea otters aren't simply playful, hungry, and tidy—they're smart, too. To open a clamshell, an otter will dive down, bring up a rock, place it on its chest, and crack open the clam against it while floating on its back. Otters are among the very few animals who have learned to make use of tools.

How did the aquarium get its otters? Those in the tank had been separated from their mothers by storms, were rescued, and were raised in the aquarium. How do you raise an orphaned otter? With a baby bottle and a waterbed when it is very young. Once it learns to dive, it is moved to a tank or a holding pen out in the bay. The aquarium's staff is the first to try to raise orphaned otters and then return them to the sea.

Look up when you leave the otter tank and you'll find yourself moving below a mixed herd of larger marine mammals. Carefully crafted models of porpoises and dolphins swim above you, along

Sea otters frolic in the chilly otter tank.

Visitors marvel at the size of a whale calf displayed overhead.

with seals, sea lions, and even a human skindiver. All are dwarfed by the models of the largest mammals of all—the whales.

The gray whale calf hanging overhead is 22 feet long. Its mother, beside it, is twice that size. Yet these giants live on plankton, the sea's smallest creatures. Instead of teeth, gray whales have strips of baleen in their mouths, which act like a sieve in straining plankton from the water.

Gray whales are the most commonly seen whales in Monterey Bay.

Each winter they migrate southward to their breeding grounds in Mexico. A few months later, with their recently born calves, they pass by again, heading north toward their summer feeding grounds off Alaska. If you look closely at the model, you'll notice scores of barnacles that have attached themselves to the whales, hitching a many-thousand-mile ride.

Are whales really related to land mammals? Look up at the gray whale skeleton nearby and you'll spot what once were finger bones, normally hidden from view within the whales' flippers. Why are whales so much bigger than land animals? Because the weight of their bodies—over 100 tons for a blue whale—is supported by the buoyant water in which they live. On land, such animals would find it too hard to support their own weight.

Unlike the gray whales, the killer whales or "orcas" pursuing them overhead have teeth, and plenty of them. If you look closely, you can even spot the marks of those teeth on the mother gray whale's tail. With high dorsal fins and striking black and white patterns, orcas are easy to recognize. They also move extremely fast, and few creatures are swift or clever enough to avoid their jaws. Fish, otters, seals, and other whales are all fair game. Hunting in groups, orcas can travel at up to 25 knots an hour. Being mammals, though, they must interrupt their sprints and come to the surface to breathe through their blowholes.

The aquarium's exhibits offer an amazing variety of sea life to be viewed. But you can do more than look—you can touch. Do you like petting cats and dogs? Here you'll have the chance to pet a bat ray. Walk over to their pool and watch them flapping their wings to stir up food from the bottom. Their long tails look dangerous, but in fact they only sting in self-defense and with the base, not the tip, of the tail. The rays in this pool are well accustomed to people and will let you reach over the side and stroke their velvety backs.

There's more touching to be done at the touch tide pool nearby. Here you can feel the rough skin of a bat star, the sharp spines of an urchin, or some feather boa kelp. Get a feel for the weight of a gumboot chiton.[3] Let your fingers explore the back of a decorator crab, which sticks bits of seaweed and other debris to its shell to camouflage itself. Move from the hard to the soft and feel the squishy, boneless sea cucumber.

Upstairs at the kelp lab you can touch some of the kelp forest's many residents. You can also observe them through microscopes. What appears to be a stone-still brittle star turns out, under the microscope, to be an animal in constant motion, its hundreds of tiny "fingers" passing bits of food down its long arms toward its mouth.

[3]chiton (kī′ tən): a mollusk

Shown at left:
Discovering sea life up close

Below, top to bottom:
*Brittle star, purple sea
urchin, northern abalone,
and a tropical sea cucumber*

At the barnacle display you can turn a crank and set its water in motion, causing the barnacles to open up and send out their feathery legs to catch food. Nearby you can turn another crank and change the direction of a current of water. Watch the fish in the tank change direction as well, always facing into the current. Can you guess why?

The aquarium extends outdoors as well. Many of the plants and animals on display can be seen outside in the Great Tide Pool. This large man-made pool was quickly occupied by the bay's marine life. Peering over the rail, you may be able to name much of what you see. Look up from the tide pool and you may see a marine mammal or two in the bay. Watch for otters dining off their chests while floating on their backs. If it's winter, you might see a baby otter lying on its mother's chest as well. You can often see harbor seals perched on nearby rocks and sea lions riding the waves.

If you visit during the months of December through May, keep an eye out for migrating gray whales. Their heart-shaped spouts are clearly visible on a calm day. After spouting several times, a whale usually makes a deep dive, often showing its tail as it descends.

Before leaving the Monterey Bay Aquarium, try scanning the water with one of the second-floor telescopes. It's a great way to glimpse a flock of ducks, a soaring pelican, or a pair of sea lions—and to realize that you now can tell a seal from a sea otter, and that the next time you see a whale, whether it's real or fiberglass, you may even know it by name.

Reader's Response

Which exhibit would you most want to see at the Monterey Bay Aquarium? How did you make your choice?

THE MONTEREY BAY AQUARIUM

Thinking It Over

1. How many different kinds of sea creatures are there in the Monterey Bay Aquarium?
2. Compare a kelp forest and a land forest. Tell how the two environments are alike and how they differ.
3. In what ways do otters depend on kelp?
4. What might have happened to sea otters if hunting laws had not been changed to protect the otters?
5. What are the main differences between gray whales and orcas?
6. What technique did the author use in writing this article to make the aquarium come alive for the reader? How did you decide?

Writing to Learn

THINK AND COMPARE   Select an interesting creature or object. Compare your choice to something else, as in this example:

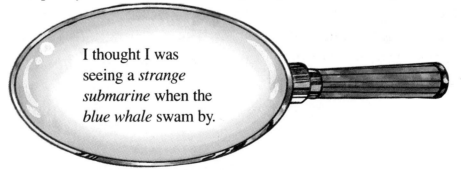

I thought I was seeing a *strange submarine* when the *blue whale* swam by.

WRITE   Compose a description that shows how the creature or object you chose is like something else.

The Lobster Quadrille

"Will you walk a little faster?" said a whiting to a snail,
"There's a porpoise close behind us, and he's treading on
my tail.
See how eagerly the lobsters and the turtles all advance!
They are waiting on the shingle— will you come and join
the dance?
Will you, won't you, will you, won't you, will you join
the dance?
Will you, won't you, will you, won't you, won't you join
the dance?

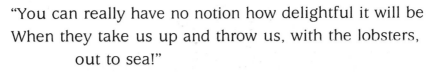

"You can really have no notion how delightful it will be
When they take us up and throw us, with the lobsters,
out to sea!"
But the snail replied "Too far, too far!" and gave a look
askance—
Said he thanked the whiting kindly, but he would not join
the dance.
Would not, could not, would not, could not, would not
join the dance.
Would not, could not, would not, could not, could not
join the dance.

"What matters it how far we go?" his scaly friend replied,
"There is another shore, you know, upon the other side.
The further off from England the nearer is to France—
Then turn not pale, beloved snail, but come and join the
dance.
Will you, won't you, will you, won't you, will you join
the dance?
Will you, won't you, will you, won't you, won't you join
the dance?"

Lewis Carroll

LITERATURE LINK

How do authors paint pictures with words?

—Winslow Homer, *Returning Fishing Boats*, 1883

What sort of day is this? Cold and damp perhaps. How does it feel to be aboard that sea-tossed boat?

Just as Winslow Homer used a brush to paint this picture, a writer can paint pictures with words. In fact, when writers paint with words, they're limited only by their imaginations. They can use words to create fantastic mental pictures for their readers.

Creating Vivid Pictures

Authors use sensory language to help readers imagine not only how something looks, but also how something sounds, smells, feels, or tastes. Here's what authors do to create vivid pictures with sensory language.

- They use concrete language that appeals to the five senses.
- They describe people, places, and things with specific and colorful details.
- They use words and phrases that draw readers into the scene.

Do you remember reading "Mafatu and the Ma'o" at the start of this unit? Here's an excerpt from that story:

> The fire crackled and snapped about the base of the tamanu tree. When at length it had eaten well into the trunk, Mafatu climbed aloft and crept cautiously out upon a large branch that overhung the beach. Then taking firm hold of the branches above his head, he began to jump up and down. As the fire ate deeper into the trunk, the tree began to lean under the boy's weight. With a snap and a crash, it fell across the sand. As it fell, Mafatu leaped free of the branches, as nimbly as a cat.

In this case, the author helps you imagine the scene by using words that appeal to your sense of hearing. What two words describe how the fire sounds while it's burning? How do the author's words help you hear the sound the tree makes when it finally falls across the sand?

On the next page is a later section of the same story. The author's vivid description helps you share Mafatu's experience.

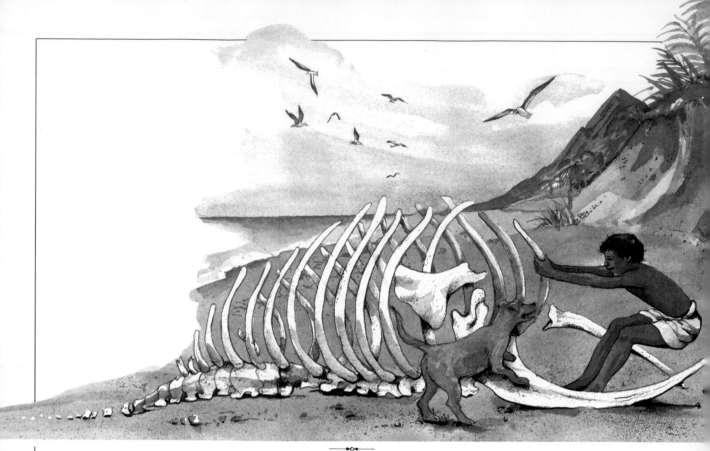

One morning, wandering far down the beach, Mafatu
came upon a sheltered cove. His heart gave a leap of joy; for
there, white-gleaming in the sun, was all that remained of the
skeleton of a whale. It might not have meant very much to
you or me; but to Mafatu it meant knives and fishhooks
galore, splintered bone for darts and spears, a shoulder blade
for an ax. It was a veritable treasure trove. The boy leaped up
and down in his excitement. "Uri!" he shouted. "We're rich!
Come — help me drag these bones home!"

His hands seemed all thumbs in his eagerness; he tied as
many bones as he could manage into two bundles. One
bundle he shouldered himself. The other Uri dragged behind
him. And thus they returned to the camp site, weary, but
filled with elation. Even the dog seemed to have some
understanding of what this discovery meant; or if not, he was
at least infected with his master's high spirits. He leaped
about like a sportive puppy, yapping until he was hoarse.

Now began the long process of grinding the knife and
the ax. Hour after long hour, squatting before a slab of basalt,
Mafatu worked and worked, until his hands were raw and
blistered and the sweat ran down into his eyes.

Learning About Literature/Author's Craft

Did the author's use of sensory language help you see the whale skeleton "white-gleaming in the sun"? Did it help you hear Uri "yapping until he was hoarse."

Now read one last excerpt from the story.

—◆—

The hammerhead approached the raft in leisurely fashion; it rolled over slightly, and its gaping jaws seemed to curve in a yawning grin. Uri ran to the edge of the raft, barking furiously; the hair on the dog's neck stood up in a bristling ridge. The shark, unconcerned, moved away. Then with a whip of its powerful tail it rushed at the bamboo fish trap and seized it in its jaws. Mafatu was struck dumb. The hammerhead shook the trap as a terrier might shake a rat.

—◆—

The author makes you feel as if you're right there looking at the "gaping jaws" and hearing Uri "barking furiously" as the shark "shook the trap as a terrier might shake a rat."

One important thing to know about sensory language is that it is not unique to fiction. Nonfiction writers, when they want readers to visualize the subjects and events they write about, often use words to create vivid and realistic pictures.

The next selection, "The Big Spring," is a nonfiction adventure of whales. The author, Jean Craighead George, is known for using sensory language to make real events come alive. Find words and phrases that appeal to your senses. Which images are so vivid that they make you feel as though you are there?

The Big Spring

by Jean Craighead George

Off the coast of Bandon, Oregon, a gray whale surfaced. Her seven-inch-long nostrils emerged first and blew a spout of air and water fifteen feet into the air. The column swooshed with a roar that could be heard for half a mile. Having exhaled, she then inhaled, and the breath came into her lungs with a whine, like wind rushing into a tunnel. Her nostrils closed over this salty gasp. A low wall of muscle arose around the nostrils like a frown and kept the water out. She submerged.

Four seconds later, her nose, which was on the top of her head, came up again. She gave four strong blows. The waves clapped around her. She snorted at them, then headed down into the corridors of the Pacific Ocean.

The female gray whale was 43 feet long. She weighed 34 tons. She was one of a group of animals that are the largest ever to live on this earth. Like all whales she was also hostess to many small beasts. On her back and over her mountain of a belly lived thousands of barnacles. They pulled their feet in and stopped kicking food into their mouths when their great hostess surfaced to breathe. They adjusted to her rising and diving, just as we adjust to the moods of the earth as it circles the sun.

This city-block-of-an-animal plunged forward for a thousand feet. Then she surfaced and peered over the ocean. She had no language, she made no vocal sounds, but she spied now and then to make sure her kinfolk were traveling with her.

Beside her swam her son, a 20-foot baby. He had been born in January in the California Bay, and now the two of them were on their way north to the Bering Sea—a long journey of 7,000 miles.

The mother plunged down into the green spring ocean and looked around. She was following a familiar canyon wall that she knew as well as you know your own street, for she had traveled along it every year for 20 years of her life. The submarine canyon was gray and dark, and lay like a great highway up the continental shelf. The whale knew exactly where she was.

Ahead of her loomed a sand barrier. She quickened her pace, for she knew she was coming to a cove. Once more she blew and looked around. She saw no other gray whales and sensed she was behind the main migration. At the sand bar she tasted the silt of Coos Bay and, because she could not feel the currents from her baby, slowed down, then stopped.

Her son was looking at a giant squid. The mother attracted his attention by crunching her wide teeth, the only sound she could make, but an effective one. The baby spurted to her side. He was eager and energetic. He whooshed friskily to the surface and peered around. He saw boats and lighthouses. This was his first trip to the summer rendezvous of the gray whales—the Bering Sea. His mother was teaching him the underwater landmarks, for in the fall he would have to travel back alone in the manner of the gray whale. Their migration was not a social affair. Each whale made the exhausting trip by itself.

The mother whale swung over the delta at the mouth of the bay and crunched her teeth again. Her son came down to her. She was taking the water from the bay in and out of her mouth. He did likewise, and the taste of the bay was forever imprinted on his senses. Each bay and cove and canyon had to be memorized in this manner, by taste, by sight, and by currents that eddied and pulled, for each was different in every inlet along the great California coast.

The mother plunged over the sand bar. The whale child followed. For a moment they lingered in the different water pressures, feeling all the details of this place with their throat grooves, the openings under their necks that were sensitive to pressures, to currents and eddies.

The mother delayed long here as if to impress this particular spot on the youngster. From here they would take out to sea, and the underwater world of the continent would be replaced by the deeps of the Pacific. From here on it would be all pressure memories. The whale child circled gently, biting the sand, filtering the water in and learning.

Then they hurried on—a thousand feet at a run. They swam to the edge of the continental shelf.

Suddenly the whale child looked back. He whirled in panic. Coos Bay appeared different from the north. He turned and flipped back to the sand bar, tasting the salts and minerals once more, feeling the texture of the water, trying to learn well. When he was satisfied with his impressions he tailed out to meet his mother. But she was gone.

The life of the gray whale is silent for the most part, a grind on their plankton-filtering teeth, a noisy blow. Over the sea canyon walls, ticking and rasping like the beat of a tin cup on a wooden table, came the rare "distress" sound made by the clicking teeth of the baby whale.

He was lost. He surfaced, blew a great column of air and water and pulled himself skyward so high his whole chest was out. All he saw was a trawling boat harvesting the bottom-

dwelling fish. He saw no mother. He glanced at the boat again. It was big, it might be a whale. He headed for it, spying tentatively as he went.

The boat was gray like his mother and covered with barnacles. Rising and blowing he came up to the object. But the whale child drew back. The wooden whale was too small, the wrong design, the wrong scent, and the water that surrounded it was not warmed by the mammal body. Oil seeped from it.

The young whale fled in terror, diving into unfamiliar hills and valleys. His eyes rolled as he searched. Schools of fish felt him on their lateral lines and wheeled away. He plunged on, but saw no sand barrier, tasted nothing familiar.

He cried into the ocean, tapping out his bleat that traveled swiftly for hundreds of yards and then faded against the coastal reefs.

As the sun went down, lopsided as it reached the horizon, the giant child circled and circled the empty waters. He spied out and looked until he was tired. Finally he slept. His flippers, once the feet of his land-walking ancestors, hung down into the sea. His nostrils were barely above the surface.

Two hours later the young whale awoke. His skin was cold and he turned sleepily to nurse. Then he remembered that his mother was not around. He swirled in panic. He breached, head in the air, fins out. He saw the land, and knew this was where he must begin to retrace his steps. He swam south.

No adult gray whales eat on the long eight-month migration, nor do they eat in the bays where they give birth to their young and remate. No other beast can go so long without eating and still be active. Woodchucks, ground squirrels, bears feed all summer, and starve all winter; but they sleep during their starvation and do not use much energy. Not the gray whale. This beast swims constantly while starving, with the exception of the babies that nurse on the trip north.

And so, the giant whale child sucked in the ocean because he was hungry and weak. He filtered out the plankton through odd rows of baleen teeth that were more like sieves than teeth. Then he rolled southward in fear and fright.

At noon he found Coos Bay. He knew its taste. His mother had taught him this. Swimming to the familiar barrier he tapped his jaws together and called. There was no answer in all the vast ocean. The young whale drifted into the cove. It was familiar. He had been born in a cove, in the low hot waters of California Bay where flats shone white in the dry land. The young whale spied upon the shore. It was different from his first home; there were tall trees and lush plants. The strangeness alarmed him, and he submerged for his ten minutes underwater. The bars, the shallows, the light that flickered from the sun down into the bay were comforting. But he saw no whales. There had been thousands in the bay of his birth. This was a desolate cove.

The young whale felt strong instincts pulling him, and occasionally he swam to the mouth of the bay and looked north, for gray whales work on appointments with their needs. They must give birth to calves in the protected lagoons. They must depart on schedule to travel the 7,000 miles to the only food they eat—the plankton of the Bering Sea—and they must get there on time, or they starve to death. Again in the fall they must leave on schedule in order to reach the bays in time to have their babies in the protected waters. Any interference with this timing means death to the whales.

The young whale child tapped his teeth and circled Coos Bay. He had been born in January, a magnificent male of sixteen feet. Upon his arrival in the whale world, he had been immediately nuzzled by his giant mother, who, without arms or feet with which to hug him, expressed her love by circling him. She led him to the surface to blow, then, tipping her body, she showed him where to find her milk.

The rest of the two months in the lagoon were reassuring to the young whale child. Hundreds of other whales slept and rolled with him, each one awakening instinctively before the tide went out and beached him, an event which means certain death to a whale, for they are helpless on the land. The whale child learned to avoid being stranded. He met other young whales, and by meeting them, knew what he was.

In March there were fewer and fewer of his kind in the bay, for the great migration had started north. Finally his mother beat her tail, crunched her teeth and led him around the sand bars, over hills, and out into the sea. He stayed close to her big side. She paused beyond the bay channel to teach him the tastes and pressures of his birthplace. Then she spanked him forward to keep her schedule with the burst of spring in the Bering Sea.

The young whale felt pressures and tastes in Coos Bay similar to those he knew as an infant, and so he lingered, blowing and swirling over the bottom. By night he would swim toward the shore, and by day he would move to the entrance, feeling the pull of his species toward the dark waters of the north. But he did not know how to go.

And so he stayed where he was.

The days passed. His mother did not return. The huge child grew weak with longing and hunger. He could not know that they had lost each other as she had spurted forward to drive a killer whale from their path. Killer whales never kill adult gray whales, but they compete for the same waters; and so to protect their rights, they molest the young. Over the eons the gray whale has learned peace by avoidance. They keep to the bottom. The killers keep to the surface.

But all life is chance. A killer whale and the whale child's mother had met, and she responded to an old instinct. She chased him. From that moment on their separation became greater as the mother moved instinctively north searching for her child in an effort to keep her schedule with June in the Bering Sea. And the child, following the instincts of the young, looked for familiar waters.

A week later the tired whale child came up to the shores of Coos Bay where people moved and boats were tied. In loneliness he watched the boats. They were almost as big as his mother. One night he nuzzled one. And close beside its purring motors he fell asleep.

But as he slept he breathed like a wind tunnel. The owner of the yacht heard the strange sound and came out to see if a storm were brewing.

He looked down into the water and saw the young whale sleeping happily against his ship. He stared again to make sure, then paced the entire length of his deck until he came to the end of the baby. An unmistakable whale tail lay under the water. He radioed the Marine Laboratory and he radioed the Fish and Wildlife Service.

At dawn the lost whale child was a captive.

The excitement was great. During the night the men had enclosed him in a great wire fence, and they all stood and stared at him as he snapped and rolled.

Gray whales had almost become extinct in the Pacific Ocean during the whaling years in the nineteenth century, but with laws prohibiting their killing, they had increased in numbers. Nevertheless the ships and boats on the Pacific often frightened them and diverted them from keeping their precise schedules with the plankton and the bays. And these delays spelled their death.

So the scientists in Coos Bay were thrilled to be able to study a live gray whale. They measured and weighed him. They noted the movements of the whale child, they put microphones in the water to record any sounds he might make, and they watched him judge the tide and swim to the deepest pocket of his cage when it went out. They took his temperature and analyzed his blood.

To feed him they poured nutrients into the water that were similar to the nutrition in the plankton. The formula came from studies made on the stomachs of other gray whales that had washed ashore in the past. The scientists were coming to a new understanding of this remarkable beast, and they were excited.

Meanwhile the remarkable beast grew weaker and weaker, for the plankton formula was not what he needed.

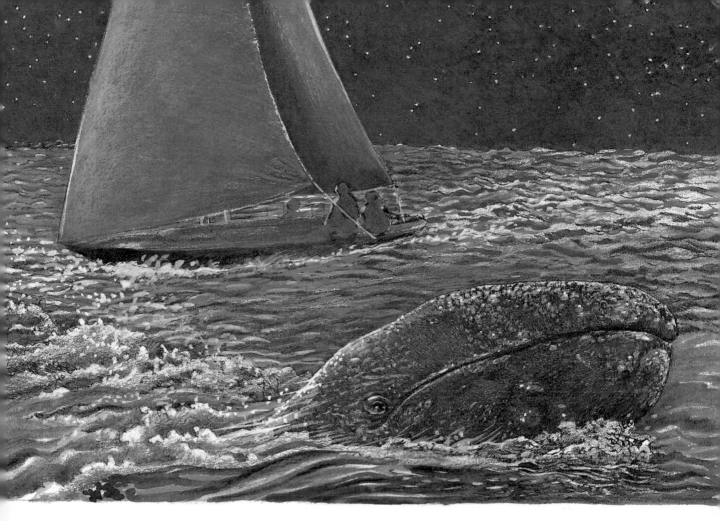

He needed his mother's milk. He cried at night, and eyed the men by day.

Then one night a small craft, sailing out into the ocean, was rocked by an enormous object just off the sand bar at the lighthouse. The boat was thrown off course by the swell. Its crew peered into the water to see if they had struck anything, but the sea was black. Only a trail of phosphorescent animals told them something big had passed down the channel into the bay. They gave the incident little thought, for their boat righted itself quickly and purred on out to sea.

The next morning when the scientists came to take a cardiograph of the young whale, they were distressed to find the fence crunched like paper—and the whale child gone.

Far out at sea a mother whale and her son blew four times and submerged to follow green currents in the depths of the Pacific Ocean. The mother lingered to teach her son the pressure and weight of these bleak waters. She was very patient, and her child was serious and obedient.

A school of sharks circled them as they plunged over the edge of the continental shelf and thundered north, for the belly of the female bore toothlike gashes—as if raked by a wire fence.

As they followed the watery highways, known only to the gray whales, the "roadsides" were spangled with the signs of spring. Diatoms bloomed, copepods glittered among the diatoms, fish glimmered as they tossed their silver eggs to the sea, and clams siphoned the bright water in and out of their valves; for it was springtime in the ocean.

◆ LIBRARY LINK ◆

Would you like to know more about the mysterious sea? Read Spring Comes to the Ocean *by Jean Craighead George, from which this selection is excerpted.*

 Reader's Response

What do you think was most remarkable about the younger whale's behavior?

The Big Spring

Thinking It Over

1. When the story began, the mother whale was taking her son to the Bering Sea. Why were they going there?
2. How did learning underwater landmarks help the baby whale?
3. Why did the baby whale return to Coos Bay?
4. Do you think it was right or wrong for the scientists to catch the baby whale? Explain your answer.
5. After he was caught, the baby whale grew weaker every day. What happened next? How did the story end?
6. Imagine that the baby whale had stayed in Coos Bay. How might the story have ended? What makes you think so?

Writing to Learn

THINK AND QUESTION   If you were going to write a question for your classmates about "The Big Spring," what would you want to ask? Add to the list of topics below.

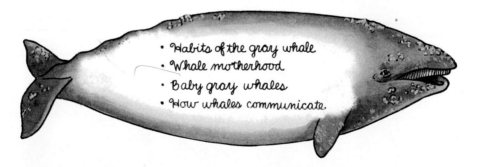

- Habits of the gray whale
- Whale motherhood
- Baby gray whales
- How whales communicate.

WRITE   Use the list of topics to focus your questions. Write three essay questions about "The Big Spring." Then write your answer to the question you think is most interesting.

Lee Bennett Hopkins
INTERVIEWS

Laurence Yep

Laurence Yep was born in San Francisco, California, where his parents owned a little grocery store. Mr. Yep, like the character Craig Chin in his novel *Sea Glass*, "wheeled piles of boxes into the store on a creaky hand truck" and did other odd jobs.

As a child he attended parochial school in San Francisco's Chinatown. He felt like an outsider at the school because he did not speak Chinese.

"Growing up as a Chinese-American in San Francisco, I found few books which dealt with my own experiences. I lived in a predominantly black area but commuted by bus every day to a bilingual school in Chinatown. Stories set on farms, or in the suburbs, or in Midwestern small towns were less real to me than science fiction or fantasy. Science fiction and fantasy dealt with strategies of survival, people adapting to strange new lands and worlds, or some fantastic or alien creatures adjusting to ours. Adapting to different environments and cultures happened each time I got off the bus.

"When I was eleven years old, I enjoyed Andre Norton's ability to conjure up other worlds; the world in her book *Star Born* was one of my favorites. For me, it was a *spellbinding* book in the fullest sense of the word. When I was fifteen, Ray Bradbury became another of my favorite authors, especially his *Martian Chronicles*."

This love of science fiction influenced Mr. Yep to begin writing short stories. At the age of eighteen, while a freshman in college, he became a published writer. He sold his first story to the science fiction magazine *Worlds of If*. He was paid a penny a word.

"The story took me about six months to write," he said. "I was paid ninety dollars for it. It sounds like a lot of money until you consider how much time I put into that story."

After the publication of the story, he began writing science fiction professionally. "I got four rejections for every acceptance," he said. "I took a lot of hard knocks from editors and publishers who told me I couldn't write, but I kept on."

A long-time friend, Joanne Ryder, a poet and writer of children's books, was working at a major New York publishing house and encouraged him to try writing a science fiction novel for girls and boys. The result was his first book, *Sweetwater*, published in 1973.

Two years later, his second novel, *Dragonwings,* appeared. *Dragonwings* garnered a host of awards including a 1976 Newbery Honor Book award. One book reviewer called the novel "an exquisitely written poem of praise to the courage and ingenuity of the Chinese-American people . . . a triumph."

Other novels followed, including *Child of the Owl*, *Dragon of the Sea*, *Dragon Steel*, *The Serpent's Children*, *The Mark Twain Murders*, and *The Tom Sawyer Fires*.

Although he is an accomplished writer, writing does not always come easy to Mr. Yep. "For me writing is a long, hard, painful process. I write about three thousand words a day. Every book I do takes about three or four rewrites. Since each novel goes about sixty- to seventy-thousand words, it takes quite a bit of writing.

"To me, however, writing is addictive. If I don't get to write at least three or four times a week, I start getting very angry with people, very annoyed. Writing is really a pleasure that I seek out actively, and I try to set out a certain number of hours for it. I have a special area where I live where I do my writing. I sit down and

things start coming. But it took me a long time to get there because it is not an easy thing to forget suddenly that you are sitting at your desk by a computer with your bedroom wall in front of you, and to imagine that you are really on Mars or in some far-away world among alien kinds of creatures. That's why it is important, I think, to have special boundaries that you set around yourself—special times, special places, special situations—where your sense of the work breaks down, when imagination starts to come."

I asked Mr. Yep if he had any advice to give to young writers.

"My advice to young writers is this: Read a lot. Read to find out what past writers have done. There are different ways of setting up characters. You can set characters by the way they look, by the way they dress; you can confine it just to the way they talk without ever describing them. One way you can find out about creating characters is to read good books. Find out how other good writers have accomplished the art of creating.

"Once you start picking up on these little techniques, you should begin to write about what you know. Write about your own

school, your class, about your teachers, your family. That's what I did. Each writer must find his or her own voice.

"As young writers, you have to keep on writing. You have to realize that even though you may feel great about what you write, it may not actually be that good at first. It may need more rewrites. You may have to rewrite one single scene four or five times before it will be interesting enough for readers to enjoy."

Besides writing novels for young adults, Mr. Yep has written books for adults and several one-act plays that were produced in California.

He still lives in San Francisco, a city he truly loves. "What fascinates you so much about San Francisco?" I asked him. As soon as I mentioned the city, Mr. Yep beamed.

"In San Francisco," he told me, "the whole world comes to you. You don't have to go anywhere for it! I love my town and my roots there."

The next selection you will read is from Mr. Yep's novel *Sea Glass*. I asked Mr. Yep how long it took him to write this book.

"With all of my novels," he said, "it takes me as long as I *feel* it. I constantly look for a challenge in my work and am always searching for new angles to old problems. *Sea Glass* was a challenge to write. But, then, all my work is a challenge. It's just like life, isn't it?"

Reader's Response

What advice given by Mr. Yep will you remember and try to use in your own writing?

LEE BENNETT HOPKINS INTERVIEWS

Laurence Yep

Thinking It Over

1. Do you think Yep's fascination with science fiction as a child had a positive effect on his life? What led you to your answer?
2. Why do you think Yep kept on writing, even though some editors told him he couldn't write?
3. How do the boundaries that Yep sets up for himself help him write?
4. Yep said that writing is "a long, hard, painful process" for him, yet that writing is a pleasure that he seeks actively. How can both statements be true?
5. How do you think Yep's writing career might have been affected if the story he had tried to publish while in college had been rejected?

Writing to Learn

THINK AND RECALL Laurence Yep, an award-winning author, gives advice to young authors. Copy and complete this cluster of his suggestions.

WRITE Choose one of Mr. Yep's suggestions about writing, and explain in a paragraph how you think this suggestion can help you as a writer.

HARPER TROPHY

The Big Wave
Pearl S. Buck

To live in the midst of danger is
to know how good life is.

from *The Big Wave* by Pearl S. Buck

Pearl S. Buck, the author of *The Big Wave*, was the first American woman to win the Nobel Prize for Literature. She lived for many years in Japan and China and helped the United States establish better relations with those countries. In *The Big Wave*, Buck introduces Kino and Jiya, two Japanese boys facing a double danger of natural disasters: Their homes lie between the menacing ocean and an unpredictable volcano.

Kino is a poor farmer's son who lives on a mountainside above the ocean. His friend Jiya, the son of a poor fisherman, lives in a small fishing village on the beach below. On hot, sunny days, the two often meet there to swim in the ocean, which Kino finds "beautiful," but Jiya sees as "the enemy." That is why the houses in the fishing village have no windows facing their "enemy," the sea. If they had had windows, perhaps the villagers would have seen signs of a huge tidal wave erupting deep in the ocean. The big wave destroys the village and leaves Jiya homeless and alone, to be taken in by Kino's family as a son. *The Big Wave* tells the story of how these two boys learn to live with the dangers their land brings them.

Craig knew his uncle would be able to teach him many things about his ocean cove. But he never dreamed he would find a secret garden there.

The
Sea Garden

by Laurence Yep
from *Sea Glass*

That Saturday Uncle was already down on the beach. He looked thin and bony and sinewy as he sat with his jacket draped around his shoulders. I turned the wagon around and pushed it before me through the gate. Then I leaned back on my heels and gently lowered it down the path, trying not to look to my right where the edge of the path was. Uncle didn't look up even though the old wagon rattled noisily down the rocky path.

I lifted the carton of groceries out of the wagon onto the porch, sliding it over toward the door. Then I put the old carton with the garbage into the wagon and parked it against the

430

porch so it wouldn't roll down. One lonely sea gull wheeled about, crying over the calm waters of the cove. "Afternoon," I called down to him. My voice echoed on the rocks but Uncle didn't turn around. He just waved his hand vaguely in the air.

I picked up my towel, which was rolled into a cylinder, and with that tucked under my arm I went down to the beach. The tide was really low today. The beach was a lot bigger and I could see a lot of the reef. At the foot of the path, I began to slog across the sand toward where Uncle sat. "I didn't squeeze the bread this time."

"I wait and see." Uncle had a small crowbar in his hand. It was tied to his wrist by a thong. I watched as Uncle slipped the end of the crowbar between the shell and the tan flesh of an abalone.

"You went diving for abalone without me." I stared at him accusingly.

When Uncle had the crowbar positioned just the way he wanted, he shoved it in hard. I suppose he must have broken the abalone's hold on its shell, because he pried it out easily, dropping it into a basket. "I walk through my gardens and I find this one."

I looked around the cove, but it looked especially empty and lifeless now. Even the gull was off to some other place. There were barnacles on the cliffsides, but they were above the water so they were shut up tight and I didn't think they counted. To me, anyway, it looked like the only living things there were me and Uncle.

"What gardens?" I asked skeptically.

Uncle smiled as if it were his secret. "I thought you were one smart boy. Can't you see them?" He slipped the thong on the crowbar from his wrist and dropped it into the basket.

"No, I can't." Sullenly I folded my arms across my chest.

"You think maybe you see, but you don't. Not really." He pointed at my eyes. "Your eyes, they tell your mind a lot of stuff. But your mind, he's one busy fellow. He say, 'I don't have time to listen. Fill out these forms.' So the eyes, they fill out the forms, but there's no place on the forms for everything they see. Just a lot of boxes they are supposed to mark or not. So your mind, he misses a lot." Uncle nodded his head firmly. "You gotta look at the world. Really look."

"Like you?" I was beginning to feel impatient with Uncle.

"No. I only do it in a small, small way. But if you can make your mind listen to your eyes, really listen, what wonders you see." Uncle searched my face, looking for some sign of comprehension, but I could only look at him in confusion. Uncle smiled to himself sadly. He pretended to become stern. "Well, you want to swim, or talk, boy?"

"Let's swim." I started to undress self-consciously on the beach. I was already wearing my swimming trunks underneath my pants, so it didn't take me long. In the meantime, Uncle had shrugged off his jacket and waded into the water to begin swimming. I stared at him in surprise.

He moved almost as quickly and easily through the water as the otter we had seen. There was nothing wasted about his motions when he swam. It was pure, simple, graceful.

"Come on." Uncle turned to me from the water. "You just remember one thing. The currents in my cove, they aren't very strong, but even so, don't fight them."

I adjusted the waistband of my trunks over my stomach, knowing that the waistband would slide back under my belly before long.

Uncle hadn't shivered or said anything when he'd walked into the water. You'd have thought it was warm bathwater to him. But I gave a yelp the moment I waded into the water. The water felt so cold that it felt like someone had been chilling it in the refrigerator. I could feel the goose bumps popping out all over my skin, and I began to shake and to huddle up and hold myself.

Uncle waved one hand from where he was floating. "Come on. You get used to it."

I nodded nervously and kept on walking. I felt the beach slope downward sharply, and I immediately found myself in the water up to my chest. The sea wasn't very pleasant to move around in, but it was better than that first moment of shock. Then a wave broke against the reef and spray went flying and the sea surged through the narrow opening. The pull of the sudden current wasn't all that strong, but it caught me by surprise so I got knocked off my feet.

I couldn't see. There was only the clouded, stinging salt water all around me. I flailed with my arms, trying to get my feet on something solid, but I couldn't find anything. And then I felt the current begin to draw me away from the beach as it began to flow out toward the sea. I really panicked then, forgetting everything I'd ever been taught. I wanted air. My lungs tried to drag it in, but all they got was salt water. I began to choke.

Then strong hands appeared magically, gripping me on either side. I tried to grab hold of Uncle. Something. Anything, as long as I could hold on to it. Somehow, though, Uncle managed to avoid me. My head broke above the surface. I could see the light for a moment before the salt water, running down my face, made my eyes close. I gasped, coughed, and gasped again, trying to get the film of seawater out of my lungs.

Uncle's strong hands pulled me steadily in toward the beach. Then I could feel firm sand under me. I stumbled. Uncle's hands held me up until I got my balance. I started to stagger toward the beach with Uncle supporting me. Gratefully I felt the air around my shoulders and then my chest and then my stomach. I stretched my arms out like a blind man and stumbled out of the surf to fall onto the beach. I lay on my stomach for a moment, coughing and spitting. I could still feel the sea pulling at my ankles, so I crawled another yard farther up the beach. The sea swept higher. I could feel it tugging at my ankles again, as if it were alive and trying to drag me back in.

Then I felt Uncle's shadow as he sat down heavily beside me. "You sure you can swim, boy?"

I sat up, beginning to shiver. Uncle covered my shoulders with my towel. With one corner of the towel I wiped at my face. "I could have told you. I'm just too fat and clumsy. Sorry."

Uncle put on his ragged jacket and sat down. "You feel too sorry for yourself. And that's not good."

"Are you crazy?" I started to shiver, so I pulled the towel tighter around my neck.

"You're the crazy one." Uncle flung sand over his legs. "You want to stay on the beach when you can be out in the water."

"Drowning isn't my idea of fun." I wiped some of the water from my face.

Uncle put his hands behind him and leaned back. "Well, maybe if you're scared . . ."

With a corner of my towel I finished drying my face. "Who said I was scared?"

"Me," Uncle said. "I say you're scared."

"Nothing scares me," I insisted.

Tunelessly Uncle hummed to himself and tapped his fingers against the sand.

"Well, even if I am," I mumbled, "it's stupid to do something just to prove I'm not scared."

"Yes, no, maybe so. Something good shouldn't scare you."

Uncle began to rub his palms together so that the sand sprinkled down. "Maybe I ask you to put your head on a railroad track, and you say no, well, that's different."

"I'm still not going in." I shook my head for emphasis.

Uncle worried at the nail of one finger. Some sand got on his lips. "You can walk on the water then?" Uncle smiled, amused.

I liked Uncle when he said that. I mean, Dad would have gone on shouting or wheedling or both, but instead Uncle turned the whole thing into a joke. He seemed to relax then. "You want to go for a walk instead?" He nodded at the beach. "I mean on solid ground?"

"Sure," I said, even though the cove wasn't more than twenty yards wide at any point.

Uncle rose and started across the wet sand toward the cliffs on one side of the cove, and I followed him. When he was by the cliffs, Uncle pointed to the walls above the water at the foot-wide bands of chalky little white bumps. "These are barnacles, and those"—he gestured at a blackish band about a foot wide below them—"are mussels." The bands looked like they were painted on both sides of the cove where the tide would reach it about a yard above its present level. "The water's out or they'd all be open to eat the little things in the water."

"And you see the starfish?" Uncle pointed at the water where there was a bright orange spot just below the surface. "He's waiting now. When the water gets higher, he will climb back up to the barnacles and mussels." We waded cautiously into the surf; and, as the water sucked at my ankles, he took my wrist and guided it under the water. I felt the rough surface of the starfish. Uncle let go of my wrist and I traced the shape of the starfish and felt the five legs, one of them curled up slightly. My fingers closed round the body of the starfish and I gave a tug; but it felt as if it were part of the cliff wall.

Uncle laughed in delight, like a kid sharing a new toy with someone else. "You want a starfish, you need a crowbar. Once a starfish sits, nobody can pull it up."

I let go of the starfish. "Is this your garden then?" I looked around the cove, feeling disappointed. The bands of mussels and barnacles and the starfish didn't make up a sea garden in my mind.

"I bet you think this is one real crazy old man, right?" Uncle asked. He bent over so that his hands were near the waterline and ran his hands lightly over the face of the barnacles that were clustered so tightly together. He did it lightly, or the rough faces of the barnacles might have cut up his hands. Suddenly he gave a yelp. He lifted out his hand, and I saw clinging to it a long, greenish-brown worm with lots of legs. And then it let go and dropped with a plunk back into the sea.

"Did it hurt?" I asked.

"No, see, not even the skin's broken." He showed me the finger. "That's the hunter that stalks and kills, and this whole place is his jungle." He indicated the bands of mussels and barnacles. "And this is just the start of my garden." Uncle smiled, both proud and pleased—like someone who knows a secret that you do not. "Too bad you don't want to see more of it."

I looked uncertainly at the cove. "You mean I have to swim?"

"Out there." He pointed to the reef that was exposed at low tide.

He was one shameless old man to tempt me that way and he knew it. I almost refused again, but I have to admit I was curious about that garden of his.

"Okay. I'll try just once more," I grumbled.

"We'll stay in the shallow end. Then, if you feel good, we can go out." Uncle walked farther into the water and half turned around as he took off his jacket. I whipped the towel off my shoulders and threw it high up on the beach. Uncle threw his jacket beside it. I waded into the sea until I was waist deep. I kept waiting for Uncle to shout instructions at me the way Dad would have, but he didn't.

I took a deep breath. Then another good one. Holding my arms ahead of me, I bent forward and kicked off from the sand. There was that shock for a moment of letting go of the land, and then I was floating. The cold water didn't feel so bad this time. I twisted my head to the side and breathed in the air and then slid over, floating on my back, letting the sun warm my face and skin.

Uncle began swimming in the water toward me. The spray from his splashing sent a drizzle over me, and then his body was floating alongside of me. He didn't shout anything at me or

tell me how to do things better; he just warned me, "Careful. Don't go out too far."

So we stayed floating on our backs for a few minutes.

"Do you want to swim out to the reef?" I asked Uncle finally.

"Oh-kay." Uncle grinned. He started to move his arms, raising a glittering shower around his head as he swam out toward the rock reef. I followed him much more slowly and clumsily. Once Uncle was at the reef, he stretched out his arms and clung to a large boulder, hoisting himself up. He perched on the boulder with all the ease of a sea gull, as if he had done this thousands of times. I suppose he had if you thought about all the years he had spent in the cove.

Aware of Uncle watching me, I kept on churning toward the reef. I thought he might have some instructions for improvement by now, but still he didn't say anything.

Instead, he only reached out one hand. I clasped it and Uncle almost pulled me up out of the water to sit beside him—I mean, as if he were as rooted as a starfish to that boulder.

"What—?" I began.

"Shhh. Listen." Uncle swept his hand along, palm downward and parallel to the sea, in a short, sharp gesture for quiet.

At first, though, my main concern was getting a better grip on that big rock, but then as I sat there, I could feel the rhythm of the sea surging against the rocky reef that protected the cove, trying to make the opening in the reef bigger. The sea wasn't pounding so much as steadily pushing, as if it knew it had all the time in the world and could be patient. But after sitting there for a while, I almost felt like the reef was living and I could feel its heart beating.

Even now at low tide, I could feel the fine mist in the air—I suppose it was spray from the waves moving against the reef. But it felt almost like the breath of the rocks around me, breathing slowly and quietly along with the beating of the reef's heart.

"We'll start up there, boy." Uncle pointed toward the top of the reef.

"What about the big waves?" I was too interested to pay attention to the cold air.

Uncle shook his head. "I don't think there will be any more. And if there are, the reef will protect us." He patted a rock affectionately. Then he turned and began climbing. I followed him more cautiously the three feet or so to the top of the reef, and then I turned my head back in toward the cove.

Uncle waved his hand to indicate both sides of the reef. "When the sea goes out, all around here—maybe in little cracks, maybe on ledges—there are pools left. And the rocks, maybe they protect the pools so the big strong waves"—Uncle pantomimed a crashing wave stopped short—"the waves can't reach the pools. Then all kinds of things can grow." He spoke slowly and proudly, as if he were just about to pry up the lid to a treasure chest.

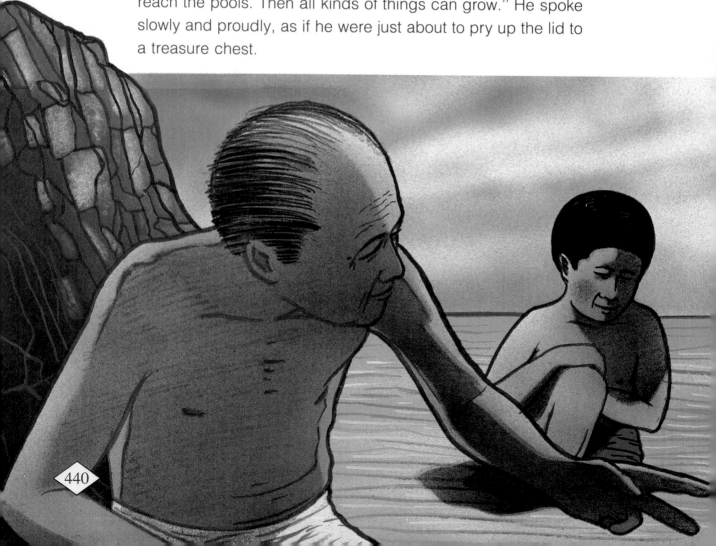

At that moment to my right—from a crevice I thought would be too small for anything to live in—a bright blue-and-purple crab scuttled out. It was only a few inches across. It paused when it saw us, and lifted its claws, ready to defend itself. Tiny bubbles frothed at its mouth.

Uncle reached across my lap to wiggle a finger above its head just out of the reach of its claws. The crab scuttled back into its crevice. "The brave, bold hero," Uncle said with a laugh. "Maybe when he goes home, he tells a lot of tales about fighting us." Carefully Uncle stood up then. He held out his hand, and I took it for support as I got slowly to my feet.

"Now do what I do." Confidently, Uncle turned his back to the sea and began to edge sideways along the top of the reef.

Uncle made it look real easy, but I found myself spreading my arms for better balance and I began to wish the rocks wouldn't vibrate. It was like walking on the back of some sleeping snake that might wake up and shake me off at any moment.

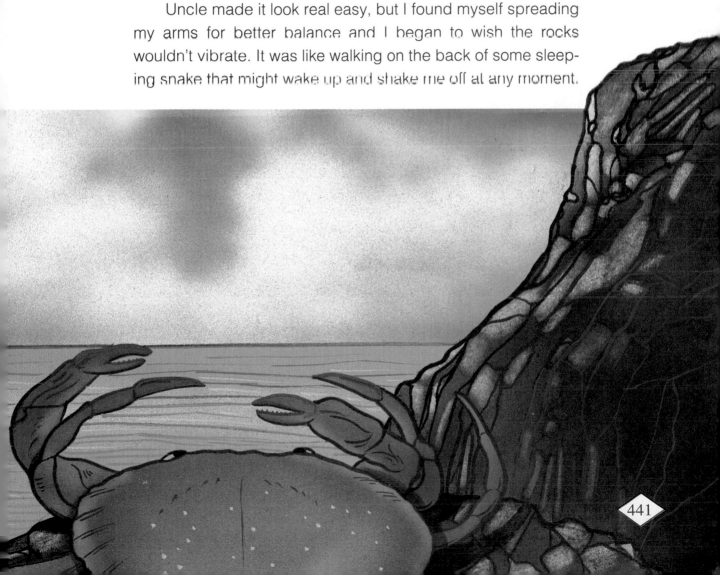

441

Uncle stopped where two rectangular slabs of rock leaned their tips against one another. One rock faced toward the sea, the other faced toward the cove. He waited shyly for me. I looked down between the rocks. There was a shallow depression on the giant boulder on which the two slabs rested. I caught my breath. The stone looked gray-black when it was wet, and the seawater was almost clear here; and in the daylight, the colors seemed even brighter. There were anemones of all colors—animals shaped like flowers, whose thin petals moved with a life of their own in the still water. Uncle leaned forward, supporting himself against the slabs. His hand barely stirred the surface of the pool as his finger brushed the petals of a red anemone. In the wink of an eye, the anemone had closed up, looking like a fat, bumpy doughnut. The other anemones closed up too. Uncle removed his hand from the pool. We waited for a little while until one by one they opened once

again. They were all kinds of bright colors—orange, red, yellow, solid colors that would make any artist ache inside to be able to use.

Uncle paused where a flat slab of rock leaned against the top of the reef. He pointed inside. "Can you see it?"

I looked in at the shadows. It looked like a big ball of spines within the water under the slab. "What is it?"

"A sea urchin," Uncle explained. "It came up into the high tide pools."

Even as we watched, the sea urchin retreated farther into the shadows by moving its needle-like spines.

From there we climbed lower on the reef to the top of a small boulder which had crumbled. Uncle squatted down. I did the same.

Uncle waited, hands clasped, arms resting on top of his thighs. He looked like he could stay in that position forever.

"There." Uncle pointed carefully to the shadow of a rock, at a slug-like thing with little stubby tubes at one end and the rest of its back covered with bright orange-red spots. It crept upside down across the pool as if the surface was a floor to it. Behind it, it left a little silver thread.

"He leaves a trail behind him. You know, like a land slug, that's his cousin. See that silver line? That's it. Watch what happens when I break it." Uncle reached down and touched the silvery thread behind the slug. The slug fell slowly through the water as if whatever invisible wires held it up had suddenly broken. When it landed gently on its back on the bottom of the pool, it slowly twisted about in the water, righting itself, and began crawling up the side again. "He keeps on trying, so I know he's gonna get cross."

Uncle stood up, wiping his hands on the side of his swimming trunks. "You know all the pools around here. Well, some of them are big. Some of them are small. And every pool is cut off from the other. Maybe the pools are this far apart." Uncle held his hands an inch from each other. "But the pools, they might as well be miles and miles apart because the animal in one pool won't know about an animal in another pool. You take any animal around here and it would probably think its own pool is the whole world, and it doesn't know there are pools and pools all around it." Uncle sounded awed by the magic and vastness of what he owned.

The sea must have been rising higher because the waves were beginning to splash over the top of the reef. I hadn't noticed the narrow little channel before—it was really more like a scratch along the surface of the rocks. But the anemones' pool at the top of the reef must have begun to fill up, because a little trickle of water began to snake its way down into the pool of the sea urchin and then slipped down the channel again, rounded a corner, and slid in a curve down the surface of a rock, into the pool of the slug and on. So Uncle wasn't exactly right. There was a little thread of water connecting the tide pools sometimes before the sea did come in.

"I never dreamed there was so much to see," I said.

Uncle leaned forward and pretended to peer at something for emphasis. "You have to learn how to pay attention to things." He added, "But first you have to like yourself." He gave a tug to his trunks and sat down. "People who don't like themselves, they spend all their time looking at their faults. They don't have time to look at the world."

He glanced up at the top of the reef. We could see the spray rising in the air. The drizzle in the air was changing to more like a shower. "Maybe we should go back now," Uncle said. "This reef's not a good place when the tide rises."

◆ LIBRARY LINK ◆

If you would like to learn how Uncle Quail helps Craig find his niche, read Sea Glass *by Laurence Yep, from which this selection is excerpted.*

Reader's Response

How would you feel about exploring Uncle Quail's sea garden?

WRITING ABOUT READING

Writing a Sea Story

The sea provided an interesting background for each story in this unit. Characters faced the dangers of the sea and experienced its power. Now you will have an opportunity to create an original character and write a sea story of your own.

Every story has three basic elements: character, setting, and plot. Characters are often, but not always, people. For example, in "The Big Spring," a whale is the main character. The setting is the time and place the story happens. Even in stories about the sea, there are many possible settings: islands, lighthouses, ships, the ocean depths, sand dunes, and more. Each setting inspires its own story. The plot is what happens. It is a series of related events or actions that make up the story. In this unit, each of the main characters faced a problem presented by the sea. As the character tried to resolve the problem, the important events took place. Finally, there was an outcome, or end, to the story.

Prewriting

Begin by identifying a setting and a hero or heroine for your story. You yourself may be a character in the story if you wish. Then think of other characters for your story. Beside each character's name, write one or two descriptive words. You can use these words as the starting-point for developing the personality traits of each character.

Second, decide on a challenge for your main character. To think of ideas, review the challenges that characters in the unit faced.

Third, look at the story chart on the next page. Use the same questions to make a story chart for your story.

Story Chart

Question	Answer
Who is the main character?	Mafatu
What is the character's problem or challenge?	He wants to overcome feelings of fear or weakness.
What does the character do to meet the challenge?	He goes to sea and overcomes his fear.
How does this happen?	He kills a shark and saves his dog's life.

Writing

Write a story of three to five paragraphs. The story chart will help you begin your story. It will also give you ideas for episodes. If new ideas occur to you while you are writing, jot them down.

Revising

Check your story for clarity. Will readers be able to understand how the character meets the challenge? Make your sea adventure come to life by using active verbs and descriptive words. Create a title for your story.

Proofreading

If there is any dialogue in your story, make sure it is punctuated correctly.

Publishing

Assemble a class collection of stories. Place them together in a book called *The Challenge of the Sea*.

WORKING TOGETHER

Preparing Interview Questions

Information in the stories in this unit answered many questions about the power, danger, and inhabitants of the sea. Is there anything else you would like to know? Are you curious about how scientists can tell the age of a whale? One way to gather information about a subject is to interview an expert on that subject. As a group, you can develop a list of interview questions about sea-related topics.

To help the group work together well, take responsibility for one or more of these tasks:

♦ Encouraging everyone in the group to share ideas

♦ Recording the group's ideas

♦ Agreeing or disagreeing in a pleasant way

♦ Making sure everyone stays on the topic

Together, agree on a selection that is of special interest to your group. Talk about what you learned from reading it and what else you would like to know. Suggest and record questions that you might use to interview a recognized authority on the topic. Select four different questions. Take turns writing the questions down on a sheet of paper.

Reread your questions. Where might you find the answers? Everyone should be prepared to explain how you could get your questions answered.

BOOKS TO ENJOY

Abel's Island by William Steig *(Farrar, Straus & Giroux, 1976)* Abelard Hassam de Chirico Flint is a mouse accustomed to leisure. But a rainstorm sweeps him away from his comfortable life, and he winds up stranded on an island. Does this pampered mouse have the spunk to survive?

The Eyes of the Amaryllis by Natalie Babbitt *(Farrar, Straus & Giroux, 1977)* They say the sea never gives up its secrets. Yet Geneva Reade continues to wait for a message from her husband, who was lost at sea thirty years before.

Carry On, Mr. Bowditch by Jean L. Latham *(Houghton Mifflin, 1955)* People in eighteenth-century Salem think Nathaniel Bowditch is too small to be a sailor. But he is good at math and astronomy and masters the art of navigation. Sailors find they can't do without his skill.

Shadow Shark by Colin Thiele *(Harper, 1988)* Twelve-year-old Joe and his cousin Meg encounter a true test of courage on the south coast of Australia due to a shark hunt and a terrible accident.

Night Dive by Ann McGovern *(Macmillan, 1984)* A twelve-year-old girl is about to scuba dive at night for the first time. Her fear turns into awe as she explores a coral reef and the remains of an old shipwreck.

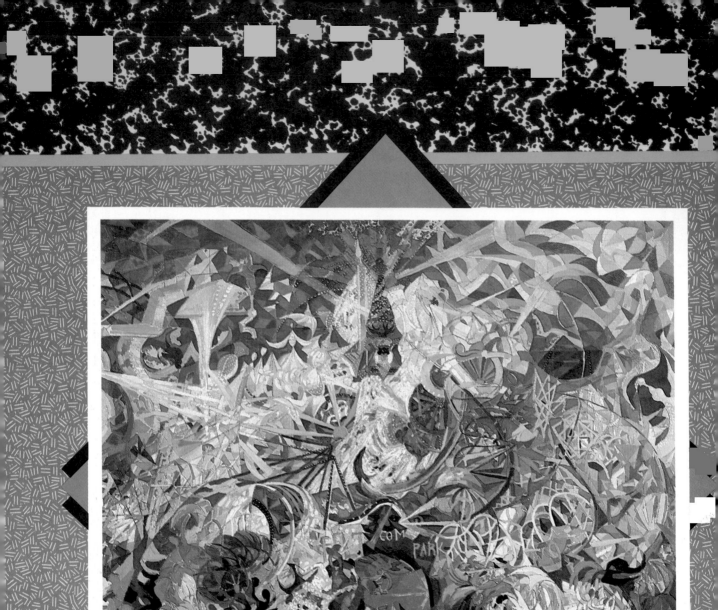

A WAY OF SEEING

*E*ach artist sees the world in a special way.

Why does art often appeal to writers as a subject for their writing?

BATTLE OF LIGHTS, CONEY ISLAND,
painting by Joseph Stella, American, 1913

Maria, a talented young artist, wants her art to be beautiful . . . but her mother insists that art must be true.

ART
MUST BE TRUE

by Jean Merrill

452

Maria had put off doing the assignment all week. Then last night, Friday night, she had opened her drawing pad on the kitchen table.

She had a new set of colored markers that Mama had bought her. She wanted to do a drawing with the markers.

She tried all the colors on the cover of the pad. Then she sat for a long time, staring at a clean sheet of drawing paper. Finally, she started to draw.

She drew a large white house with picture windows. The windows looked out over a wide lawn that sloped down to a pond.

Maria sketched in a winding driveway with birch trees on either side. To one side of the house, she drew a stone terrace and colored in some chairs, covered in a gay, striped cloth.

She wondered if she should put a car in the driveway. Or a station wagon.

No, she decided. Miss Lindstrom might have seen her getting off the Eastside bus in front of the museum.

At the far end of the driveway, Maria drew a figure of a girl on a bicycle.

Mama, who was ironing one of Maria's smocks, looked over at the drawing.

"Pretty," Mama nodded. "Like a picture in the magazines. But what are you drawing for the art class?"

"This is for class," Maria said.

"A *magazine* picture?" Mama said.

Mama was used to Miss Lindstrom's giving more interesting assignments. Things like: "A Bad Dream." Or, "The Way the World Would Look to Me, If I Were a Rabbit." Or, "The Loneliest Place in the World." Or, "The Way I Feel on the First Day of Spring."

The first time Maria came home with one of these assignments, Mama was puzzled.

"How you feel on the first day of spring?" she said. "How can you draw a feeling? Daffodils maybe. But how you *feel*—?"

But when Maria showed Mama her painting of lilacs in Highland Park and parents and children out walking in their best clothes, Mama said, "Ah— how you feel in the spring—nice and pretty and happy, smelling the lilacs. I see."

Mama understood about Miss Lindstrom's assignments now. She could explain to her friends all of

Maria's pictures that she had pinned up in the apartment.

"Picture of a bad dream," Mama would tell Mrs. Katz. "Not what happens in the dream maybe. Just how it makes you feel. A lot of big dark shapes pressing in on you."

Mrs. Projansky from across the hall thought at first that the cabbages in the picture that Mama called *The Rabbit's World* were bushes. Or big green clouds.

"Bushes!" Mama said. "Big green clouds!"

Mama explained to Mrs. Projansky that she must try to see as a rabbit would see. "To a rabbit, a cabbage could look as big as a bush."

Mama had learned a lot about art, and she knew by now that art was not like a picture in a magazine. So when she asked about the house, Maria could not lie to her.

"We have to draw a house this week," she said.

"Just a house," Mama said. "Any house? Not a house in a bad dream? In the spring? The way a house looks to a rabbit? Just a plain house?"

Maria did not answer for a minute. Then she told Mama, "It's supposed to be a picture of the house where we live."

"Oh," Mama said. She looked at Maria's picture again.

"Our house?" she said.

"No," Maria said. "I can't draw our house."

"Can't *draw* it?" Mama said. "Before you ever went to art class, you could draw a whole block of houses burning down and five fire engines and ten cops and a hundred people in the picture. Now you can't draw one house?"

"That's not what I mean," Maria said.

Maria tried to explain to Mama that a three-room apartment on Market Street wasn't the same as a house. And so to do the assignment she would have to imagine a house.

"But a three-room apartment is *in* a house," Mama said. "So it's a big house. Apartment house. Your teacher means draw where you live."

Maria jabbed a pencil into the kitchen table.

"Oh, Mama!" she said. "This house is no good to draw. How can I make a beautiful picture of this house? I was trying to make a beautiful picture."

Mama looked down at the house Maria had drawn and shook her head.

"It's nice that art should be

454

beautiful,'' Mama said. ''But it should also be true. Your teacher asks you to draw what you know.''

Mama pointed to the picture of the bad dream.

''When you painted the bad dream,'' Mama said, ''did you paint Papa's bad dream? My bad dream?

''No,'' Mama said. ''You painted *your* bad dream. How *you* feel with a bad dream.''

Maria scribbled circles on her drawing pad.

''Is a bad dream beautiful?'' Mama asked. ''No. A bad dream is a bad dream.''

Maria scribbled more circles.

Mama sighed. ''I am not an artist,'' she said. ''All I know is—art must be true.''

Mama went on talking to herself as she ironed a shirt. ''True to how you feel,'' she muttered. ''True to how you see. And if you're a rabbit—true to how a rabbit sees. But true. Always true. Art must be true.''

Maria did not say anything.

Mama was stubborn. Especially about art.

She was very stubborn with Papa about the classes at the museum. Maria had heard Mama arguing with Papa late at night. Papa did not like Mama ironing shirts to pay for the classes.

"I don't like my wife to work," Papa said. "I make enough for food. For rent. For clothes. Why should my wife work?"

"You're a good man," Mama always told Papa. "You make enough. I only iron for a little extra. For the art classes. If you have an artist in the family, you need art classes."

"But at the museum?" Papa said. "At school they got art classes."

"*Those* classes!" Mama said. "Those classes are for anybody. If you can draw like Maria, you need real artists' classes. With real artists for teachers."

Mama could be very stubborn.

Maria watched Mama packing the shirts she had been ironing all day into a carton for Papa to carry down to the Overnite Laundry. Then she looked again at the house she had drawn.

What was wrong with using her imagination? An artist should be able to imagine things, too.

But the picture did look like a magazine picture. Mama was right about that.

Maria tore the picture from her drawing pad and slipped it into her portfolio. She started another drawing.

She sketched in the outline of the house she lived in. With angry slashes

of a marker, she drew the rusted fire escape zigzagging down the front of the building. She drew the sagging window frames and the crumbling cement steps leading up to the front door.

There were the broken windows in Mrs. Sedita's apartment on the ground floor. The landlord had refused to fix them, and Mrs. Sedita had had cardboard tacked over the missing panes for a year.

On the windowsill outside the Durkins' apartment, Maria drew three milk cartons. The power company kept turning off the Durkins' electricity, and Mrs. Durkin had to put her milk on the windowsill to keep it cool.

Maria drew Mrs. Katz leaning out of a third-floor window, screaming at a bum slumped on the steps below. Then she took a marker and lettered on the front of the building the words some kids had painted there in a nasty green color a long time ago.

She was drawing very fast. Putting in all the things that made the building look so sad, old, tired, dirty, and ugly. Mama would see that she could not take a picture like this to Miss Lindstrom.

Maria paused and looked at her drawing.

It was 79 Market Street all right. And she hadn't had to go out and look at the building. She knew exactly how it looked.

Except that she had forgotten to put in the carved stone heads. They were the only thing she really liked about the building.

Between the first and second floors, just above the first-floor windows, were four carved stone heads. When the building was built, eighty or ninety years ago, the four stone heads had been set into the brickwork to decorate the building.

Under the heads were four names carved into the stone bases: BACH, MOZART, BEETHOVEN, and WAGNER. Mr. Bocci, the super, had told Maria that they were the names of four famous musicians.

"This was probably some fancy building when it was built," Mr. Bocci said.

If the man who built it could see it now, Maria thought as she chose a gray marker and carefully drew in the stone heads.

She knew the exact expression on each musician's face, and how each musician's hair was carved. She was just finishing Bach's funny little sausage curls when Mama came over.

Mama studied the picture for a long time. "It's true," she said finally. "It's Market Street."

Mama sighed. "You take to art class?"

"Mama! I can't."

It *was* true. It *was* Market Street. And Maria was afraid she was going to cry.

She ripped the picture off the pad and stuffed it into her portfolio. She put away her markers and pencils, washed and went to bed.

Maria heard Mama come into her room much later to hang a freshly ironed smock in her closet. Mama stood at the foot of her bed for a minute, as if she wanted to say something. But Maria pretended to be asleep.

What difference would it make which drawing she showed Miss Lindstrom? Miss Lindstrom would not know that the first drawing was an imaginary house. Only Mama knew.

Only Mama. Mama, who never complained about the hours she spent ironing for the Overnite Laundry. Working sometimes until long after Papa and Maria were asleep.

But last night Maria had not been able to sleep. Even so, morning had come too fast. And now she lay in bed listening to the Sanitation Department throwing the garbage cans down on the sidewalk, and could not make herself get up.

Maria heard Mama calling her for the second time.

No, she could not tell Mama she was sick.

Maria dressed, braided her hair, and put on her yellow smock.

When Mama said, "Pretty," as Maria came into the kitchen, Maria could not look Mama in the eye.

Mama did not say much at breakfast. And when she took down the brown teapot and fished out the three quarters, Maria wanted to say, "Please, Mama, try to understand."

But she couldn't say it. And when Mama went to wake up Papa, Maria knew what she had to do.

She opened up her portfolio and took out the drawing of the white house with the picture windows. She looked at the drawing for a minute. Then she tore it up and put it in the garbage can.

Mama must have known. She nodded her head in a proud stern way as Maria went out the door.

Maria felt better as she walked to the bus stop. But once on the bus, she began to think about Miss Lindstrom again, and wished she had stayed home.

She hunched down in her seat and stared out the window. It wasn't like watching a movie this morning. The city streets flashed by in the crazy way they do in a dream that is going too fast and is going to end in a terrible way. And suddenly the bus was at the museum.

Maria walked quickly through the big entrance room. Usually, she walked very slowly through this room. She loved its high ceilings and the sunlight slanting down through windows placed high on the outside walls. The sound of her footsteps echoing from the stone walls and the serious faces of the six lions who guarded the hallway that led to the art class made Maria feel as if she were a distinguished person arriving at a great palace for an important occasion.

But this morning Maria hurried past the lions without a glance.

Most of the kids in the class were already at their easels when Maria came in, and were pinning up the drawings they had done during the week.

If only she'd come a few minutes earlier, Maria thought, she might have gone up and explained quietly to Miss Lindstrom that she'd forgotten to bring her drawing. Had forgotten to do the assignment even.

Coming in late, though, Maria felt as if everyone was watching her. Quickly, she opened up her portfolio and took out her drawing.

Her hands were clumsy as she tacked the drawing to her easel, afraid someone might laugh. But no one did.

Glancing over her shoulder, Maria saw that the other students were looking at their own work, some of them adding a few lines to their pictures. Or trying to smudge out bits they didn't like.

Miss Lindstrom was already walking around, looking at what everyone had done. At one easel, she would nod and smile. At another, she would ask a question. Now and then she would call the whole class to look at something unusual in someone's drawing.

Maria trailed behind the others, hardly hearing what the silvery voice was saying.

Most of the drawings on the easels were of houses with yards and trees, as Maria had expected. But many of the houses pictured were less grand than she'd imagined. None as grand as the one she'd wanted to draw for Miss Lindstrom.

And there was one picture that surprised Maria because the house in it looked quite old and shabby. The house was set in a big yard and had a funny tower on one side, which perhaps had made it look very handsome at one time. But the house looked now as if it needed painting, and there was one very messy-looking corner of the yard with a lot of boards and boxes scattered around.

A redheaded boy named Jasper had painted the picture. Jasper pointed to the house in the painting.

"This is where I live," he told Miss Lindstrom. "But over here is where I'm *going* to live." He pointed to the boards and boxes.

"That's the most important part of the picture," he explained. "I'm building my own house out here. I'm

designing it myself, and it's going to be really beautiful.''

Miss Lindstrom laughed. ''Is it going to have a tower?'' she asked.

''Certainly not,'' Jasper said. ''It's going to be a very modern house. With see-through walls that you walk through to get outdoors.''

The whole class laughed, and then Miss Lindstrom talked a little about how it was clear from the way Jasper had placed the house off to one side in the picture that the messy pile of boards *was* the most important part of the picture.

There was always something funny in Jasper's paintings, a crazy way of looking at things. But Miss Lindstrom seemed to like Jasper's work.

Maria was puzzling over this when Miss Lindstrom moved over to her easel. Maria's hands felt cold. Her mouth felt dry. She wanted to run down the hall to the washroom and hide. But she just stood there by Jasper's easel, watching Miss Lindstrom.

Maria caught the brief look of surprise on Miss Lindstrom's face and wished she could sink through the floor.

Miss Lindstrom did not say anything for a minute. Then she looked around for Maria.

''Maria,'' she called. ''Come.'' She put an arm around Maria's shoulder.

''Everyone come here,'' she called.

The rest of the class crowded around Maria's easel.

"Maria didn't quite understand the assignment," Miss Lindstrom was saying. "But it doesn't matter. Look what she's done."

Miss Lindstrom stepped back so that everyone could see.

"I'd meant for you to draw your own house," Miss Lindstrom said to Maria. "But what you've done is very interesting."

Miss Lindstrom asked the class whether any of them had ever driven through Carpenter Street, Market Street or Water Street—the old part of town down near the river.

"I have," Jasper said. "My uncle goes there to buy fish."

"If any of you have," Miss Lindstrom said, "you will see how perfectly Maria has caught the feeling of the crowded tenements in that part of town.

"Look." Miss Lindstrom bent over Maria's drawing. "See here," she said, "—and here—and here—" The art teacher's beautiful hands touched the paper lightly.

"So many beautiful things," she said.

Miss Lindstrom pointed to Mrs. Katz's laundry strung across the fire escape on the third floor. To the cats fighting over a spilled garbage can in front of the house. To a tired figure leaning on a windowsill. To the milk cartons on another sill.

"I can almost hear the kids yelling in the street," Miss Lindstrom said. "I can hear people yelling, laughing, and crying inside the apartments. I can smell spaghetti cooking. And chicken soup."

"Not me," Jasper said. "I smell fish."

Miss Lindstrom laughed. "You're right, Jasper. I can smell that, too. There's so much going on in this house."

Now Miss Lindstrom was looking at the stone heads.

"And these heads," she said. "When this building was built years ago, someone lovingly carved those heads, and Maria has drawn them so lovingly that you can feel the care the stone-cutter took in carving them."

"Hey, that's Beethoven!" Jasper said, pointing to one of the heads.

"How did you know?" Maria asked in surprise. Because she had not put the musicians' names under the heads.

"I saw his picture in a book once," Jasper said.

Miss Lindstrom asked the class if they knew that there was an exhibition of carved stone heads, like those in Maria's drawing, on the top floor of the museum. They were taken from old buildings in the city, before the buildings were torn down, she said.

Maria looked at her drawing. Would Bach, Mozart, Beethoven, and Wagner be in the museum someday? She tried to imagine their faces looking down on museum visitors instead of her friends on Market Street.

Miss Lindstrom was talking to the class again.

"Does everyone see what is so good about Maria's drawing?" she asked.

"All those little details," one girl said. "The heads, the cats, the milk cartons, and the writing on the front of the building."

"No," another girl said. "All those bits are nice. Maria can draw anything. But what's really good is that her picture isn't just a picture of a building. You feel as if you know the people who live in it."

"Yes," Miss Lindstrom said. "That's it. It's a beautiful drawing, Maria. Full of life and feeling. The nicest thing you've done this year." She gave Maria a hug and moved on to another easel.

Maria stood staring at her picture.

Miss Lindstrom had hugged her and told her that her picture was beautiful. But it wasn't Miss Lindstrom with her spun-gold hair that Maria was seeing as she stared at her picture.

She was seeing Mama. Mama standing dark and stern over the ironing board. Mama saying stubbornly, "Art must be true." Mama standing and nodding gravely as Maria would tell her what Miss Lindstrom had said about her drawing today . . .

Then Maria heard Miss Lindstrom say her name again.

"Maria's picture gave me an idea for next week's assignment," Miss Lindstrom was saying.

"Next week," she said, "I want each of you to visit a part of the city where you have never been before and to draw a picture of the houses there— or the stores—or the street."

"Except Maria," said Miss Lindstrom.

"Since you have already done that, Maria," she said, "maybe you would like to draw your own house next week."

Maria felt as if Mama's grave eyes were on her as she looked up at her art teacher and said in a clear, sure voice, "But that *is* my house in the picture."

 Reader's Response

What will you remember about this story? Explain why.

ART
MUST BE TRUE

Thinking It Over

1. Why didn't Maria want to draw a picture of her own house for art class?
2. How did Mama feel about Maria's picture of the make-believe house?
3. How did Maria feel when the art teacher looked at her drawing? How do you know?
4. How did Miss Lindstrom respond to Maria's drawing?
5. Do you think Maria had the necessary qualities to be a good artist?
6. If Maria had taken her other drawing to art class, what might have happened?

Writing to Learn

THINK AND DISCOVER Maria discovers that honest details make a picture. Writers, like artists, depend upon details to make their work realistic. Sketch a possession that you enjoy owning. Label all the details you see.

WRITE Write a description of the possession that you sketched. Be sure to include details to make your writing realistic.

465

Thinking ◆ Reading ◆ Writing

Evaluating Qualities

Many stories deal with people who are successful in one way or another. When you read, it is interesting to think about the qualities that make a person successful.

Learning the Strategy

A chart can be a useful tool for evaluating a person's qualities and judging how important those qualities are to success in a particular field. Think about Maria in "Art Must Be True." She has many qualities that contribute to her success as an artist. She also has qualities that may make her a better person but are not necessarily important to being a good artist. The chart below lists and evaluates some of Maria's qualities.

Quality	Important to being a good artist?	Reason
Observant	Yes	She could see things others would miss.
Practiced drawing a lot	Yes	Art is a skill that requires practice.
Communicated well with her mother	Not necessarily	Good quality but not important for an artist.

Artists must be able to observe the world around them and remember all of the details. Then, they must practice so that they can skillfully paint or draw those details. Although Maria's ability to talk to her mother might make her a better person, this quality may not be as important as the others in terms of her success as an artist. Do you agree or disagree? How would you have filled in the chart?

Using the Strategy

The following chart lists qualities that may be important for someone who wants to succeed in ski jumping. Evaluate the qualities and decide which you think are important and why. Complete the chart on your own paper.

Quality	Important?	Reason
Courage		
Coordination		
Willingness to practice		
Good natured		

Applying the Strategy to the Next Selection

The next selection you will read, "Pueblos and Pow-Wows," tells about the lives of two Native American artists. As you read, make a chart for each of them to evaluate which qualities are important to their success.

◆◆◆ The writing connection can be found on page 555.

Pablita Velarde and Patrick Des Jarlait are two successful artists whose work is both beautiful and true, but their success was not easily won.

PUEBLOS AND POW-WOWS:
Two Native American Artists

by Helen Strahinich

A pueblo in Taos, New Mexico

Pablita Velarde[1] and Patrick Des Jarlait[2] are two Native American artists who painted scenes from the lives of their peoples. By the time Pablita and Patrick were born—Pablita in 1918 and Patrick in 1921—settlers had built farms and towns across the American continent, and Native Americans no longer roamed freely across the land. Nevertheless, these artists grew up in communities that had kept much of their Native American heritage. Both hoped to keep alive the traditional ways of life that they had learned as children. Their paintings show their pride in their rich heritage. ◄◆►

◄◆►

What quality is described here? Is this quality important to their success as artists?

Although both are Native Americans, Pablita and Patrick come from very different cultures that are hundreds of miles apart. For centuries, Pablita's people farmed in the American Southwest, while Patrick's hunted, fished, and gathered rice along the forested shores of Lake Superior.

[1]Pablita Velarde: (pu blē′ tu ve lär′ de)
[2]Des Jarlait (dā zhär lā′)

Shoreline of Lake Superior

469

Pablita Velarde's Childhood

Pablita's people—the Pueblos—live in the Southwest. Since the area is hot and receives little rain, much of the land is desert. The main crop of the Pueblos is corn, which can grow in a hot, dry climate. The people used to live in pueblos, or towns, where all the homes were joined together, a little like apartment buildings of today. These pueblos were often located on mesas—flat-topped mountains common in that part of the Southwest.

Pablita's early childhood was spent on the reservation of Santa Clara where her family lived on the edge of the pueblo. As a child, Pablita suffered from an illness that took away her sight for two years. During that time, she developed a habit of storing in her memory images of things she had seen.

Only three years old when her mother died, Pablita often stayed with her grandmother. It was her grandmother who taught her many of the old Pueblo arts. Pablita learned to roast gypsum rock and to make a white powder that was the basis for a house paint. She learned to paint the designs that bordered the windows and decorated the fireplaces. She also learned to make fine pottery in the Pueblo tradition.

Near Santa Clara were the ruins of an ancient cliff dwelling—Puye,[3] the "Pueblo of Clouds." Pablita loved playing in the ruins of the old pueblo. Sometimes she found rocks there with pictures on them. She made up stories about the pictures and stored their images in her memory. Later, the mental images became material for her art work.

When there were festivals, traditional Kachina dancers wore strange masks and bright costumes, carried drums and rattles, and performed at the plazas around town. Pablita remembered every detail of the colorful dances. One of her famous paintings shows a plaza where a traditional dance is going on. In this painting, Pablita captures the excitement of her people watching the dancers from the rooftops.

[3]Puye (poo' yā)

Patrick Des Jarlait's Childhood

Patrick's people are the Chippewas. His ancestors lived in small bands in the forests along northern Lake Michigan and Lake Superior. Their homes were wigwams—oval shelters covered with strips of birch bark. Summers were mild, but winters were harsh, and there was abundant rain and snow. The Chippewas hunted the forest animals and gathered wild rice that grew in the lakes.

Patrick grew up on the Red Lake Reservation in northern Minnesota. His earliest memories were of forest scenes, of beautiful Red Lake, and of the animals that lived there. As an artist, these scenes figured in his work throughout his life.

Like Pablita, Patrick had a childhood illness that took away his sight. Although the doctors said he would not recover it, he never lost hope or the desire to draw. When his sight did return, he said it was like a miracle. Also like Pablita, Patrick's mother died when he was a child.

Is Patrick's memory important to his success as an artist?

At Red Lake, activities and festivals changed with each new season. The wild rice harvest was in the fall. In the winter, there was hunting, trapping, and ice fishing. In the spring, the Chippewas gathered for the maple sugar harvest, an activity that Patrick loved to draw. The harvesters called him "little boy with a pencil."

For the Chippewas, the great summer event was the July Pow-Wow. Long ago the Pow-Wow had been a meeting time when Chippewa leaders would gather to solve problems. By the time Patrick was a boy, the Pow-Wow had become a social event, like a fair. There were booths with food and handicrafts, as well as games and dancing. The dancers wore traditional costumes with beadwork that took hours to sew. Years later, Patrick returned to these scenes to tell the story of his people. One of his paintings, called *Chippewa Dancer*, shows the feathers, beadwork, and colorful face paint worn during a traditional dance.

School Experiences

Like many Native American children who lived on reservations, Pablita and Patrick went to mission schools—Pablita in Santa Fe, New Mexico, and Patrick in Redby, a village near his home in Minnesota. They lived at the mission schools and rarely saw their families. They were not allowed to speak their own languages or to take part in activities related to their peoples' past, because the schools wanted them to give up their traditional ways. Both Pablita and Patrick, however, kept their love for their peoples' ways in their hearts.

Later, Pablita went to a government school in Santa Fe, where she was fortunate enough to meet Dorothy Dunn, a teacher who was trying to revive Native American art. Under Dunn's guidance, Pablita learned the principles of color. She experimented with traditional methods of grinding rocks and clay to make earth colors, and she used chalk and charcoal to paint Pueblo scenes.

One of her favorite subjects was the activities of Santa Clara women. Some of these paintings were shown in a school exhibit at the end of eighth grade. A woman who was preparing a mural for the Chicago Exposition of 1933 saw Pablita's paintings and selected one for the New Mexico Exhibit. Soon after receiving this honor, Pablita was asked to make a mural of Pueblo life for a national art project.

In his early years in school, Patrick Des Jarlait did not receive the kind of encouragement for his art that Pablita Velarde received. Patrick assumed he would make his living as a lumberer like his father, or in the fisheries. Still, he continued to have a strong interest in painting, drawing, carving, and woodwork. Finally, one of his high school teachers, Miss Ross, recognized his talent. "Some day I want to hear great things about you," she told him. She gave him art supplies and books, and her interest in the Chippewa way of life freed Patrick to explore his people's past.

Pablita and Patrick were each fortunate to find a teacher who encouraged their talent. This experience was important for both of them.

Becoming an Artist

Pablita had turned to her Native American heritage as the subject of her art. Becoming a painter, however, meant a conflict with her Native American past, as well. Among the Pueblos, painting was an art practiced only by men, so Pablita's success as a painter shocked the people of Santa Clara. Pablita's father tried to get her to give up painting and encouraged her to learn to type instead. Pablita did take business courses from a nearby high school and after graduation got a job as an assistant teacher. Still Pablita was drawn to the art world and she soon left the reservation to demonstrate pottery making on a lecture tour. After that, she received a variety of art assignments. One of her favorites was painting a mural at Bandelier[4] National Monument Museum, the site of an old cliff dwelling. The mural showed how Native Americans had lived there long ago.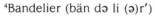

[4]Bandelier (bän də li (ə)r')

Santa Clara Growth Dance by Pablita Velarde

What quality is shown here?

Santa Clara Basket Dance by Pablita Velarde

Although Pablita married and had two children, she continued to paint. She was becoming known for her paintings made of earth colors. She collected clays and stones, ground them into powders on an Indian grinding stone, and then mixed the powders with glue and water to make her special paints. During this period, Pablita won many prizes. In 1954, she even received the *Ordre des Palmes Academiques*[5] from the French government, along with twelve other Native American artists. This was the first time a foreign government had recognized Native Americans as artists.

When Pablita Velarde was a child, her father told traditional stories from the past. Many years later, when her father was an old man, he helped her write down the stories, and she illustrated them. When their book was published in 1960, it created a lot of interest among other Native Americans in preserving their old tales. Storytelling was her father's way of passing on his people's traditions, and one of Pablita's most famous paintings shows her father telling stories to a group of children. Pablita, too, had a story to tell; the rich traditions of the Pueblo people live on through her paintings.

The path toward becoming a painter was difficult for Patrick Des Jarlait as well, since it is not easy to make a living as an artist. However, after graduating from high school, Patrick

[5]Ordre des Palmes Academiques (ôr′ drə dā pälmz′ ä kä dā mēk′)

served in the Navy Visual Aids Department during World War II. Working with artists from both MGM and Walt Disney studios helped him to develop as a commercial artist. On weekends, Patrick and other artists set up studios in old garages, and he painted his memories of Red Lake. He also had a one-man show of his paintings in a San Diego gallery.

After leaving the Navy in 1945, Patrick returned to Red Lake Reservation. He felt the need to develop his own style of art by returning to his heritage. Bright colors with little water, and short brush strokes that created a feeling of motion, became his trademark. During the year he spent back at Red Lake, Patrick observed and recorded everything he could about the Chippewa way of life. Many of his paintings from that time, such as *Wild Rice Harvest*, show the seasonal activities of Red Lake. ◆◆◆

◆◆◆

What quality does Patrick show here?

The scene of the rice harvest is especially interesting, because it shows all the different skills that were needed to harvest and prepare the rice for eating. In the background on the far left, you can see Chippewas in a boat harvesting the wild rice from the shallow lakes. On the front left, you can see a kettle filled with rice. The rice is being heated over the fire so its hulls will burst open. Next to the kettle, a trampler is

Wild Rice Harvest by Patrick Des Jarlait

475

Chippewa Dancer
by Patrick Des Jarlait

dancing on the rice to separate the hulls from the kernels. On the right is a woman who is winnowing the rice. She is pouring the rice back and forth between two baskets, so the wind will blow the hulls away from the kernels.

Later Patrick went to St. Paul, Minnesota, where he worked as a commercial artist. Each night he set aside time to paint scenes of his people. Over time, many galleries and private collectors bought his art work and eventually he was able to devote all of his time to painting the Chippewa way of life.

In the end, both Pablita Velarde and Patrick Des Jarlait were rewarded for their hard work and determination. In spite of personal difficulties and prejudice, they both achieved fame as artists. They also succeeded in keeping alive the memory of the rich traditions in which they were raised. Their work helped to renew interest in the great Native American cultures of North America. Through their paintings, the stories of their peoples' pasts and their own experiences will continue to reach future generations of Americans. ◄◆►

Complete your chart for each artist. Be sure to evaluate each quality in terms of its importance to Pablita and Patrick as artists and give a reason why.

Reader's **Response**

Have you ever overcome an obstacle similar to those that faced Pablita Velarde and Patrick Des Jarlait?

PUEBLOS AND POW-WOWS:
Two Native American Artists

Thinking It Over

1. In what ways were the childhoods of Pablita Velarde and Patrick Des Jarlait alike?

2. Do you think going to mission and government schools helped or hurt Pablita and Patrick as artists? Explain your answer.

3. Find facts, opinions, or both, in this sentence: Pablita and Patrick were fortunate to find teachers who encouraged their talent. How did you decide what was fact and what was opinion?

4. What was the main problem Pablita faced in becoming an artist on a Pueblo reservation?

5. If Patrick had not returned to Red Lake Reservation, how might his art have been changed or affected?

6. Why do many people feel the art of Pablita Velarde and Patrick Des Jarlait is important?

Writing to Learn

THINK AND INVENT Pablita Velarde and Patrick Des Jarlait received encouragement for their work. Name a person who encourages your efforts. Look at the ''Thank-you Gram'' below and think of how you might thank the person you named.

Thank-You Gram!

To you a teacher of the past.
Hello once again.
Always your kind words remain.
Never will I forget them.
Know that I appreciate YOU!

WRITE Design, write, and decorate a ''Thank-you Gram'' for the person you named who encourages you.

478

My People

The night is beautiful,
So the faces of my people.

The stars are beautiful,
So the eyes of my people.

Beautiful, also, is the sun.
Beautiful, also, are the souls of my people.

Langston Hughes

A Thing of Beauty
from *Endymion*

A thing of beauty is a joy forever;
Its loveliness increases; it will never
Pass into nothingness; but still will keep
A bower quiet for us, and a sleep
Full of sweet dreams, and health, and quiet
        breathing.

John Keats

WORLD OF READING
Magazine
News About Reading

Computer Graphics for Books

In years past, illustrators such as the Englishman Sir John Tenniel and the American N. C. Wyeth worked with pen and ink or brush and paints to create beautiful illustrations for books.

Today, many book and magazine illustrators use another tool—the computer. The new field of computer graphics, as it is known, has grown very rapidly in the last few years. Experienced artists have been helped by computers. In addition, even

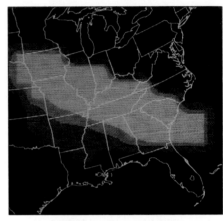

A computer-generated weather map needs to be drawn only once. Information can be added without redrawing the entire map.

people who are not artists can use the computer to create art to go along with the words they write.

Computer-generated art is being widely used by publishers. You probably have seen computer illustrations in books and magazines but may

Just imagine being able to use a computer to paint a picture with sixteen million colors to choose from!

480

Computers can generate art that cannot be created in any other way.

not have realized that they were produced on a machine. That's because advances in computer technology have made it possible to create art that is as varied as anything that can be done with a paintbrush and canvas.

In addition, computers can generate art that cannot be created in any other way. For example, mathematical

Advances in computer technology have made it possible to create art of the highest quality.

information can be shown in picture form. Using numerical data, computers can create landscapes with three-dimensional qualities. They can also use numerical data to generate maps that appear in newspapers and books. A computer is a perfect tool for map-making because details can be changed and information can be easily added with little expense.

Computers have given graphic designers greater flexibility in designing books and magazines. They can experiment with layouts and designs and see the results instantly. These pages and others in this book were designed on a computer.

☞ **Many magazines have current information about computer graphics. Look for articles on computers in such magazines as Current Science and Compute!**

Computers have allowed people to create graphics for materials as varied as greeting cards, newsletters, and books.

481

Have you ever watched the clouds move across the sky? They form certain shapes, and then drift apart to look like something else. They are white, then change to red and gold. It is almost as if an artist in the sky is creating a special effect for you to enjoy!

C.L.O.U.D.S.

written and illustrated
by Pat Cummings

Chuku had just come to work at the department of Creative Lights, Opticals, and Unusual Designs in the Sky.

The supervisor had assigned someone to show him around. He had spent the morning learning where the gossamer and lightbeams were kept. He'd received a key to the Hue Room, where all the colors were stored.

And now he sat at his drawing table waiting for his assignment. Finally a messenger knocked on his door and, with a sarcastic "Congratulations," dropped off a large manual. Attached to the front was a memo.

 CLOUDS

CREATIVE LIGHTS, OPTICALS, AND UNUSUAL DESIGNS IN THE SKY

From: The Supervisor

To: Chuku

Welcome to our department. As you will read in the manual, it is our policy to start junior artists in the less demanding areas. You'll be designing skies for the city of New York. I hope you will see this as the good training program it is. I'm confident that you'll be able to work your way up in no time at all. The manual should answer all your questions. Good luck!

He read the memo twice. New York did not sound like what he had hoped for: It sounded like a job no one else wanted. He quickly leafed through the pamphlet, occasionally reading the rules that were starred.

*Only those with two years of experience may use the special effects laboratory.

*Absolutely no words or numbers allowed!

*Please submit all sketches for Spectacular Sunsets no later than noon for approval. (Check section 7 for geographical limitations.)

And so on . . .

Chuku was anxious to get started. Consulting the maps in the back of the manual, he immediately left for the western sector to inspect the New York sky.

It was a pale gray when he arrived and a slight drizzly rain was falling. The sky seemed terribly low and the buildings poking through at the center of the city made it seem even lower. Chuku sighed. Pulling out his notebook, he took a seat on a convenient ledge and began to take notes. He made two columns on the paper and marked one "Advantages" and the other "Disadvantages." He looked around for a few minutes and then began to write in the "Disadvantages" column:

—Not much room to work in
—Tall buildings could get in the way.
—The air is dirty. (Check manual to see if that affects the colors.)
—Nobody ever looks up!

And under the "Advantages" column he could only think to write:

—Nobody ever looks up!

Then he put away his pad and returned to his office.

Once at his table, he took out a large sheet of paper and sent to the Hue Room for a bottle of Classic Sunny-Day Blue. He spent the rest of the afternoon sketching a very plain blue sky that would cover the city the next day.

The supervisor called Chuku to his office before he left work to look at the sketch. "Lovely," said the supervisor.

"But it's just plain blue," said Chuku.

"Well, son," the supervisor answered, "you're just starting. Can't get too carried away. It'll be just fine." And he smiled a knowing smile as Chuku left.

The next day the weathermen beamed on televisions and boomed over radios: "What a lovely day, not a cloud in the sky!" When Chuku heard that, he decided the supervisor must have known what he was talking about.

Soon his days assumed a pattern. He spent his mornings looking over the city, deciding where to sprinkle a few clouds or throw a little color at sunset. By afternoon he was back at his table sketching the next day's sky. He made sure to include the rainy and gray days the manual insisted must occur. They usually followed days on which he felt angry or bored.

One day, after a whole week of rain, he was passing over Central Park when something shiny on the ground caught his eye. A little girl was lying atop a grassy hill. Her hands were clasped behind her head, and she was staring up. Around her neck a piece of string held a gold star that had flashed up at him. She was smiling and watching the sky with such intent that even Chuku looked upward. But she was only looking at the plain blue sky that he had sketched the day before.

She watched the sky, and Chuku watched her. In the early afternoon her brother came running from the nearby ball field and pulled her to her feet. She was reluctant to leave and he had to tug her hand constantly. As they disappeared among the trees, Chuku heard the boy say, "We can come back tomorrow, Chrissy. Now come on!"

Chuku hurried back to his office. He felt incredibly good. He picked up jars of Oh So Turquoise and Peacock's Tail Blue. He chose two small tubes of Cloud-Lining Silver and Unbelievable Brilliant Gold. On a small tray he collected daubs of Sea Mist Green, Midsummer White Dream, and Awfully Pretty Rose.

Returning to his desk he pulled out his largest sheet of paper and began to sketch a cloud-filled sky. First he drew a flurry of gold-speckled clouds . . . hundreds of them that would cover the sky. Then he worked on a cloud sequence: The clouds would change into birdlike shapes and scatter. A larger cloud would dramatically roll in, looking like a tiger about to pounce. The tiger would roll and unfold, stretching out his front paws to make an elephant's trunk. The elephant, in turn, would stretch his trunk up, up into a long giraffe neck. Finally it all would pull apart into a patchwork of wispy clouds.

Chuku was exhausted. He had nine drawings before him. The entire thing would last a couple of hours, he figured. Then he'd end with a Lovely Light Lavender sunset, and throw in traces of the U.B.Gold and A.P.Rose.

When the supervisor saw the sketches, he raised his right eyebrow slightly, but said no more that his usual "Fine with me."

Then he stamped all nine designs with his special seal and sent them down to the Production Department, as usual.

APPROVED

The next morning Chuku was back at the park, in an excellent spot for viewing both the sky and the little girl's reactions. She arrived shortly before the first tentative clouds rolled into place. Stretching out on the grass, she watched the bird shapes grow and fly off in all directions. As the tiger appeared, her mouth opened to a wide smile and only closed as the last shreds of the giraffe stretched apart.

This time as her brother took her hand and led her home, her eyes remained glued to the quickly lavendering sky.

After they left, Chuku returned to his office. He felt terribly good again and immediately set to work.

Flowers sprouted from boats, and snakes turned into ladders. He constructed castles that would dissolve into schools of fish at the slightest gust of wind. And with a well-placed breeze, he would send a swarm of butterflies into a huge outstretched hand.

Chrissy loved it. She was there every day, except when it rained—and there were still rainy days. Chuku was careful to stick to the rules: He made sure that something was happening all over town, not just in the park. He found that the sky around tall buildings with reflecting glass windows was an excellent place to use bright colors. Over the rivers he often created his best rainbows and sunsets. He had truly begun to enjoy his job.

The supervisor had taken notice of this sudden burst of creativity, and eventually he sent word for Chuku to come to his office.

"You've been doing some lovely work, son," he said. "That's a particularly uninspiring area, but you've made advantages out of your disadvantages."

"Thank you, sir," Chuku replied modestly.

"In fact, the director himself has noticed. We've decided you're ready for a really nice location."

"B-but—" Chuku stammered.

"Don't thank me, son," the supervisor continued. "The director recognizes talent and told me personally that I could give you a tropical location. Now there's a winner! The colors they use in that area! You finish up the week in New York and next week I'll show you your new office."

Chuku was distressed. He knew it would be a mistake to refuse such a well-intentioned offer, but even the thought of leaving New York and Chrissy upset him.

"Thank you, sir," he said softly.

Chuku returned to his office. For a long time he sat at his desk staring at the paper he'd painted Ballet Slipper Blue. Then he picked up a piece of soft chalk and wrote across the center:

Hello down there.

He knew this would never be approved. The supervisor stuck to the rules strictly and words were absolutely forbidden. But he had to at least say something to Chrissy before he transferred to the tropics. So when the supervisor had left his office to inspect the new shipment of thunderbolts and rainbow parts, Chuku slipped in and used his rubber stamp.

The next afternoon he sat in the park watching Chrissy watch the sky for the last time. Slowly the words rolled into place. No airplane had written them and very few people even seemed aware of them. But Chrissy jumped to her feet and pointed at each word. She'd only recently been learning to read and her lips formed each word carefully as she read "Hello down there."

She began jumping and waving and jumping and smiling. Then the bird pattern he had used the first time he had drawn for her came drifting in. And as the birds flew apart in every direction, Chrissy's brother came and led her away. Just at the edge of the trees, she turned and waved again at the sky.

Chuku didn't feel like going back, so he wandered over the city taking his last look. He passed the Empire State Building where people were watching the sky through telescopes. He paused downtown at the Manhattan and Brooklyn Bridges and marveled at the reflections of his sky in the water. Everywhere people seemed to be looking up. In the World Trade Towers, executives stood at the windows dictating letters, and people on coffee breaks chatted and watched small clouds drift by. Uptown at the library park and in Columbus Circle, musicians were playing and couples leaned back on park benches, their dark glasses reflecting the sun. And up in Morningside Park, children of all sizes dotted the grass and pointed at his cloud formations. Chuku had never felt so good about his job and so bad about leaving. He remembered that only a short while ago, he had looked forward to being transferred.

Sadly, he returned to work only to find a memo pinned to his drawing table.

CLOUDS

From: The Supervisor
To: Chuku

COME SEE ME!!!

Holding the memo, Chuku stepped into the supervisor's office.

"Sit down!" The supervisor's tone was threatening. "Do you realize what you've done? Have you read your manual—section 3, number 17? Absolutely *no* words allowed!"

"But sir, I . . ." Chuku interrupted.

"You not only disregarded the rules, but you had the nerve to sneak in here and use my stamp! I am shocked. The director is shocked. There is no excuse for your behavior!"

"But sir, I can . . ." Chuku tried again.

"You can go back to your office is what you can do! And you can forget about the tropics and forget about the new office. You can stay where you are till you've learned some responsibility."

"Yes, sir," Chuku whispered, feeling very good indeed.

As he left the supervisor yelled after him "And you had better forget your sudden love of words, young man!"

Chuku smiled all the way back to his office. He felt so good that he hardly noticed all the disapproving frowns that peered at him through open doors marked MIDWEST and DOWN UNDER and FAR EAST.

He went in his office and painted a fancy sign to hang on his door. Then he sat down at his drawing table with a very contented look on his face and opened a new jar of Twilight Blue.

Reader's Response

If you were Chuku, what message would you send to people on the earth?

C.L.O.U.D.S.

Thinking It Over

1. What does C.L.O.U.D.S. stand for in the story title?
2. Chuku began his New York assignment by making a list of the advantages and the disadvantages of the New York sky. Do you agree with his list? How did you decide?
3. What happened to make Chuku enjoy his job?
4. What was the difference between the skies Chuku drew when he first started his job and the skies he drew later?
5. Why do you think Chuku broke the rules about drawing words?
6. How did Chuku feel about not being transferred to the tropics? What clues tell you this?

Writing to Learn

THINK AND INVENT   Imagine that you have the responsibility for naming colors in Chuku's paint cabinet. Look at the ideas below. Notice how certain words make you think of certain colors. Create five new color names of your own.

WRITE   Write a paragraph describing the scene outside your classroom window, a night sky, or any scene you like. Use the new names you created for the colors in your scene.

LITERATURE LINK

What kind of story is a myth?

Picture a bright sunny day, too beautiful to be true. All of a sudden, storm clouds roll in. The sky turns black and a crash of thunder pierces the air. How do you feel? Now, think how you might feel if you believed, as ancient people did, that lightning was a warning from the gods. The rumble of thunder and the flash of lightning filled these people with awe.

People have always tried to explain things they couldn't understand. An old Scandinavian tale, for example, explains thunder as the rolling chariot wheels of the Norse god Thor. Chinese stories describe how Mother-Lightning uses mirrors to help produce flashes of light, while the Master of Rain sprinkles water over the earth.

How to Recognize a Myth

Stories like these are myths, which come to us from many cultures. Myths often provide explanations of how and why natural events occur. Here are some other common features of myths:

- They tell about the lives of ancient gods, goddesses, and heroes.
- They may describe what seem to be supernatural events.
- They may convey a message or warning.

If you keep these features in mind, you'll be better prepared to grasp the meaning of the myths you read.

Read this adaptation of a myth about Demeter, the Greek goddess of agriculture, and her only daughter, Persephone. What features make this a myth? What natural events does it explain?

———•◦•———

Persephone was picking flowers one day when Hades, ruler of the underworld, suddenly seized her and carried her down to his kingdom. Overcome with sorrow at the loss of her daughter, Demeter turned her grief upon the earth. Crops would not grow, and the land turned barren.

Zeus, mightiest of the gods, finally commanded that Hades set Persephone free. Hades obeyed, but first he tempted Persephone to eat a pomegranate seed. This fruit was a symbol of marriage, and after Persephone ate it, she had to return to Hades after visiting her mother.

From then on, Persephone lived with her mother nine months of each year and with Hades for the remaining three. Whenever Persephone descended to the dark underworld, Demeter's grief turned the world cold and bare, and winter began. But with her daughter's return three months later, the flowers of spring bloomed once more.

———•◦•———

Watch for the features of a myth as you read the next selection, "Arachne." Does it explain a natural event or convey a special message?

Arachne

by Doris Gates

Arachne, a young woman of ancient Greece, is famous for her skill at weaving.

Arachne was a country maiden who was famous throughout the land for her skill at weaving. No person on Earth, it was said, could weave so skillfully as she. There were some who said that not even Athena, goddess of all household arts, could weave so well as Arachne.

Among these arrogant boasters was Arachne herself, who was not at all modest about her skill. She never bothered to consider it a gift of the gods, nor was she ever humbly grateful for it. Instead, she was foolishly

proud of it and even made fun of the work of girls less
gifted than she. But then, one had to admit it was a
wondrous sight to see her fingers moving lightly and
swiftly back and forth across her loom. Her designs were
intricate and beautiful, and she wove the colors of her
threads with the ease and smoothness of an artist working with brush and paint. So graceful was she in all her
motions that often the wood nymphs left their shadowy
hiding places to watch her at work.

In time Arachne's fame and her boasting reached the
ears of Athena, and the goddess decided to draw the girl
into a contest that would cure her arrogant pride.

One day, when Arachne was weaving in a pleasant
grove, there suddenly appeared beside her a bent old
woman. She gazed for a moment at Arachne's loom and
then said, "That is a pretty piece of weaving, my dear,
and yet I have seen the time in my youth when I could
have done as well."

At this Arachne threw up her head and said in a
scornful tone, "Never did any mortal weave as I am
weaving now, old woman."

"Those are rash words," said the old woman, and a strange angry light came into her gray eyes, which were exceedingly youthful for one so bent with years. "It is foolish to take too great pride in what one can do, for surely there is always someone who can do the task even better."

"Not so," cried the angry girl. "There is no one who can weave better than I."

The old woman smiled and shook her head doubtfully. "Allowing that no mortal can weave as well as you, at least among the Immortals there is one who can surpass you in the art."

Arachne left off her weaving to stare at the old woman. "And who is that, pray?"

"The goddess Athena," replied the old woman.

Arachne laughed scornfully. "Not even Athena can weave as well as I."

At these words, the wood nymphs who had come to watch Arachne began to whisper among themselves. They

were frightened, for it was dangerous for mortals to set themselves above the gods in anything. Foolish Arachne!

On hearing the boastful words, the old woman's eyes again flashed angrily. But in a moment they softened, and she said, "You are young and have spoken foolishly and in haste. Surely you did not mean what you said. I will give you a chance to take back your words."

But Arachne flung up her head defiantly. "I did mean what I said, and I shall prove it."

"Prove it then," cried the old woman in a terrible voice. A cry went up from the encircling crowd, and Arachne's face turned white as a cloud bank. For the old woman had vanished, and in her place stood the shining form of the goddess Athena.

"For long," she said, "I have heard your boasting and have watched your growing vanity. Now it has led you to defy the gods. It is time you received a lesson from which other mortals as foolish and vain as you may profit. Let the contest begin."

Another loom was set up in the pleasant grove, and
Arachne and the goddess began to weave. News of the
contest spread through the quiet meadow and up the
mountain heights. Soon a large crowd of shepherds drew
near to watch the weavers.

Athena wove upon her loom a bright tapestry that
told the story of other foolish mortals who had thought
themselves greater than the gods, and who had been punished for their pride. Arachne pictured on her loom the
stories that told of the foolish acts of the gods.

The colors used by the two weavers were so bright
they might have been plucked from the rainbow. The
weaving was so perfect that the figures on each loom
seemed to be alive and breathing. The watchers marveled
that such skill could be on Earth or in heaven.

At last the tapestries were finished, and the two contestants stood back to see what each had wrought upon her loom. Athena was so angered by what the girl had dared to picture in her work that she struck the tapestry with her shuttle, splitting the cloth in two. Then she struck Arachne on the forehead. Immediately there swept over the girl a deep remorse at her vanity in setting herself above the very gods. Athena took pity upon the foolish Arachne.

"Live," she said, "but never must you be allowed to forget the lesson you have learned today. You must hang throughout all eternity—you and all who come after you and are of your flesh and blood."

With that, she sprinkled Arachne with bitter juices, and at once Arachne's hair and ears and nose disappeared. Her whole body shrank. Her head grew small, and she took the shape of a spider. And to this day, from her body she draws the thread with which she spins her web. And to this day, often we come upon her hanging by that thread, just as Athena said she must hang throughout all eternity.

◆ LIBRARY LINK ◆

Doris Gates retold Greek myths as a radio storyteller. Later, she published retellings of Greek myths in a series of books. "Arachne" appears in the book entitled The Warrior Goddess: Athena.

The next time you see a spider, take a closer look at its delicate web. You may see what you never knew was there.

Spider Silk

by Penelope Naylor

Spiders' silk is one of the most delicate-looking products of nature. It can be found collecting dust in quiet corners, or sparkling in the morning when it is covered with beads of dew. Sometimes the silk is difficult to see when the threads are freshly spun, or when a spider dangles from a ceiling in an unlit room. At other times, the threads shimmer in the sunlight, creating tiny prisms of rainbow-colored bands.

What is the frail-looking material known as spiders' silk, and how do spiders use it to survive?

Deep inside the spider's abdomen are little glands that produce the liquid known as silk. This liquid is a fiber-like protein named *fibroin* (fī'brō in). It looks like egg white, and is made of the same substance as the silk used for weaving cloth.

The fibroin flows from the silk glands, through narrow tubes, to the spigots on the openings called spinnerets. When the spider wants to make some silk, it opens one or more of the spigots so that a narrow stream of liquid is discharged. As soon as the liquid is exposed to the air, it hardens to form a silken thread, much finer than a strand of human hair.

Once it has hardened, spiders' silk will not break unless it is pulled with considerable force. It can be stretched into different shapes, and can withstand the struggle of entangled prey. The silk does not dissolve in water, and in spite of its delicate appearance, it can be extremely strong.

In fact, the silk of the tropical Golden Silk Spider is about the sturdiest natural fiber known to man. Silk from this spider's huge webs is used on some South Pacific islands as rope for weaving fishing nets.

Spiders use their silk for many different purposes. They wrap insects in silk to trap them as food, and they make silken sacs for their eggs. They release strands of silk for the wind to pick up. Then they fly like eight-legged balloons.

Some spiders lay down their silk threads to mark their

paths, or make silk nurseries for their young. Others line their burrows with silk and cover them with silk trapdoors.

But the most unique way in which spiders use their silk is for building a variety of intricate webs as snares for catching prey.

Many spiders do not build webs. But among those that do, the greatest architects in the spider world belong to the family of Orb-Weavers.

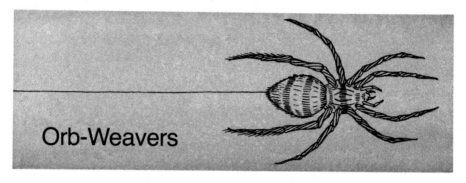

Orb-Weavers

Orb-Weavers are a large family of spiders, with more than two thousand species. They do not necessarily look alike, but they are grouped together because they all make a similar circular web.

Most Orb-Weavers construct their webs during the night. To begin, the spider hangs onto a firm object, and releases a strand of silk from its spinnerets. Currents in the air carry the strand until it catches on another object. If the silk does not connect with anything, the spider draws it back and sends out another strand. (See Illustration 1.) Once a steady line, or bridge, is secured, the Orb-Weaver makes it stronger by putting down more lines of silk. Then the spider attaches a strand to the middle of the bridge, and drops on it until a sturdy anchor is found (2). As the vertical strand is tied, a thread from the bridge is pulled down to form the shape of a Y. The center of the Y will become the hub of the entire web (3).

Next the Orb-Weaver builds radial lines from the hub to the outer edges of the web. It fixes silk threads in the center, one at a time, and carries them along a line of the Y back to the original support (4). The spider climbs down the support, then tightens and secures the thread (5).

This operation is repeated many times until a frame is constructed that looks like a wagon wheel, or a sliced, but lopsided, pie (6).

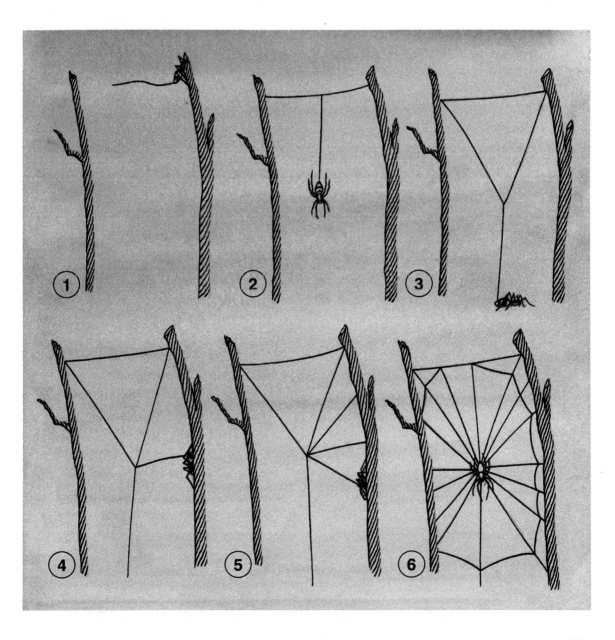

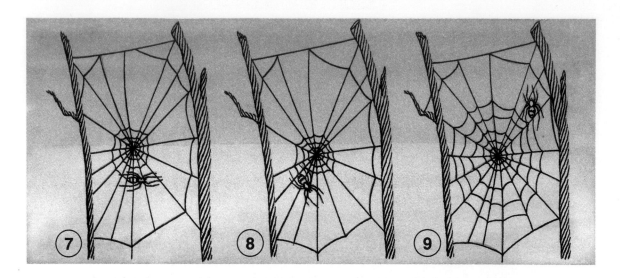

To complete the web, the Orb-Weaver lays down a spiral of silk from the hub to the edge of the frame (7). As it circles, it measures the distance between spirals with its legs. When the spiral is large enough, the spider turns around and goes back the way it came (8). It picks up the guiding spiral and lays down a new one, with the threads much closer together (9).

There are many kinds of orb webs, as each Orb-Weaver places the threads in a certain manner. Some spiders also spin a special design on the finished web as a badge of their species. But most orb webs, no matter what their variations, are constructed in the same basic way.

◆ LIBRARY LINK ◆

The Spider World, *from which this selection was taken, will amaze you with descriptions of spiders and their habits, particularly how they weave webs with Arachne-like perfection!*

Reader's Response

Which selection did you enjoy more, the myth about how spiders came to be or the article about how they spin their webs? Explain the reasons for your choice.

Arachne Spider Silk

Thinking It Over

1. How were Arachne's and Athena's tapestries alike? How were they different?
2. What lesson do you think Arachne learned from Athena?
3. Could Arachne have avoided her punishment? What might she have done to change her fate? How did you decide on your answer?
4. How does a spider produce silk? Tell what happens first, next, and last.
5. Why is it important for spiders' silk to be so strong?
6. The author states that orb weavers are "the greatest architects in the spider world." Is this a fact or the author's opinion?

Writing to Learn

THINK AND COMPARE   Arachne wove with colored threads. Spiders weave with colorless silk. Compare Arachne with the spider she became. Copy and complete the diagram below by adding more of your ideas about how Arachne and the spider are alike and different.

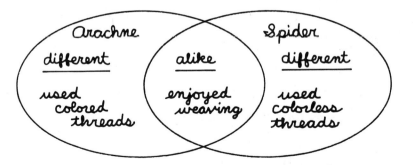

WRITE   Write a paragraph about Arachne. Tell how she resembled the spider she became.

507

LITERATURE LINK

What can you do when you get lost in facts and details?

This photographer is in for trouble. He got stumped by too many tracks, and he's missing the big picture. Reading can be like that, too. Do you find yourself muddled in facts and details at times? You may think: Wait a minute! I'm lost. What is this article really about?

Zero in on Key Points

Getting lost in details can happen to any reader. But there are ways to get back on track. If you're reading along and begin to lose sight of what's important, get a sheet of paper and a pencil. Then try these steps:

- Find the part where you first got lost and begin rereading.
- If there are no headings, read until you see a change in topic. Think about a good heading for that part and write it down.
- Write key ideas for each of the parts. Use your own words.
- As you go, think about how each part fits in with the topic of the article. Use your notes to help.

Strategy for Reading

Below is part of "Spider Silk" with notes taken by a student who was having trouble keeping track of key points.

Once it has hardened, spiders' silk will not break unless it is pulled with considerable force. It can be stretched into different shapes, and can withstand the struggle of entangled prey. The silk does not dissolve in water, and in spite of its delicate appearance, it can be extremely strong.

In fact, the silk of the tropical Golden Silk Spider is about the sturdiest natural fiber known to man. Silk from this spider's huge webs is used on some South Pacific islands as rope for weaving fishing nets.

> Spiders' silk is strong
> —hard to break
> —can be stretched
> —doesn't dissolve in water.
> —silk from the Golden Silk Spider
>   is strongest natural fiber

Did this student pinpoint the key ideas? Do you think making notes like this will help you when you get stuck?

The next selection, "Goose Tracks and Blazing Stars," is full of interesting information. If you have trouble as you're reading, stop and ask yourself: What is most important in what I just read? If you don't know, try the steps you learned in this lesson.

The fabric of history is preserved through goose tracks and blazing stars.

GOOSE TRACKS AND
BLAZING STARS

by Joanne Morgan

A talented quiltmaker shows her handicraft to a young admirer.

"I'll be taking out today," said the first woman.

"Really? I'm just putting in," answered the second. "I hear Liza's on her fourth roll. Are you still working on the half?"

What kind of jargon are they speaking? Is it some kind of fast-food service slang? No, these women are using phrases American quilters have been repeating since George Washington was a boy. Once you understand the background of their story, their odd-sounding remarks will seem as aptly worded as a modern newspaper headline.

The story of American patchwork quilts begins with early English settlers—the Pilgrims. They crammed the hold of the tiny *Mayflower* with the food and tools they needed to survive in their new home. No passenger could take more than the most essential household goods. Everyone aboard ship, however, brought bedding. So quilts, a common bedcovering in England in 1620, probably arrived in America on the *Mayflower*.

The Pilgrims expected the London merchants who were supporting their settlement to send more food, clothing, and other supplies in the spring. But when a ship finally arrived, it did not bring supplies. Instead, it brought more settlers to be fed—settlers with only the clothing on their backs.

As the settlers searched for food, worked the fields, and built houses, scraps of cloth became almost as precious as scraps of food at Plymouth. The days of hard labor rapidly wore holes through the colonists' few garments. They had no cloth to make new clothing, so the women patched and reworked the torn garments until they were too tattered to mend. Then the practical Pilgrims stitched the rags together to make blankets, thus creating the first American "crazy quilts."

Nearly a century later, by the early seventeen hundreds, seaport towns had grown up along the coast. Trading ships were bringing expensive English and Indian cotton prints to these seaports. Since the average settlers could not afford these imported

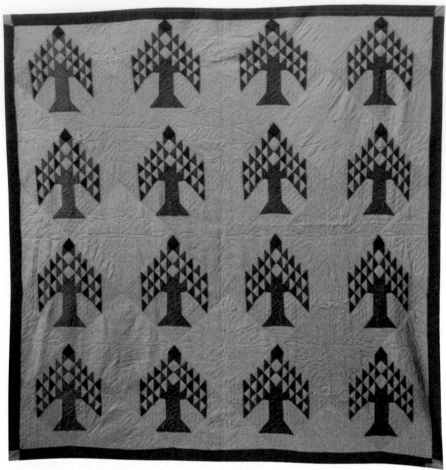

Pieced quilts are made by stitching bits of cloth together.

fabrics, the clever colonists learned to create similar patterns from their own homespun cloth.

Some women cut scraps of fabric and stitched them together to create fanciful flowers and trees. They stitched one tree patch to the next until they had enough pieces sewn together to make a quilt. Patchwork patterns made of bits of cloth stitched together are called *pieced work*.

Other women started with a length of material large enough to cover a bed. They stitched scraps of fabric onto this cloth to make designs that formed pictures of flowers and trees. Patchwork patterns made of bits of fabric sewn onto a larger piece of cloth are called *appliqué work*. All patchwork quilts are made of *pieced work* or *appliqué work* or a combination of both.

With appliquéd quilts, fabric is sewn onto larger cloth to form designs.

Many of the wealthier colonists used designs printed on the imported fabrics to make their appliquéd quilts. They cut the bright flower and beautiful tree designs from the prints and stitched them onto lengths of homespun cloth. The Tree of Life design, a common motif in English and Indian cottons, appears on many eighteenth-century American quilts.

The word *quilt* means layers of fabric stitched together. The patterned layer is called the quilt top. A finished quilt also needs a backing, or lining, layer. Usually a quilt has a third filling layer between the top and the backing. The stitches, often fancy, which hold the layers together are called *quilting*.

Boys as well as girls learned to sew as soon as their chubby baby fingers could hold a needle. Men alone in the wilderness often had to repair their own clothing. Women in colonial villages usually had to make every garment their families owned.

Once a girl could sew well enough to do the mending, she began learning how to put quilt blocks together. At first she worked on simple four-patch, with four parts to each block. Then she moved onto the nine-patch, with nine parts to each block. At least half of all American patchwork patterns are four-patch or nine-patch designs.

Before a girl could marry, she was expected to make a chest full of quilt tops. Most experts agree that the magic number was twelve—twelve everyday quilt tops. When the young lady became engaged, she would begin work on her thirteenth quilt top—an elaborate quilt for best use, known as the Bride's Quilt.

Once a girl became engaged, she needed all the help she could get to finish her thirteen bedcovers before the wedding. What better way to get help than to invite all her friends to a stitching party, or quilting bee?

The first quilting bees took place long before the American Revolution began in 1776. They remained a popular form of entertainment in cities and towns until after the Civil War ended in 1865. In rural areas, neighbors gathered from miles around to enjoy the festivities. The women stitched from dawn till dark. Small children threaded the needles. At suppertime, the men and boys joined the women. After supper, everyone sang, danced, and played games. Sometimes the bee went on for days until all the quilts were finished.

Often the groom added his own best quilt to the bride's collection. Worked by his mother, sisters, or friends, a lad's Freedom Quilt was a symbol of his economic independence. To mark this event, he received a suit of clothes, known as his Liberty Suit, and the elaborate Freedom Quilt.

Not every woman waited for a quilting bee to complete her work. Most homes had a quilting frame, a simple device made of four hardwood poles which were pegged, tied, or clamped at the corners. A quilter "putting in" was putting her layers of fabric into the quilting frame. The lucky lady "taking out" was removing her finished work from the frame.

When "putting in," the quilter first stretched the lining across the frame. Then she patted the filling into place. Finally, she "coaxed" the top into position, making certain every seam was smooth.

The stitcher started at the edge and worked toward the middle of the quilt. All she could comfortably reach was a twelve-inch width. When the first width was done, she unfastened the side rail, rolled the quilt around it, and repegged the frame. Then she did the next width. The average quilt took about six rolls, so a quilter on her fourth roll was more than halfway finished.

Throughout the nineteenth century, women continued to save every odd bit of cloth for patchwork—scraps left from cutting a dress, a child's worn-out smock, a set of tattered drapes. Each piece brought a special memory to the finished quilt. In some rural areas, the salvaged fabric was so valuable that an expert quilter would make patchwork "on the half" for her neighbors. The quilter sewed half the neighbor's scraps into a quilt for the neighbor and kept the other half of the cloth as payment for her work.

Boys sometimes helped with the quilt making as well. They sorted fabrics, cut pieces, and occasionally set blocks together. Calvin Coolidge, president of the United States from 1923 to 1929, pieced a quilt in 1882 at the age of ten. The President Calvin Coolidge Homestead in Plymouth Notch, Vermont, owns this quilt.

Dwight David Eisenhower, president of the United States from 1953 to 1961, recalled helping his mother and brothers with a quilt. He remembered cutting the stripes for the blocks from old shirts and the checks and prints from fabric left from his mother's dresses. The President Eisenhower Birthplace Museum in Denison, Texas, displays that quilt.

The names given to American patchwork patterns are almost as colorful as the quilts themselves—Goose Tracks, Blazing Star, Road to Oklahoma. Although some patterns definitely originated in specific regions, most patterns found their way across the entire country as settlers moved from East to West, or as peddlers carried the latest designs from North to South.

One pattern which began on Cape Cod as the Ship's Wheel became Blazing Star as it traveled inland and Harvest Sun when it reached the Midwest. What Pennsylvania frontiersmen called Bear's Paw, their Quaker neighbors named Hand of Friendship. Long Islanders knew the same pattern as Duck's Foot in the Mud.

Superstition haunted some patterns. No mother wanted her children to sleep under the Wandering Foot. They might grow up

Road to Oklahoma

Blazing Star

Goose Tracks

with an unsettled personality or a constant desire to roam. But when quilters renamed the design Turkey Track, the spell was broken! Likewise, the girl who dared to use a heart motif in a quilt top before her engagement was courting disaster. Superstition said she would never marry.

Quilts carefully handed down from one generation to the next often bear a history as colorful and intricate as their patchwork. Quilts made for special occasions—Presentation Quilts, Album Quilts, Liberty Quilts, and Bride's Quilts—usually carry the signature of their maker. Some quilts have the initials of the quilter and a date in one corner.

But not all beautiful quilts are old. The story of American patchwork quilts continues today. Many community centers and craft shops offer courses in quilting. Libraries and bookstores have books full of quilt patterns. Sewing shops sell quilt kits that take the guesswork out of choosing fabrics. All across the country, quilters are still ''putting in'' and ''taking out,'' although few if any are willing to work ''on the half.''

Reader's Response

In what way would you like to preserve your family's history?

GOOSE TRACKS AND
BLAZING STARS

Thinking It Over

1. When did the story of American patchwork quilts begin?
2. Why were quilts popular in colonial America?
3. What are some similarities and differences between pieced work and appliqué work? How did you identify these similarities and differences?
4. Why do you think quilts played an important role in American family life?
5. Why do you think the quilt pattern known as Ship's Wheel on Cape Cod was renamed as it traveled to the Midwest?
6. Do you think that quilts serve as good preservers of family memories? Explain your answer.

Writing to Learn

THINK AND PREDICT   Think of five names of quilt patterns that could reflect the world as it will be when you grow up.

WRITE   Write a paragraph telling about one of the patterns that you named.

517

The Haste-Me-Well Quilt

by Elizabeth Yates

Simon lay very still in his bed. Outside, birds were singing in the apple tree; cows were mooing by the pasture bars as they did when it was time to be milked.

Sometimes the wind flapped a little at the drawn shade, lifting it and letting in a flash of sunshine to frolic through the darkened room. But Simon only turned restlessly on the bed, kicking at the sheet and sending his books and toys onto the floor. He was tired of lying still, tired of being sick. He was cross at the world.

A set of crayons that his father had brought him that morning toppled off the bed. The blue one lay broken. Simon was glad it was broken and wished they all were. He did not want to use them. He hated crayons. He hated everyone. He—

Then the door opened slowly. It was Grandmother, with something over her arm. She went quietly across to the window, raising the shade so the sunlight could come into the

room. The scent of lilacs came, too, and the song of birds.

Simon screwed up his eyes and said crossly, "Don't want any light, want darkness."

Grandmother laid the quilt she was carrying across the end of his bed; then she sat down on the bed and took one of Simon's hands in hers. She put her other hand on his forehead. Her touch was cool and gentle, like the water of a brook on a summer day. Simon opened his eyes and stared at her.

"Truly the light is sweet, and a pleasant thing it is for the eyes to behold the sun," Grandmother said slowly. "That's in the Bible, Simon. Grandfather read it to me this morning before he went out to plant the corn."

Simon opened his eyes wider. Grandmother had put something at the end of his bed. It was a patchwork quilt. Simon looked at it curiously. It was made not of odd-shaped patterns sewn together, but of tiny pictures of real things.

"Granny, what have you got?" he asked, forgetting how cross he was at the world, forgetting his hot, heavy head.

"This, Simon, is a quilt that we have always laid on the bed of sickness. Because of that it is called the Haste-Me-Well Quilt."

Deftly she shook it out of its folds and spread it over Simon, saying as she did so, "Grandfather needs you to help him on the farm. Your father wants to take a strong boy back to the city with him. It's time that you got well."

"Is it a magic quilt?" Simon asked, fingering it warily.

Grandmother nodded. "Perhaps, but a very special kind of magic."

Then something happened to Simon. He smiled. And because he had not smiled for a week but only thought how sorry he was for himself, his lips were a little stiff at the corners. But the smile lived on in his eyes, dark and deep, almost as dark as his thick black hair.

"Tell me about it, please," he said, snuggling down under the quilt and pulling Grandmother's hand up to his chin.

"Long ago, Simon," she began, "more than a hundred years ago, my grandmother—"

"*Your* grandmother!" he exclaimed—such a long way that seemed to reach back into the past.

"Yes," Grandmother nodded, "Lucy, her name was, made that quilt. She lived on a farm on the moors close to the Scottish border. She was not much older than you when she started it, and she finished it when she was seventeen—in time for her marriage. All of her friends were making quilts, but they made them out of bits and pieces of calico cut into squares or circles or triangles and sewed together into pretty patterns. Lucy was gay and strong, with quick fingers and a lively mind. She wanted to do something different, so she cut out her bits of calico into little pictures."

Grandmother bent over the quilt, and Simon propped his head up to follow her finger's journey across it.

"See, here is the farmhouse where she lived on the edge of the moors. Here are the chickens and the old tabby. Here is the postman, the muffin man with his bell, and the peddler who came with trinkets and ribbons and pots and pans. Here is her father, going off with his crook for the sheep. Here is a teakettle and the footstool at her feet, tables and fire tongs, watering cans and a bellows, horses and snails, a great castle, and a coach with dashing horses. Things she read about in books are here, like dragons and kangaroos and gladiators, as well as the latest fashion in bonnets and a mirror to try them on before"—Grandmother got more and more excited as her fingers flew across the quilt and she pointed out its wonders.

"It *is* a magic quilt," Simon agreed.

"Whatever young Lucy saw as interesting, useful, or amusing," Grandmother went on, "she snipped out of calico and sewed onto a white square, which was sewed to all the other white squares. Then, see, Simon, around the border she planted an old-fashioned garden!"

"It's like your garden, Granny, here at Easterly Farm!" Simon exclaimed.

"That's because it was *her* garden," Grandmother said quietly.

"It was?"

"Yes. When Lucy married, she and her husband came to America, here to this New England countryside. It was close to wilderness then, you must remember, but with their own hands they built this house; and while Silas cleared the fields and planted his crops and raised his stock, Lucy brought up her family—five boys and five girls, each one with a name from the Bible."

"And the quilt?"

"It must have meant everything to her in those days, for it was all her past—beautiful and orderly and gracious—and she brought it forward into a life of hardship and toil and privation. To her it was the tale of an age that was gone forever, costumes and customs, the little things used in a house and the larger things that, though never seen, were talked about; and she made it the background of a new life."

"How did it get its name, Granny? You haven't told me that."

Grandmother smiled. "The quilt used to lie on the guest bed, for all to admire it and for its occasional use. Then one day Peter was sick. He was the eldest of the five boys. He was wracked with chills, and nothing they could do seemed to warm him. Lucy put all the blankets she had over him, and finally the quilt. Soon, oh, much sooner than anyone thought possible, the chills shivered themselves away and he went to sleep. Ever after that the quilt was put on the bed of a child who was sick."

"Was it ever on my father's bed?" Simon asked.

"Yes." Grandmother looked away. "Once when he fell from the barn during the haying and hurt his back, the doctor said that he could not do anything for him because he could not keep him still long enough." Grandmother smiled and turned back to look at Simon. "Grandfather and I didn't give up so easily. We put the quilt on his bed and for days and days afterward your father had wonderful adventures with it. He was always going to tell me about them, but he always forgot to."

Simon was looking drowsy, so Grandmother smoothed the folds of the quilt as it lay over him and stole softly from the room.

Simon moved his fingers lovingly over the quilt. He stroked the furry rabbit and called to the horse galloping across the field. He waved to the coach as it dashed along the road to London, and he bought a muffin from the muffin man. Then he opened the gate in the white fence that enclosed the farmhouse from the rolling moors and went up to the wide front door. Seeing it from a distance, he had not thought he could possibly go through the door, but the nearer he got to it the more of a size they were, and he found himself going into the house.

Inside, it was cool and quiet. His steps echoed a bit on the polished brick of the floor, but the sound did not disturb the tabby sleeping by the hearth. On the hob hung a fat kettle with a wisp of steam coming from its spout, saying as clearly as any words that whoever might be passing would be welcome to a dish of tea.

Simon went to the end of a passage and pushed open another door. A young girl was sitting by an open window. Grandmother had not told him what Lucy looked like, but Simon knew right away that this was Lucy. The quilt lay in a heap on the floor beside her; on a table nearby were scissors and thread, and bits and pieces of cloth. Simon crossed the room and stood beside Lucy. She looked up at him.

"I have a little boy in the quilt," she said. "There's no room for you."

"That's all right," Simon replied, "but mayn't I sit down and watch you?"

"If you wish," she smiled, "but it's all finished."

Simon sat down, tailor fashion, before her, cupping his chin in his hands. "Two hundred and seventy-four squares around a center panel, bordered by flowers," Lucy went on.

"It's all done, but it's well it is for I'm going away next week."

"Where are you going?" Simon asked.

"To the New World," Lucy looked out of the window and Simon thought her voice throbbed, like a bird's on a low note. "I shall never see England again, never the rolling moors, nor the mountains of Scotland."

"*Never?*" Simon echoed. What a long time that was.

She shook her head slowly. "Ever since I was a little girl I have been cutting out and patching together the things that are my world. Now I can take my old world with me into the

new. Once I wished I could draw pictures, go to London, and study to be an artist, but—"

"Why didn't you?" Simon demanded.

"If I had been a man I should have, but a girl doesn't do those things. Scissors, thread, thimble, calico—those are my artist's tools. Fingers are wonderful things, aren't they, little boy? You put a tool in them—it doesn't matter what it is—a hoe, a churn, a needle, a spoon—and they do the rest."

"My father gave me crayons to draw with," Simon confided. "I want to be an artist someday."

"Crayons?" Lucy looked as if the word were strange to her. "They'll not make you an artist, but fingers will."

"Why?"

"Because they are friends to all you're feeling. I didn't know when I started this quilt that it would mean so much to me. Now, though I'm going far away, everything I love is going with me."

Simon stroked the quilt. "It will be nice to have it on your bed, won't it?"

She laughed. "Oh, it won't ever be on my bed. It's too good for that! It'll be in the spare room, for guests to use when they come to stay with us."

"And it will be on the children's beds whenever they are sick," Simon went on.

Lucy looked at him, amazed. "What a strange idea!"

"It will make them well."

"Do you really think so, little boy?" Lucy looked incredulous, then her eyes gazed far away as if she did not see Simon at all and she said slowly, "The quilt could never do that, but perhaps the thoughts I have sewed into it could." Her eyes came back from the faraway place and she looked closely at Simon. "What is your name, little boy? I would like to know in case we meet again."

"Simon."

She wrinkled her brows. "Yes, Simon. For a moment I thought you were one of my boys." She went on looking at him as if wondering why he seemed so familiar, then she shook her head.

"There's magic in the quilt," Simon commented, reaching out and touching it.

"Magic? What strange words you use."

"But there is," Simon insisted. "How did you put it in?"

She laughed gaily. "What you call magic is just being happy in what you are doing, loving it the way you love the morning or the new lambs every spring. There's strength in happiness."

The blind was flapping at the window. The scent of lilacs filled the air. The sun, dropping low over the hills, was coming into the room like an arrow of gold. Simon drew his hands over the quilt and propped himself up on his elbows. On the floor lay his crayons, one of them broken.

He slipped out of bed and gathered the crayons together into their box, then he pushed the pillows up straight and climbed back into bed. Leaning against the pillows, he curved his knees up so his drawing pad might rest against them. He was sad that the blue crayon was broken, for so much blue was needed to arch the sky over the rolling moors and give life to Lucy's eyes. But he would manage somehow.

Quickly he worked, his fingers strong and free, eager with happiness, hurrying to do something for Grandmother so that he might have a present for her when she came back.

The door pushed open a little, then wider as Grandmother saw Simon. On the table by his bed she laid a small tray.

"There's a glass of milk from the afternoon's milking,
Simon," she said. "Grandfather sent it up to you, and I
thought you'd like a molasses cookie from a batch I've just
made."

Simon finished his picture quickly.

"See, Granny, I have a present for you!"

Grandmother smiled as she took the drawing. It was a happy picture, well-done, too. Simon's father would be pleased with it. A young girl and a patchwork quilt, and in the background a small stone farmhouse. Grandmother looked closer. It was the Haste-Me-Well Quilt and Lucy looking at the world with eyes of wonder.

"Thank you, Simon, thank you very much, but I did not tell you my grandmother's eyes were blue, did I?"

Simon shook his head. "Were they?"

"Yes, blue as morning light on the mountains, and her fingers were fine and strong."

Fingers were wonderful things, Simon thought. It didn't much matter what they held if they held it with joy. Simon looked dreamily across the room. He was trying to remember something to tell Grandmother, but whatever it was it was slipping from him like a rainbow before full sunshine.

"May I get up now, Granny, please?" he asked.

A surprised smile lighted Grandmother's face. She nodded and began to fold up the Haste-Me-Well Quilt.

◆ LIBRARY LINK ◆

You may enjoy other historical stories by Elizabeth Yates such as Under the Little Fir *and* Amos Fortune Free Man.

Reader's Response

Which part of the Haste-Me-Well Quilt would you like to see in your dreams?

The
Haste-Me-Well Quilt

Thinking It Over

1. At the beginning of the story, why was Simon feeling cross with the world?
2. What did Grandmother do to comfort Simon?
3. Simon believed he met Lucy in England. Explain what you believe really happened. How did you reach this conclusion?
4. How did Simon feel by the end of the story?
5. What made the Haste-Me-Well Quilt so special?

Writing to Learn

THINK AND INVENT   Simon discovered his great-grandmother's memories stitched in the Haste-Me-Well Quilt. On the chart below, read the names of items that made the quilt personal. Make your own list and name items that have a personal significance for you.

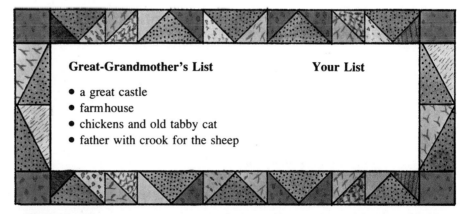

Great-Grandmother's List   **Your List**

- a great castle
- farmhouse
- chickens and old tabby cat
- father with crook for the sheep

WRITE   Simon enjoyed a gift from the past. Your ideas are a gift for the future. Use your list to write a letter to your future grandchildren. Tell them what you want them to remember about this time and this place.

The Land of
COUNTERPANE

When I was sick and lay a-bed,
I had two pillows at my head,
And all my toys beside me lay
To keep me happy all the day.

And sometimes for an hour or so
I watched my leaden soldiers go,
With different uniforms and drills,
Among the bed-clothes, through the hills;

And sometimes sent my ships in fleets
All up and down among the sheets;
Or brought my trees and houses out,
And planted cities all about.

I was the giant great and still
That sits upon the pillow-hill,
And sees before him, dale and plain,
The pleasant land of counterpane.

ROBERT LOUIS STEVENSON

British Infantry regiments, ca. 1800-85

LITERATURE LINK

How do illustrations in an article help you understand the text?

Have you ever had to write directions telling someone how to get to your home? Maybe you drew a map to be sure the directions were clear and easy to understand. If so, you discovered firsthand the truth of the old saying "A picture is worth a thousand words." Information is frequently made clearer by pictures.

Authors use photographs, drawings, and diagrams to help readers visualize complicated information. Notice how the pictures help explain the information about birds in the text below.

Wing Shapes

gull

pheasant

The shape of the wings affects the way a bird flies. The pheasant, for example, can rise quickly from the ground by flapping its short, wide wings. They are very effective for a quick takeoff when the bird is frightened.

Fast-flying birds, such as the swallow, have thin, pointed wings. Swallows move swiftly and turn sharply in the air. Other birds, with long wings, make use of wind currents to glide and soar on. They travel great distances on their long, outstretched wings. But it takes a lot of effort for the bird to keep its wings spread against the force of the wind.

swallow

While flying, a bird changes the angle of its wings to change direction; it beats its wings faster to increase speed. The tail is used to steer with and the alula (thumb) feathers lift to prevent the bird stopping or stalling suddenly.

eagle

from *Birds*, Franklin Watts, 1984

Does looking at the pictures help you understand how different kinds of wings affect the flight of birds? Which birds are shown and described but not mentioned by name?

Paying close attention to diagrams and other illustrations as you read will make new information clearer. You'll enjoy it more, learn it faster, and remember it longer. Follow these tips for combining text and illustrations:

- Look at all the illustrations before you begin reading.
- Carefully read captions that accompany illustrations.
- Look again at the illustrations as you read.
- After reading, use the illustrations to remember main points.

Use these tips as you study the text and illustration below from "Tides at the Seashore," an article you read in Unit 3. Notice how the diagram and the information in the text work together to help you understand how the moon causes tides.

The moon pulls hardest on the part of the earth nearest it. The pull lifts the water on that part of the earth. The water bulges out toward the moon. Where the bulge is greatest, it is known as high tide. When the moon is on the horizon, and the bulge is the lowest, it is low or ebb tide.

At the same time that the moon lifts the water up on the part of the earth nearest it, the moon pulls least on the opposite side of the earth. The water on the opposite side of the earth bulges away from the moon, because of the lessening of the pull.

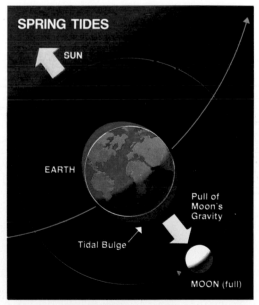

SPRING TIDES
SUN
EARTH
Pull of Moon's Gravity
Tidal Bulge
MOON (full)

The illustrations are the main focus of the next article, "Reading a Picture." As you read, combine text with illustrations to understand the paintings.

READING A PICTURE

BY SHIRLEY GLUBOK

Terrace at Sainte-Adresse, 1867, by Claude Monet (1840-1926)

Have you ever heard the saying "a picture is worth a thousand words"? You will really appreciate its meaning once you learn how to read a picture.

A work of art has a language of its own. Paintings and drawings can speak to us without words. Sometimes an artist has a message for us and when we look at the picture we can read it easily. But sometimes a work has different meanings to different people, and each person looking at it can see it in a different way.

Claude Monet: Observing Nature Directly

The French artist Claude Monet[1] spent the summer of 1867 in the seaside resort town of Sainte-Adresse. He always had his paints and brushes with him. The water and sky made an interesting background for his compositions. One day when his family and a friend were relaxing on the terrace overlooking the sea, he composed a picture of the scene.

By looking carefully at the painting it is possible to gain a great deal of information. The bright flowers and green grass and the crisp white dresses on the women tell us it is summer. We know it is

[1]Claude Monet (klōd mō nā′)

537

a fine day because the sky is blue with a few light clouds floating across the sky. The sun casts shadows and the women are holding parasols to shield their faces from its rays. The slight ripples on the water, and the full sails on the boats in the distance tell us there is a gentle breeze. The breeze can also be seen blowing through the flags.

There is much more to be learned by looking at the picture a little longer. It is apparent that the time of day is late afternoon because the shadows are long. And we can tell that the people know each other. They have been sitting together, and two of them got up from their chairs to walk to the edge of the terrace where they are having a conversation.

We can also tell that it is the late 1860s by the style of clothing and by the combination of sailboats and steamboats in the distance. The steamboat had begun to take the place of the sailing ship, but large sailing vessels were still being used for transportation as well as for pleasure. Sainte-Adresse is located on the English Channel that separates England from France.

The artist focuses our attention on the man and woman standing on the terrace by placing them in the center and framing them between the two flagpoles. The seated gentleman sits with his chair facing in their direction, drawing our attention to them. The round shapes of the flowers in the center, the ladies' parasols, and the frames of the chairs balance the rectangular shapes of the flags.

Claude Monet painted *Terrace at Sainte-Adresse* when he was a young man. It is known that the bearded gentleman represents his father, the woman seated under the parasol is his aunt, and the young woman standing is his cousin. However, his interest was in the outdoor scene and not in the features of the people.

As time went on the artist grew more and more interested in painting only what he saw in nature. He especially wanted to show the shimmering color effects of sunlight on flowers and on the surface of the water. He would often paint the same scene over and over again in different seasons and times of day. Monet exhibited his work with a group of artists known as Impressionists, who liked to paint outdoors, observing nature directly.

Still Life with Puppies, 1888, by Paul Gauguin (1848-1903)

Paul Gauguin: Painting the World of Feelings

Paul Gauguin[2] was not interested in observing nature to record what his eye saw. He wanted to discover the hidden world of his own feelings and to express them without attempting to show things as they appear to our eye. In his paintings Gauguin made the shapes of objects simpler and flatter than they would be in nature. So we can tell immediately that they are not true to life. When we see three tiny puppies with orange or yellow ears drinking milk from a pan, we expect them to be on the ground. When we look more closely we realize we do not see what we expect to see. The puppies are standing on a tablecloth. The rounded form of the table can be seen at the very bottom of the picture.

Three blue glasses and three objects that could be little apples are lined up in front of the puppies. The artist did not want to tell us what these objects are by showing them realistically, so we are forced to guess. We also wonder why the objects are in threes. When we look at the fruit on the napkin in front of the glasses we see another group of three . . . three pieces of fruit. And then two are left over. When we try to count the pieces of fruit in the bowl it is difficult to tell just how many there are. Then our eye gets another surprise . . . the upper rim of the bowl is flattened. The patterns on the tablecloth do not seem to have any special arrangement, and the markings on the dogs are just as puzzling. Yet the overall pattern of the composition is balanced and pleasing to the eye.

The painting is full of puzzling things. Every object has a dark outline with no shadows. And the table top tilts to show everything with equal interest, in sizes that have nothing to do with real life. The puppies' bodies are no bigger than the blue glasses, which in turn are not much larger than the pears on the table. When Gauguin made this painting, he was working in a new style and he wanted to free himself from reality.

In his own life, Gauguin attempted to free himself from the everyday world. He was a successful businessman in Paris who was always attracted to faraway countries. At first he painted and collected works of art as a hobby, but when he was thirty-five he quit his job to take up painting as a career. After moving about here and there, he sailed for Tahiti in the South Pacific to escape from civilization. He spent almost ten years in the tropics but failed to find the earthly paradise he had sought.

Marc Chagall: Creating from Dreams and Memories

Marc Chagall's[3] childhood in Russia was a constant theme that he used in his paintings throughout

[3]Marc Chagall (mark shə gäl')

540

Green Violinist, 1923/24, by Marc Chagall (1887–1985)

his lifetime. The colorful works that are memories of his childhood sometimes show strange combinations of figures that seem like dreams. When he was a boy, Chagall learned to play the violin from his uncle, who was a fiddler. Fiddlers were important in Russian village life because there were no orchestras. They played their cheery music at weddings and other gatherings. The painter's love of music shows in his works; violins appear over and over.

Chagall painted *Green Violinist* in the early 1920s, when he was living in Paris. He made the fiddler's form huge while everything else, even the houses at the bottom of the picture and the church between them, is tiny. These homes with snow all around represent the square in the Russian village where he grew up.

The painting is full of surprises. The first is to see a man with a green face. The artist himself said this has no meaning. Checked trousers worn by the violinist remind us of Chagall's interest in the circus. Hebrew words are written on the bottom of one of the legs. The words mean "Oh Father!" The artist would rather paint what was in the private world of his mind than what he saw in the world outside. The natural colors of objects did not matter to him, and it also did not matter that the positions of the objects do not seem to make sense.

In this strange composition people defy the laws of gravity by floating or jumping in the air, against clouds that are shaped like balloons. A tiny man standing with his feet outspread is waving his violin. A ladder resting against a tree may stand for Chagall's wish to be taller when he was a child. The horse propping itself against a house and peering upward at the fiddler may have the same meaning. Another horse pulling a cart appears at the top of the picture. The artist once said, "All my life I have drawn horses that look more like donkeys or cows. I saw these animals in Lyozno[4] at my grandfather's, where I often asked to go along to the neighboring villages when he went to buy livestock for his butcher shop."

Marc Chagall carried his childhood memories with him all his life. He was born in the town of Vitebsk,[5] Russia, in 1887. He went to art school in Russia and then moved to Paris. Afterwards he returned to Russia, where he painted set designs and costumes for the theater. Later in his life he visited Israel often. He made stained glass windows for a hospital in Jerusalem and huge paintings for Lincoln Center in New York. Chagall spent most of his life in France, where he died in 1985.

[4]Lyozno (lyōz′ nō)
[5]Vitebsk (vē′ tebsk)

541

Cat and Bird, 1928, by Paul Klee (1879–1940)

Paul Klee: Making the Imagination Visible

The images in Paul Klee's[6] paintings came from his imagination, not from what he saw. To show that a cat has a bird on his mind, Klee drew a large figure of a cat that fills the entire picture. A small bird is perched on the animal's forehead, just above its eyes. The cat stares straight ahead as it thinks about the bird. All of the cat's features are drawn with clear-cut lines in geometric shapes that connect with each other. The eyes and nose could almost be human. The tip of the nose shaped like a tiny heart, the triangular mouth, and the animal's whiskers stretching into the corners of the picture, remind us this is a cat.

Paul Klee was born in Switzerland to a German father and Swiss mother who were musicians. As a boy he showed talent as a violinist, but he chose to go to art school in Germany, where he lived during

[6]Klee (klā)

World War I. He was teaching art in Germany when Hitler rose to power in the 1930s. His art school was closed by the Nazis, and he was forced to return to Switzerland where he continued to work for the rest of his life.

Georgia O'Keeffe: Communicating Through Colors and Shapes

Forms and shapes that she saw around her were the inspiration for Georgia O'Keeffe's paintings. She chose skyscrapers as her subject when she was in New York City, barns when she was in the country, and adobe houses and churches in New Mexico. O'Keeffe had wanted to be an artist since childhood, and as a young woman decided to paint in her own way, not like other people. She said, "I found I could say things with color and shapes that I couldn't say in any other way . . . things that I had no words for."

Sometimes she concentrated on a single flower and enlarged it to enormous proportions until the form filled an entire canvas. When she first began visiting the New Mexican desert, she missed flowers. As she took long walks she began collecting animal bones she found on the ground and piled them up on the patio of her house. She said, "To me they are as beautiful as anything I know . . . to me they are strangely more living than the animals walking around."

She felt close to the world of nature . . . sun, sky, trees, mountains, and desert. Once she said about her life, "I have picked flowers where I found them—have picked up seashells and rocks and pieces of wood where there were seashells and rocks and pieces of wood that I liked. When I found the beautiful white bones on the des-

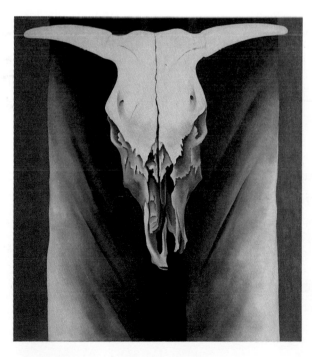

Cow's Skull: Red White and Blue, 1931, by Georgia O'Keeffe (1887–1986)

543

ert, I picked them up and took them home, too. I have used these things to say what is to me the wideness and wonder of the world as I live in it."

When she returned to New York she took a barrel of bones with her as symbols of the desert. A cow's skull that was worn smooth by wind and water and bleached white by the sun became the subject of one of her finest works. She painted the skull against a blue cloth background, then added red stripes down the sides of the painting to make it "a great American painting" in the colors of the flag. She wanted people to notice it, and they did. The cracked skull of a cow with smooth horns, empty eyes and jagged edges is an interesting form. Sometimes she painted something even more unusual—an animal skull and a fresh flower together.

Georgia O'Keeffe was born on a wheat farm in Wisconsin in 1887. She studied art in Chicago and New York, and taught art in schools and colleges. O'Keeffe's paintings were considered "modern" and they were exhibited in New York at an art gallery that showed modern art before it became popular. The gallery was owned by Alfred Stieglitz, who was one of the world's great photographers. He made hundreds of photographs of O'Keeffe. Stieglitz and O'Keeffe were married in 1924.

O'Keeffe discovered the wonders of New Mexico on a visit. She loved the empty space and the peace and quiet, and said the country fitted her exactly. She spent her summers there. After Stieglitz died, she moved to New Mexico where she lived and worked until her death in 1986.

◆ LIBRARY LINK ◆

Shirley Glubok has written several art books for young readers. You may enjoy The Art of Ancient Greece, The Art of Africa, *and* The Art of Colonial America.

Reader's Response

Which of the paintings discussed in the selection did you like best? Why?

READING A PICTURE

Thinking It Over

1. When did the scene in Claude Monet's painting *Terrace at Sainte-Adresse* take place? How can you tell?
2. What did Paul Gauguin try to express by painting three tiny puppies with orange or yellow ears?
3. Make up another title to describe Chagall's painting *Green Violinist.*
4. If the cat in Klee's painting *Cat and Bird* could talk, what do you think it would say?
5. What did Georgia O'Keeffe want you to see and experience with *Cow's Skull: Red White and Blue*?
6. What do you think is the difference between "reading" a painting and looking at one?

Writing to Learn

THINK AND VISUALIZE   Select a favorite picture from this article. Imagine that you are in the painting. Close your eyes and find answers to the questions below.

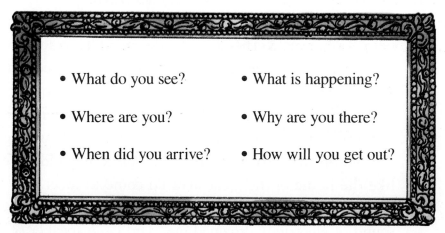

- What do you see?
- Where are you?
- When did you arrive?
- What is happening?
- Why are you there?
- How will you get out?

WRITE   Use the answers to these questions to write a postcard that you might send from this place.

Jōi's ambition to be a cartoonist takes him to another part of town—and a conversation he'll never forget.

The Cartoonist's Apprentice

by Allen Say

ENGLISH CONVERSATION SCHOOL, said a small hand-painted sign on the door. I looked at the crumpled newspaper article in my hand to check the address, and my heart sank. No mistake, I'd come to the right place.

I had never been in this part of Tokyo, and the shabbiness of the neighborhood depressed me. The dead-end street was full of cracks and puddles, and the two-storied office building in front of me looked more like a run-down barracks than a place of business. I looked blankly at the rain-soaked side shingles and thought of rows and rows of decaying teeth stacked on top of one another. The place just didn't seem like the home of the great man I'd come to meet.

Suddenly a deafening noise exploded, and the screeching sound of electricity drowned me. The large speaker of a nearby movie theater began to blast away the theme music, announcing the start of the first afternoon show. I looked

back toward the bustling train station where I'd gotten off a train only a few minutes before, and wondered if I should go back. Bicycles darted every which way, enormous shiny foreign cars cruised like the lords of the avenue, charwomen rummaged among the ruins of bombed buildings to bag whatever trash they could find. In between the blasts from the speaker I heard the calls of the shoeshine boys, and felt a chill. I didn't know what to do.

I stood there a good five minutes, hoping for someone to come out of the building—for anything to happen. But nobody came out, and nothing happened. Finally, more to get away from the noise than anything else, I rushed through the front door.

The long hallway was dark and empty, smelling of mildew. The evenly spaced doors along the corridor had windows of milky glass, and ghostlike figures moved behind them, whispering in small, dull voices. I went from door to door, reading the nameplates, but the man I was looking for was not on the first floor. It was almost a relief.

The second floor wasn't much better, except a dirty skylight in the ceiling cast a shaft of light along the corridor and made the place seem a little more cheerful. Another ENGLISH CONVERSATION SCHOOL sign was posted on the wall at the top of the staircase, with an arrow pointing to the far end of the hallway. I followed the arrow, and went past the school until there was only one door left. Something small and white glowed on the door, right below the frosted glass. It was an ordinary calling card, pinned there with a thumbtack.

Noro Shinpei,[1] read the four characters. At first glance the name looked like any other, but when it was read aloud it was nonsense. Noro, the surname, means slow, and Shinpei is an army private. Slow Army Private. It was obviously a pen name, but it looked very official and dignified on a printed card. I looked at it again and touched the crisp card to see if it was real. My heart began to beat fast, then I laughed silently. Not because of the comical name, but because I'd finally found the man I'd come to meet.

Feeling weak in my knees, I tapped twice on the glass.

"Enter," said a man's voice. It was more like an order than an invitation. I cracked open the door and peeked inside. Two figures were seated at a long desk, peering up at me with curiosity.

"A-are you Master Noro?"

"You've found him. Come in and close the door before you catch TB."

Quickly I closed the door and looked around the room. Books and magazines and pieces of paper were scattered everywhere. The desk was cluttered with pens and nibs and

[1]Noro Shinpei: (nō′ rō shin′ päē)

548

pencils, brushes of all sizes, and more inkpots than anybody could use in a lifetime.

"The squalor impresses you" Noro Shinpei smiled. His two front teeth were crowned with gold.

"No, sir. I mean it looks fine, sir," I said with a shaky voice.

"We had a visit from the local authorities this morning," he said and laughed. "Well, pull up a chair and sit. Put the books on the floor, anywhere. Hand me a pen, Tokida,[2]" he told the youth sitting next to him. I put the pile of books on the floor and sat down.

Noro Shinpei was in his late thirties. His long hair looked as if it was always combed with fingers, and he wore a long, cotton-filled winter kimono. Not many men wore kimonos anymore and he looked old-fashioned, sitting there with his hands inside the long sleeves, samurai-style. There was something about Noro Shinpei that reminded me of an old-time *ronin*.[3] I say old-time because in the old days a *ronin* was a samurai without a master. A samurai was a warrior, an expert swordsman who dedicated his life to serving a master. Today a *ronin* is someone without a job.

Tokida looked three or four years older than I. His hair was cropped close to the skull, and his sharp face was full of pimples. He wore a pair of round steel-rimmed glasses, and his shirt was crinkled as if he'd slept in it. He stared at me suspiciously.

"And your name?" asked Noro Shinpei.

"Jōi,[4] sir."

"That's an unusual name. How do you write that?"

I wrote the two characters on a piece of paper.

"Kiyoi.[5]" He misread my name.

"It's Jōi, sir." I corrected him.

"And what can I do for you?"

[2]Tokida (tō kē′ du)   [4]Jōi (jō′ ē)
[3]ronin (rō′ nēn)   [5]Kiyoi (kē′ yō ē)

"I want to be a cartoonist, sir."

"I see. . . ."

A long pause.

"And you want to be my pupil, is that it?"

"Yes, sir."

My ears felt hot and the shirt collar tightened around my neck.

"How old are you, Kiyoi?"

"Thirteen, sir. I'll be fourteen in August."

"How tall are you?" He looked me up and down in disbelief.

"A hundred and seventy-three meters, sir."

"Centimeters, you mean."

"Yes, sir."

"Remarkable. A giraffe-boy, the chosen one," he said. He was being polite, punning on giraffe-child which also means a wonder child. Telephone pole was what they called me at school.

"Where do you go to school?"

"Aoyama[6] Middle School, sir."

"A very good school. Is this spring vacation?"

"Yes, sir, two weeks."

"Where do you live?"

"Shibuya,[7] sir."

"Near your school. Were you born in Tokyo, then?"

"Yokohama, sir."

"Do your parents know you came to see me?"

"Yes, sir."

"Did you tell them why?"

"Yes, they don't mind, sir."

"You're quite sure about that? Even if you are a genius, you're a minor and I have to respect your parents' wishes. What is your father's occupation?"

"He's a merchant, sir."

"Now that's a sly answer. He could be anything from a street peddler to a department store tycoon. I get the feeling you're the oldest son."

"Yes, sir."

"Where is your sense of filial duty?"

"What do you mean, sir?"

"What does your father feel about his heir wanting to become a cartoonist?"

"He doesn't mind, sir, he really doesn't. He only wants me to stay in school. He says I'm going to change my mind when I grow older," I said desperately.

"And do you think you'll change your mind?"

"No, sir," I admitted.

"Of course not. At least that's what you think now. What about your mother?"

[6]Aoyama (ou yä′ mu)   [7]Shibuya (shē bōō′ yu)

"She doesn't mind either, sir, as long as I do well in school."

"You're blessed with a wise mother. So tell me, why do you want to be a cartoonist?"

The question surprised me. Somehow I didn't expect such a question from a famous cartoonist.

"I'm not sure, sir, but I've always drawn. I'm not good at anything else. I'd rather draw cartoons than anything, sir."

"Drawing before dumplings." He rephrased an old saying. "Tell me, if I don't take you on, what will you do?"

"I don't know . . . I'll do it on my own, sir," I said defiantly, though I suddenly felt tired and hopeless.

"I like your spirit," he said and began to laugh. His laughter took me aback.

"So what have you been drawing?"

"I've been copying mostly, sir. I've copied a lot from your strips."

"Draw something for me then," he said, handing me a drawing pad. "Let's say a horse. Yes, draw a horse, and don't try to imitate my style—or anybody else's for that matter. I want you to draw it in your own way. Tokida and I will go about our business, so relax and take your time."

I didn't move. I couldn't. My knees would have buckled under me if I tried to stand up. I picked up a pencil. I wished Tokida would leave the room, but he showed no sign of getting up. He's probably enjoying the scene, I thought, waiting for me to make a fool of myself. What if my hand shakes, I thought suddenly. Then I heard the theater speaker for the first time since I'd been in the room. The noise was faint, but the mumbling dialogue and the background music comforted me.

The first thing I drew was an ear, the side view of it, then I drew another ear, slightly overlapping the first. Then the slanting line of the forehead, a little bump over the eye, and the dipping "dish nose" of an Arabian horse. I heard the soft lead of the pencil sliding over the paper. My hand didn't shake, and I wasn't afraid anymore.

Soon a side view of a horse appeared on the page. I could have drawn the horse from some other angle but didn't think of it. I was happy with the way the horse was coming out. The snout was about the right length, the legs had all the joints, the tail turned out a little too bushy, and the eye was a bit like a human eye, but it was a horse, all right, and not a bad one. I shaded the animal here and there and handed the drawing to the great cartoonist.

He looked at it, squinting his eyes. He had a very large nose for a Japanese, pitted with pores, and his jowl was blue though it was freshly shaven. Maybe he's part Ainu,[8] I thought, one of those people who lived in Japan long before the Chinese and the Koreans came to claim the land for themselves.

Tokida craned his neck to peek at my drawing but the cartoonist closed the sketchbook.

"The horse was an excuse," he said. "I wanted to see how you draw. Most boys your age draw like this," he said, drawing a straight line with many jerky strokes. "You seem to have survived your art teachers."

I thought he was paying me a compliment, but wasn't sure, so I said nothing.

"So you want to devote your life to the serious business of cartooning," he asked.

"Yes, sir."

"What can I do to dissuade you?"

"Nothing, sir."

"Then I have no choice but to take you on."

"You mean I can be your pupil, sir?"

"If that is what you want."

[8]Ainu (ī′ nōō)

553

Speechless, I nodded my head.

"Then I accept you as my pupil. But there's one thing, Kiyoi. Any talk about money and out you go; is that clear?"

"Yes, sir."

"Don't worry, Kiyoi, I'll make you earn your keep." He laughed. "Tokida here is three years older than you. At least that's what he tells me. Think of him as your partner, an older brother."

Tokida gave me a thin smile. I knew very well he resented me for barging in to share his master. I had read about him in the paper, the youngest budding cartoonist.

"If you have nothing else to do, stay for supper," said my new master.

"Thank you, sir, but my family is expecting me," I said, and bowed several times to the two of them and walked out of the door as calmly as I could. I floated down the dusty staircase, swam through the hallway, and burst out the front door.

Puddles were still there on the pavement, but now the rainbow of the oil slick caught my eye. The speaker was still blasting away, but now it sounded as though it was celebrating my triumph. I looked up at the ugly building and somehow the shabbiness of it seemed wonderful.

◆ LIBRARY LINK ◆

Would you like to know what happens to Jōi after he becomes Noro's pupil? Find out by reading The Ink-Keeper's Apprentice, *by Allen Say.*

Reader's Response

What does this story say to you about the importance of having someone to guide or teach you?

The Cartoonist's Apprentice

Thinking It Over

1. Why did Jōi want to work for the famous cartoonist?
2. Why do you think Noro told Jōi to draw in his own way and not anyone else's?
3. How did Jōi's feelings about Noro's neighborhood change after he was accepted as the cartoonist's apprentice?
4. Define *ronin* and *samurai*. Would you describe Jōi as a *ronin* or a *samurai*? Explain your reasoning.
5. What do you think Jōi would have done if Noro had not accepted him as a pupil? What makes you think so?

Writing to Learn

THINK AND EVALUATE   Becoming a good cartoonist isn't easy. You must have certain qualities and learn certain skills. On your paper, complete the chart below that evaluates qualities that are important for being a good cartoonist.

Quality	Important for being a good cartoonist	Reason
Witty	+	So cartoons will be funny

WRITE   Use the information on your chart to write a paragraph about the qualities you would find in a good cartoonist.

HARPER TROPHY

PATRICIA MacLACHLAN

The Facts and Fictions of Minna Pratt

By the Newbery Medal-Winning Author of *Sarah, Plain and Tall*

There are times, more often lately, that Minna feels she knows Mozart better than she knows herself.

from *The Facts and Fictions of Minna Pratt* by Patricia MacLachlan

When Minna Pratt rides the bus to her cello lesson or browses in her mother's writing room or listens to Willie the street musician, she ponders some puzzling questions. Are her brother's favorite tabloid headlines fact or fiction? Why doesn't her mother ask Minna normal questions like "What did you have for lunch today?" instead of "What is the quality of beauty?" And then there is Minna's daily question to herself: When will she be able to play the cello with a trembling vibrato like a real string player?

When Minna meets Lucas Ellerby, who plays the viola and has a great vibrato, her questions grow as their friendship blossoms. Why, Minna wonders, is Lucas so interested in her messy, peculiar family? Why can't her family be more like Lucas's, where dinner-table conversation revolves around facts, the house is always clean, and everyone wears matching socks? But Minna's questions remain unanswered even when she writes anonymous letters to her mother (about wrong questions) and fervent pleas to Mozart (about the missing vibrato). In Patricia MacLachlan's funny novel about music and frogs and different kinds of truth, the answers that finally come to Minna Pratt are the truths she eventually realizes for herself.

More than a hundred years ago, an artist named John Audubon decided to travel throughout North America to find and paint every species of bird—an undertaking that required special help.

Down the Mississippi with Mr. Audubon
by Barbara Brenner

October 11, 1820 *The Beginning*

My name is Joseph Mason.

Most likely you never heard of me, or of my teacher, Mr. John James Audubon. He is a painter around these parts and teaches drawing to young persons like myself. He also works at the museum here in Cincinnati, where his job is preparing birds for the museum's displays.

Mr. Audubon has a regular passion for birds. He has a notion to paint *every bird* in America and make a big book or portfolio of them for folks to marvel at. Right now he is planning a trip down the Ohio and Mississippi to search for birds to paint. And now here is where Joseph Mason comes into the picture. John James Audubon has asked me to go with him!

I am to help Mr. Audubon find bird specimens and to do

other chores for him as he may need me. In return, he will provide my board and also teach me drawing. I hope to be a painter
when I grow up, but while Mr. Audubon's specialty is birds, mine
is plants and flowers.

Both Mr. Audubon and I like nothing better than to hunt and
fish and tramp through the woods; we are much alike in that. I
think that may be why Mr. Audubon chose me to go on this trip
with him.

I aim to set down in this journal all that happens to us on this
trip. I shall do it as truly and faithfully as I can, because I know
that although Mr. Audubon is only a poor painter now, someday
he will be famous. Then people will want to know all about how
he made his bird paintings. And maybe they will also want to
know something about Joseph Mason and this frontier journey.

At half past four this afternoon we stepped aboard a flatboat bound for New Orleans. The dock was crowded with boxes and bales, as well as with voyagers and their families come to see them off.

We made a goodly crowd ourselves: There was Mama and Papa, Mr. Audubon, Mrs. Audubon, and Victor and John, who are the Audubons' sons. There was a lot of hugging and kissing all around, which embarrassed me no end. I got caught by both ladies, who patted and fussed at me as if I were a boy of six instead of an almost full-grown lad of thirteen.

Papa, however, treated me like a man. We shook hands, and he talked to me earnestly. Told me to work hard and to pay heed to what Mr. Audubon can teach me. I will do that. I think Papa would be proud for me to become a painter. He values all forms of culture highly.

Seemed like before we knew it, the crew was casting off. A few last words and our families were hustled ashore. By five o'clock we were drifting out into the channel—on our way.

Now it's late. Way past my bedtime at home. I'm in the cabin of the flatboat, sitting with Mr. Audubon. We are both writing in our journals.

I guess I'm lucky. Not many thirteen-year-old boys get the chance to travel down the Ohio and Mississippi all the way to New Orleans. Scares me a mite, though. Never was this far from home before. I keep thinking of my mother and father. Mama's cheek was wet with tears when she kissed me this afternoon. And Papa suddenly looked so old and frail. . . .

I wonder when I'll see them again. I asked Mr. Audubon how long he figured we'd be away. Maybe six months, maybe a year, he says. Mr. Audubon says he misses his family already. He brought with him a painting that he made of Mrs. Audubon, whose name is Lucy. He says his wife is his best friend. "She eez my bast fraind." That's the way he said it. Mr. Audubon has an odd way of speaking. He's French, I believe.

We're going to sleep now. Mr. A. says we shall sleep on deck. The air is better out there, he says. We have buffalo robes to roll ourselves in, so we shouldn't be cold.

And so to bed. More about this boat tomorrow, when it's light enough for me to see.

October 13   The Flatboat

Sun in my eyes woke me this morning. Mr. Audubon was already up and off somewhere. I sat on the deck for a spell, getting a closer look at my new home. I've seen many a flatboat from the shore, but this is the first time I've seen one from the deck.

A flatboat is really a large raft with sides. It's about forty feet long. Both ends are squared off, and it has some cabin space

as well. Most of the passengers stay on deck. Many of them are taking their livestock down the river to sell or to trade, so the deck looks like a regular Noah's Ark or a traveling barnyard. *Smells* like a barnyard, too. Can't hardly get a whiff of the river for all the pig and chicken smell.

This kind of boat has no sails or steam, so we're at the mercy of the wind and the river current. On a brisk day we can travel up to fourteen miles or so. But if there's no wind, we have to sit like a big clumsy cow in a mudhole, until the breeze or current takes us again.

We got stuck like that this afternoon, which sorely provoked Mr. Aumack, our captain. Mr. Aumack is a young man, but he has an old face which is weather-beaten and leans to sour expressions. When he is angry or upset, as he was when the boat stopped moving, his face changes color. It sometimes goes red and sometimes as purple as an iris. I couldn't take my eyes from him at supper. Felt quite shy when he caught me staring.

The other people on the boat seem used to our slow progress. The children run and play on the deck as if they were at home, while their mamas work at their washtubs or sit knitting in the sunshine. Some of the passengers are squatters, going downriver to find new homes. Others are tradespeople with goods to sell. They will set up shop whenever the flatboat stops at a town. And when they have nothing more to sell, they will leave the boat and begin the long walk home.

The sailors are a rough crew. Whenever a keelboat or steamboat passes us, they line up on the side of the boat to yell at it. The sailors on the other boat do likewise and everyone seems to make good sport of it.

Mr. Audubon laughed when he saw me listening to that coarse talk. He says it's a custom, called blackguarding. The game is to call the loudest and worst insults. Some of the passengers join in, too. But not Mr. Audubon; he is too much of a gentleman for that. He has fine manners and always speaks in a soft, polite voice, although he looks like the roughest frontiersman. He dresses in boots and buckskins and wears his hair long, down to his shoulders. With his beard and his piercing blue eyes, he is quite handsome, save for his teeth, which are rotting.

Mr. Audubon and I spent a good part of this day sitting on deck sketching. The rest of the time we were busy oiling our guns and getting ready for our first hunting expedition, which will take place tomorrow. And Mr. Audubon told me more about his plans for this trip.

Now here I got a surprise. It seems that Mr. A. hasn't a penny to his name. He has got us passage on this boat with the promise that we will supply game for the captain and his crew! So I shall be *hunting*, if not *singing*, for my supper. And for everyone else's, too.

Now about the birds for Mr. Audubon's paintings. He needs examples of every species of bird common to these parts, including those that have never been named in other bird books. He calls these nondescripts—which means that no one has described them. Mr. A. has a book with him by a Mr. Alexander Wilson, which he uses as a guide. But Mr. Audubon hopes to include in *his* bird book many species that Mr. Wilson does not picture. If I find a new species, Mr. Audubon says he may name it for me. Mason's hawk! Mason's flycatcher! Even Mason's eagle! How fine that sounds. I shall look sharp for new birds, you may be sure.

We are all ready. Powder dry, boots greased, guns in order. Tomorrow we start hunting in earnest. I hope that game is plentiful; otherwise two artists and the crew of this flatboat will be going hungry.

And so to bed on deck, where we sleep on stretched buffalo hides. The cows and pigs are never very far away, but it is better out there than in the cabin, which is always full of smoke from the hearth where we do our cooking.

I can't help thinking what a long way I am from my cozy bedroom under the eaves.

Mr. Audubon and I have gone hunting every day this week. We start out as soon as the sun is up. We leave the flatboat and arrange to meet it at an appointed place downstream. The first day we did this I couldn't believe that the boat wouldn't move faster than we did. But at dusk, when we came out of the woods, there it was.

We have found plenty of game as well as many birds to draw. Today, for example, we started out by taking care of our food supply. We shot seven partridges and a few grebes, which are a kind of duck. Later we came on a group of wild turkeys. Mr. Audubon showed me how he calls them. He has a whistle of bone on which he blows. As soon as they hear the sound, they begin to flock around. He shot one, and it went into our game bag with the other birds.

As for our drawing collection, I first shot a fish hawk, which I wounded. Mr Audubon killed it with a pin through the breast, so it would be whole for him to draw.

Soon after this we added a hermit thrush to our collection.

When the game bag became heavy, we decided to head back toward the river. That walk back to the boat seemed powerfully long to me, but Mr. A. stepped along as sprightly as if we were just starting out. By the time we saw the outlines of the boat looming out of the dusk we had covered more than thirty miles. How does Mr. Audubon do it? He is almost forty years old, but I confess he can outlast me.

Right now he is sitting across from me in the cabin, setting up his drawing materials. He has everything the best—Whatman's paper, chalks, brushes, watercolor paints of the finest quality. When I marveled at his rich supplies, he told me, "Joseph, these are the tools of my trade. For these and a good gun I will spend my last penny."

He lays out his supplies so lovingly—the way a man about to

564

have a feast would set his table. How Mr. Audubon loves his work! He will labor all evening drawing the fish hawk and the hermit thrush. *He* is not a bit tired. But Joseph Mason is more than ready for sleep.

October 21   Working

Worked all day today. Practiced my flower drawing. Audubon is still drawing a fish hawk and the hermit thrush. He only made sketches of the hawk, but he has drawn the hermit thrush in detail and plans later to make a painting of it. Mr. A. makes sketches of everything as preparation for painting later. But if he makes a painting of a bird and later feels he can do it better, he will abandon or destroy the first one. At this rate, I wonder, will he ever finish his portfolio?

It is very interesting how John James Audubon does his bird drawings, so I will tell it here. He has a wooden frame which is covered with wire. The wire is made of small squares. He wires the bird on this frame in some interesting and lifelike position. Sometimes he attaches threads to the wings and tail so he can raise or lower them. Then he takes fresh paper and rules it into squares the exact size of those on the frame. He then begins to draw the bird, true size, using the squares as a guide. He pays careful attention to every part, measuring bill and claw and length of wing. You might think all this measuring would make the drawing stiff and dull. But no. When Mr. Audubon is finished with the drawing, the bird looks so lively it seems that any moment it will fly off the paper.

After Mr. Audubon finished the drawing of the hermit thrush, he cut it open to examine the contents of its stomach.

This way he can see what a bird has been eating and make note of it. Mr. A. makes a note of everything. He may someday write a book of life histories of the birds of America to go with his paintings.

I learned that we still weren't finished with the hermit thrush. After he had finished examining it, Mr. A. put it into the fire and roasted it for our lunch! It was hardly enough for two, but what there was tasted tender and delicious. Still . . . .

I think I would rather hear a thrush sing than eat one. Mr. Audubon agreed.

October 28   In the Mud

Weather cold and colder. Glad to have those buffalo robes.

Yesterday we met a steamboat and tied up to it. It pulled us along at a good clip. Mr. Audubon says we are like baby ducklings paddling after our mama. Except that in this case we do no paddling; the wheel of the steamboat does the work. But it seems that nothing is gotten for nothing. Last night we paid dearly for our free ride. We had just curled up in our robes prepared to spend a quiet night when there was a terrible grinding sound. It threw everyone into an uproar, sent the hens skittering and clucking all over the deck. We had gone aground on a sandbar!

All the men had to turn out of bed to help get both boats unstuck. We climbed over the side and waded into the water, which was icy cold. The feeling left my legs altogether even though I was wearing my buckskins. Finally, after much pushing and shoving, we moved them both off the bar. Everyone clambered wearily back on deck and went into the cabin, where we hung our clothes in front of the fire and stationed ourselves there as well. We wrapped ourselves in the buffalo robes and waited for our breeches to dry; there was much chattering of teeth in the meantime.

Tired as I was, I remembered to remind Mr. Audubon that this dunking took care of my weekly bath. We bathe in the river on Sunday and wash our clothes. But I made him promise that I wouldn't have to face that cold water again for a full week!

It has been a while since I last wrote. I have been sick, having suffered an accident. But let me tell it from the start.

It began with my wish to shoot a wild turkey. As I have mentioned, the woods here are filled with these handsome birds. And they make a fine dinner; the very thought of roasted turkey is enough to set my mouth to watering.

Everyone on the flatboat had managed to shoot a turkey. But

the day that I got mine a poacher ran off with it. I had hung my game bag on a tree while I was stalking, not knowing that the woods are full of thieving scoundrels. Came in for a lot of teasing on that account—"Ah, Joseph! Did you really shoot a bird or is it a tall tale?" Even Mr. Audubon, who *saw* me shoot the turkey, joined in the sport, for he is a great teaser. I was smarting from all of that and determined to get another one.

Came a crisp morning, I set out. Mr. Audubon was busy painting, so I went with Captain Aumack. We had fine luck, and by the middle of the afternoon we had each bagged a pair of turkeys. As we approached the boat, I hallooed and held up my prizes for everyone to see. I was rewarded by cheers from the sailors on the deck. Then wasn't I proud!

But "Pride goeth before a fall," says the Good Book. As we waded toward the boat, another flock of turkeys came from the woods. The crew began shooting at them from the boats, and one of the birds fell into the water quite near me. Like a good bird dog, I went to retrieve it from the water. Little did I know that the creature was only wounded. As I came on it, the turkey lunged at me and fetched me a good clap on the side of the head with its beak. Startled, I dropped my bag and tumbled backward into the shallows, where my head and a rock met with a hard how-de-do.

The next thing I knew I was on the deck of the flatboat and some sailors were bending over me. Mr. A. was there, looking worried, and so was Mr. Aumack, his face lit up apple-scarlet.

I was spitting water like a well pump and feeling mighty dizzy. Nobody looked to be settling down to stay in one place, so I closed my eyes again. Didn't open them up until the following day. By this time I had a lump on my head the size of a potato and a pain to match.

It has taken several days for my noggin to heal. I never did find out what happened to my turkeys. Burns me to think that someone else ate them. But there are plenty more wild turkeys between here and New Orleans, and I vow that one will find its way into range of my gun before this trip is out.

Mr. Audubon was very kind to me when I was ill. Whenever I was awake, he was at my side, watching over me. Often he would play music for me. He is a fine musician on both the fiddle and the flute. It was most pleasant to lie in bed and have Mr. Audubon entertain me. But it must have been hard on him. Mr. A. is a great outdoors man. It makes him seasick to be cooped up in the cabin when the boat is moving. Also the smoke from the poor cooking hearth bothers his eyes and makes it difficult for him to work. Gives him a headache, he says. Only he calls it a "haddack," in his French way.

My being sick has had one benefit. It has given me a chance to watch John James Audubon at work. I never did see a man work as *hard* as he does. I have watched him sometimes sixteen hours a day, bent over the little drawing table in the cabin. And this place so cramped he can't even stand up straight to stretch his legs!

When my head is better I hope to copy Mr. Audubon's ways and work harder at my own drawing.

I feel sorry for Audubon. I think it a shame that he works so hard and makes such fine pictures, yet is so poor. Perhaps when these paintings are finished, he will get the fame he deserves.

◆ LIBRARY LINK ◆

Barbara Brenner used Audubon's journals to create On the Frontier with Mr. Audubon. *You may want to read the rest of her book to share more of Joseph's and Mr. Audubon's adventures.*

Reader's Response

Imagine you worked for John James Audubon and traveled down the Mississippi with him. What would you have enjoyed and not enjoyed about your work?

Writing a Description

In this unit you read about different kinds of artists: painters, a quilter, a weaver, and a cartoonist. Although these artists worked with a variety of materials, they all chose subjects that had personal significance for them.

In this lesson you will write a description of a room that you would like to design. Like the artists you read about, you will use your own experiences. Think especially of a room that would make you happy and comfortable and that would appeal to your interests.

Prewriting

Decide on the kind of room that you want to design. Consider a wide variety of choices, including a living room, a kitchen, a den, a bedroom, a study, a sun room, a powder room, a library, a recreation room, an enclosed patio, or a studio.

Study the floor plan shown below. Note the round and square objects, which indicate the placement of furniture. Also, look at the illustration on the next page. Notice the details, such as the bookshelves, the desk, and the lamp.

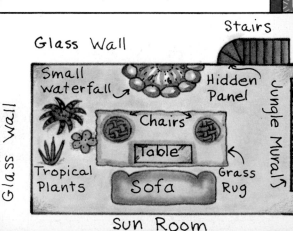

Next, draw the shape of the room you want to design. Put in some round and square blocks to represent furniture and other fixtures that will be in the room. Be sure to label the furniture and decorations you select. Let your imagination roam—the sky's the limit!

Writing

Write a three-paragraph description of your room. Explain to your readers the function and purpose of everything in your ideal room. Tell why the things you included are important to you. What personal experiences did you use to create your design?

Revising

Have you described the objects and details in your room as completely as you can? Your readers will get a vivid picture of your room if you include sizes, shapes, colors, and textures in your description.

Proofreading

Check your description closely to make sure you have used commas correctly.

Publishing

Use several of the floor plans and descriptions to make an architectural magazine entitled *A Way of Seeing: The Magazine of Creative Rooms.*

WORKING TOGETHER

Planning an Art Exhibit

In this unit you learned that art takes many forms, from clouds in the sky to patchwork quilts. Imagine that a museum is planning an exhibit that features works of art from this unit. Your group will plan the exhibit and prepare a program that describes the exhibit for people who come to the museum.

As you work, make sure that people take responsibility for one or more of these tasks:

♦ Inviting others to talk
♦ Contributing ideas
♦ Recording the group's ideas
♦ Getting the group back to work, if necessary

Together, recall the stories in this unit and the works of art that are described in them. Make a list of the stories and of the art that goes with them. Discuss which works of art you might include in an exhibit. Can you think of a theme for the exhibit? For example, you might choose as a theme the art of different cultures, North American arts and crafts, or art of the twentieth century. As a group, choose a theme for your exhibit and decide on the art you would include.

Next, each of you can draw a page for a program that describes the exhibit. On the page draw one of the works of art. Write a sentence below it that tells about the artist.

Put the pages together to make the program. Do you think your classmates would like to attend your exhibit?

Puppeteer by Kathryn Lasky (*Macmillan, 1985*) Paul Vincent Davis plans, produces, and performs puppet shows—all by himself. Follow him for a year as he creates a production of *Aladdin and His Wonderful Lamp*.

The Revenge of the Incredible Dr. Rancid and His Youthful Assistant, Jeffrey by Ellen Conford (*Little, Brown, 1980*) Short, skinny Jeffrey is always being picked on by the class bully. But in the fantasy stories Jeffrey writes, he is always the hero.

Drawing from Nature by Jim Arnosky (*Lothrop, Lee & Shepard, 1982*) When you draw from nature, you develop a sense of wonder at how varied life is. Drawing becomes a way of seeing deeply into things.

Portrait of Ivan by Paula Fox (*Macmillan, 1987*) Miss Manderby reads to Ivan while Matt Mustazza paints his portrait. As the portrait nears completion, Ivan gets a clearer picture of who he is.

The Horse in the Attic by Eleanor Clymer (*Bradbury Press, 1983*) Caroline dreams of having a horse. One day in the attic, she finds a painting of a wonderful racehorse. She sets off to discover the history behind the painting.

BROWSING FOR BOOKS

Sharing Your Reading

You have followed Frodo Baggins every exciting step of the way to Mt. Doom and back, in *The Lord of The Rings*. Six times you've journeyed through the wardrobe with Peter, Susan and the others to the magical land of Narnia. You have gobbled up every Susan Cooper book, and can't wait for a new adventure in the lives of the Drews.

One of the best things about books is that they allow you to escape into times and places more exciting than your own. How wonderful it is to spend an hour or two with The Great Brain at the end of a long, hard day, or to read just one more time about Charlotte, and Fern's efforts to save Wilbur, in *Charlotte's Web*.

Sometimes, reading is even better when you share it with others. What fun it is to see which part of *The Pushcart War* everyone likes best, or argue about which Natalie Babbit book is the best one of all.

Some people have found that having a book pal is a terrific way to enjoy reading even more. What is a book pal? It's someone who likes to read as much as you do, or who likes the same kinds of books that you do. You both might love books about horses or baseball, cooking or mysteries, science fiction or history. A book pal is someone with whom to go to a library or bookstore to browse on a rainy day. It's someone to swap books with, or get suggestions from when you don't know what to read next.

If you love reading, think of someone you know who feels the same way you do. Maybe he or she will be your book pal.

A Game of CATCH

by Helen Cresswell

"**I**sn't it deep and *dangerous*!" Kate bent over the parapet to peer at the moat below. "And the smell!"

She sniffed in the strong, dark-green smell of moat and stone, remembering piers and seaweed. Hugh followed suit and their gasps made white smoke about them in the frosty air.

"One day we'll bring a rope and scale the walls," Hugh said.

"Someone'd see us and stop us," Kate said, hopeful.

"It's winter. Tour buses don't visit museums in winter."

"There's the caretaker."

"Let's find him." Hugh swung down from the wall. "He'll be old and hoary. Far too hoary to notice us. We'll get him to let us in and have a look round."

"But we hate museums," Kate pointed out.

"Usually, yes. This is different."

He tilted back his head and stared up at the great stone ramparts rearing to the blank winter sky. Suddenly he could feel echoes all around him and shouted "Oy!" and heard *oy . . . oy . . . oy* dying back into the cold stone.

"That made me jump," Kate said.

"Try it."

"Hello!" *Hello . . . lo . . . lo . . .* The syllables rang in the bitter air. A storm of rooks was roused overhead. They fell out of the sky like great black gloves. Involuntarily Kate put up her arm as a shield but they caught themselves in flight and lifted back up, yelling hoarsely and starting their own echoes.

"I'm Kate!" *Kate . . . Kate . . .*

"I'm Hugh!" *Hoo . . . hoo . . . hoo . . .*

"Hello!" *Hello . . . lo . . . lo . . .* "I'm Kate!" *Kate . . . Kate . . . .*

They were seized with excitement; the whole bare place was suddenly peopled for them.

"What's all the noise?"

They were bemused by the volleys of echoes, and a strange human voice, close at hand, took them by surprise. Besides, they weren't looking. They had their heads tilted back to the battlements and the sky.

"Oh!" Kate said. "Good morning."

"Morning."

"I hope we weren't making too much noise," said Hugh, who always knew how to be polite enough to get himself out of trouble. "We didn't know anyone was about."

"I don't mind a bit of noise myself," said the man. "Not ordinary noise. But echoes are best left be."

They stared at him. "Best left be?" repeated Kate.

"Echoes are funny things. Best left where they belong. Particularly in an old place like this. I don't believe in rousing up echoes, myself."

Kate shivered and pulled up her scarf around her throat.

"I expect you'll be the caretaker, sir," said Hugh, keeping up the politeness—even overdoing it a little, Kate thought.

"Joe Whittaker, caretaker," he replied. "One man with a castle to keep singlehanded."

"It must be very hard work," said Hugh.

The caretaker said nothing.

"We thought we'd like to have a look round inside, if it's no trouble," Hugh went on. "We're staying down in the village, and our aunt said we ought to look round the museum. She said it was very interesting."

"Oh, it's that, right enough. They come in busloads like swarms of blessed wasps in the summer."

Kate, picturing a busload of wasps, almost giggled. The echoes had left her feeling like giggling. Instead she said, "I expect you know our Aunt Grace. Her name's Miss Fairley and she lives at the White House."

"Aye," he agreed, "I know Miss Fairley, right enough. And this place is open all days and all weathers, if you don't count Christmas. Open to the public ten till five, admission ten pence and half-price children."

He turned and led the way over the flags to the great studded gate. They followed him, exchanging eyebrows. Cut into one of the doors was another, smaller opening, and they passed through this into the courtyard. It was cold as a cell, a cellar, the high walls cutting out all but a square of sky. Grass grew between the cracks of the paving stones and Kate, shivering again, half longed for a tour group to break the thin, ringing silence.

The caretaker halted by an arched doorway.

"Main entrance," he said. "I'll get your tickets."

They followed him into a different silence and a different cold. A tiny room, lit by a bare electric light bulb, led off from the hallway. This was evidently the office, for he was busy unlocking drawers and rattling cash boxes.

They waited in the doorway. The room was quite cosy,[1] as much a living room as an office. Coconut matting covered the flags and two paraffin heaters threw little red ruffs of light about them that at least looked warm. There was an old wooden rocking chair, a wireless, and a sink with a shelf of crockery and a half-silvered mirror above it. In one corner was a small stove and kettle and near it an oilcloth-covered table. The shelves against the far wall were stacked with newspapers and magazines and what looked like boxes of jigsaws.

"Oh! You like jigsaws!" cried Kate.

She was a champion herself, with nearly a hundred in her cupboard and a subscription to a club promised for her birthday.

"Aye."

The caretaker had the tickets ready now, and Hugh handed him the money. "They make the evenings go, do jigsaws."

"I'll send you some of mine, when I get home," Kate promised. The moment she had said it she was surprised at herself. But she had had a sudden picture of the little room at night, one electric light bulb in a great stone well of dark and silence.

[1]Some words in this selection are spelled in the British style.

"Would you, miss?" His anonymous caretaker's face began to break up now. His eyes began to see them, really see them as people, instead of just two half-price tickets.

"Of course. I've got plenty that I've finished with."

"I'd be grateful, and that's the truth. I *like* a puzzle I've done before—it comes halfway to meet you, so to speak. But a new one— well, it's a real treat, miss, as you'll know yourself."

Kate did. She knew exactly what he meant. There was nothing quite to match the moment when you sat at the table, tipped a brand-new puzzle out of its box and began turning the pieces the right way up. She smiled at him and he smiled back for a moment before his caretaker's face came shuttering down again.

"You'll want to go up those stairs"—he pointed to the far end of the hall—"and turn left. After that, just keep going and in the end you'll come out again at the other side of the stairway. Go in a circle round the square, so to speak. There's arrows, anyhow. You can't go wrong."

"Thank you. We'll go and have a look. Come on, Kate."

They walked down the hall, up the stairs, took a last look at Joe Whittaker's figure outlined against the dim light of his doorway, and went left.

They were in a wide, long gallery. To the right were tall slit windows, set deeply into the wall. On the other side were doors leading off.

A worn runner of red carpet ran like a road before them. They trod it because the sound of their footsteps on the stone made them feel like intruders. Hugh's fingers closed over the tickets in his pocket. After all, they had paid their money. At the first door they stopped. It was closed.

"Are we meant to go in?" Kate whispered. "It might be private."

"If it was, there'd be a notice."

They stepped off the carpet and tiptoed to the door. Hugh lifted the heavy iron handle and turned it. The door swung slowly open.

"But it's empty!" cried Kate. There was nothing to see but stone walls, stone floor, a large mullioned window and beyond it walls again at the other side of the courtyard. The windows might as well have been of looking glass, offering no view, reflecting only stone.

"We'll try the next one," said Hugh.

They closed the door behind them and walked slowly up the gallery, politely meeting the stares of the bearded men and plump, bare-shouldered ladies. They looked at them out of habit, feeling it was expected of them. They looked at everything—the pieces of tattered tapestry, the crossed pikes, the pottery in glass cases—as if they were on a school outing and supposed to be learning something.

The next room was full of life-size models in glass cases wearing shabby, jewel-encrusted robes. They stared silently at them for a minute and then were back in the gallery, trudging toward the next door. This time it was pictures—etchings of the castle, views of the battlements among the trees, the courtyard swarming with soldiers. Doggedly they followed the red carpet.

By the time they reached the end of the gallery, where it took a right-angled turn to the left, Kate was beginning to feel the old museum-feeling stealing over her. It was a boredom so enormous that it hurt. It was a feeling that if she had to go on looking at dull things with an interested expression on her face for a moment longer she would either go mad or begin to break things. They turned the corner. There before them lay another gallery, another strip of red carpet, another row of blank doorways.

"Oh, *Hugh!*"

"What's the matter?"

"It's horrible, you know it is. Just like all museums. There are three more of these galleries to get through yet. Let's go back."

"No," said Hugh.

"*Please.*"

"No. Look!" He pointed. The door of the first room stood open. Beyond it they could see steps rising up as if through the very ceiling. "That'll be to the battlements."

Kate's eye fell on a notice and a black arrow.

"It is! There's a notice: *To the battlements.*"

Throwing their echoes to the winds, running now and even shouting, they raced to the stairs.

"We can go right round the castle up on top!" cried Hugh.

"We'll be able to see for miles!" cried Kate.

The stairs spiraled up, and they reached a heavy studded door. Hugh gave it a push, and the next minute fresh air was on their faces and they were out in the welcome frost and among the scolding rooks, right on the very roof of the world, it seemed. They ran to the outer edge of the battlement and found that they could just see over the top at the lowest parts, though Kate had to stretch a little to manage it.

"Oh!" she gasped. "Isn't it high!"

The moat that had seemed so deep and dangerous an hour ago lay far and away below, no more than a dyke. Beyond were the stubbled brown fields powdered with frost, the dull pewter of the lake, the broomstick trees.

"There's the church," said Hugh.

"And there's the White House. We're miles above everything. Let's go right round. Let's look from the other side."

They ran to find a new view from the far side, stopping now and then to peer between the cut-out edges of the ramparts.

"I'm actually hot!" Kate gasped when at last they had gone the four sides of the square and were back to the staircase.

"We haven't looked over the other side," said Hugh.

There was a level wall, and they peered over it down into the deep well of the courtyard.

"Hello" *lo . . . lo . . .* "I'm Kate!" *Kate . . . Kate . . . .*

The echoes rang like bells; they seemed to strike out of the very stones and spin freely in the upper air. And with them there came again the excitement, the strong feeling that the place was suddenly peopled and alive. They both felt it, and Kate suddenly touched Hugh's arm and cried, "Catch! You're on!" and sped toward the studded door.

She spun giddily down the steps and heard the clatter of Hugh's footsteps following. Out into the wide gallery she sped and heard Hugh's voice following her—"Kate, Kate!"—and the echoes of her name running around her. Then among the echoes she thought she heard another voice saying her name, close at hand. So she ran faster, and heard too the laughter of children, near and clear. But the laughter had no echoes, it simply faded, went swiftly away as if into a great distance.

"Catch me! Catch me!" she cried. But the excitement had gone with the crowding laughter. As she stood still, straining her ears, Hugh was touching her arm and shouting, "Catch! You're on!"

"Hugh! Wait! Hugh!"

But he was away, racing up the gallery under its cold, shafting light. And Kate, without the least desire to catch him, ran after him.

Mr. Whittaker was still in his office when they reached the entrance hall again. He was seated at the oilcloth-covered table, his hands cupping a steaming mug of tea. He looked up.

"Finished?" he asked.

"We've seen what we want to, thank you," said Hugh

truthfully. They had seen one gallery and played catch through the other three.

"Is that all?" asked Kate. "I mean, isn't there a downstairs?" She could have bitten off her tongue. As there was an upstairs, there *had* to be a downstairs. There could be another slice of that endless square to trudge, and she was out of breath and tired of playing catch.

"Stables, mostly. That and storerooms. There's just the one room, over yonder." He nodded his head and they turned to look.

"Sort of a banquet hall. Go on, have a look."

They crossed the hall and turned the knob of one side of the great double doors.

"Oh!" said Kate softly. "A real room!"

The door swung to behind them and they advanced a few paces, looking about them. They were in a hall rather than a room, with long mullioned windows running down to the floor on one side. On the other sides a carved wooden gallery ran, with flags and banners hanging from poles at intervals. A refectory table stood in the middle with twenty or more chairs set around it. On the walls hung the usual tapestries, the usual portraits. There was certainly nothing homelike about it. And yet the room was not hushed as the others had been; the air was less cold.

"It might only have been yesterday," said Kate to herself.

"What might?" asked Hugh. He was wandering over by the great stone fireplace, and for a moment found himself putting out his hands as if to warm them at a blaze. Hastily he pulled them back and put them in his pockets, taking a quick look to see if Kate were watching. She was.

"It *is* warmer in here," she said.

"Probably something to do with it being on the ground floor," he replied. "Not so high up, and all that." It sounded lame, even to him.

"No. It's nothing to do with that at all. Hugh, did *you* hear the voices?"

"What voices?" He threw himself down in a padded chair, his legs stretched out in front of him.

"Up in the gallery, just after we came down from the roof. Voices calling my name, and then children laughing. Didn't you hear?"

"It was me calling, idiot," he said.

"And someone else."

"Echoes."

"There *were* echoes," she agreed. "But these were real. At least, not exactly real, because they didn't have echoes."

"What *are* you talking about?" he said.

"I told you. You did hear them. You must have. Didn't you?" For a moment he did not reply.

"Yes, I did," he said at last. "I was testing you."

"Thank you very much."

"You know what I mean. You're always imagining things."

"Not this," she said.

For a while neither of them said anything. Even the silence was ordinary now, just any silence in any room.

"It's something to do with the echoes," said Kate. "As if in calling and making them answer we were making something else answer, too. Some*one* else."

"So we'll ask old Whittaker," Hugh said. "He said something about the echoes when we first saw him."

"Echoes are best left be."

"That's it. You see? He'll know what's going on."

He got up.

"But, Hugh, wait a minute."

He turned.

"Do you think we should? We don't want to spoil it. Perhaps telling might spoil it for them."

"Them?"

"Whoever they are. The children. They seemed so happy and excited. They were laughing."

"Look, if there's anyone here, he'll know about it. He lives here. Telling him won't make any difference."

"I suppose not."

They went back across the entrance hall and stood in the doorway of the caretaker's room waiting for him to notice them.

He did not look up, but he evidently knew they were there.

"Seen everything, then?"

"Yes, thank you."

"We liked that room," Kate told him. "It seemed—lived in."

He did look up then, but said nothing, merely looking hard at their faces as if trying to read something there.

"Staying here long?" he asked.

"Only three more days," Hugh replied. "We're just staying while our parents finish tidying things up. We've sold our house."

"We're going abroad to Canada," Kate said. "For five years."

"Not that we particularly want to," added Hugh.

The caretaker was silent. Kate could feel the situation slipping away and with sudden inspiration said, "I've just thought, I'd better bring those jigsaws up to you. Most of them have been packed, but I've got some with me. You can have those."

"You make sure you want to part with them first. An old jigsaw is an old friend. I know that."

"Oh, I'm sure," she replied. "I'll bring them tomorrow."

"It must be lonely here, Mr. Whittaker," said Hugh.

"It don't matter how much you're alone if you don't feel alone," he replied.

"I don't think I'd feel alone here, either," Kate said.

He looked sharply at her, and she met his gaze.

"I heard someone calling my name, up in the galleries," she said. "And children, laughing."

He seemed to let out a long-held breath.

"Did you, now?" he said at last.

"And everything came alive, as if the whole place was suddenly crowded. It was after we'd been on the battlements making echoes."

"Ah, echoes. It'd be the echoes you heard."

"No," put in Hugh, "they called Kate's name. I heard them as well."

"Kate!" replied the old man. "You're called Kate, are you? It's the name!"

For a minute nobody spoke, then Hugh boldly said, "You do know what we're talking about, don't you?"

"Oh, yes," he agreed slowly. "I know, right enough. Here, look."

He got up and came out into the hall. Silently he pointed behind them and they turned and saw a picture. It showed two children, a girl and a boy of about their own ages. The girl wore a long, apple-green dress tied with a sash of dark olive. She was laughing and stretching out her hands to catch the ball that the boy was holding up as if to tease her. He was all in brown, trimmed with lace at the neck and cuffs, and his dark hair curled to his shoulders. He, too, was laughing.

Hugh, moving closer, read out the inscription set into the wide gilt frame.

"*The Lady Katherine Cottam and her brother, Charles, painted by the local artist, James Hammond. Their father, Lord Cecil Cottam, was the last resident of Bottrel Castle, and left in*

1790 for the family seat in Cumberland, where the Cottam family still lives."

"But they didn't really leave at all," said Kate then. "They're still here."

The caretaker nodded.

"It's the name, isn't it?" she went on. "We're both called Katherine."

"And we kept calling our names to start the echoes," added Hugh.

"Things latch themselves on to names. Names mean more than most people suppose. And echoes can only give back what you give 'em. You got to give an echo the right name."

Footsteps sounded in the courtyard and the door was pushed open. They swung around.

"Customers," said the caretaker, and went back to his office.

"We'll come again tomorrow," Kate called after him. They went past the three ladies delving in their purses for coins, and on into the cold stone well of the courtyard. They walked in silence through the main gates, over the ramparts and across the drawbridge. Neither of them spoke until they were on the path toward home over the meadows, where there were no echoes.

That night it froze. It was not a hard black frost that merely took the sky and trees from the lake and darkened the puddles in the ruts. It stole reflections but it brought its own, too. It had come combing softly down in the night through the bare trees and been caught among their boughs in straws. It was like salt on the stubble.

Kate and Hugh went out to test the ice on the lake, the castle forgotten in the huge excitement of the frost. They left their skates behind, afraid of taking too much for granted.

Now they stood in the stiffly furred grasses by the water's edge and banged the ice with their heels, delighted that they could not break it. Hugh found a stick and hammered, but the stick broke.

"It might be all right," he said.

"In another day, Aunt Grace said. She said leave it another day."

They were alone in that white, silent landscape, and the thought of a sudden dark hole in the ice was terrifying.

"We'll come down again after dinner and bring a hammer," he said. "We can't tell for sure like this."

"We've got to come back again, anyway," said Kate. "I told Mr. Whittaker I'd bring those puzzles."

"You and your castle," he scoffed. "You and your old echoes."

"They're no more mine than yours!" cried Kate defensively. "You were there, too. I thought you said you heard them."

"I might have *thought* so, at the time. But not now."

She stared at him, dismayed.

"But it was real," she cried. "You know it was. And the picture! And Mr. Whittaker! He knew it was real."

"Look," he said, "when people live on their own, they start imagining things. It's only natural, if you think about it. Day after day in that great old place with nothing to do but jigsaws and hardly a customer a week in the winter."

"The trouble with you is that you never want to believe anything," said Kate. "Even when it's right under your nose you don't want to believe in it."

"I've just got common sense, that's all. If you think for a minute, the whole thing's impossible, Kate. There's two hundred years between them and us. And all the echoes in the world can't bridge *that*."

"They can, they can!" insisted Kate. "And nothing's impossible!" But she said it to herself.

"We'll go and make that slide in the drive," said Hugh. He gave the ice a final thwack with the stick and hared[2] off over the crunching turf.

After dinner they took a hammer and went to the lake again.

"Better give it another day, I suppose," said Hugh reluctantly. "So we may as well go up to your castle."

They hid their skates under a bush and set off, Kate with a large parcel under her arm. But the visit was a disappointing one. Yesterday they had been caught unawares; there had been the sheer magic of surprise. But today the echoes were locked in by

[2]hared (herd): ran

590

more than just the frost, and though Kate longed to stand and call her name out of the stones, she could not.

It was not only that Hugh was there beside her, unbelieving now and half ready to mock; it was that she felt quite certain that the whole thing was not so simple as it seemed. It was not just a matter of calling up echoes as if they alone were the key to a secret lock. There was something else besides. And she knew, quite certainly, that she could shout her name a thousand times today without the least stir from the stone. The centuries had settled back into place again.

Even the caretaker seemed aware of it. He thanked her for the jigsaws, unwrapping the parcel eagerly and stacking the boxes neatly on his shelves along with the others.

"That'll take care of a good few hours," he said with satisfaction.

But he said nothing about their conversation of the day before. He was in a talkative mood. Hugh asked him what he thought about the ice on the lake, and he launched into stories of his own childhood and the winters he could remember, with snow high as barn doors and ice you could light fires on. Hugh and Kate listened, fascinated—until, when at last they walked away over the drawbridge, the whole landscape seemed to have shrunk since they last saw it. They walked rapidly home, thinking of a hot fire, tea and television, tired of frost.

Next morning they had to go into the nearby town to shop. Their aunt wanted to buy them clothes for Canada.

"We can buy things over there," Kate protested. "There are shops, aren't there?"

"There's nowhere like England for woolies," replied their aunt. "And you'll need plenty of those where you're going."

And so there was only an hour of daylight left when at last they reached the lake. Hurriedly they pulled up the laces on their boots, delighted to find that no one had been before them. There was not a scar, not a mark on the whole wide sweep of it, and it beckoned them with the perfection of untrodden snow.

Hugh was the first on, with a few swift, thrusting strokes, and by the time Kate had tied her last lace he was already in the distance, making straight across the middle to the far side.

Kate looked about her at the flawless ice and followed him, her eyes fixed on the furrows left by his blades. But as her fear of the tracklessness vanished, she too was ranging the whole lake, like a bird with the whole vast air of the sky to choose from. Once, years ago, she could remember skating on a frozen canal, sweeping straight up a long white endless road between the stiff sedges until darkness fell. But she had never before been let loose in a freedom like this, with infinite possible paths spoking about her, endless choice. It was almost too much, like a new dimension.

"Kate! Kate!" She heard Hugh calling and turned to see that he too was skating in great arcs, greedily, as if trying to print his signature over the whole blank page of the lake. He beckoned, but she would not go to him, and sped into new distances, staking her own claim.

As the afternoon wore on they hardly met or even came close to each other, spellbound in their private mazes. But the dusk began to gather swiftly, and the sun suddenly appeared at the rim of the meadows, huge and orange in a sky surprisingly tender and tinged with green.

"Kate! Kate!" Hugh was calling again from the far side of the lake. "Catch me! Kate!"

And in that moment the frost released its echoes and she heard her name go folding away across the darkening meadows— *Kate . . . Kate . . . Kate . . .* —and on into silence.

"Kate! Kate!" She checked, turned, and drove fast toward him. "Catch me!" *Catch . . . catch . . . .* Then again her name, nearer now, "Kate, Kate!" without echoes, and the sound of steel blades tearing the ice.

Slowing, she looked over to her right, and saw, impossibly, furrows moving across the ice, turning, wheeling, curving like smoke tracks in the sky. Forgetting Hugh, she veered to follow, but always they were beyond her, furling out of the ice ahead, curving mischievously aside, doubling back, elusive as smoke.

"Kate! Kate!" She no longer knew who was calling her, nor cared. Intent on the beckoning tracks she sped and thought she heard laughter beyond the hissing of her own skates and the pounding in her ears.

"Kate!" It *was* Hugh's voice now, close by, and she lifted her eyes to look at him, a stranger for a moment after the spellbound hour when only their paths had crossed.

"You're not even trying to catch me!" he cried. "What are you playing at? Kate!"

But she was away again, panic-stricken now because she had lost track of the unreeling thread and was left with a maze of thin lines, crossing and recrossing endlessly. She stopped and looked about her, listening for the sharp scything of blades that would betray her quarry. There was nothing. She strained her eyes into the dusk and could just make out her brother's figure away again at the far end of the lake. The sun had dropped. It was impossible to un-ravel the skein on the ice. Everything had gone away into darkness and silence.

She skated to where Hugh was already on the bank changing his boots. He did not look up. If she was ever to tell him what had happened now was the time, with the frost falling, the cold translating into whiteness, and anything possible after the long spell on ice.

But with her first steps onto the bank the world seemed to dip and then steady again, as it did after a day at sea. Her head spun; she sat down fumbling with her laces, and felt the delicious cold of the hoar against her hot legs.

"I forgot my gloves," Hugh said. "I shall get hot-aches when we get in."

"Serve you right," she heard herself say. Served him right for what? She hardly knew. But the moment had passed, and she said no more. They went home between the dark hedges of the lane which was all metal now, silver and iron.

"Another frost tonight," said Hugh. Kate smiled.

It did freeze again. It was as if everything were conspiring with the echoes, ground and water turning to stone, the air thin and bitter. Kate woke to see it and knew that she must spend the day seeking. In particular she knew that she must go to the castle alone.

It was easy to get away that morning. Hugh had heard that there was a canal beyond the village, and intended to skate along it right into the next village.

"I don't feel like skating again," Kate said when he told her.

"Come on," he urged. "Aunt Grace says it's a snow sky today. If it snows you won't get another chance."

"I don't want to, Hugh. Honestly."

"I know where you'll go," he told her. "Up to your old castle."

"I might."

She waited until he had left and then set out up the lane toward the castle. There was a mist as well as the frost, and at first she could not see even the castle's outline, in a curiously shrunken world, a world with walls now.

As she walked it seemed as if everything about her contained a secret from which she alone was shut out. Even the cattle, kneeling in the frosty grass, turned their heads to stare after her curiously as she passed, slowly blowing out their white breath.

All the time she was asking herself questions.

"Is it the picture on the wall that matters? If the picture was taken away, would they go with it?"

She did not know the answer.

"Yesterday, on the lake, whose time was it, theirs or ours? Had they come forward to meet us, or were Hugh and I skating two hundred years ago?"

There was no answer to this either. The frost and the ice and the landscape were all anonymous. Yesterday might have been any day taken from all time. It might have been yesterday or it might have been a thousand years ago.

She looked about her and realized that the same was true today. The mist had swallowed the village behind her. She saw not a single landmark of time, only the fields, the sky, and the weather. She hurried her steps toward the castle and Joe Whittaker, who stood with his feet firmly planted in the twentieth century and could anchor her safely there, too.

As she went under the high archway into the center courtyard she could see his light bulb burning through the dusty window. She tiptoed into the hallway, not wanting him to know that she was there yet. She gazed up at the picture, looking for clues. But the children were not even looking at her, they were looking at each other, intent on their game and the ball in the boy's hand. There was only one clue, and even that was hardly more than a hint.

"They're wearing warm clothes—velvet and wool," she thought. "And the girl has a muff hanging from her wrist. It was winter. It could have been this very time of year."

If the girl had been wearing muslin and a straw hat, at least Kate would have known the answer to one of her questions. At least she would have known that yesterday on the frozen lake it had not been Hugh and herself who had stepped out of their time and into that of the picture.

"It's you again, is it, miss?"

She found Joe Whittaker at her elbow, muffler tucked in his jacket, steaming mug of tea in hand.

"Oh! You made me jump. Yes. I wanted to look at the picture again." They stared up at it together.

"It *is* a mystery," remarked the caretaker at last. "No doubt about it. Even to me, and I live with it."

Kate said nothing.

"Have a cup of tea," he invited. "I've only just mashed."

She followed him into the office and sat in the rocking chair near the oil stove. She hugged her knees and watched him busy with the crockery, waiting for the right moment to tell her story. The opening came easily, as it happened.

"You put trust in the ice yesterday, then," he said. "I saw you away down there from up top. Good little pair of skaters you are."

"Did you watch long?" she asked quickly. "What time was it?"

"Time? I can't say. I don't reckon much by the clock myself. Near dusk, I suppose."

She bent forward.

"Did you—I don't suppose you saw the others, too?"

"Others, miss?" He came over with a cup and saucer and set it down on the table beside her.

"Yes, the other two. There were four of us—in the end, at any rate."

He shook his head.

"I didn't see four of you. Must've been after."

"Must've been," she agreed. After all, why should he have seen them? Even she had seen only the unfurling of their tracks. But she had half hoped that the caretaker, who lived with echoes and knew that time had nothing to do with clocks, might have taken the centuries in his stride.

"What I suppose is," he went on surprisingly, "that your friends weren't there to *be* seen."

"But they were!" she cried. "I heard them!"

"Oh, they were there, right enough," he agreed. "No one knows that better than me. But not to be *seen*."

"I saw their marks on the ice. I heard them. Do you think I'll ever actually see them? Do you?"

"Depends how much you want to, I suppose."

"Oh, I really want to, Mr. Whittaker. Just for a moment, even. I want to believe in them."

"Seeing is believing," he said. "We've always to see before we'll believe."

"I don't think Hugh would believe even if he *saw*," she said. "That's really why I want to see them so badly. It always seems to be Hugh that's right and me that's wrong. I'm not saying anything against him, mind, it's just that we're different. But I was so sure about this, and at first I thought Hugh was as well. But now he's gone all sensible, as usual, and says I'm imagining things."

"So far as *I* know," said Joe Whittaker slowly, as if airing an opinion to which he had given a great deal of though, "there isn't all that much difference between seeing and imagining. In the end you might say the two was one and the same thing."

"You mean that if a thing *feels* real, it is?"

"Something like that," he said.

Kate drank her tea and stared at him over the top of her cup. There was something she meant to ask him, something that was at the very tip of her tongue but she couldn't quite remember. He too sat sipping his tea, and just then the electric light suddenly paled as a shaft of sunlight flooded the little room.

"The sun's out!" Kate cried. "And I wanted to skate again! We go tomorrow. If I don't see them today, I never shall!"

"Gone for five years you'll be, you say?"

"Yes. But I'll tell you this. If I don't see them, I'll come back. The minute we get back from Canada I'll come straight down here and . . . "

She broke off. He was shaking his head.

"You'll be five years older," he said.

"What of it?"

"And they won't."

Suddenly she saw what he meant. *Their* time was standing still, but hers was still moving. She was not playing an endless game of ball in a gilt frame and waiting for an echo to bring her back to life. She stood up. "I'll have to be going."

He went with her into the hall and suddenly she remembered the question she had been going to ask him.

"What did you mean when you said you knew they were down there, Mr. Whittaker? You said, 'Nobody knows it better than me.' What did you mean, please?"

He looked up at the picture and that, too, was bathed in sunshine now, kindling the dark oils, bringing the two children forward out of their dark background.

"I knew by that," he said.

She stared at him. She half thought she knew what he was going to tell her, but it seemed impossible.

He jerked his head toward the picture.

598

"They'd gone."

Now that he had actually said it, it was still impossible.

"So you see, miss, you were right. And that brother of yours was wrong."

So they said their good-bys and the caretaker went back to his little room and got out the sweeping brushes, because the sun had lit up the corners and more dust than even he could bear. As for Kate, she walked home with a head full of questions again, because in the puzzle she was trying to solve, every answer brought a new question with it. It was like trying to do a jigsaw with half the pieces missing.

The sun stayed out for an hour or two and then suddenly went in. The sky filled, a soft, gray snow sky.

"We might be able to skate, if we hurry," Kate said after dinner. "The snow might not come for hours, yet. It might not even come at all."

"It'll come, all right," said their aunt. "It'll come thick and heavy. You get down to the lake, if that's what you want. Though you'll be getting all the skating you want over there."

"Not this kind of skating," thought Kate.

As they went up the now familiar lane she was filled with unbearable excitement. It seemed certain to her now that today time would finally run free and unfetter all the echoes and the unseen voices.

When they reached the lake they saw that the sun had wiped the slate of the ice clean, and it was brand new again. And this time it was Kate who was away first, making a beeline for the far side. She heard Hugh's voice, "Kate, wait! Kate!"

She skated on, pretending not to have heard. She wanted Hugh to make his own tracks, to leave her alone. She wanted to make the same patterns as yesterday's all over again, history to repeat itself. She was making toward the moment just before dusk when the invisible blades would come scything out of nowhere and the game of catch would begin again.

But things went wrong. Hugh had been skating all morning, had followed the frozen canal to Withenshaw and back alone, and was tired of the sound of his own skates and the endless white of ice. He started to follow.

"Look out! I'm coming!"

She checked and looked back over her shoulder to see him coming after her with long, swift strokes, and she cried, "No, I'm not playing! Go away!"

But he came on, so she turned and sped away and found herself playing catch without meaning to at all, the wrong game of catch.

But even this was more than just a game, because if he caught her it would be all up. She would have to chase him, too, and then the whole thing would begin all over again, and the afternoon would waste away. She drove fast along the length of the lake, heading for the tiny, reed-trimmed islands that scattered the ice. She could dodge him there. Hugh was a better skater, and it was her only chance.

He was still a good way behind her when she reached the first island, caught a blade in a tuft that still showed through the ice, and fell. For a moment she lay there, her face pressed against the ice, seeing the crust of hoar on the rush spears that were bent under her.

Then Hugh was standing over her.

"Kate! Are you all right? Can you get up?"

She lifted herself slowly onto her hands and knees, but as soon as she tried to get to her feet she groaned and fell to her knees again.

"My foot hurts," she said. "No, my ankle."

She turned sideways to a sitting position and looked up into his worried face.

"You must have sprained your ankle."

"Not actually sprained it. It just hurts."

"Can you make it to the bank, if I help you?"

She did not reply. She was looking beyond him to the other side of the lake, where a group of figures had just appeared.

"Look!"

He followed her gaze.

"Looks like the Lewises. I can see their sled. Lucky dogs."

So the afternoon was lost, after all. There was no need now to go on pretending about her foot. Whether she played catch or not, whether she skated fast or slowly, it made no difference.

"I'll see if I can get up now," she said.

Hugh held her hands and she got to her feet.

"How does it feel?"

She took a testing step forward.

"All right, I think." Her ankle did hurt a little. She hadn't really been going to pretend it was sprained, just twisted, so that she couldn't play catch with Hugh. He was looking in the other direction again, and they could hear shouts and laughter floating over the ice.

"See if you can make it over to the other side," he said. She could tell that he was impatient, hoping that she wasn't going to spoil things. She skated slowly off, careful not to go too fast, and he came up alongside.

"You must have just given it a twist," he said. "I expect it'll wear off in a bit if you go carefully."

"I'll just go slowly round till it does," she said. "You go over to the others. They're taking turns on the sled, by the look of it."

Three of them were towing long ropes, harnessed like horses. Deborah, the youngest Lewis, was sitting bolt upright on the sled, waving her arms and shouting.

"Sure you'll be all right?" He hesitated.

"Positive."

She watched him skate over to join them, wondering why she didn't go herself now that the lake was crowded and the last hope of a game of catch had gone.

She was gliding dreamily around the circumference of the lake when the snow began to fall. She paused, and stood by the row of pollards,[3] scenting the change, feeling the blotting-out of frost that was almost like warmth. The flakes were large and tissue-thin, they floated like white skeleton leaves, and the thicker they fell the

---

[3]pollard (pol′ ərd): a tree with its top branches cut back to thicken the growth

faster they seemed to spin. She blinked as they melted on her hot face and ran into her eyes, and when she moved off again she was giddy with their swirling motion.

She realized that she was just by the fence where they had left their things, and stopped again. There was no sign of the others and she listened for their voices, but there was only the enormous blanketing silence of falling snow. They seemed to have gone right away.

She climbed onto the bank and unlaced her boots. Then she hung them on the fence beside Hugh's boots and overcoat and went again to the rim of the lake, straining her ears and eyes into the dizzy mist of whiteness. And as she stared, she did hear voices, and laughter, very faint and muffled. They seemed to be coming not from the ice, but from behind her, and once, quite clearly, she heard her name being called, "Kate! Kate!"

She began to run, stumbling here and there over roots and tussocks because now the snow was falling so thickly that she could see only a yard or two ahead.

"Kate! Catch! Catch!"

"I'm coming! Wait, I'm coming!" she cried, and although there were no echoes here, even in the muffling snow she knew that her voice was ringing, carrying, crossing centuries.

"Catch!" The voice was close by, and as she strained her eyes into the spinning snow something came flying toward her and fell at her feet with a soft thud.

She stared down. It was a ball.

"So *this* is the real game of catch," she thought, and picked it up.

For a moment she stared down at the ball in her hands. It was quite soft and made of dark red leather, sewn together in segments. Then she looked up and they were there, both of them.

Though they were divided from her by the falling snow she saw them clearly, and they were watching her, too, expectantly. Suddenly the girl stretched out her hands and without thinking Kate tossed the leather ball back straight into her waiting palms. The girl laughed and shook her hair, then darted off.

"Don't go!" she cried. "Kate!" She called the name again. "Kate!"

"Things latch themselves on to names," Joe Whittaker had said.

But the girl had already turned; she threw the ball to the boy, who leaped nimbly forward to catch it before it touched the ground. He straightened up and looked at Kate.

"Catch!" he cried suddenly, and again the ball was in her hands. She threw it back to him and the girl came running from behind the curtain of snow again to catch it in her turn. They tossed it backward and forward, backward and forward, and all the time Kate, watching the ball, watching them, was thinking fast and furiously. And as the ball came to her the next time she held it firmly between both hands and waited. If she kept it, the spell would be broken and they would stay forever. It was the ball in flight that bridged the centuries. Without it they could never return.

They stood waiting, watching her. The girl, puzzled, smiled

and held out her hands. Kate shook her head and put the ball behind her back. They waited, all three of them, the game of catch suspended and the snow falling silently all about them.

"Kate! Kate!" Voices were calling in the distance. She saw the girl stiffen, listening. "Where are you? Kate! Kate!"

The voices were nearer; Kate could hear Hugh's among the yells of the Lewises. What would *they* make of the girl in green velvet and the boy with his long hair brushing his shoulders and shirt frilled at his thin wrists? She stared at their white, frightened faces, and hesitated. Then she brought the ball from behind her back and held it up.

The girl's face cleared, she nodded delightedly and ran forward a few paces from her brother, and Kate, smiling back, threw the ball straight into her cupped hands. For an instant the girl stood there and then with a swift wave turned and ran, the boy after her. They swam into blurs in the snowstorm and were gone.

"Kate! Kate! Where are you!"

She began to run, playing a new game of catch. Now she was hunter and hunted together. She kept her eyes down at first, looking for footprints, but there was nothing to guide her but laughter ahead and now and again a glimpse of pale green or brown. The farther she ran the fainter the laughter grew, and as it dwindled for the last time she halted, panting for breath, and found herself right on the drawbridge of the castle.

Through the great stone arch she hurried and across the high courtyard with its strange snow-light and muffled echoes. The caretaker's bulb burned behind his long window, but as she ran into the entrance hall and stopped in front of the picture she saw that the room was empty. Joe Whittaker was making the lonely rounds of his castle, battening it against the snow.

She stared up. They were there ahead of her, posed and careless as if nothing had ever happened. They had stepped back into the gilt frame and another time and now they did not even look at her, absorbed in their private game of catch.

And yet, as she stared, Kate felt that there was something different. The children were the same, their clothes, their faces.

Impossible to explain—and yet different. Still the girl held up the ball and the boy waited for her throw.

"Perhaps he'll wait another hundred years," Kate thought. She knew that the game was over for her now. Slowly she turned and went out into the snow. It was falling lightly now, the flakes went drifting dreamily with all the time in the world. Over the drawbridge she went and started across the darkening meadows. Down by the lake she could see the outline of a small figure approaching. It was Hugh, alone. The others had gone home, but he had waited. He had seen her, too, because he waved and she heard him call, "Kate! Kate!"

And in those moments as they ran toward each other she suddenly knew what had been different about the picture. *The girl had been holding the ball!* Surely, *surely*, before it had been she who was stretching out her hands to catch it, while the boy held it aloft, teasing her? She, Kate, had been the last to throw it in that strange, triangular game of catch. And she had thrown it not to the boy, but the girl.

"Kate!" Their paths met. "Where have you been? I've been looking everywhere."

"I lost my way in the snowstorm," was all she said, and they went together through the last gate of the fields and into the lane. And still she was trying to remember how the picture had looked yesterday. Surely it had been the boy who held the ball? And the girl had it now, and would have it for who knew how many years to come. Perhaps forever?

A herd of cows was being driven home along the lane. Kate and Hugh pressed against the hedge and watched them lumber by, bringing a strong, summer hay-smell into the pure air of the frost. Snowflakes settled on their warm leather foreheads and fringed their round brown eyes.

When the cows had passed, the two of them had the lane to themselves again. It gleamed ahead of them in the dusk, showing their tired legs the way home.

"Surely the ball has changed hands," Kate thought again. The snow went on falling.

GLOSSARY

Full pronunciation key* The pronunciation of each word is shown just after the word, in this way:
abbreviate (ə brē′vē āt).

The letters and signs used are pronounced as in the words below.

The mark ′ is placed after a syllable with a primary or heavy accent as in the example above.

The mark ′ after a syllable shows a secondary or lighter accent, as in **abbreviation** (ə brē′vē ā′shən).

SYMBOL	KEY WORDS	SYMBOL	KEY WORDS
a	ask, fat	b	bed, dub
ā	ape, date	d	did, had
ä	car, father	f	fall, off
		g	get, dog
e	elf, ten	h	he, ahead
er	berry, care	j	joy, jump
ē	even, meet	k	kill, bake
		l	let, ball
i	is, hit	m	met, trim
ir	mirror, here	n	not, ton
ī	ice, fire	p	put, tap
		r	red, dear
o	lot, pond	s	sell, pass
ō	open, go	t	top, hat
ô	law, horn	v	vat, have
oi	oil, point	w	will, always
oo	look, pull	y	yet, yard
o͞o	ooze, tool	z	zebra, haze
yoo	unite, cure		
yo͞o	cute, few	ch	chin, arch
ou	out, crowd	ŋ	ring, singer
		sh	she, dash
u	up, cut	th	thin, truth
ʉr	fur, fern	*th*	then, father
		zh	s in pleasure
ə	**a** in **ago**		
	e in **agent**	′	as in (ā′b′l)
	e in **father**		
	i in **unity**		
	o in **collect**		
	u in **focus**		

*Pronunciation key and respellings adapted from *Webster's New World Dictionary, Basic School Edition,* Copyright © 1983 by Simon & Schuster, Inc. Reprinted by permission.

606

A

a·but (ə but′) *verb.* to touch or join at one end; border. **abutted, abutting.**

ac·com·plice (ə kom′plis) *noun.* a person who helps another commit a crime.

ac·com·plish (ə kom′plish) *verb.* to do; complete. —**accomplished** *adjective.* **1.** something done or finished. **2.** skilled or practiced; artful: She is an *accomplished* musician. **accomplished, accomplishing.**

ac·cus·tom (ə kus′təm) *verb.* to become familiar with; to be in the habit of. —**accustomed** *adjective.* usual: Tom was in his *accustomed* good mood.

a·dapt (ə dapt′) *verb.* **1.** to make usable, especially by changing size, color, etc. **2.** to change one's own behavior, attitude, etc., to fit new conditions. **adapted, adapting.**

ad·dic·tive (ə dik′tiv) *adjective.* contributing to the development of an almost unbreakable habit.

ad·ver·tise·ment (ad′vər tīz′mənt *or* əd vur′tiz mənt) *noun.* a public notice, usually paid for, announcing things for sale, wanted, etc.

ad·vis·er or **ad·vi·sor** (əd vī′zər) *noun.* one who gives advice or opinions to someone else. **advisers, advisors.**

ag·gres·sive (ə gres′iv) *adjective.* **1.** prepared to start a fight. **2.** active; full of energy; forceful.

ail (āl) *verb.* to be sick; to feel ill. —**ailing** *adjective.* not well.

al·ba·tross (al′bə trôs) *noun.* a big sea bird with webbed feet, long narrow wings, and a hooked beak.

an·ces·tor (an′ses tər) *noun.* someone from whom one is descended; a forebear: Two of my *ancestors* were artists. **ancestors.**

an·chor (ang′kər) *noun.* **1.** a heavy object held by a chain or rope and lowered into the water to keep a ship or boat from drifting. **2.** anything that keeps or seems to keep something else steady. —*verb.* **1.** to keep from drifting or coming loose. **2.** to fasten securely to something.

an·noy (ə noi′) *verb.* to disturb, bother, or make slightly angry. —**annoyed** *adjective.* irritated: They all gave her an *annoyed* look when she kept talking.

ap·point (ə point′) *verb.* **1.** to make definite; decide upon. **2.** to name or choose for an office or position. —**appointed** *adjective.* selected; agreed upon.

a·quar·i·um (ə kwer′ē əm) *noun.* **1.** a tank or bowl with transparent walls in which fish, other water creatures, and plants can live. **2.** a building in which such tanks are displayed for visitors to observe. **aquariums** *or* **aquaria.**

ar·chi·tect (är′kə tekt) *noun.* one who designs and draws plans for buildings and other structures and oversees their construction. **architects.**

ar·ro·gant (ar′ə gənt) *adjective.* overly proud and indifferent to the wishes of others; haughty; overconfident; conceited.

ar·se·nal (är′s′n əl) *noun.* a place to make or store weapons such as guns and ammunition.

ar·ti·fi·cial (är′tə fish′əl) *adjective.* **1.** manufactured or made by a person; not natural. **2.** false; insincere.

as·set (as′et) *noun.* **1.** anything owned that has value. **2.** something that is valuable or desirable to have. **assets.**

as·ton·ish·ment (ə ston′ish mənt) *noun.* great surprise; full of wonder; amazed.

a·stride (ə strīd′) *adverb.* with one leg on either side, as when straddling a horse.

as·trol·o·ger (ə strol′ə jər) *noun.* a person who attempts to predict the future by studying the motions of the planets, stars, and other heavenly bodies.

as·tron·o·my (ə stron′ə mē) *noun.* the science of the motion and composition of stars, planets, and other heavenly bodies.

awe·struck (ô′struk′) *adjective.* filled with wonder; awed.

ax·is (ak′sis) *noun.* **1.** the real or imaginary straight line about which a sphere or other object revolves. **2.** a straight central line about which other parts of a thing are arranged in a balanced fashion.

anchor

◇

Aquarium comes from the Latin word *vivarium* in a round-about way. A *vivarium* was where any live animals were kept. So, put together the first part of *aquarius*, Latin for "a water carrier," and the last part of *vivarium*. What results is a place where animals that live in water are kept.

aquarium

B

bal·ance (bal′əns) *verb.* **1.** to compare to see which is heavier, better, etc. **2.** to keep from falling; keep steady. **3.** to make things or parts equal in weight, value, importance, etc.: You should *balance* the objects in your picture. **balanced, balancing.**

ba·leen (bə lēn′) *noun.* a stiff, flexible material that grows from the upper jaws of certain whales.

bam·boo (bam bo͞o′) *noun.* a tropical plant of the grass family with hollow, jointed, woody stems which are used to make canes, furniture, etc. **bamboos.**

ba·o·bab tree (bā′ō bab′ trē) *noun.* a tree found in Africa and India that has a tall, thick trunk. The bark yields a fiber used for making rope, paper, etc., and the fruit is edible.

bar·ri·er (bar′ē ər) *noun.* **1.** something that blocks the way. **2.** something that keeps people apart or hinders progress.

ba·salt (bə sôlt′ *or* bās′ôlt) *noun.* a hard, dark volcanic rock.

bed·ding (bed′iñg) *noun.* **1.** mattresses, sheets, blankets, pillows, etc. **2.** straw, leaves, hay, etc., used for animals to sleep on.

be·head (bi hed′) *verb.* to cut off the head of someone or something.

be·lay (bi lā′) *verb.* **1.** to make secure by winding around a pin, cleat, etc. **2.** in mountain climbing, to secure a person at one end of a rope or to secure the rope to an object or person for support.

be·ware (bi wer′) *verb.* to be on guard; be careful of.

bi·lin·gual (bī liñg′gwəl) *adjective.* **1.** able to speak two languages with ease. **2.** written or spoken in two languages. **3.** having or using two languages, as in a bilingual country.

blade (blād) *noun.* **1.** a flat, broad part of an object. **2.** the sharp cutting edge of a knife, sword, etc. **3.** the flat, broad part of a leaf. **blades.**

boar's-tooth (bôrz′to͞oth) *adjective.* made from the teeth of a male pig or hog: He wore a *boar's-tooth* necklace.

boast·er (bōst′ər) *noun.* a person who brags or praises too highly. **boasters.**

breach (brēch) *verb.* **1.** to make a break in something; to break through. **2.** to jump above the water's surface, especially as a whale does. **breached, breaching.**

bulge (bulj) *noun.* something that swells out. —*verb.* to swell out; protrude. **bulges, bulged, bulging.**

bul·lion (bo͞ol′yən) *noun.* gold or silver bars, especially before they are made into coins.

bur·den (burd′′n) *noun.* **1.** a load that a person carries. **2.** something one has to put up with. —*verb.* to put a burden on; load; weigh down.

bur·ro clam (bur′ō klam) *noun.* a kind of large clam with a tightly clamping shell.

bush (bo͝osh) *noun.* **1.** a plant with many branching stems, smaller than a tree and without a trunk. **2.** land that has been left wild and not cleared or settled.

by·stand·er (bī′ stan′ dər) *noun.* a person who stands by or near while something is happening but does not take an active part in it. **bystanders.**

C

cal·i·co (kal′ə kō) *noun.* a cotton cloth usually printed with a colored pattern.

cam·ou·flage (kam′ə fläzh) *noun.* **1.** the act of changing the appearance of soldiers, ships, etc., to make them hard for enemies to see by coloring them to fit in visually with their surroundings. **2.** any disguise of this kind. **3.** anything used to disguise or mislead. —*verb.* to disguise in order to conceal: The hunters *camouflaged* themselves. **camouflaged, camouflaging.**

ca·nal (kə nal′) *noun.* **1.** a constructed waterway used by ships or to carry water for irrigating crops. **2.** a tube in the body. **canals.**

baobab tree

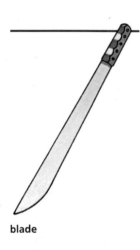

blade

Camouflage comes from French *camoufler*. It was originally a slang term for smoke blown into the eyes of someone to keep the person from seeing what was going on. In World War I, it referred to a smoke screen used to hide a ship from an enemy. Later, *camouflage* came to refer to the painted designs, which were found to provide a better disguise. Now it refers to anything that disguises.

ca·pa·bil·i·ty (kā′pə bil′ə tē) *noun.* skillfullness; ability to do things well: The writer's *capabilities* were well known. **capabilities.**

car·toon·ist (kär tōōn′ist) *noun.* a person who draws cartoons which can be (a) a newspaper or magazine drawing showing how the editor or artist feels about some event or person; (b) a comic strip; (c) a funny drawing.

cau·tious·ly (kô′shəs lē) *adverb.* in a careful way; in a manner that avoids danger.

ce·leb·ri·ty (sə leb′rə tē) *noun.* **1.** a well-known or famous person: After winning, she became a *celebrity*. **2.** fame; renown.

cham·ber·lain (chām′bər lin) *noun.* **1.** an officer in charge of a ruler's household. **2.** a high official in some royal courts.

cham·pi·on (cham′pē ən) *noun.* **1.** someone or something that wins or is judged best in a competition. **2.** a person who fights for or defends another person or a cause: The mayor was the *champion* of the poor. —*adjective.* winning first place; being the best of its kind. —*verb.* to defend or support.

char·ac·ter (kar′ik tər) *noun.* **1.** any letter or other symbol used in writing, printing, or by a computer. **2.** a person's pattern of behavior or personality. **3.** a person's special qualities. **4.** a person in a story, play, etc. **characters.**

chock (chok) *noun.* a wedge or block made of wood, metal, etc., used to fill a space and hold an object steady, stop it from moving, etc. It may be wedged into cracks, placed under wheels, and so on.

cit·a·del (sit′ə d′l *or* sit′ə del) *noun.* **1.** a fortress on a high place for the defense of a city. **2.** a place of safety; refuge.

cit·y room (sit′ē rōōm) *noun.* the room where local news is handled at a newspaper, television, or radio station.

clam·ber (klam′bər) *verb.* to climb with effort, especially by using the hands as well as the feet. **clambered, clambering.**

clev·er (klev′ər) *adjective.* **1.** quick thinking; intelligent, witty. **2.** skillful. **3.** showing intelligence or skill. **cleverer, cleverest.**

cli·ent (klī′ənt) *noun.* **1.** a person or business for whom a lawyer, accountant, etc., is acting: My *client* was pleased with my work. **2.** a customer.

coast·al (kōs′t′l) *adjective.* of, near, or along a coast.

coax (kōks) *verb.* **1.** to try to get someone to do something, particularly by being very agreeable, flattering, etc. **2.** to push or press something, especially when it will not go into place easily. **coaxed, coaxing.**

col·lapse (kə laps′) *verb.* **1.** to fall down as when sides no longer hold. **2.** to break down suddenly; fail: There was no warning before the bridge *collapsed*. **3.** to fold into a small space. **collapsed, collapsing.**

col·lec·tor (kə lek′tər) *noun.* a person or thing that gathers, as a person who collects coins. **collectors.**

col·li·sion (kə lizh′ən) *noun.* **1.** sudden, forceful contact; crash. **2.** a clash of opinions, interests, etc.

com·mer·cial art·ist (kə mur′shəl är′tist) *noun.* a graphic artist who does work used for advertisements, publications, etc.

com·mon de·nom·i·na·tor (kom′ən di nom′ə nāt′ər) *noun.* **1.** a number that can be divided with no remainder by each denominator of two or more fractions: A *common denominator* for ½ and ⅓ is 6. **2.** something shared by two or more persons or things.

com·pass (kum′pəs) *noun.* **1.** an instrument that shows direction, especially one with a needle that points to magnetic north. **2.** an instrument with two hinged legs used for drawing circles or measuring. **3.** boundary; circumference. —*verb.* **1.** to go around. **2.** to achieve; gain. **3.** to grasp mentally; understand.

com·po·si·tion (kom′pə zish′ən) *noun.* **1.** a putting together by combining a number of parts. **2.** the putting together of words or musical notes to make a complete piece of writing or a musical work. **3.** the parts or materials of a thing and the way they are put together.

com·pound (kom pound′) *verb.* **1.** to mix together; combine: The druggist *compounded* the ingredients for the medicine. **2.** to make greater or add to. **compounded, compounding.**

a	fat	oi	oil	ch	chin
ā	ape	oo	look	sh	she
ä	car, father	ōō	tool	th	thin
e	ten	ou	out	*th*	then
er	care	u	up	zh	leisure
ē	even	ur	fur	ng	ring
i	hit				
ir	here	ə =	a *in* ago		
ī	bite, fire		e *in* agent		
o	lot		i *in* unity		
ō	go		o *in* collect		
ô	law, horn		u *in* focus		

Clever started out, as nearly as anyone can tell, as a locally used word in certain parts of Great Britain. It has been used to mean "skillful," "active," and "handsome" at different times. It is an example of how a slang word can become accepted over time.

compass

computer

crags

com·pute (kəm pyo͞ot′) *verb.* to arrive at an answer by arithmetic; calculate. **computed, computing.**

com·put·er (kəm pyo͞ot′ər) *noun.* **1.** a person who computes. **2.** a machine that performs calculations and can select, store, and manipulate data.

con·ceit·ed (kən sē′tid) *adjective.* having an exaggerated opinion of oneself; vain.

con·fide (kən fīd′) *verb.* **1.** to tell or discuss one's secrets: Mark *confided* his surprise to Josie. **2.** to give to someone for safekeeping, as a secret, money, etc. **confided, confiding.**

con·fine (kən fīn′) *verb.* **1.** to keep within limits; restrict. **2.** to keep locked away, as in prison.

con·found (kon found) *verb.* to mix up or confuse. **confounding.**

con·jure (kon′jər *or* kun′jər) *verb.* to make appear as if by magic; *often* **conjure up.**

con·quer (koṅg′kər) *verb.* **1.** to gain something by using force. **2.** to overcome by physical or mental force; defeat: He *conquered* his fear of water by swimming every day. **conquered.**

con·quest (koṅg′kwest) *noun.* **1.** the act of gaining something by use of force. **2.** something gained by use of force, such as a country, or by trying hard.

con·scious·ness (kon′ shəs nis) *noun.* **1.** awareness. **2.** all the thoughts and feelings a person has when awake: The bad memory was gone from her *consciousness*.

con·stel·la·tion (kon′stə lā′shən) *noun.* a group of stars named after something they seem to resemble: The North Star is in the *constellation* of the Little Dipper.

con·struct (kən strukt′) *verb.* to put together according to a plan; make; build.

con·tem·pla·tion (kon′təm plā′shən) *noun.* **1.** the act of looking at something with concentration. **2.** the act of thinking about something with concentration; study. **3.** a looking forward to (doing) something.

con·ti·nen·tal shelf (kont″n en′t′l shelf) *noun.* an underwater shelf of land sloping gradually from the above-water edge of a continent to the point where a steep drop to the ocean bottom begins.

con·tin·gen·cy (kən tin′jən sē) *noun.* **1.** the state of being uncertain or happening by chance. **2.** an accidental happening; uncertain event. —*adjective.* an alternative for unexpected events: She had a *contingency* plan in case of rain.

con·ver·sa·tion·al (kon′vər sā′shən'l) *adjective.* of, for, or like a conversation: His easy, *conversational* way of talking was pleasant to hear.

cor·ri·dor (kôr′ə dər) *noun.* a long hall; any narrow passageway or route. **corridors.**

cos·tum·er (kos′ to͞om ər) *noun.* **1.** a person who makes, sells, or rents costumes. **2.** the shop where such a person works.

cour·te·ous·ly (kur′tē əs lē) *adverb.* in a well-mannered way; politely and thoughtfully.

cove (kōv) *noun.* a small bay or inlet.

cov·er (kuv′ ər) *verb.* **1.** to put one thing over another. **2.** to guard or defend a particular place. **covered, covering.**

crafts·man (krafts′mən) *noun.* a worker in a skilled trade; artisan. **craftsmen.**

crag (krag) *noun.* a steep, rugged rock that rises above or projects from others. **crags.**

cram (kram) *verb.* **1.** to pack full or too full. **2.** to stuff or force. **3.** to stuff the mind by studying a lot of things in a hurry, as for a test—*colloquial in this use.* **crammed, cramming.**

cramp (kramp) *noun.* **1.** a sudden, painful tightening of a muscle. **2.** abdominal pain (usually *plural*). **3.** a metal bar with bent ends for holding stone blocks or timbers. —*verb.* **1.** to cause a cramp. **2.** to keep from moving; confine.

cre·a·tiv·i·ty (krē′ā tiv′ə tē) *noun.* the ability to bring about or make; originality; inventiveness.

crev·ice (krev′is) *noun.* a crack or split making a narrow opening, as in a rock.

610

D

dan·gle (daṅg′g'l) *verb.* **1.** to hang loosely with a swaying motion. **2.** to cause or to hold so that something dangles. —**dangling** *noun.* state of hanging loosely.

daub (dôb) *verb.* **1.** to cover or smear with soft, sticky material such as an ointment. **2.** to paint sloppily. —*noun.* **1.** anything painted coarsely with large strokes. **2.** a badly painted picture. **daubs.**

de·code (dē kōd′) *verb.* to uncover the meaning of something written in code. **decoded, decoding.**

de·duce (di dōōs′ *or* di dyōōs′) *verb.* to figure out something from known facts; infer.

deft·ly (deft′lē) *adverb.* skillfully; in a quick, sure way.

de·scent (di sent′) *noun.* **1.** a descending, going down to a lower place. **2.** a downward slope. **3.** the family from which one comes, ancestry.

de·sert (di zurt′) *verb.* **1.** to leave someone or something when one should not. **2.** to leave military service without permission. **deserted, deserting.**

des·per·ate·ly (des′pər it lē) *adverb.* **1.** in a reckless, hopeless way. **2.** desiring or needing greatly. **3.** very seriously; dangerously. **4.** very greatly.

des·tin·y (des′tə nē) *noun.* **1.** something that is bound to happen; one's fate: No one knows one's *destiny.* **2.** the power that makes things happen; fate.

de·tect (di tekt′) *verb.* to discover the presence of something hidden or not easily seen.

di·lem·ma (di lem′ə) *noun.* a situation where a choice must be made between two equally unpleasant things; difficult choice.

dim·ple (dim′p'l) *noun.* **1.** a small hollow spot, particularly on the cheek or chin. **2.** any slight depression. —*verb.* to form dimples. **dimpled, dimpling.**

dis·ad·van·tage (dis′əd van′tij) *noun.* **1.** an unfavorable situation or circumstance: Being unable to read is a *disadvantage.* **2.** loss or harm. **disadvantages.**

dis·be·lief (dis bə lēf′) *noun.* the state of not believing; lack of belief: The child expressed *disbelief* in elves.

dis·cern (di surn′ *or* di zurn′) *verb.* to see or recognize; make out clearly: It is hard to *discern* the road in fog.

dis·charge (dis chärj′) *verb.* **1.** to release from something. **2.** to release from a job; fire. **3.** to remove a burden. —**discharged** *adjective.* given forth; let out: The *discharged* soldiers waited for the train home.

dis·re·gard (dis′ri gärd′) *verb.* to pay no attention to. **disregarded, disregarding.**

dis·solve (di zolv′) *verb.* **1.** to become part of a liquid. **2.** to break up or come to an end; finish: Our club *dissolved* because too many members moved away. **dissolved, dissolving.**

dis·suade (di swād′) *verb.* to change a person's course of action by persuasion or advice.

dis·tin·guish (dis ting′gwish) *verb.* **1.** to separate by differences; show the difference in. **2.** to see the difference in. **3.** to sense clearly. —**distinguished** *adjective.* famous or outstanding: The *distinguished* guest gave an excellent talk after dinner. **distinguished, distinguishing.**

dis·tress (dis tres′) *verb.* to make full of pain or misery; to cause worry, suffering, etc. —**distressed** *adjective.* troubled.

dou·ble-cross (dub′ 'l krôs′) *verb.* (*informal language*) to trick or cheat someone by not doing what was agreed on or promised.

dra·mat·i·cal·ly (drə mat′ik lē) *adverb.* having to do with the theater; in a striking or exciting way.

drift·wood (drift′wŏŏd) *noun.* wood that is or has been drifting in water.

drow·sy (drou′zē) *adjective.* **1.** being sleepy or half asleep. **2.** making one feel sleepy or half asleep.

du·ra·ble (dŏŏr′ə b'l *or* dyŏŏr′ə b'l) *adjective.* lasting even under hard wear or much use.

dwell (dwel) *verb.* to make one's home; live. —**dwellers** *plural noun.* people who live in a place.

a fat	oi oil	ch chin
ā ape	ŏŏ look	sh she
ä car, father	ōō tool	th thin
e ten	ou out	*th* then
er care	u up	zh leisure
ē even	ur fur	ṅg ring
i hit		
ir here	ə = a *in* ago	
ī bite, fire	e *in* agent	
o lot	i *in* unity	
ō go	o *in* collect	
ô law, horn	u *in* focus	

dangle

◇

Deduce comes from the Latin word *deducere* meaning "to lead down." When facts lead us to a conclusion, we are deducing.

descent

611

E

Easel comes from the Dutch word *ezel*, which means "donkey." A donkey is a good, solid animal which can carry or support a load. In the same way, an easel can support a picture.

erupt

exhibit

ease (ēz) *noun.* **1.** ability to do, without trying hard: The problem was solved with *ease.* **2.** rest; relaxation. **3.** freedom from pain, worry, etc. —*verb.* **1.** to reduce pain, worry, etc. **2.** to reduce strain or pressure; loosen. **3.** to move slowly and carefully.

ea·sel (ē′z′l) *noun.* a standing frame used to hold an artist's canvas, chalkboard, etc.

e·lab·o·rate (i lab′ər it) *adjective.* worked out carefully; done in great detail; complicated. —*verb.* (i lab′ ə rāt) **1.** to work out carefully; do in great detail. **2.** to say or write something in detail; give more information; be more specific.

eld·est (el′dist) *adjective.* oldest.

el·i·gi·ble (el′i jə b′l) *adjective.* having the qualities required; suitable; desirable.

e·lude (i lood′) *verb.* **1.** to avoid or escape by using speed, cleverness, etc. **2.** to keep from being seen, understood, or remembered.

en·deav·or (in dev′ər) *verb.* to try hard; make a good attempt. —*noun.* an attempt or effort.

ep·i·dem·ic (ep′ə dem′ik) *noun.* the rapid spreading of a disease among many people at the same time. —*adjective.* widespread, as a disease: We had an *epidemic* from a new contagious disease.

e·quiv·a·lent (i kwiv′ə lənt) *adjective.* equal in amount, value, etc. —*noun.* something that is equal; the same: One-half is the *equivalent* of two-fourths.

e·rupt (i rupt′) *verb.* **1.** to burst forth. **2.** to throw out lava, water, etc. **3.** to break out in a rash. **erupted, erupting.**

ex·hib·it (ig zib′it) *verb.* **1.** to show or display publicly. **2.** to present for viewing; show. **exhibited, exhibiting.** —*noun.* **1.** something displayed, particularly publicly. **2.** something presented as evidence in a court of law.

ex·hi·bi·tion (ek′sə bish′ən) *noun.* **1.** the act of showing publicly. **2.** a public showing, as of a collection of things.

ex·pect·ant (ek spek′ tənt) *adjective.* waiting for something to happen; **expecting.**

ex·qui·site·ly (eks′kwi zit lē *or* ik skwiz′it lē) *adverb.* **1.** done in a careful or elaborate way. **2.** very beautifully done, especially in a delicate or careful way. **3.** in a manner that shows the best quality. **4.** very greatly; intensely.

ex·tinct (ik stiŋkt′) *adjective.* **1.** no longer living; having died out: The passenger pigeon is an *extinct* species. **2.** died down or gone out: The fire is *extinct.*

F

fab·u·lous (fab′yoo ləs) *adjective.* **1.** of or like a fable; imaginary; mythical: A dragon is a *fabulous* beast. **2.** hard to believe; astounding; incredible.

famed (fāmd) *adjective.* well-known; famous.

fan·ta·sy (fan′tə sē) *noun.* **1.** imagination or fancy. **2.** a play, story, daydream, etc., with much imagination and very unreal.

fea·ture (fē′chər) *noun.* **1.** any part of the face, as the eyes, nose, chin, etc. **2.** a distinct or special part or quality. **3.** a main attraction at a show, sale, etc. **4.** a special story or column in a newspaper or magazine. **features.**

fee·ble (fē′b′l) *adjective.* not strong; weak.

fence (fens) *noun.* **1.** a railing or wall placed around a field or yard. **2.** a person who buys and sells stolen goods.

fi·ber (fī′bər) *noun.* **1.** any of the thread-like parts forming animal and plant tissue. **2.** anything that can be separated into threads for weaving, etc. **3.** character; nature; quality. **fibers.**

fid·dler (fid′lər) *noun.* **1.** a person who plays the violin. **2.** a person who toys or plays with something or moves their fingers in a restless way.

field (fēld) *noun.* **1.** a wide piece of open land. **2.** a piece of land with a special use or that produces some natural resource, as a landing field or oil field. **3.** the area in which something can be seen, as a field of view. **4.** the space in which magnetic or electrical lines of force are

active: The magnetic *field* erased the tape.
5. a branch of learning.

fil·i·al (fil′ē əl) *adjective.* of, suitable to, or due from a son or daughter.

fil·ter (fil′tər) *noun.* **1.** a device that removes solid particles from a liquid or gas. **2.** any material used in such a device, as sand, charcoal, etc. —*verb.* **1.** to pass through a filter. **2.** to act as a filter for. **3.** to remove with a filter. **4.** to move or pass slowly. **filtered, filtering.**

fiord (fyôrd) *noun.* a long, narrow inlet of the sea bordered by steep cliffs.

for·bid (fər bid′) *verb.* to rule against; not to allow; prohibit. —**forbidden** *adjective.* against the law or the rules.

form (fôrm) *noun.* **1.** the shape or outline of anything. **2.** a mold used to give something shape. **3.** the way in which something is put together; arrangement. **4.** a printed paper with blank spaces to be filled in. —*verb.* **1.** to give a shape to. **2.** to train. **3.** to develop, as habits. **4.** to come together; organize.

for·mi·da·ble (fôr′mə də b'l) *adjective.* **1.** causing fear or dread: The general's manner was *formidable.* **2.** hard to do.

for·tu·nate (fôr′chə nit) *adjective.* having, bringing, or coming through good luck.

fra·grance (frā′grəns) *noun.* a sweet or pleasant smell.

freight·er (frāt′ər) *noun.* a ship that carries goods.

fu·ri·ous (fyoor′ē əs) *adjective.* **1.** full of fury or wild anger. **2.** moving violently; overpowering.

G

gai·ly (gā′lē) *adverb.* **1.** in a happy manner; merrily. **2.** brightly; in bright colors.

gal·ax·y (gal′ək sē) *noun.* **1.** any vast grouping of millions of stars. **2.** any group of famous people. **galaxies.**

gar·ment (gär′mənt) *noun.* any piece of clothing. **garments.**

gar·ner (gär′nər) *verb.* to gather up and store. **garnered, garnering.**

gen·er·os·i·ty (jen′ə ros′ə tē) *noun.* **1.** the quality of being willing to give; unselfish or noble and forgiving. **2.** an unselfish or forgiving act.

ge·o·met·ric (jē′ə met′rik) *adjective.* **1.** having to do with geometry, the branch of mathematics that deals with points, lines, planes, and solids. **2.** made up of straight lines, triangles, circles, etc.

gi·gan·tic (jī gan′tik) *adjective.* like the size of a giant; very big; huge; enormous.

glimpse (glimps) *verb.* to get a quick look at. —*noun.* a brief look.

god·dess (god′is) *noun.* **1.** a female being thought of as living forever and having more than human powers. **2.** a woman of great beauty or charm.

gold·smith (gōld′smith) *noun.* a person skilled in making gold objects.

gra·cious (grā′shəs) *adjective.* **1.** having or showing kindness, charm, politeness, etc. **2.** having grace and comfort: It is a *gracious* home.

grat·i·tude (grat′ə tōōd *or* grat′ə tyōōd) *noun.* the feeling of being thankful for some favor; thankfulness: She showed her *gratitude* by thanking me.

grave·ly (grāv′lē) *adverb.* **1.** in a way that requires serious thought. **2.** seriously; solemnly; in a dignified manner. **3.** dangerously; in a threatening way. **4.** somberly; dully.

grav·i·ta·tion·al (grav′ə ta′shən'l) *adjective.* of or having to do with the force by which every mass or particle of matter attracts and is attracted by every other mass or particle of matter: The planets are held in their orbits by *gravitational* attraction.

greed (grēd) *noun.* the desire to take all one can get without thought of others. —**greedy** *adjective.* wanting to have more than one needs or deserves.

guar·an·tee (gar ən tē′) *noun.* **1.** a promise to return one's money or to replace an item if it is not what the seller says it is. **2.** a promise that something will be done. **3.** a promise to pay another's debt or do something that the person is not able to do. —*verb.* **1.** to give a guarantee. **2.** to promise: I *guarantee* that you will like it.

a fat	oi oil	ch chin
ā ape	oo look	sh she
ä car, father	ōō tool	th thin
e ten	ou out	*th* then
er care	u up	zh leisure
ē even	ur fur	n̄g ring
i hit		
ir here	ə = a *in* ago	
ī bite, fire	e *in* agent	
o lot	i *in* unity	
ō go	o *in* collect	
ô law, horn	u *in* focus	

fiord

gigantic

guide (gīd) *verb*. **1.** to show the way, conduct, or lead to. **2.** to control the course of; steer. —*noun*. **1.** a person who leads or shows the way. **2.** something that controls, directs, or instructs.

H

hard·ship (härd′ship) *noun*. something that is hard to bear; trouble; pain; suffering, etc.

haste (hāst) *noun*. **1.** quick movement; hurrying. **2.** hurrying carelessly.

head·long (hed′lôṉg) *adverb*. **1.** with the head first. **2.** with uncontrolled speed; recklessly.

heart·bro·ken (härt′brō′k′n) *adjective*. filled with sorrow or grief.

her·it·age (her′ət ij) *noun*. something received from one's ancestors or the past, such as certain skills, rights, or a way of life: America has a *heritage* of freedom.

her·o·ine (her′ə win) *noun*. **1.** a woman or girl admired for doing something brave. **2.** the most important female character in a story.

his·to·ri·an (his tôr′ē ən) *noun*. a writer of or an expert on history. **historians.**

hold·fast (hōld′fast′) *noun*. **1.** any device that holds a thing in place, as a catch, hook, nail, etc. **2.** any of a number of rootlike or suckerlike parts that serve to attach plants to the surface on which they grow.

home·spun (hōm′spun) *noun*. **1.** cloth made of yarn spun in the home. **2.** a coarse, loosely woven cloth. —*adjective*. **1.** spun or made at home. **2.** made of homespun. **3.** plain; homely; simple.

hon·or·a·ble (on′ər ə b′l) *adjective*. **1.** worthy of honor; respectable. **2.** having a sense of right and wrong; integrity. **3.** bringing honor.

hor·i·zon·tal (hôr′ə zon′t′l) *adjective*. parallel to the horizon; not vertical; flat; level.

host (hōst) *noun*. **1.** one who has guests at home or who pays for their entertainment away from home. **2.** one who runs a

hotel. **3.** a living thing in which another living thing lives. **4.** a great number: There was a *host* of things to do. **5.** an army. —*verb*. to act as a host as at a party.

hub (hub) *noun*. **1.** the center part of a wheel. **2.** a center of interest; activity.

hue (hyo͞o) *noun*. a color, usually a particular shade or tint.

hum·ble (hum′b′l) *adjective*. **1.** showing an awareness of one's own weaknesses and faults; not proud; modest. **2.** low in rank or position; unimportant. —*verb*. to lower in pride; make humble; take away power.

hu·mil·i·ate (hyo͞o mil′ē āt) *verb*. to lower the pride or dignity of; hurt the feelings of by making to seem foolish. —**humiliated** *adjective*. felt ashamed: The *humiliated* man regretted his past behavior. —**humiliation** *noun*. the condition of feeling foolish, ashamed, without pride.

hurl (hurl) *verb*. **1.** to throw with force. **2.** to speak in a forceful or angry way.

hys·ter·i·cal (his ter′i k′l) *adjective*. **1.** having to do with a wild fit of crying, laughing, etc.; emotionally uncontrolled. **2.** very funny or comical.

I

il·lu·sion (i lo͞o′zhən) *noun*. **1.** a false idea or belief. **2.** a false or misleading appearance: The water gave the *illusion* of being pure.

il·lus·tra·tive (i lus′ trə tiv) *adjective*. that illustrates or explains: The strings attached to the globe were *illustrative* of the earth's division into zones.

i·mag·i·nar·y (i maj′ə ner′ē) *adjective*. existing only in the mind; not real: The monsters were all *imaginary*.

im·meas·ur·a·ble (i mezh′ ər ə b′l) *adjective*. too large or too much to be measured.

im·mor·tal (i môr′t′l) *adjective*. **1.** never dying; living forever. **2.** having fame that will last. —*noun*. **1.** a being that lives forever. **2.** a person who has fame that lasts. **immortals.**

holdfast

Hue comes from the Old English word *hew*. "Form," "shape," "look of," "color," and "beauty" were all meanings of *hew*. Over the centuries, the meaning changed until only one of the original meanings remained.

hurl

im·pres·sion·ist (im presh′ə nist) *noun*.
1. a painter who seeks only to capture an overall impression or a momentary glimpse of a subject without showing every detail. **2.** a writer or composer who works in that style. **3.** an entertainer who does impersonations. **impressionists.**

in·cred·i·bly (in kred′ə blē) *adverb*. in such an unusual or improbable way that it is not easy to believe.

in·fan·try (in′fən trē) *noun*. soldiers trained and equipped to fight on foot.

in·flu·ence (in′floo wəns) *noun*. **1.** the power persons or things have to affect others. **2.** a person or thing that has influence. **3.** the power a person or group has to affect things because of wealth, social position, etc. —*verb*. to have influence; affect the behavior of; affect the action or thought of; modify.
influenced, influencing.

in·ge·nu·i·ty (in′jə noo′ə tē *or* in′jə nyoo′ə tē) *noun*. **1.** the quality of being clever, skillful, inventive, etc. **2.** the quality of being made in a clever or original way. **3.** cleverness, originality, skill, etc.

in·hab·it·ant (in hab′i tənt) *noun*. a person or animal that lives in a particular place.
inhabitants.

in·her·it (in her′it) *verb*. **1.** to get something from someone after that person dies; become an heir: You will *inherit* this house after I die. **2.** to have certain characteristics from parents or ancestors who had them.

in·let (in′let) *noun*. **1.** a narrow strip of water running into the shore from a river, lake, ocean, etc. **2.** an entrance or opening.

in·nate (i nāt′ *or* in′ āt) *adjective*. that seems to be born in one; natural: She has *innate* talent in writing.

in·sep·a·ra·ble (in sep′ ər ə b′l) *adjective*. that cannot be separated or parted: The friends were *inseparable*.

in·spect (in spekt′) *verb*. **1.** to look at carefully; examine. **2.** to examine or review officially.

in·spi·ra·tion (in′spə rā′shən) *noun*.
1. a reason or urge to do something.
2. something that causes thought or action: The beautiful sunset was an *inspiration* to the artist. **3.** an inspired idea. **4.** a breathing in.

in·stinct (in′stiṅkt) *noun*. **1.** a way of behaving that an animal or person is born with. **2.** a natural or learned ability or knack; talent.

in·ter·mit·tent (in tər mit″nt) *adjective*. stopping and starting again from time to time: We had *intermittent* rain all day.

in·tri·cate (in′tri kit) *adjective*. complicated, detailed.

in·va·sion (in vā′zhən) *noun*. an entrance of an attacking army; a breaking in on: The *invasion* of the island was not successful, and the army was forced to leave.

J

jar·gon (jär′gən) *noun*. **1.** talk that is not understandable; gibberish. **2.** special words used by people in the same kind of work, way of life, etc.: Auto mechanics have their own *jargon*.

jest·er (jes′tər) *noun*. a person who jokes, makes joking remarks, etc.; especially a sort of clown hired by a ruler in the Middle Ages to do tricks and tell jokes.

jew·el·er (joo′ əl ər) *noun*. **1.** a person who makes, sells, or repairs jewelry. **2.** the shop where such a person works.

jowl (joul) *noun*. **1.** the fleshy, hanging part below the lower jaw. **2.** a jaw, especially the lower jaw. **3.** the cheek.

K

keen (kēn) *adjective*. **1.** having a sharp edge or point. **2.** sharp, cutting. **3.** very sensitive; sharp in hearing, seeing, etc. **4.** eager, enthusiastic: We were *keen* to get the job finished. **5.** intense, strong.

a fat		oi oil	ch chin
ā ape		oo look	sh she
ä car, father		ōo tool	th thin
e ten		ou out	*th* then
er care		u up	zh leisure
ē even		ur fur	ṅg ring
i hit			
ir here		ə = a *in* ago
ī bite, fire		e *in* agent
o lot		i *in* unity
ō go		o *in* collect
ô law, horn		u *in* focus

Infantry had its beginnings in a Latin word for child, *infans*. It came into English from the French *infantrie*. Foot soldiers are usually young, and the word for child came to be used for them.

inlet

ledge

Ledge, a narrow shelf, is related to the Middle English word *legge*. *Legge*, however, meant "lay" as in laying eggs. How the one word was turned into the other is one of the mysteries of word usage.

lute

kelp for·est (kelp fôr′ist) *noun.* a large amount of kelp, a large brown seaweed, growing in one undersea area.

ki·mo·no (kə mō′nə) *noun.* **1.** the traditional Japanese loose outer garment with wide sleeves and a sash about the waist. **2.** a woman's loose dressing gown in this style.

kin·ship (kin′ ship′) *noun.* the state of being related or connected; relationship.

knead (nēd) *verb.* **1.** to mix by folding, pressing, and squeezing dough, clay, etc., to prepare for use. **2.** to rub, squeeze, or press with the hands; massage. **kneaded, kneading.**

L

la·goon (lə gōōn′) *noun.* **1.** a small, shallow body of water, especially one that joins a larger one. **2.** a body of water surrounded by an atoll. **3.** a body of shallow salt water cut off from the sea by sand dunes. **lagoons.**

land·lord (land′lôrd) *noun.* **1.** a person who leases or rents land, houses, etc., to others. **2.** a person who runs a rooming house, inn, etc.

land·mark (land′märk) *noun.* **1.** any large thing such as a house, tree, etc., that makes a particular place easily recognized: The old barn is a good *landmark.* **2.** a very important event. **3.** an object that marks the boundary of a piece of land. **landmarks.**

laugh·ing·stock (laf′ing stok′) *noun.* a person or thing that everyone laughs at or makes fun of.

league (lēg) *noun.* a number of persons, groups, or countries joined together for some reason, as to protect or help each other.

ledge (lej) *noun.* a flat, shelf-like part coming out of a cliff, wall, etc.

leg·a·cy (leg′ə sē) *noun.* **1.** money or property left to someone in a will. **2.** anything handed down from one person, especially an ancestor, to another.

less·en (les′′n) *verb.* to make or become less; decrease. **lessened.** —**lessening** *noun.* a decreasing amount.

li·a·ble (lī′ ə b′ l) *adjective.* **1.** obligated by law; responsible. **2.** likely to happen, usually referring to something unpleasant.

life·like (līf′līk) *adjective.* as in real life; that looks real.

list·less·ly (list′lis lē) *adverb.* in a way that shows no interest in what is going on around one because of sickness, sadness, tiredness, etc.

look·out (look′out) *noun.* **1.** the act of watching carefully for something or someone. **2.** a person who keeps watch; guard; sentry. **3.** a place, usually high up, from which watch is kept. **4.** concern; worry.

lon·er (lō′nər) *noun.* (*American informal language*) a person who would rather be alone or work alone than with other people.

loy·al·ty (loi′əl tē) *noun.* the state of being loyal; faithfulness.

lute (lōōt) *noun.* an early musical stringed instrument held and played like a guitar.

M

ma·neu·ver (mə nōō′vər *or* mə nyōō′vər) *noun.* **1.** large scale practice movement of troops, warships, etc. **2.** any change of movement or direction done with skill as in driving a car or flying an airplane. **3.** a skillful move or trick. —*verb.* **1.** to do maneuvers with. **2.** to plan or manage skillfully. **3.** to move, get, make, etc., by some trick or scheme. **maneuvered, maneuvering.**

man·u·al (man′yōō wəl) *adjective.* made, done, or used by the hands. —*noun.* a book of facts or instructions; handbook.

mar·vel (mär′v′l) *noun.* a wonderful or astonishing thing. —*verb.* to wonder; be astonished. **marveled, marveling.**

mas·sage (mə säzh′ *or* mə säj′) *noun.* a rubbing or kneading of the body to loosen muscles and stimulate circulation. —*verb.* to give a massage.

math•e•ma•ti•cian (math′ə mə tish′ən) *noun.* an expert in the science known as mathematics, which uses numbers and symbols in dealing with the relationships of amounts, sizes, and forms.

maw (mô) *noun.* **1.** an animal's stomach. **2.** the throat, gullet, jaws of an animal, such as an alligator.

mem•o•ran•dum (mem′ə ran′dəm) *noun.* **1.** a short note written to help someone remember or to remind of something. **2.** an informal written note often used in business. **memo.** *short form.*

men•tal im•age (men′t'l im′ij) *noun.* a picture, feeling, memory, etc., that exists only in the mind: The actual house did not meet his *mental image* of it. **mental images.**

mi•cro•scope (mī′krə skōp) *noun.* an instrument with a lens or combination of lenses used to make things seem larger so that they may be easily observed. **microscopes.**

mi•gra•tion (mī grā′shən) *noun.* **1.** any movement from one place to another. **2.** a movement from one region to another with the change of seasons, as some birds do: Their *migration* took them north.

mill (mil) *noun.* **1.** a machine for grinding, crushing, pressing: a pepper *mill.* **2.** a building with machinery for grinding, such as grain into flour or meal. **3.** a factory: a steel *mill.* —*verb.* **1.** to grind, make, or form. **2.** to move slowly in a mixed-up way, referring to the action of a group or crowd. **milling.**

mis•sion (mish′ən) *noun.* **1.** a special duty or errand someone is sent out to do by a church, government, etc. **2.** a group of people sent on such an errand, or the place where they live and work: The building of the *mission* was finished at last. **3.** a group of people sent to a foreign government to negotiate something.

mod•est (mod′ist) *adjective.* **1.** not vain or boastful about oneself; humble. **2.** not forward; shy. **3.** behaving, dressing, speaking, etc., properly. **4.** not extreme. **5.** quiet and humble in appearance.

mo•men•tum (mō men′təm) *noun.* **1.** the force with which an object moves: The ball gained *momentum* as it fell. **2.** any strength or force that keeps growing.

mon•i•tor (mon′ə tər) *noun.* **1.** a student chosen to keep order in some schools. **2.** something that reminds or warns. **3.** in radio, TV, and sound studios, a receiver or loudspeaker used to check the broadcast or recording. —*verb.* to listen or watch; to keep check on: I *monitor* their progress. **monitored, monitoring.**

moor (moor) *noun.* an area of open wasteland, often marshy and covered with heather. **moors.**

mor•tal (môr′t'l) *noun.* a being that must die at some time, especially a person.

mo•tif (mō tēf′) *noun.* a main idea or theme, feature, etc.; specifically in art, literature, and music, a main theme or subject that is developed; a repeated figure in a design.

mo•tion•less (mo′shən lis) *adjective.* not moving; unable to move.

moun•tain•eer (moun t′n ir′) *noun.* a person who climbs mountains for sport.

mourn•ful•ly (môrn′fəl ē) *adverb.* sadly; in a way that shows grief.

mu•ral (myoor′əl) *noun.* a picture, usually large, painted or put on a wall.

microscope

N

ne•go•ti•ate (ni gō′shē āt) *verb.* **1.** to bargain or discuss in the hope of reaching an agreement. **2.** to make arrangements for, settle, or finish a business deal, treaty, etc.: *Negotiate* a fair agreement. **3.** to transfer or sell negotiable papers, as stocks, bonds, etc. **4.** to succeed in doing something, as climbing, crossing, etc.

nib (nib) *noun.* **1.** a bird's bill or beak. **2.** a point; especially the point of a fountain or artist's pen. **nibs.**

nos•tril (nos′trəl) *noun.* either of the two outside openings of the nose. **nostrils.**

nos•y (nō′zē) *adjective.* (*informal language*) too curious about other people's business; interfering.

migration

O

o·blige (ə blīj′) *verb*. **1.** to force to do something by reason of law, circumstances, conscience, etc. **2.** to make one feel something is owed because of a favor or kindness received. **3.** to do a favor for. **obliged, obliging.**

ol·fac·to·ry (ol fak′tər ē *or* ōl fak′tər ē) *adjective*. of the sense of smell.

op·por·tune (op′ ər to͞on′ *or* op′ ər tyo͞on′) *adjective*. just right for the purpose or situation; suitable; timely.

out·go·ing (ou͞t′gō′iṅg) *adjective*. **1.** going out; leaving. **2.** sociable; friendly.

patchwork

P

pam·phlet (pam′flit) *noun*. a small, thin book, usually with a paper cover.

pan·try (pan′trē) *noun*. a small room near a kitchen, used for storing food, dishes, and other kitchen items.

par·cel (pär′s'l) *noun*. **1.** wrapped-up object; package; bundle. **2.** a piece of land. —*verb*. to separate into parts for giving away or selling. **parcels.**

parch·ment (pärch′mənt) *noun*. **1.** an animal skin prepared for writing or painting on. **2.** a document written on parchment.

patch·work (pach′wurk) *noun*. **1.** anything made from odd-shaped, unmatching, or mixed parts; jumble. **2.** a quilt or other needlework made from odd patches of cloth sewn together. **3.** any design like this.

pawn·bro·ker (pôn′brō′kər) *noun*. a person who lends money at interest to people who leave personal property with him or her as security.

peace·ful·ly (pēs′fəl ē) *adverb*. **1.** in a quiet and calm way; not noisily or disorderly. **2.** in a manner suited to a time of peace.

pen name (pen nām) *noun*. a name used by an author in place of his or her own.

Pirogue is a secondhand borrowing from the Carib people (who gave their name to the Caribbean Sea). It came into English directly from the French *pirogue*. This word dates from Colonial times when England, France, and Spain were exploring the Americas.

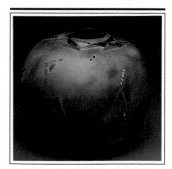

pottery

per·sist (pər sist′) *verb*. **1.** to refuse to give up; go on steadily. **2.** to keep doing over and over. **3.** to continue to exist; last. **persists, persisted, persisting.**

phy·si·cian (fə zish′ən) *noun*. a medical doctor, especially one who is not a surgeon.

pil·lar (pil′ər) *noun*. **1.** a long, slender, vertical support for a roof, etc., or as a monument; column. **2.** a person who is the main support for an organization, community, etc. **pillars.**

pi·rogue (pi rōg′) *noun*. **1.** a canoe made from a hollowed log. **2.** any boat shaped like a canoe.

pitch (pich) *verb*. **1.** to throw; toss. **2.** to erect; set up. **3.** to slope downward. —*noun*. **1.** a throwing or way of throwing. **2.** the amount or angle of slope. **3.** in mountaineering, one part of the climb.

pit·i·ful (pit′i fəl) *adjective*. **1.** causing or deserving pity. **2.** causing or deserving contempt or scorn.

plain·clothes (plān′klōthz′) *adjective*. not wearing a uniform on duty, usually referring to a police officer.

plank·ton (plaṅk′tən) *noun*. microscopic animals and plants that float or drift in a body of water and are used as food by larger sea animals.

pla·za (plä′zə *or* plaz′ə) *noun*. a public square or marketplace in a city or town.

pleas·ing (plēz′iṅg) *adjective*. giving a feeling of delight or satisfaction.

plod (plod) *verb*. **1.** to walk or move heavily and with effort. **2.** to work slowly and steadily, especially on a dull task. —**plodding** *adjective*. in a laborious manner.

plum·met (plum′it) *verb*. to fall straight down. **plummeted, plummeting.**

pore (pôr) *noun*. a tiny opening, as in the skin or plant leaves, through which fluids may be taken in or released. **pores.**

port·fo·li·o (pôrt fō′lē ō) *noun*. **1.** a flat carrying case for loose papers, drawings, etc. **2.** a list of stocks, bonds, and other investments owned.

pot·ter·y (pot′ər ē) *noun*. **1.** pots, bowls, dishes, etc., made from heat-hardened clay. **2.** a place where pottery is made.

pouch (pouch) *noun.* **1.** a small bag or sack. **2.** a loose fold of skin forming a pocket on the abdomen of certain female animals, such as the kangaroo. **3.** anything in the shape of a pouch. —*verb.* to make into a pouch.

prac·ti·cal joke (prak'ti k'l jōk) *noun.* a trick played on someone in fun.

pre·cau·tion (pri kô'shən) *noun.* care taken beforehand, as against danger, failure, etc.

pre·dict (pri dikt') *verb.* to state what one thinks will happen in the future.

pre·dom·i·nant·ly (pri dom'ə nənt lē) *adverb.* mainly, most frequently, noticeably.

prej·u·dice (prej'ə dis) *noun.* **1.** an opinion made without knowing or by ignoring the facts; unreasonable opinion. **2.** dislike or distrust of people because of their race, religion, etc. —*verb.* to cause to have prejudice.

pre·scrip·tion (pri skrip'shən) *noun.* **1.** an order or direction: This diet is a *prescription* for weight loss. **2.** a medical doctor's written instructions for preparing and using a medicine; a medicine made according to a doctor's instructions.

pre·sume (pri zōōm') *verb.* **1.** to assume permission where none exists; dare. **2.** to take for granted; suppose. **3.** to be too bold; to go beyond what is right or expected.

prey (prā) *noun.* **1.** an animal hunted for food by another animal. **2.** any person or thing that is a victim of someone or something. —*verb.* **1.** to hunt other animals for food. **2.** to rob by force. **3.** to get money from by dishonest means. **4.** to have a harmful influence upon.

print (print) *noun.* **1.** a mark made on or in a surface by pressing or hitting with something. **2.** cloth printed with a design or clothing made of this cloth. **3.** letters, words, or pictures made on paper from inked type, plates, wood blocks, etc. **prints.**

pri·va·tion (prī vā'shən) *noun.* the absence of things needed for life or comfort: Lack of money is a *privation*.

proc·ess (pros'es) *noun.* **1.** development over time involving a series of changes. **2.** a way of making or doing something involving a number of steps. **3.** the act of doing something over a period of time.

pro·claim (prō klām') *verb.* to make known publicly; announce. **proclaimed, proclaiming.**

pro·jec·tion (prə jek'shən) *noun.* **1.** a sticking out or being made to stick out. **2.** something that sticks out from. **3.** a prediction based upon known facts. **4.** an image seen on a surface such as a motion picture.

pro·por·tions (prə pôr'shənz) *plural noun.* comparative relations with respect to size, amount, degree, etc.

pro·vi·sions (prə vish'ənz) *plural noun.* a supply of food for future use.

pun (pun) *noun.* the humorous use of words having the same sound or spelling that mean different things; play on words —*verb.* to make puns. **punned, punning.**

pun·ish (pun'ish) *verb.* **1.** to make undergo pain, loss, suffering, etc., for doing something wrong. **2.** to set a penalty for. **3.** to treat in a harsh way.

pun·ish·ment (pun'ish mənt) *noun.* **1.** a punishing or being punished. **2.** a penalty for a crime or wrongdoing.

pur·su·er (pər sōō'ər *or* pər syōō'ər) *noun.* someone or something that follows so as to catch, or as in a course of action. **pursuers.**

a fat	oi oil	ch chin
ā ape	oo look	sh she
ä car, father	ōō tool	th thin
e ten	ou out	*th* then
er care	u up	zh leisure
ē even	ur fur	ng ring
i hit		
ir here	ə = a *in* ago	
ī bite, fire	e *in* agent	
o lot	i *in* unity	
ō go	o *in* collect	
ô law, horn	u *in* focus	

prey

Projection has its roots in the Latin *projectum*, "to throw away from" or "force out." With a little imagination it is not hard to see how it came to mean "sticking out" or "predicting from known facts."

Q

quilt·er (kwil'tər) *noun.* **1.** a person who makes quilts. **2.** a machine that quilts. **quilters.**

R

rappel

reel

range (rānj) *noun.* **1.** a row or line of, as a series of connected mountains. **2.** the greatest distance a gun can shoot, or something can move or be heard. **3.** the limits of possible differences of amount, degree, etc.: The *range* in price is from one to five dollars. **4.** a large, open area of land used by grazing animals. —*verb.* **1.** to travel about; roam. **2.** to stretch or lie in a particular direction. **3.** to be within certain limits.

rap·pel (ra pel') *noun.* a way of going down a mountain by using a double rope anchored above the climber who loops it around the body and plays it out slowly. —*verb.* to go down by using a rappel. **rappelled, rappelling.**

re·al·is·ti·cal·ly (rē'ə lis'tik lē) *adverb.* **1.** in a practical manner. **2.** in a way that uses the technique of picturing things in art and literature as they really are.

re·as·sure (rē ə shoor') *verb.* to take away doubts about; to make feel secure once again. **reassured, reassuring.**

reb·el (reb"l) *noun.* a person who resists authority or control. —*adjective.* fighting against authority. —*verb.* (ri bel') **1.** to resist authority or control. **2.** to have a strong dislike for. **rebelled, rebelling.**

re·cede (ri sēd') *verb.* to move back; slope backward. **recedes, receded, receding.**

re·cess (rē'ses *or* ri ses') *noun.* **1.** a hollow place, particularly in a wall. **2.** a shut off or inner place: Who knows what secrets are in the *recesses* of the mind? **3.** a stopping of work, study, etc., for a short rest. **recesses.**

rec·ol·lec·tion (rek' ə lek' shən) *noun.* **1.** something that is remembered or recalled; a memory. **2.** the act or power of remembering.

re·cov·er (ri kuv'ər) *verb.* **1.** to get back something lost, stolen, etc. **2.** to get well again. **3.** to save oneself from falling, slipping, etc. **4.** to restore to useful condition; reclaim.

reef (rēf) *noun.* a ridge of rocks, coral, or sand just below or at the surface of the water.

reel (rēl) *noun.* **1.** a frame or spool on which something is wound. **2.** the amount of something wound on a reel. —*verb.* to wind on or off a reel. **reeled, reeling.**

ref·uge (ref'yōoj) *noun.* **1.** shelter or protection from danger, etc.: We found *refuge* from the storm. **2.** a safe place to be; shelter.

reg·is·ter (rej'is tər) *noun.* **1.** a record or list of names or things; also, a book in which the record is kept. **2.** a device for counting and keeping a record of, such as a cash register. **3.** the range of tones of a voice or musical instrument. —*verb.* **1.** to keep a record of something in a register, as to register a birth. **2.** to put one's name in a register, as of voters. **3.** to show, as by a look on the face. **4.** to make an impression: I saw it, but it was some time before it *registered*. **registered, registering.**

re·gret (ri gret') *verb.* to be sorry about or feel troubled over something done or not done: Do you *regret* spilling the paint? —*noun.* a feeling of being sorry or troubled.

re·luc·tant (ri luk'tənt) *adjective.* **1.** not wanting to do something; unwilling. **2.** showing unwillingness.

rem·e·dy (rem'ə dē) *noun.* **1.** any medicine that cures, heals, or relieves. **2.** something that corrects a wrong or helps make things better. **remedies.**

re·morse (ri môrs') *noun.* a deep feeling of sorrow or guilt over having done something wrong.

rep·u·ta·tion (rep'yoo tā'shən) *noun.* **1.** what is generally thought about a person or thing, good or bad. **2.** good things thought about a person or thing. **3.** fame.

re·sem·ble (ri zem'b'l) *verb.* to be or look like. **resembles, resembled, resembling.**

res·er·va·tion (rez'ər vā'shən) *noun.* **1.** the act of keeping aside or back. **2.** something withheld, as a thought, objection, etc. **3.** public land put to some special use. **4.** an arrangement by which something is set aside until called for, as a hotel room, tickets, etc.

rest·less·ly (rest′lis lē) *adverb.* **1.** in a way that is never or almost never at rest or quiet. **2.** nervously; in a way that is not relaxed. **3.** in a disturbed manner.

re·venge (ri venj′) *verb.* to damage, hurt, etc., in return for damage, hurt, etc., received; get even for. —*noun.* **1.** the act of taking revenge or wish to do so. **2.** a chance to get even, especially a return match after having lost one.

re·view·er (ri vyo͞o′ər) *noun.* a person who examines or evaluates and writes opinions of books, plays, movies, etc., for a newspaper or magazine or who broadcasts such opinions on radio or television.

re·vive (ri viv′) *verb.* **1.** to come or bring back to life or consciousness. **2.** to come or bring back to a healthy, active condition. **3.** to come or bring back into use or notice, as to revive an old movie or song.

re·write (rē rīt′) *noun.* something written in a different way; a revision. **rewrites.** —*verb.* to write again or in different words; revise. **rewrote, rewriting.**

rheu·ma·tism (ro͞o′mə tiz′m) *noun.* any disease in which the joints are swollen and painful.

rid·dle (rid″l) *noun.* **1.** a problem or puzzle in the form of a question or statement whose meaning or answer is hard to guess. **2.** any person or thing that is hard to understand. **riddles.**

rile (rīl) *verb.* **1.** to make a liquid muddy by stirring up solids from the bottom. **2.** to make angry.

rob·ber·y (rob′ər ē) *noun.* an act of robbing; a theft. **robberies.**

ro·tate (rō′tāt) *verb.* **1.** to turn around a point or axis in the middle. **2.** to change in a regular and repeating order, as in a farmer rotating crops. **rotates, rotated, rotating.**

ro·ta·tion (rō tā′shən) *noun.* **1.** a movement around an axis. **2.** a regular and repeating series of changes.

rou·tine (ro͞o tēn′) *noun.* **1.** a regular way of doing something according to rules, habit, etc. **2.** a repeated act or performance such as a dance routine. **3.** a set of coded instructions for or series of operations performed by a computer.

S

sal·vage (sal′vij) *noun.* **1.** the saving of a ship, crew, and cargo from fire, shipwreck, etc. **2.** the act of saving any goods or property from fire. **3.** the property so saved, especially that brought up from a sunken ship. —*verb.* **1.** to save from shipwreck, fire, etc. **2.** to use what can be saved from damaged goods or property. —**salvaged** *adjective.* saved from destruction.

scan (skan) *verb.* **1.** to look at closely; examine: Carefully *scan* this contract. **2.** to glance at. **3.** to break down poetry into its rhythm pattern. **scanned, scanning.**

scroll (skrōl) *noun.* **1.** a roll of paper or parchment on which there is writing. **2.** a decoration in the form of a scroll.

sen·ti·nel (sen′ti n'l) *noun.* a person or animal who guards a group; sentry. **sentinels.**

sen·try (sen′trē) *noun.* a person, usually a soldier, who keeps watch to protect property or a group of people.

se·vere (sə vir′) *adjective.* **1.** strict or harsh: It was a *severe* winter. **2.** serious; forbidding. **3.** very plain and simple; unornamented. **4.** violent, extreme, as pain, etc. **5.** hard to bear.

shaft (shaft) *noun.* **1.** the long stem or handle of an arrow or spear. **2.** an arrow or spear. **3.** something that seems to be thrown like an arrow or spear. **4.** a long, slender thing or part, such as a handle.

shim·mer (shim′ər) *verb.* to shine with a flickering light. **shimmered.** —**shimmering** *adjective.* unsteady or wavering.

shut·tle (shut″l) *noun.* **1.** a device that carries the thread back and forth between the vertical threads when weaving. **2.** a device that carries the lower thread back and forth in a sewing machine. **3.** a bus, train, or other vehicle that makes short trips back and forth. —*verb.* to move quickly back and forth.

sing·let (sin͡g′glit) *noun. British.* an undershirt or jersey.

a fat	oi oil	ch chin
ā ape	o͞o look	sh she
ä car, father	o͞o tool	th thin
e ten	ou out	*th* then
er care	u up	zh leisure
ē even	ur fur	n͡g ring
i hit		
ir here	ə = a *in* ago	
ī bite, fire	e *in* agent	
o lot	i *in* unity	
ō go	o *in* collect	
ô law, horn	u *in* focus	

Scan developed from the Latin *scandere* – "to climb." It also meant "to measure verses." How did measuring verses come from climbing? It is an indirect reference to raising and lowering the foot to mark the rhythm. From the concept of measuring came the idea of examining and looking at.

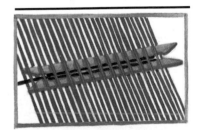

shuttle

smock

stipes

sin•is•ter (sin′ is tər) *adjective*. that threatens something bad: He saw a *sinister* figure on the dark street.

slab (slab) *noun*. a broad, flat, and fairly thick piece of something.

slack (slak) *adjective*. **1.** loose; not tight; relaxed: The rope was *slack*. **2.** careless; negligent. **3.** not active or busy. **4.** moving in a slow or sluggish way. —*noun*. the part of a rope, etc., that hangs loose.

slash (slash) *verb*. **1.** to cut by using broad strokes, as with a knife. **2.** to whip hard; lash. **3.** to make cuts to show the material below, especially in cloth. **4.** to lower or reduce sharply. **5.** to criticize strongly. —*noun*. a sweeping stroke or blow, or a cut made with such a stroke. **slashes.**

slew (sloo) *verb*. to turn sharply around a fixed point or pivot: The skiers *slewed* around the marker. **slewed, slewing.**

smock (smok) *noun*. a loose shirtlike piece of clothing worn to protect the clothes beneath. —*verb*. to decorate with stitching so as to make the cloth hang in even folds.

smudge out (smuj out) *verb*. to blur, make less distinct as by rubbing and spreading.

snout (snout) *noun*. **1.** an animal's nose and jaws that stick out, as of a dog or pig. **2.** something that looks like this, as a nozzle.

soar (sôr) *verb*. **1.** to go up into or fly high in the air. **2.** to rise above the ordinary.

so•lar e•clipse (sō′lər i klips′) *noun*. an eclipse, or blocking, of the sun by the moon.

so•lar sys•tem (sō′lər sis′təm) *noun*. the sun or another star and all the planets and other bodies that move around it.

sol•emn•ness (sol′əm nis) *noun*. a condition of being grave, serious; very earnest or formal.

spasm (spaz″m) *noun*. **1.** a sudden, uncontrollable tightening of a muscle or muscles. **2.** any short, sudden burst of activity or feeling.

spec•tac•u•lar (spek tak′yə lər) *adjective*. of or like a strange and remarkable sight; showy; striking.

spike (spīk) *noun*. **1.** a pointed piece of metal, wood, plastic, etc. **2.** a very large nail. **spikes** —*verb*. **1.** to fasten a spike or

spikes to. **2.** to pierce with a spike or spikes. **3.** to stop or block.

spi•ral (spī′rəl) *adjective*. circling around a center in a curve as the thread in a screw or bolt. —*noun*. a spiral curve or coil.

splin•ter (splin′tər) *verb*. to break or split into thin, sharp pieces. **splintered, splintering.** —*noun*. a thin, sharp piece of wood, bone, etc.

spout (spout) *noun*. **1.** a pipe or protruding lip from which a liquid pours. **2.** a stream or jet as of a liquid coming from a spout. —*verb*. **1.** to shoot out a liquid, etc. **2.** to speak in a loud, self-important way.

squal•or (skwol′ər) *noun*. a foul or unclean condition; filth; wretchedness.

stal•lion (stal′yən) *noun*. a full-grown male horse that is able to breed.

stead (sted) *noun*. the place of a person or thing as filled by a replacement: Since he could not make it, she went in his *stead*.

stern (stʉrn) *adjective*. **1.** severe; unyielding; strict. **2.** grim; forbidding. **3.** firm; full of resolution; unable to be moved by persuasion.

stim•u•late (stim′yə lat) *verb*. to excite or make more active. **stimulated, stimulating.**

sti•pes (stī′pēz) *noun*. a stalk or other short, thick support of a plant.

stout (stout) *adjective*. **1.** fat. **2.** strong in build; firm. **3.** powerful. **4.** brave; courageous: He was the *stoutest* hero of all. **stouter, stoutest.**

strand[1] (strand) *verb*. **1.** to run aground, as a ship. **2.** to put or be left in a difficult, helpless position. **stranded, stranding.**

strand[2] (strand) *noun*. **1.** any of the bundles of or single fibers that are twisted together to make rope, string, cable, etc. **2.** anything like a string or rope. **3.** a shore, especially of an ocean. **strands.**

strat•e•gy (strat′ə jē) *noun*. **1.** the science of planning and directing military operations. **2.** skill in managing or planning anything, especially by using tricks and schemes. **strategies.**

stride (strīd) *verb*. **1.** to walk taking long steps. **2.** to take a single, long step over or across. **3.** to sit or stand with a leg on either side of. **strode, striding.**

strum (strum) *verb*. to play by running the fingers across the strings, as a guitar. **strummed, strumming.**

stub·born (stub'ərn) *adjective*. **1.** determined to have one's own way; unwilling to give in. **2.** hard to handle, treat, or deal with.

sub·ject (sub'jikt) *adjective*. **1.** under the control of another. **2.** likely to have; liable. **3.** depending upon something in order to happen. —*noun*. **1.** a person under the control of another, as a ruler or government. **2.** a person or thing being talked about or otherwise dealt with: He did not like being the *subject* of their talk. **3.** the word or words in a sentence about which something is said. **4.** a course of study.

sub·merge (səb murj') *verb*. to put or go under the surface, especially water. **submerged, submerging.**

sum·mit (sum'it) *noun*. the highest point; top.

sum·mon (sum'ən) *verb*. **1.** to call together. **2.** to call forth; rouse; gather. **3.** to order to appear, as at a court of law. **summoned, summoning.**

su·mo (soo'mō) *noun*. Japanese wrestling in which the winner forces his opponent out of the ring or causes him to touch the ground with any part of his body except the soles of his feet. **sumo wrestler.**

sunk·en (sungk'ən) *adjective*. **1.** below the surface of water or other liquid. **2.** below the surface of whatever is around it. **3.** pushed in; forming a hollow.

su·per·sti·tion (soo'pər stish'ən) *noun*. any belief or practice that comes from fear and/or ignorance and is not supported by the known laws of science.

su·per·vi·sor (soo'pər vī'zər) *noun*. a person who directs or manages a group of people.

sur·name (sur'nām) *noun*. **1.** the family name, usually the last name in Western cultures. **2.** a special name added to a person's name as a description. —*verb*. to give a surname to.

sur·pass (sər pas') *verb*. **1.** to be better or greater than. **2.** to go beyond in quantity, amount, ability, etc. **3.** to go beyond the limit, capacity, etc., of.

sus·pi·cious (sə spish'əs) *adjective*. **1.** seeming to be guilty of a wrong. **2.** feeling or showing that another person is guilty of a wrong.

swerve (swurv) *verb*. to turn aside from a straight course. **swerved, swerving.**

swim·ming nose (swim'ing nōz') *noun*. a term for a shark, used because of the animal's extraordinary sense of smell.

swin·dle (swin'd'l) *verb*. to get money, property, etc., by cheating or tricking. **swindled, swindling.**

swol·len (swō'lən) *adjective*. increased in size or volume; enlarged.

a	fat	oi	oil	ch	chin
ā	ape	oo	look	sh	she
ä	car, father	ōo	tool	th	thin
e	ten	ou	out	th	then
er	care	u	up	zh	leisure
ē	even	ur	fur	ng	ring
i	hit				
ir	here	ə	= a *in* ago		
ī	bite, fire		e *in* agent		
o	lot		i *in* unity		
ō	go		o *in* collect		
ô	law, horn		u *in* focus		

T

talk·ing-to (tôk' ing too') *noun*. a scolding or reprimand.

tap·es·try (tap'is trē) *noun*. a heavy cloth used as a wall hanging, furniture covering, etc., woven with decorative designs and pictures.

tar·pau·lin (tär pô'lin *or* tär'pə lin) *noun*. **1.** waterproof material, usually canvas. **2.** a sheet of this for protecting something.

tat·tered (tat'ərd) *adjective*. **1.** torn and ragged. **2.** wearing clothes that are torn and ragged.

tel·e·scope (tel'ə skōp) *noun*. an instrument for making far-off objects seem closer and larger. It consists of one or more tubes that contain lenses or lenses and a mirror. —*verb*. **1.** to slide into one another as do the tubes of a small telescope. **2.** to force together in this manner.

tem·pest (tem' pist) *noun*. **1.** a wild, stormlike burst of feeling, action. **2.** a wild storm with high winds, often with rain.

ten·e·ment (ten'ə mənt) *noun*. **1.** a rented apartment or rooms. **2.** a building divided into apartments, especially one with poor living conditions in a poor section of a city.

Swindle came from *swindler*, which came from the German *schwindler*— a frivolous or heedless person, or a cheat. The latter meaning was taken into the English language.

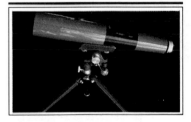

telescope

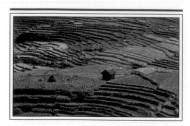

terrace

thatched

---◇---

Toil is another word that shows how meanings change. In the 1200s it meant "a verbal dispute," "strife," and "turmoil." About three hundred years later it meant "hard labor" as well. As a verb in the 1300s, *toil* meant "to fight in a lawsuit" as well as "to work hard."

term (tʉrm) *noun.* **1.** a period of time during which something lasts, often set by agreement or law. **2.** a word or phrase with a special meaning in some field. —**terms** *plural noun.* conditions of a contract, agreement, treaty, etc.

ter·race (ter′əs) *noun.* **1.** a flat platform of earth with sloping sides; also, a series of such platforms, one above the other, as in going up the side of a hill. **2.** an uncovered, paved area near a house overlooking a lawn or garden. **3.** a nearly level piece of land that then slopes sharply to a body of water.

ter·rain (tə rān′) *noun.* ground or an area of ground, usually with reference to its landforms or usability: They rode over rough *terrain*.

thatch (ᵺach) *noun.* roofing made of straw, rushes, palm leaves, etc. —*verb.* to cover with thatch. —**thatched** *adjective.* covered with straw or other plant material.

the·at·ri·cal (ᵺē at′ ri k′l) *adjective.* **1.** having to do with the theater, actors, plays, etc. **2.** overly dramatic or artificial in manner.

three-di·men·sion·al (ᵺrē′di men′shə n′l) *adjective.* having, or appearing to have, the dimension of depth in addition to width and height.

tid·al wave (tīd′′l wāv) *noun.* a very large, destructive wave caused by an earthquake or very strong wind. **tidal waves.**

tire·some (tīr′səm) *adjective.* **1.** tiring; boring. **2.** annoying.

toil (toil) *verb.* **1.** to work hard and steadily. **2.** to go slowly or with pain and effort. —*noun.* hard, tiring work or effort: We were tired after a day's *toil*.

to·ken (tō′kən) *noun.* **1.** a sign or symbol, as in a token of affection. **2.** a keepsake or souvenir. **3.** a piece of stamped metal used instead of money. —*adjective.* only pretended, as in token integration.

top·knot (top′not) *noun.* a tuft of hair or feathers worn at the top of the head.

tot (tot) *noun.* a young child.

tra·di·tion·al (trə dish′ən′l) *adjective.* handed down by word of mouth from generation to generation; customary.

trai·tor (trāt′ər) *noun.* a person who betrays his or her country, friends, cause, etc.: The *traitor* sold the country's secrets.

treas·ure trove (trezh′ər trōv′) *noun.* **1.** something of value found hidden, whose owner is not known. **2.** any valuable knowledge or thing that is discovered.

truce (trōōs) *noun.* a temporary stop of warfare or fighting by agreement between the sides.

ty·rant (tī′rənt) *noun.* **1.** a person who rules with complete power as in some ancient Greek cities. **2.** a cruel and unjust ruler. **3.** a cruel or unjust person.

---

u

un·at·tend·ed (un′ə tend′id) *adverb.* **1.** not taken care of or waited upon. **2.** alone; not accompanied. **3.** neglected or ignored.

un·bear·a·ble (un ber′ə b′l) *adjective.* that cannot be put up with: She found their teasing *unbearable*.

un·com·pre·hend·ing (un′kom prə hend′iŋ) *adjective.* not understanding.

un·in·spir·ing (un′in spīr′iŋ) *adjective.* **1.** failing to appeal to the imagination. **2.** failing to arouse to action. **3.** failing to create a feeling or thought.

u·nique (yōō nēk′) *adjective.* **1.** one and only; single. **2.** having no like or equal. **3.** unusual; rare.

un·pre·dict·a·ble (un′pri dikt′ə b′l) *adjective.* not able to tell what will happen; not to be made known beforehand.

un·trod·den (un trod′′n) *adjective.* **1.** not walked upon, along, etc. **2.** not pressed with the feet; untrampled.

un·war·y (un wer′ē) *adjective.* not cautious; not on one's guard.

un·will·ing (un wil′iŋ) *adjective.* **1.** not ready or inclined to do something. **2.** done without really wanting to.

V

va·can·cy (vā'kən sē) *noun.* **1.** a job or position that needs a person to fill it. **2.** a place to live in or stay at that is not occupied. **3.** the condition of being empty.

vague·ly (vāg' le) *adverb.* not clearly or definitely.

van·ish (van'ish) *verb.* **1.** to disappear; go suddenly from sight. **2.** to stop existing. **vanished, vanishing.**

ver·ti·cal (vur'ti k'l) *adjective.* straight up and down; perpendicular to the horizontal.

vex (veks) *verb.* to disturb, annoy, or trouble. **vexed, vexing.**

vi·bra·tion (vī brā'shən) *noun.* a rapid back-and-forth motion.

Vi·king (vī'king) *noun.* Scandinavian warrior of the 8th, 9th, and 10th centuries. **Vikings.**

vol·ca·no (vol kā'nō) *noun.* **1.** an opening in the earth's surface from which dust and ash, or molten rock, is thrown out. **2.** a cone-shaped hill or mountain made of volcanic material built up around such an opening.

vul·ner·a·bil·i·ty (vul'nər ə bil'ə tē) *noun.* the condition of being able or likely to be hurt; open to criticism or attack; a weak spot.

W

weave (wēv) *verb.* **1.** to make by passing threads, grass, reeds, etc., over and under one another. **2.** to twist into or through. **3.** to put together in the imagination, as in putting events into a story. **4.** to spin, as a spider does its web. **weaving, wove, woven.** —**weaving** *noun.* something that has been woven.

wedge (wej) *noun.* **1.** a wood or metal piece narrowing to a thin edge that can be driven into something to split it. **2.** anything so shaped. **3.** anything that opens the way for some action, change, etc. —*verb.* **1.** to split or force apart. **2.** to hold in place with a wedge. **3.** to force or pack in tightly, especially in a narrow place. **wedged, wedging.**

will (wil) *noun.* **1.** the mind's power to choose, decide, control one's own actions, etc. **2.** something wished or ordered by a person. **3.** strong purpose; determination. **4.** the way a person feels about others. **5.** a legal document stating what should be done with a person's money and property after death. —*verb.* **1.** to decide; make a choice. **2.** to control or make happen by the power of the will. **3.** to leave to someone by a will.

wilt (wilt) *verb.* **1.** to become limp; wither as from heat or lack of water; droop. **2.** to become weak. **wilted, wilting.**

wis·dom (wiz'dəm) *noun.* **1.** the quality of being wise. **2.** the ability to judge correctly based on knowledge and experience. **3.** learning; knowledge.

wiz·ard (wiz'ərd) *noun.* **1.** a magician; sorcerer. **2.** one who is very skillful or clever at something: *used only in everyday talk.*

wiz·ard·ry (wiz'ərd rē) *noun.* that which a wizard does; magic; sorcery. **wizardries.**

wrack (rak) *noun.* **1.** ruin; destruction as used mainly in the phrase *wrack and ruin.* **2.** seaweed or other plant material washed up on shore. —*verb.* to cause pain and suffering; torture. **wracked, wracking.**

wrench (rench) *noun.* **1.** a sudden, sharp twist or pull. **2.** an injury caused by a twist, as to the back. **3.** a sudden feeling of sadness, grief, etc. **4.** a tool for holding or turning nuts, bolts, pipes, etc. —*verb.* **1.** to twist or pull suddenly. **2.** to injure by twisting. **3.** to distort or twist a meaning, statement, etc.

a fat	oi oil	ch chin
ā ape	o͞o look	sh she
ä car, father	o͞o tool	th thin
e ten	ou out	*th* then
er care	u up	zh leisure
ē even	ur fur	ng̍ ring
i hit		
ir here	ə = a *in* ago	
ī bite, fire	e *in* agent	
o lot	i *in* unity	
ō go	o *in* collect	
ô law, horn	u *in* focus	

Volcano takes its name from the Roman god of fire, Vulcan or Volcanus. It came into English from the Italian *volcano* sometime in the 1600s.

wilted

The authors listed below have written some of the selections that appear in this book. The content of the notes was determined by a survey of what readers wanted to know about authors.

LLOYD ALEXANDER

LLOYD ALEXANDER

Lloyd Alexander has written many books and stories for young people. He's won several awards, including the Newbery Medal for his book *The High King* and a National Book Award for the *Marvelous Misadventures of Sebastion.* He said that he learned to read when he was quite young and has been "an avid reader ever since, even though my parents and relatives were not great readers." One of his favorite authors was Charles Dickens, who provided both encouragement and refuge when Lloyd Alexander was growing up. "If he helped me escape from my daily life, he also sent me back somehow better able to face up to it." *(Born 1924)*

ISAAC ASIMOV

ISAAC ASIMOV

Isaac Asimov has written stories, essays, fiction, and nonfiction books about dozens of different subjects. He says that he became interested in science fiction back in 1929 when he was a boy and saw an issue of *Amazing Stories.* "From then on I was hooked. I was a science-fiction fan of the most confirmed variety." Isaac Asimov says that he works at his writing every day. "I start early each day and continue typing till the number of typographical errors reaches an unacceptable concentration." From this work pattern, Isaac Asimov has become one of the most prolific writers in America. *(Born 1920)*

BARBARA BRENNER

Barbara Brenner's mother died when she was one year old. She was brought up in a household of loving aunts, uncles, grandparents, and cousins. She says about her writing: "Most of my books have a natural history component; I write about what I like—snakes, spiders, mules, roosters, dogs, cats, ants, gorillas, bears—all of these creatures have found their way into my work." She has received several awards for her books, including Outstanding Science Book awards from the National Science Teachers Association and the Children's Book Council. Barbara Brenner now writes material to be used on computers, as well as continuing to write books for young people. *(Born 1925)*

BARBARA BRENNER

LEWIS CARROLL

Lewis Carroll is the pen name for Charles Lutwidge Dodgson, who was a mathematics professor in England. He is best remembered for his book *Alice's Adventures in Wonderland.* The book began as stories told to the Liddel girls, daughters of the dean at the college where Dodgson taught. The girls enjoyed the stories so much they asked him to write them down. Later, Dodgson wrote *Through the Looking Glass,* which told more about Alice and her fantastic adventures. *(1832–1898)*

LEWIS CARROLL

ELIZABETH CLEMONS

Elizabeth Clemons is the pen name for Elizabeth Cameron Nowell. She has written many books under the name Elizabeth Clemons and some under the name Elizabeth Cameron. She says about her writing: "The books I have written have all been about things in which I am interested—animals, rodeos, seas and beaches, rocks, transportation, travel. Most of my books are factual but I have written a few simple fiction books for young people." Elizabeth Clemons loves the sea, and her home is on the beach in Carmel-by-the-Sea in California.

HELEN CRESSWELL

HELEN CRESSWELL

Helen Cresswell was born in England. She says that from the time she was very young she wanted to be a writer. "I began writing at the age of six or seven," she says, "in fact I don't remember ever *not* writing." Her earliest works were poetry, and at the age of fourteen, she won her first literary award for the best poem in the annual Nottingham Poetry Society. Since then, she has won several awards for her fiction. *(Born 1936)*

EMILY CROFFORD

EMILY CROFFORD

Emily Crofford says that one of the things she particularly likes about being an author is talking with students. Her advice to students who want to write is, "Take time to daydream." She says, "People are so busy, busy, busy. They don't take time to daydream—to sit and look at things around them. I did a lot of daydreaming when I was young. That's where writing comes from." Before becoming a writer, Emily Crofford was a newspaper reporter and editor.

PAT CUMMINGS

PAT CUMMINGS

Pat Cummings is both an author and an illustrator. She has illustrated her own books as well as those of other authors. She says, "I like to incorporate personal things: people I know, things I use around the house, or places I've been." Although she was born in Chicago, she grew up in Okinawa and Japan. She speaks some French and Italian and enjoys traveling. *(Born 1950)*

SIR ARTHUR CONAN DOYLE

Sir Arthur Conan Doyle was the creator of Sherlock Holmes, one of the most famous of all fictional detectives. Doyle said about the process of writing the Holmes stories: "People have often asked me whether I knew the end of a Holmes story before I started it. Of course I do. One could not possibly steer a course if one did not know one's destination. The first thing is to get your idea. Having got that key idea, one's next task is to conceal it and lay emphasis upon everything which can make for a different explanation." According to Doyle, he kept a notebook with a list of the names that he thought about using for his detective. One of the names was Sherringford Holmes. Later this was changed to Sherlock Holmes. *(1859–1930)*

SIR ARTHUR CONAN DOYLE

RACHEL FIELD

Rachel Field was an editor for several publishing companies before she became a full-time writer. She said that she spent time writing before she did much reading. "It wasn't that I could not have learned to read earlier. I knew the letters and all that, but it was so much pleasanter to have my mother read books to me." Rachel Field was the first woman to be awarded the Newbery Medal, which she won for *Hitty: Her First Hundred Years. (1894–1942)*

RACHEL FIELD

PAUL FLEISCHMAN

Paul Fleischman said that his father wrote books for young people, so writing always seemed to him like an "honorable and possible profession." He also said that he was very interested in music and would compose it if he had the talent to do so. He tries to bring musical elements into his writing. He says, "My sentences all scan (or are supposed to), as if set to music. I spend half my time attending to sound (alliteration and internal rhyme)." One of his books was a Newbery Honor Book; others have been Golden Kite Honor Books. *(Born 1952)*

PAUL FLEISCHMAN

About the Authors 629

ROY GALLANT

ROY GALLANT

Roy Gallant's special interest in the physical sciences is astronomy. As a science writer and teacher, he believes that no subject is too complex to present to children. "If a writer has command of the scientific concept he is dealing with, and if he knows the capabilities of his audience, he can communicate with them." Roy Gallant has been a co-recipient of the Thomas Alva Edison Foundation Award for the best children's science book of the year. *(Born 1924)*

DORIS GATES

DORIS GATES

Doris Gates grew up on a prune ranch in the Santa Clara Valley of California. Her first-hand knowledge of the fruit farmers and the migrant fruit pickers has formed the background for many of her stories. Besides writing stories and telling stories on the radio, she has written six volumes retelling the Greek myths. *(1901–1987)*

JEAN CRAIGHEAD GEORGE

JEAN CRAIGHEAD GEORGE

Jean Craighead George is an award-winning author who has written many books for young people. Among her most popular books are *Julie of the Wolves,* which was a Newbery Medal winner, and *My Side of the Mountain,* which was made into a movie. Jean Craighead George says she writes "about children in nature and their relationship to the complex web of life." She does careful research for all her books, which she calls "documentary novels." She believes that books for young people should be "accurate and faithful to the truth." *(Born 1919)*

NIKKI GIOVANNI

Nikki Giovanni is best known as a poet, but she has also written essays and an autobiography titled *Extended Autobiographical Statement on My Twenty-Seven Years of Being a Black Poet*. She has received grants for writing from the Harlem Cultural Council, the Ford Foundation, and the National Council of Arts. Nikki Giovanni says, "I think children are an exciting audience to both read to and write for. I hope my poetry reaches both the heart and mind of a child who is a child and the adult who still nurtures the child within." *(Born 1943)*

NIKKI GIOVANNI

SHIRLEY GLUBOK

Shirley Glubok has lectured at the Metropolitan Museum of Art and has written books on art history and archaeology for young people. Several of her books have been named as Notable Books by the American Library Association. Several have been chosen for the Child Study Association book list. Among her writings are books about the Aztecs, the Incas, and the Etruscans as well as about Peru, Ancient Mexico, Africa, India, Ur, and Colonial America. *(Born 1933)*

SHIRLEY GLUBOK

NIKKI GRIMES

Nikki Grimes has been a college instructor in English, a researcher, and a photographer, as well as a writer. She decided to become a writer when she was a teenager. Speaking of that time, Nikki Grimes has said, "I was most influenced by James Baldwin who, when I was just seventeen, offered me his advice and counsel. He taught me the value of mastering the mother tongue." She is now an avid student of languages, among which are Spanish, Swahili, and Arabic. She summarizes her writing by saying, "In general, my fiction is autobiographical." *(Born 1950)*

NIKKI GRIMES

About the Authors 631

LANGSTON HUGHES

LANGSTON HUGHES

Langston Hughes wrote award-winning poems, short stories, and novels. He said he began to write poetry because he was elected class poet when he was in grammar school. "The day I was elected, I went home and wondered what I should write. Since we had eight teachers in our school, I thought there should be one verse for each teacher, and since the teachers were to have eight verses, I felt the class should have eight, too. I said our class was the greatest class ever graduated. So at graduation, when I read the poem, naturally everybody applauded loudly. That was the way I began to write poetry." *(1902–1967)*

HENRY WADSWORTH LONGFELLOW

HENRY WADSWORTH LONGFELLOW

Henry Wadsworth Longfellow was a descendant of Priscilla and John Alden. He wrote about them in his poem, "The Courtship of Miles Standish." He went to college with Nathaniel Hawthorne and Franklin Pierce (fourteenth president of the United States). He was a teacher, a translator, a poet, and a writer of prose. Among the many poems he wrote, some of the best known are "The Song of Hiawatha," "The Village Blacksmith," and "Paul Revere's Ride." His work was greatly admired in England, as well as in the United States. A bust of Longfellow was placed in the Poets' Corner of Westminster Abbey in London, England. The poet T. S. Eliot is the only other American to be recognized at Westminster Abbey. *(1807–1882)*

MARIE McSWIGAN

MARIE McSWIGAN

Marie McSwigan's father, uncle, and sister all worked on newspapers. Therefore, it was natural that she became a newspaper reporter. She said that her work as a reporter helped her develop a respect for accuracy and for discipline in writing. It also developed her ability to do research on a topic. Her book *Snow Treasure* won national acclaim when it was published and has remained popular with readers. It has been in print for more than forty years. *(1907–1962)*

JEAN MERRILL

JEAN MERRILL

Jean Merrill grew up on an apple and dairy farm on the shores of Lake Ontario in New York. She said that most of her waking hours, when she was not in school, were spent outdoors. She added, "The only thing that could detain me indoors was a book." She thinks her interest in writing children's books probably came from the importance that certain books had during her own childhood. "I read any book that really moved me—not once—but twice, three, six, a dozen times." Several of her books have been chosen as Junior Literary Guild selections and American Library Association Notable Books. *(Born 1923)*

PENELOPE NAYLOR

Penelope Naylor has written several books and illustrated the books of other writers. She has also studied sculpture and is a professional painter. She says, "My greatest interests are art, nature, and travel. My only ambition in life is to continue to learn—and to convey some of the beauty and excitement of what I discover to others." *(Born 1941)*

ROBERT O'BRIEN

ROBERT O'BRIEN

Robert O'Brien was the pseudonym of Robert Leslie Conly. He published books under both names. He began creating imaginary worlds at a very young age, but he was in his late forties before he began to write and publish. When he was asked why he wrote books for children he said, "I write them because a story idea pops up in my mind. Since I am in the writing business, when I get a story idea I write it down before I forget it." Robert O'Brien's books won numerous honors and awards, including the Boston Globe–Horn Book honor list and American Library Association Best Young Adult Book. *(1918–1973)*

SCOTT O'DELL

SCOTT O'DELL

Scott O'Dell said that writing is hard work. He agreed with another writer who said that the most important tool for a writer to have is a piece of sealing wax so he or she will be stuck to the chair and will have to sit and work. Scott O'Dell was a boy in the early 1900s. He said, "Los Angeles was a frontier town with more horses than automobiles and more jack rabbits than people. That is why, I suppose, the feel of the frontier and the sound of the sea are in my books." Three of Scott Odell's novels are Newbery Honor books. Scott O'Dell was a recipient of the Newbery Medal and the Hans Christian Andersen Award. *(1903–1989)*

ALLEN SAY

ALLEN SAY

Allen Say is a commercial photographer and an illustrator, as well as an author. He studied for three years in Tokyo, Japan. He has illustrated a number of books, including several of his own. About his work he says, "Most people seem to be interested in turning their dreams into reality. Then there are those who turn reality into dreams. I belong to the latter group." Some of his books have been selected as Notable Books by the American Library Association. *(Born 1937)*

ARMSTRONG W. SPERRY

ARMSTRONG W. SPERRY

Armstrong W. Sperry was an illustrator for ten years before he became a professional writer. He has said that it was combining drawing and writing that led him "into the field of children's books." Armstrong Sperry, who spoke French and Tahitian, spent two years in the French-owned islands of the South Pacific. The themes for many of his books, including the Newbery award-winning novel *Call It Courage,* come from his experiences in these islands. *(1897–1976)*

ROBERT LOUIS STEVENSON

Robert Louis Stevenson was born in Scotland. He was a sickly child and often had to stay in bed instead of going out to play with other children. When he grew up, he wrote many poems about his childhood. He also wrote exciting adventure stories, including *Treasure Island.* Stevenson said that the idea for that book came after he drew a map of a make-believe island. "I made the map of an island; it was elaborately colored; the shape of it took my fancy beyond expression." He said that when he looked at the map, the "characters of the book began to appear among imaginary woods." *(1850–1894)*

ROBERT LOUIS STEVENSON

JAMES THURBER

James Thurber wrote short stories, humorous articles, and books for young people and adults. His book *Many Moons* won the Randolph Caldecott Medal. Thurber was also a cartoonist, and he illustrated many of his articles and stories with cartoons. As the result of a childhood accident, Thurber lost the vision in one eye. His vision in his other eye grew worse as he got older, until he was almost totally blind. He had to stop drawing cartoons. But he could dictate his stories and articles, and he continued to write until his death. *(1894–1961)*

JAMES THURBER

JAMES RAMSEY ULLMAN

James Ramsey Ullman, in addition to writing books, was also a newspaper reporter and a theatrical producer. He and his co-producer won the Pulitzer Prize for the play *Men in White.* Ullman was also a world traveler and a mountain climber. He was a member of the first American expedition to Mount Everest. Seven of James Ramsey Ullman's books have been made into motion pictures and his book *Banner in the Sky* was a Newbery Honor Book. *(1907–1971)*

JAMES RAMSEY ULLMAN

MILDRED PITTS WALTER

MILDRED PITTS WALTER

Mildred Pitts Walter taught in an elementary school in Los Angeles for a number of years. She was a delegate to the Second World Black and African Festival of the Arts and Culture held in Lagos, Nigeria. She has also traveled to many different places as an educational consultant. One of her novels, *The Girl on the Outside,* is a re-creation of the 1957 integration of Central High School in Little Rock, Arkansas. Another of her books received honorable mention from the Coretta Scott King Award committee.

ELIZABETH YATES

ELIZABETH YATES

Elizabeth Yates was born in Buffalo, New York, but said that the most memorable days of her childhood were spent on her father's farm south of Buffalo. She was the next to youngest of seven children, so she always had someone to play with. After she married, she and her husband lived in London for about ten years before they came back to live in the United States. She said: "Writing is my joy, but gardening claims much of my time as do community activities." The John Newbery Medal and the William Allen White Children's Book Award are among the honors she has received. *(Born 1905)*

LAURENCE YEP

LAURENCE YEP

Laurence Yep is well-known for his science fiction writing for both children and adults. Yep said of children's writers that they "are still in touch with the magical power of words and pictures to capture the world in a way that many who write for adults are not." Laurence Yep is a Newbery winner and a Boston Globe–Horn Book winner. Some of his books have been selected as American Library Association Notable Books. *(Born 1948)*

AUTHOR INDEX

639